GERMANY'S DRIVE TO THE EAST AND
THE UKRAINIAN REVOLUTION, 1917–1918

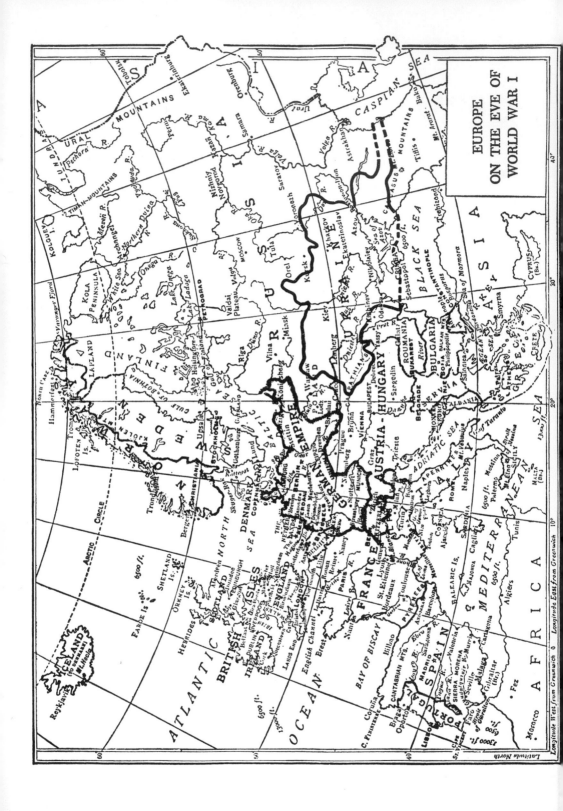

EUROPE
ON THE EVE OF
WORLD WAR I

GERMANY'S DRIVE

TO THE EAST AND

THE UKRAINIAN

REVOLUTION,

1917-1918

by OLEH S. FEDYSHYN

RUTGERS UNIVERSITY PRESS

New Brunswick, New Jersey

TO IRYNA

Preface

The aim of this book is twofold: to explain a somewhat neglected aspect of Germany's *Ostpolitik* of the World War I period and to contribute to a better understanding of the most critical phase of the Ukrainian national revolution—the years 1917 and 1918. This was a period during which the Ukrainian movement achieved some of its most impressive victories, yet suffered its most severe setbacks.

It has been my intention to provide a comprehensive and fully documented treatment in depth of both the German occupation of the Ukraine and the Ukrainian movement in this period. In fact, the German and Austrian archival materials on which the book is largely based were not available to scholarly researchers until after World War II. The relevant documents were captured by the Allied armies after the fall of Berlin and were brought to the United States for study and microfilming. In due course they were turned over to the West German government in Bonn.

Although the subject matter of this book was essentially unexplored at the time I began my research, I benefited from two excellent studies of the Ukrainian revolution which appeared in the 1950's: John S. Reshetar's *The Ukrainian Revolution, 1917–1920*, and Richard Pipes' *The Formation of the Soviet Union: Communism and Nationalism, 1917–1923*. The first contains a valuable analysis of the German occupation of the Ukraine based on published sources, and the second treats the Ukrainian developments of this period in a larger context of social and national revolutions among the non-Russian peoples of the former Czarist Empire. It was only while my book was in preparation that German historiography was enriched by Fritz Fischer's massive study of the Reich's war aims of the period, *Griff nach der Weltmacht: Die Kriegszielpolitik des kaiserlichen Deutschland, 1914–18* (unquestionably the most ambitious undertaking in this area today) and by Winfried Baumgart's fine monograph entitled *Deutsche Ostpolitik, 1918*. These and scores of other recent works in the field of modern German history and politics were consulted; however, my principal sources were the archival materials of Germany and the Dual Monarchy, and other primary sources.

The bulk of the book is devoted to the period from the March, 1917, Revolution in Russia to the collapse of the Central Powers in November, 1918. The pre-Brest-Litovsk period and peace negotiations are treated rather extensively, inasmuch as they reflect the development of German plans for the east in the face of the rapidly changing situation in that region. An even greater emphasis has been placed on the period from March to November, 1918, when the Germans were in actual control of the Ukraine, the Crimea, and other eastern territories and pursued their plans with a certain degree of consistency, incomplete and contradictory though these plans were.

The emphasis in this book is on the plans, rather than on their implementation. By this I mean the German plans for the Ukraine, the chief prize of the German's drive to the east during this period, and for the Crimea, an area in which they developed a special interest following the occupation of the Peninsula. The Reich's occupation policies in the Ukraine and the various Ukrainian developments are treated more fully than are similar events in the Crimea. The Ukrainian revolution, however, is discussed chiefly in connection with Germany's drive to the east in general, and its Ukrainian venture in particular. Such an important problem as, for example, the anti-German resistance in the Ukraine receives no more than passing attention.

German plans and policies in the Baltic area, Byelorussia, and the Caucasus are touched upon primarily for purposes of comparison. German-Soviet relations, German dealings with the Russian monarchists, German plans for the Don region and the Kuban, and the Polish problem are described only to the extent that they contribute to a more complete understanding of the Reich's plans and policies in the Ukraine and the Crimea. On the other hand, I have dealt at some length with the conflict between the Reich's war lords and the Foreign Office, inasmuch as their disagreements repeatedly complicated Germany's Ukrainian undertaking.

Austrian aims in the Ukraine are also discussed in various sections of this book, although Austria-Hungary clearly played a secondary role in the whole undertaking. In spite of greater familiarity with the east, the Dual Monarchy lacked both means and determination to pursue an independent policy in the Ukraine. Vienna's differences and misunderstandings with Berlin and its usually cool and strained relations with Kiev nevertheless offer important clues to a better understanding of Germany's Ukrainian venture.

I have used the term *east* and its derivatives as they are used in German and Austrian writings on the subject. *Ost* refers to the vast and not always clearly defined areas of the European part of the former Czarist Empire and adjacent regions. Numerous additional German, Ukrainian, and Russian terms have been preserved in the text mainly because of the lack of good English equivalents. In all cases unfamiliar foreign terms are explained as they occur.

Slavic titles and names have been transliterated according to a modified Library of Congress system used at Columbia University. Ukrainian authors, family names, and geographic terms appear in their Ukrainian version, and the Russian ones in Russian. Whenever possible, the Anglicized form of well-known people has been used (for example, Hrushevsky, Trotsky). This method was also followed with regard to place names (for example, Kiev, Vistula, Chernigov).

The preparation of this book was greatly facilitated by a research fellowship from the Ford Foundation in 1958–59 and by two summer grants from Rice University. The project originated in Philip E. Mosely's seminar in Russian foreign policy at Columbia University some years ago. Professor Mosley has remained a source of encouragement ever since. I should also like to thank Hans W. Gatzke and Fritz T. Epstein for their helpful suggestions in the early stages of my research, and Henry L. Roberts for his counsel and guidance when I was a doctoral candidate at Columbia University. My friend and colleague Ivan L. Rudnytsky of the American University deserves special thanks for helpful suggestions during the final review of the manuscript.

I should also like to express my gratitude to E. Zyblikewycz, director of the W. K. Lypynsky East European Research Institute in Philadelphia for his assistance in obtaining the necessary Austrian documents. My thanks also go to the staff of the Columbia University Library, the New York Public Library, the Library of Congress, and the National Archives for professional assistance rendered during the various stages of this project. It goes without saying that these individuals and institutions are in no way responsible for the views expressed in this study.

—OLEH S. FEDYSHYN

Staten Island, New York
October, 1969

Contents

GERMANY'S DRIVE TO THE EAST AND
THE UKRAINIAN REVOLUTION, 1917–1918

CHAPTER I

The Ukrainian National Movement and the Outbreak of World War I

The Ukraine, once known as the "granary of Europe," still evokes an image of endless wheat fields. To this an informed reader and observer of today would also add huge industrial complexes such as the Donbas and the rich mineral deposits of Kryvyi Rih and Nikopil. The general impression is still that of great industrial and agricultural wealth. Not so apparent is the political importance of a people who constitute approximately one-fifth of the U.S.S.R.'s population and inhabit an area larger in size than that of a united Germany.

Although few people today would dispute the ethnic, linguistic, and cultural distinctiveness of the Ukrainians, the historical past of this nation is still poorly understood by the outside world, and its recent political record is viewed quite often as simply a part of the Russian story that does not need a separate treatment. And yet, twice within this century, during the two World Wars, the Ukrainians heroically, albeit unsuccessfully, rose in the struggle for national and political independence from Russia. Indeed, the past three centuries of Ukrainian history have been dominated by this desire for freedom and independence from the powerful northern neighbor.[1] Undoubtedly this struggle will continue in the future, even though it will probably be waged in a less overt fashion.

The outside world's lack of interest in the Ukraine is attributable in part to the complexity of the problem. After all, it is very much easier to think of Russia as a united state, a homogeneous nation, than to delve into the confusing and complex affairs of the various non-Russian peoples of the U.S.S.R., who now constitute more than 50 percent of the Soviet Union's population.[2]

Even though few people in the outside world were aware of the existence of the Ukrainian nation at the outbreak of World War I, and even though the Ukrainians themselves were generally only beginning to think in terms of independence or separation, their elected leaders—the Ukrainian Central Rada (Council) meeting in Kiev—proclaimed the Ukraine an independent state in January of 1918. In the following month, in a desperate attempt to preserve this independence, the Rada proceeded to conclude a separate peace with Imperial Germany, thereby preventing the Russian Bolsheviks from imposing their control over this rich land. Had the Ukrainians succeeded in preserving their independence in the post-World War I period, Russia would have lost its principal food and raw materials base. Moreover, Russia would have been deprived of a direct access to the Balkans as well as East Central Europe, and would have been pushed away from the Black Sea. In short, Russia would have ceased to be a great power. Certainly, European history would have followed a very different course, and the Ukraine, with its vast mineral resources, sophisticated industries, agricultural wealth, and a people sufficiently trained to exploit these advantages, would surely have become one of the leading European powers.

This book deals with the first attempt made by the Ukrainians to achieve this goal during World War I. The aim of this chapter is to provide a brief analysis of the Ukrainian problem on the eve of this crucial period and to review the impact of World War I on the Ukrainians with respect to their preparations for this struggle.

The keys to understanding the Ukraine's past are its great wealth and the lack of natural and easily defensible frontiers. Throughout its history the Ukraine has been the highway of invasions and the prey of hungry roving marauders. During the Middle Ages it was the easternmost outpost of the west in its endless clashes with the east; then a part of this area came under Tatar and Turkish sway; next the weakening of the Ottoman Empire caused it to become the bone of contention between Poland and Russia; and finally, in this century, the Ukraine became the most coveted object of Germany's designs and ambitions in the east.

The Ukrainians were not a historical nation even though they proudly traced the origin of their independent statehood to the Kievan principality, a state that collapsed under the impact of the Mongol invasion of 1240. In the Lithuanian period that followed the idea of independent Ukrainian statehood was not revived. Moreover, the center of the political life of this region soon moved from Lithuania to Poland, thus bringing the Ukraine under Polish sway. It was not until the 1640's that the Ukrainian Cossacks under Hetman Bohdan Khmelnytsky made an effort to overthrow Polish control. The Cossacks' struggle for political independence from Poland was at first quite successful. Soon, however, after a series of bloody but inconclusive battles, Khmelnytsky decided to conclude an alliance with Moscow. This eventually resulted in complete political domination of the Ukraine by its better-organized and more determined northern neighbor. The secret alliance of the Cossack leader Hetman Ivan Mazepa with Charles XII of Sweden against Peter the Great, which ended in the disastrous battle of Poltava in 1709, marks the end of the effort of the Ukrainians to regain their independence during the Cossack period.

In the course of the eighteenth century, most of the Ukraine came under Russian control as a result of the Polish partitions, and within a short period of time all these lands became fully integrated into the Czarist Empire.[3] This in itself was not as tragic as was the almost total loss, through Russification and political and social integration, of the Ukrainian landed aristocracy, a group which had sustained similar losses through Polonization in the earlier period. In the wake of this development, the cultural, educational, and political life of the Ukrainian cities became distinctly foreign (mostly Russian or Polish, sometimes Jewish). This circumstance was the principal weakness of the Ukrainian movement in the later period and in large measure explains the failure of the Ukrainian national revolution of 1917–1921.

The process of political and social integration of the Ukrainian lands into the Russian Empire coincided with the Ukrainian cul-

tural revival that began with the publication of Ivan Kotlyarevs'kyi's travesty of the *Aeneid* in 1798. It was composed in the
discarded vernacular Ukrainian, a language then used only by the
peasantry. The appearance of this work not only marked the turn-
ing point in the Ukrainian cultural revival but laid the basis for
the development of modern Ukrainian as well. These processes
soon found their greatest champion in the person of Taras Shevchenko (1814–1861), the foremost Ukrainian poet of the nineteenth century. Shevchenko was also destined to become the
champion of the revival of the Ukrainian national idea; this process, however, gained momentum only toward the end of the
century, after Shevchenko's death.

Thus for many decades the Ukrainian national renaissance
was mainly literary and cultural. The secret diplomatic mission
of a Ukrainian nobleman, Vasyl Kapnist, to Prussia in 1791 to
seek aid against Russia must be viewed as an epilogue to the Cossack era rather than as the prelude to the struggle for national
liberation of the Ukraine, for this struggle did not get fully under
way until the second half of the nineteenth century. Such seemingly propitious events as Napoleon's invasion of Russia in 1812
stirred the Ukrainians but little, and the Polish revolt of 1830–31
produced only renewed expressions of loyalty and support of the
throne in the hope that the Czar would become more receptive to
the perennial request for the restoration of the ancient Cossack
autonomy and especially various privileges considered to be due
the descendants of former Cossack officers.[4]

It was this class approach to the Ukrainian problem—the desire by former Cossack officers to be treated as members of the
Russian gentry—which gave rise to the development of the aristocratic school in Ukrainian historiography. Thus the Ukrainian
national renaissance did not have much popular support initially,
and the Ukraine continued to serve as the battleground for the
Poles and the Russians as they contended for cultural and political domination over this area. The fact that many noblemen of
Ukrainian descent were involved on both sides of this struggle
had a negative effect on the Ukrainian movement. On the other
hand, it considerably weakened Moscow's effort to integrate and
Russify the Ukrainian provinces; furthermore, the activities of
the Polish minority of the Right Bank Ukraine (provinces to the
west of the Dnieper) provided the Ukrainians with a useful lesson

and made them more conscious of their own national identity.

The Ukrainians understandably had difficulty choosing between Poland and Russia. Consequently, they sought repeatedly a third power's support in the struggle against their more aggressive neighbors. Hetman Khmelnytsky enlisted Tatar help against Poland and then called in the Muscovites; and Mazepa cooperated with Sweden against Russia. Vasyl Kapnist's secret mission to Prussia in 1791 was also a move to get aid against Moscow. During the Crimean War (1854–1856), a Polish-Ukrainian adventurer, Michal Czajkowski, also known as Sadyk Pasha, organized in Turkey a Ukrainian Cossack legion that was to be used in the struggle against Russia. And during World Wars I and II the Ukrainians cooperated with Germany.

However, these temporary alliances with outside powers were usually arranged and promoted secretly, and they seldom enjoyed wide popular support. In fact, some of them were clearly unpopular and poorly understood by the masses; such, for example, seems to have been the case with Mazepa's secret agreement with Charles XII of Sweden. Consequently, in the modern period, the leaders of the Ukrainian movement came to rely more and more on their own resources and sought to widen their base at home. The beginning of the popularization of the Ukrainian national idea in the modern period is associated with the rise of the Populist intelligentsia in Russia in the 1840's; and its broadening from the narrow dimensions of Little Russian regionalism to a movement with definite political overtones is attributable to the influence of Taras Shevchenko.

Shevchenko was not merely the greatest Ukrainian poet of the period but a national prophet as well. This former serf, whose fiery poems called for the national and social liberation of the Ukrainian people, established, together with a small group of Ukrainian intellectuals, a federalist association known as the Brotherhood of Saints Cyril and Methodius. Even though the Czarist police soon broke up this organization and arrested its leaders, the idea of a Slav federation continued to dominate Ukrainian political thinking well into the twentieth century, until finally it was destroyed by Lenin's Bolshevik centralism.

The emancipation of 1861 (this was also the year of Shevchenko's death) provided further impetus to the development of a more politically oriented Populism in the Ukraine, as in other regions of the Russian Empire. The Populists, known in the Ukraine as *khlopomany* (peasant lovers), were generally as unsuccessful as were their Russian counterparts in winning the peasantry over to their cause. Thus the Ukrainian movement failed to develop the solid popular base that it needed to become a real political force in the country. Aware of its weakness, the leaders of the movement were extremely modest and restrained in their plans for the future. In fact these plans hardly constituted a political program since they did not go beyond "the furthering of Little Russian literature and the publication of educational materials in the Little Russian language, in order to extend useful knowledge among the people." [5]

But even this program was too much for the Russian bureaucracy. Infuriated by the Polish uprising of 1863, they decided to crush the "Ukrainian peril" in its infancy before it too could raise its head against Moscow. The result was the notorious ukase of 1863 issued by the Czarist Minister of the Interior, Count P. A. Valuev. This was an administrative decree banning all popular educational and religious works published in Ukrainian. Although this measure seriously hindered the work among the masses, the growth of the movement at the top continued and a number of secret educational organizations known as *hromadas* sprang up in the Ukrainian cities. These associations were neither politically radical nor narrowly nationalistic. In the Russian reality, however, they could only exist clandestinely and their activities were viewed by the Czarist police with great suspicion. The *hromadas* were seldom well organized, and their activities remained largely uncoordinated. Unofficially, the Kiev *hromada* was considered the central one, and its leading members, political theorist Mykhailo Drahomanov and historian Volodymyr Antonovych, were regarded as the leaders of the movement. It was the former who developed an impressive political program based on the democratization and federalization of both the Austro-Hungarian and Russian monarchies, which then divided the Ukrainian lands between them. The plan guaranteed equal rights to the three major Slavic peoples—the Russians, the Ukrainians, and the Poles. It was also Drahomanov, a respected scholar known throughout Russia, who was chosen by the *hromadas* to leave the country in order to establish a center of Ukrainian political and scholarly activities abroad. (Drahomanov remained in his post in

Geneva for a number of years, and then in 1889, six years before his death, returned to academic life by accepting a professorship at the University of Sofia, Bulgaria.) Drahomanov's stay abroad was necessitated by the even more restrictive Czarist ukase of Ems (1876), which imposed a complete ban on all Ukrainian publications as well as on all Ukrainian cultural and educational activities. These measures further weakened the Ukrainian movement in the Russian Empire and reduced even more its ties with the masses, but also eventually caused it to become more radical.

It would be wrong to associate the development of western interest in the Ukraine with the increased Czarist persecution of Ukrainophilism of the 1860's and 1870's. Strictly speaking, the Ukrainian question never entirely disappeared from the European political scene. (For those who discussed the subject publicly in a later period the Ukrainian "question" involved the quest for separate national identity and cultural autonomy, and ultimately the struggle for political independence for the Ukrainian people.) Khmelnytsky's and Mazepa's efforts to regain the Ukraine's independence were not forgotten in the west. Moreover, there were able and dedicated Ukrainian political exiles such as Mazepa's associate and successor, Pylyp Orlyk, who, following the disastrous battle of Poltava (1709), went to Turkey to continue the struggle against Russia.

An equally important contribution to the task of keeping the outside world informed about the Ukraine was made by scores of foreign visitors and travelers in Russia who were impressed with the differences between the northern part of the Empire and the more cheerful, wealthier, and above all more rebellious and independent south populated by the Ukrainians.[6] Some of these early observers of the Slavic world were greatly impressed with the richness of the Ukrainian folklore and began to study it systematically long before the native scholars. Several decades before Shevchenko's birth, at a time when even the designation Ukraine was being forgotten, the German philosopher Johann Gottfried von Herder, writing in the time of Catherine the Great of Russia, made the following remarkable statement: "The Slavs had been the stepchildren of history, but this would change in the course of time, and the Ukraine might become one day a new Hellas."[7]

In the nineteenth century the number of foreign visitors to the Ukraine increased considerably. Many were businessmen, and a high percentage of these were German. During this period the Germans also produced an impressive number of scholars in the Russian field and Slavic studies in general. German political writers and observers were likewise among the first foreign students of the Ukrainian national movement. Some of them went so far as to advocate the breakup of the Russian Empire and the formation of a separate Ukrainian state. One of the first groups to draft a plan for the dismemberment of the Russian Empire and to seek support for such a plan from the German Chancellor, Prince Otto von Bismarck, was the Wochenblatt party, a group of liberal aristocrats who regarded England as their model. The party became especially active during the Crimean War and counted among its members distinguished Germans such as Moritz August von Bethmann Hollweg, Sr., a former member of the Prussian cabinet.[8]

From London at about the same time (March, 1854), the Prussian Envoy, Karl Josias von Bunsen, made a similar suggestion in a secret memorandum submitted to his government.[9] The separation of "Little Russia from Great Russia," that is, the establishment of an independent Ukraine free of Russian control, was again advocated in 1861 by Kurd von Schlötzer, Second Secretary of the Prussian Embassy in St. Petersburg.[10] And then shortly before Bismarck's retirement, the German philosopher Eduard von Hartmann openly called for the formation of a separate Ukrainian state, which he proposed to call the Kingdom of Kiev.[11]

Neither Chancellor Bismarck nor his successors ever showed much interest for such bold plans for the east. Recent studies of Bismarck's *Ostpolitik* fully support this conclusion. Gustav Rein, in a book dealing with the revolutionary element in Bismarck's policy, shows quite convincingly that the Chancellor consistently opposed revolutions and in general pursued a peaceful foreign policy. According to another writer, Reinhold Wittram, Bismarck not only refused to support any plans aiming at Russia's dismemberment but went along with the Czarist Russification policy in the Baltic provinces, which had strong and well-organized German communities.[12]

German eastern experts, in the meantime, continued to follow Ukrainian political, social, and literary developments closely, and even those who belonged to the Russian school and opposed the dismemberment of Russia came to consider "the existence of Little Russiandom and its political movement [Ukrainian nationalism] a very serious issue." [13]

Although numerous, the German settlers in the Ukraine contributed little to the growth of the Reich's interest and influence in this area. In the prewar period they totaled about 600,000 (something like 2 percent of the Ukrainian population and roughly one-fourth of the Germans of the Russian Empire).[14] Neither the German government nor most private organizations of the Reich showed interest in the fate of their compatriots in the east, possibly because most belonged to families which had emigrated long ago, in the days of Catherine the Great. The German "colonists" in the Ukraine, who lived mostly in prosperous and well-organized communities of their own, preserved their language, religion, and customs, but rarely maintained close ties with relatives at home.

Nor did German financial interests generate much concern about the political status of the Ukraine, although at the outbreak of World War I Germany was the third largest foreign investor in Russia, with an investment of 441.5 million rubles, constituting 19.7 percent of the total foreign capital investment. That German economic interests in the Ukraine were extensive is evident from the fact that more than one-third of the German capital (160.69 million rubles) was invested in Russia's mining and metallurgical industries, of which the Ukraine was then one of the principal centers.[15] Recent Soviet studies of the problem suggest that the influence of German capital in the Ukraine was substantial. They stress the significance of individual German investments in various Russian and foreign enterprises, German financial control of or influence in French, Belgian, and other firms in Russia, and the influence of German technical experts and German-Russian businessmen on the Empire's economic life as a whole.[16]

Still, there is no evidence that these German interests exerted any real influence on the Ukrainian national movement or in any way affected the Reich's policies in this part of the world, repeated Soviet claims to the contrary notwithstanding. As is well known, Soviet authors are unanimous in maintaining that Germany worked actively for the dismemberment of Russia and the creation of an independent Ukraine from the mid-nineteenth century on. One of the foremost proponents of this thesis (which incidentally has never been substantiated by any reliable sources) has been A. S. Yerusalimskii, a well-known Soviet student of German diplomacy, who has asserted time and again that the expansionist plans of German imperialists always enjoyed the complete support of the Reich government and the Supreme Army Command and that German colonists were sent to the Ukraine and the Crimea to settle down along railroads, these being of strategic value.[17] (Of course, any schoolboy knows that the steam engine had not been invented in the reign of Catherine the Great, and that is precisely when the German colonists came into these areas.)

On the eve of World War I only a small circle of Germany's eastern experts was familiar with the Ukrainian problem. The general public as well as most members of that country's official circles were introduced to it only after the opening of hostilities in the east. At the outbreak of the war German *Ostpolitik* contained no definite designs on the Ukraine or any other part of the Russian Empire.

In the last decades before World War I the Czarist regime had continued its efforts to suppress all national movements within the Empire. However, even though tighter and tighter restrictions were imposed, the Czarist authorities proved less and less capable of coping with the challenge from the non-Russian popular movements, especially in such areas as the Ukraine. The Ukrainian movement received strong support and encouragement from Ukrainian leaders in exile and even greater support from areas not subject to Russian control, notably East Galicia.

Another important development of the late nineteenth century was the rapid industrialization of the Ukraine. This was accompanied by an unprecedented growth of the cities, progressive proletarianization of the Ukrainian masses, and an impressive growth of foreign capitalism with all its economic, social, and political implications. The Ukraine was rapidly becoming not only the seat of a growing national movement but also one of the principal centers of economic and social revolution in the Russian Empire.

The Ukrainian national movement in this post-Populist period continued to be dominated by the intelligentsia, but it was a more sophisticated group, and many of its members were increasingly drawn to socialism as well. The two trends found a common focus in the 1905 Revolution, and the Ukrainian leaders of this period were destined to play a decisive role in the Russian Revolution of 1917 as well as in the Ukrainian national revival that followed.

The development of political parties in the Ukraine can be traced back to the last two decades before World War I. Even more important was the growth of Ukrainian national consciousness among the workers, some groups within the middle class, the Ukrainian landed gentry, and also the peasant masses. During this period Ukrainian literature came into its own, and Ukrainian historiography and other social sciences also reached an impressive level of development. This period produced such Ukrainian scholarly giants as the historian Mykhailo Hrushevsky and such internationally known literary figures as I. Franko, L. Ukrayinka, and M. Kotsyubyns'kyi. Unquestionably, the Ukrainian cultural, literary, and scholarly achievements provided a powerful impetus to the national movement in this crucial period of its development.[18]

Nevertheless, at the outbreak of World War I and the collapse of Czarist Russia the Ukrainian movement was still poorly developed and thus not prepared to take full advantage of the opportunities that presented themselves to the Ukrainians at this point. Conscious of the weakness of their movement and aware of the new social reality in Russia, the Ukrainians were closely connected with the general socialist and democratic movement in the Empire. With very few exceptions (for example, M. Mikhnovs'kyi's RUP—Ukrainian Revolutionary Party), Ukrainian national leaders of the pre-World War I period were autonomists and in their writings and pronouncements were confined to advocating a democratic and decentralized federal Russia. Of course, many of them dreamed of glory and independence for their nation, but this was a very distant goal and one that could not even be discussed in public.

Thus the outbreak of World War I found the Ukrainian leaders calm and cautiously optimistic. They openly proclaimed their loyalty to Russia and sincerely hoped to solve the Ukrainian problem within the context of Russian domestic policies without interference from the outside. However, Russia did not try to enlist the Ukrainians for the struggle against the common enemy; on the contrary, they were subjected to further persecution and abuse. The Czarist regime, instead of allowing the Ukrainians a degree of freedom in their cultural life in order to strengthen the loyalty and morale of this second largest people of the Russian Empire, used the outbreak of the war as the pretext for an all-out attack on the Ukrainian national movement. Ukrainian institutions were closed, their publications were again suppressed, and a number of Ukrainian leaders were arrested and deported, among them Professor M. Hrushevsky, who had just returned to Russia from abroad.

This renewed attack on the Ukrainian movement by the Czarist regime coincided with the advance of the Russian armies into Galicia, where the Ukrainian movement had a much broader base. This area, also known as West Ukraine, had since the mid-fourteenth century been under Polish rule. The fact that it became formally a part of the Austro-Hungarian Empire following the first partition of Poland in 1772 did not change the political relations in this area very much. Nevertheless, in the subsequent period the Galicians enjoyed a considerably greater degree of freedom than the Ukrainians under the Czars.

By mid-nineteenth century the Ukrainian national awakening in Galicia, originally mainly literary and cultural in form, had begun to assume a definite political coloring. (It may be noted that throughout the nineteenth century the Ukrainian inhabitants of Galicia, of both nationalist and pro-Russian orientation, continued to refer to themselves as Ruthenians.) The existence of a limited parliamentary democracy in the Dual Monarchy, the example of the better-organized and more politically oriented Poles, and the general liberal and enlightened atmosphere in the monarchy under Franz Josef gave further impetus to the Ukrainian movement there. Later in the century the development of pro-Russian Ruthenian organizations in Galicia (whose members referred to themselves as Russians) and the growing tensions between Vienna and St. Petersburg also improved the position of national Ukrainian circles in Galicia. East Galicia, with its Ukrainian majority, however, remained largely under Polish control and domination with the full knowledge and approval of the central government in Vienna.

The Ukrainians in Galicia were also helped by their compatriots from the east. In the 1870's and 1880's, when the Ukrainian national movement in Russia was subjected to further limitations and restrictions, some of its leaders went abroad and others continued their activities clandestinely; but by far the largest group transferred its activities to Galicia. This made West Ukraine into a veritable Piedmont of the Ukrainian movement, brought Galicia closer to the mainstream of Ukrainian life, and thus prepared it for eventual unification with the rest of the Ukrainian lands in 1919. It was, for example, Mykhailo Drahomanov who laid the foundation for the Ukrainian socialist movement in Galicia. And later, distinguished scholars and national leaders, such as the Ukrainian historian Mykhailo Hrushevsky, who was destined to become the father of the Ukrainian national revolution and the first President of the Ukrainian People's Republic, were active in this area until the outbreak of World War I.

In spite of consistent pro-Polish policies in Ukrainian Galicia on Vienna's part, the Ukrainians of this region manifested a remarkable degree of loyalty and devotion to the Habsburgs at the outbreak of World War I. Since the Ukrainians were aware of the relative advantage they enjoyed in Austria and viewed the possibility of a Russian victory in the east as the most dangerous prospect for the future of the Ukrainian movement as a whole, their attitude was fully understandable.

Consequently, when in the first days of the war Vienna permitted the Ukrainians to organize a volunteer corps for the struggle against Russia, as many as 28,000 men either under twenty years of age or over forty, that is, those not then subject to the draft, offered their services to the Habsburgs. Soon however, yielding to Polish pressure, Vienna allowed a mere 2,500 of these volunteers to remain in the Ukrainian Sharpshooters Legion (Sichovi Stril'tsi), whereas the Poles were permitted to form as many as five brigades under the command of Jósef Pilsudski.[19]

To make things worse, Polish and Hungarian troops and military commanders in East Galicia (which became the front zone) responded to rumors of "Russian agents" and pro-Russian sympathies among the Ukrainian peasants and resorted to mass arrests and executions. Rapid Austrian retreat from this area because of Russian pressure in late 1914 made such practices even more widespread. According to an estimate made by a Ukrainian historian of the period, thousands of Ukrainians were executed and well over 30,000 were sent to special detention camps in Austria during the first months of the war.[20]

Following the Russian occupation of East Galicia in late 1914, this unhappy land was subjected to another period of oppression and persecution. A systematic physical destruction of all Ukrainian cultural and educational institutions was ordered by Petrograd. The use of the Ukrainian language was expressly forbidden, and the Ukrainian Greek Catholic Church of Galicia was subjected to severe and systematic persecution. Count A. G. Bobrinskii was placed in charge of this operation, which aimed at the Russification, conversion to the Orthodoxy, and eventual integration of this area into the Russian Empire. Soon, thousands of prominent Ukrainians were arrested and deported, including the Metropolitan of the Ukrainian Greek Catholic Church, Count Andrii Sheptyts'kyi. The withdrawal of Russian troops from East Galicia in mid-1915 was accompanied by forced evacuation of thousands of Ukrainian peasants under the most difficult conditions.

Little wonder that the Austrian excesses previously perpetrated in this area by the Hungarian and Polish troops came to be viewed as merely unfortunate aberrations. In spite of the persecution and continuing favoritism of the Poles, the Galician Ukrainians maintained their unshakeable loyalty to the Dual Monarchy and continued to look to Vienna. Whereas the oldest Austrian military unit, the famous Prag Regiment, defected to the Russians in 1915, the Galician Ukrainian Volunteer Legion distinguished itself time and again as one of the best fighting units of the Austro-Hungarian army. Yet, following the Russian withdrawal in 1915 the Galician Ukrainians, to their dismay and embarrassment, were again confronted with Vienna's complete indifference to their long-standing hope and expectation for greater cultural and educational autonomy. Instead, in October 1916, in a festive "Manifesto to the Poles," the Austrian and German emperors promised to reconstruct a Polish state comprised of the Polish provinces freed from Russia and Galicia, including the eastern portion that was populated mainly by Ukrainians.

World War I was not a happy experience for the Ukrainians. Their land became one of the principal battlegrounds of the war and the people suffered heavy casualties in the course of these operations, without any assurance that their suffering and sacrifices would ultimately be rewarded. Of all the fighting powers, only the Germans manifested some sympathy for the Ukrainian movement, but their interest was largely academic and did little to improve the lot of the people. The two principal powers of the east—Russia and Austria-Hungary—remained unalterably opposed to Ukrainian aspirations and each in its own way continued to oppose them. This, of course, presented the Ukrainians with almost insurmountable obstacles in their struggle for independence, though at the same time it gave them their national martyrs and supplied the movement with an aura of heroism. The rise of Ukrainian nationalism during World War I was not the result of strength and maturity; it was made possible by the weakening and ultimately the collapse of the movement's most determined opponents—Austria-Hungary and Russia—especially the collapse of Russia.

CHAPTER II

German War Aims in the East and the Ukraine, 1914-1916

The outbreak of World War I found German *Ostpolitik* rather vague. It is not surprising, therefore, that the Reich had no clearly defined war aims in the early phase of the war in the east. Indeed, during the first two years of the conflict a German-Russian understanding on the basis of the *status quo* was a very real possibility. Officially, neither the Germans nor the Russians made any specific statements during this period to destroy the basis for a separate peace. The German plan to annex Russia's Baltic provinces was not made public until 1916, and the Imperial Chancellor, Theobald von Bethmann Hollweg, who never showed much enthusiasm toward such a plan, continued to work, at least through the summer of that year, for a peace with Russia on the basis of the *status quo*.

Nevertheless, insistence on what was innocently called "improved frontiers in the northeast" was one of the early demands advanced by various private organizations and influential individuals in wartime Germany. Virtually from the beginning of the war, therefore, Bethmann Hollweg was under heavy pressure to seek territorial aggrandizement in the Baltic provinces and western Poland. Yet, in mid-1915 Bethmann Hollweg confined himself to a cautious declaration that "previous conditions" in Europe were not to be restored and that if Europe was to achieve peace, the means lay in allowing Germany to assume a stronger position on the continent. In another Reichstag speech, in April, 1916, the Chancellor was more specific, stating that Russia should never again be allowed to march its armies through the unfortified boundaries of East and West Prussia.[1]

It was not until late 1916, however, that Germany committed itself definitely to territorial expansion in the northeast. This was in fact the only territory that Germany openly sought to annex at Russia's expense prior to March, 1917. Bethmann Hollweg agreed to this policy mainly for strategic and security reasons.[2] German plans for the Ukraine, the Black Sea region, and other areas of the southeast were developed later, in the spring of 1918.

The thesis that Germany entered World War I without any clear program in general, and particularly with respect to the east, has long been prevalent among German and many other western students of this period.[3] Fritz Fischer's recent study of German war aims boldly challenges this thesis. In Fischer's view, the Germans pursued a policy of "economic expansion" in Poland, Rumania, and South Russia long before the outbreak of World War I, and from early August, 1914, on, the German government followed a concrete plan aiming at the creation of several buffer states in the west, as well as in the east, including a Ukrainian state, in close political, military, economic, and cultural association with Germany.[4]

Most German historians have been critical of Fischer's sweeping reexamination of the old thesis on Germany's war aims developed by Erich Otto Volkmann in 1929. One of Fischer's critics was Ludwig Dehio, at one time the editor of the most influential historical journal in Germany, *Historische Zeitschrift*, who wrote in 1959: "Our anti-Russian mission, then, was anything but long-standing. Before 1914 we had obviously not taken the Russian peril seriously, and even after the beginning of the war we would have preferred to exorcise it by cooperation, either on the basis of the Conservative, Prussian, Continental tradition or on the basis of our new wartime ambitions (Tirpiz)."[5] Indeed, even at the height of the German advance in the east in 1918, the possibility of German-Russian reconciliation was never lost sight of; even

General Erich Ludendorff, the principal architect of German expansion in the east during this period, did not rule out such a possibility.

An even more impressive case for the old thesis on Germany's war aims—an even more passionate defense of the Reich's wartime Chancellor Bethmann Hollweg, on whom Fischer lavished most of his criticism—was produced by Gerhard Ritter in his monumental *Staatskunst und Kriegshandwerk.* The entire third volume of this distinguished German historian's major work is devoted to the wartime period of Bethmann Hollweg's chancellorship. It is a masterful attempt to defend and restore the Chancellor's image as a genuine statesman who remained forever true to his policy of moderation and accommodation.[6]

It is the contention here that official German war aims and plans for the postwar period remained very much in flux as long as Bethmann Hollweg continued in the position of the Reich's Chancellor. He may have been correct in remaining deliberately vague on the Central Powers' war aims in the hope of coming to terms with at least one of their adversaries; however, by doing so he allowed the unofficial, and often irresponsible, plans and programs of various German organizations and individuals to be presented gleefully by Allied propaganda as official views of the Central Powers. Inside Germany, too, these private plans were frequently regarded as reflecting the thinking of the German government, and this is still a source of confusion and controversy today.[7]

Many of Fritz Fischer's critics were quick to note that he ascribed too much significance to the private memoranda, petitions, and other such documents prepared at various stages of the conflict, and they pointed especially to Fischer's treatment of Bethmann Hollweg's "September, 1914, Program." In Fischer's view the program contained most of the expansionist plans that the Germans were to develop in the course of the war, but such an interpretation must be regarded as "too sweeping." [8]

The fact that Bethmann Hollweg's papers were destroyed in 1945 deprives us of the possibility of settling these disputes once and for all. Nonetheless, there does exist the diary of his assistant and secretary—a man who was privy to the Chancellor's innermost thoughts and feelings—Kurt Riezler. The diary itself has not yet been published, but a sophisticated and reliable discussion of it has been provided by an American student of German history, Fritz Stern. Granting that Riezler's diary cannot take the place of Bethmann's papers, no one was closer to the Reich's wartime Chancellor on a day-to-day basis than Riezler, and his diary is a valuable source for the study of German aims during World War I.

It is of interest that "the September, 1914, Program" (which Fischer presents as one of the most revealing and fateful German documents of World War I) is not even mentioned by Riezler. Consequently, careful study of the Riezler diary by Stern prompted the latter to conclude that there is no evidence that Bethmann cherished expansionist aims and that "the diary reveals neither the heady atmosphere of victory nor the certainty of some master plan of conquest; rather it suggests gloom, confusion, uninspired improvisation in planning, and endless wrangling in execution." [9]

The continued fluidity and confusion surrounding Germany's official war aims contributed greatly to the fortunes of various political "schools" which competed on the German scene during the war period in an attempt to influence the Reich's *Ostpolitik*. The term "school" is used here somewhat loosely, since such activist groups were never formally organized, and their membership and leadership cannot always be clearly determined. Nevertheless, one may speak of five major schools or concepts:

1) The annexationist school, most closely associated with the *Drang nach Osten* idea.

2) The *Mitteleuropa* project (or projects).

3) The Polish school, which in some ways was a branch of the *Mitteleuropa* movement.

4) The *Osteuropa* school, which advocated the so-called border states policy (*Randstaatenpolitik*).

5) The Russian school, which defended the idea of the unity and indivisibility of Russia and its natural accompaniment, close friendship with Germany's great eastern neighbor—a concept which had deep roots in German thinking.

The most dynamic force within the annexationist school consisted of the Pan-Germans (*Alldeutschen*) organized around the Fatherland party; they were especially active in promoting the *Drang nach Osten* idea. Their leader, Heinrich Class, in a memorandum presented to Bethmann Hollweg in September, 1914, urged the German government to commit itself to a bold, aggressive plan calling for the creation of an independent Ukraine to be closely associated with Germany and to share a common frontier with it. Although the Chancellor was not receptive to such plans and ordered the memorandum to be suppressed, the Pan-Germans refused to desist from advocating such a solution for the east.[10]

Though influential from the beginning of the war, the Pan-Germans did not become an important force on the German political scene until late 1917. Their influence, however, cannot so easily be evaluated and is susceptible of exaggeration. According to some earlier studies, the German government maintained a sympathetic attitude toward the Pan-German annexationists.[11] Fischer, who puts the Pan-German membership at 25,000, maintains that this group exerted a strong and permanent influence on all aspects of German political, social, and cultural life throughout the war.[12] Alfred Kruck, however, who studied this problem much more thoroughly than Fischer, shows rather convincingly that Germany's wartime chancellors—Theobald von Bethmann Hollweg, Georg Michaelis, Georg von Hertling, and Max Prince von Baden—successfully resisted the pressure exerted on them by the Pan-Germans throughout the war. Moreover, the Pan-Germans were not even able to present their views to Kaiser Wilhelm II, let alone win him over. Similarly, their attempts in October, 1917, to induce General Erich von Ludendorff to take over as Germany's dictator also failed completely, in spite of the fact that the general had often been sympathetic with many of the Pan-German ideas.[13]

According to Henry Cord Meyer, a long-time American student of the problem, the idea of *Mitteleuropa*—a plan for an economic community which was to consist of a German-Austro-Hungarian customs union and which was to include most of the small and medium-sized European states—"played a subordinate role in the official war aims of Germany and was resisted by a majority of the Hapsburg military and diplomatic leaders." Meyer also concluded that "the German Foreign Office alone gradually developed a sympathetic interest for some form of mid-European economic integration." [14] Fritz Fischer, in his more recent study based on German archives, ascribes considerably more importance to the *Mitteleuropa* agitation and regards it as a powerful element in the formulation of the Reich's war aims. Bethmann Hollweg, according to Fischer, repeatedly spoke of a *Mitteleuropa* comprising small East European states between Germany and a "reduced Russia." In Fischer's view, both Bethmann and Richard von Kühlmann, his Secretary of State for Foreign Affairs, regarded *Mitteleuropa* as the most convenient way of strengthening Germany's power position on the continent and as a precondition for the conduct of the Reich's *Weltpolitik*.[15] Stern, in his study of Riezler's diary, came to the same basic conclusion. Riezler fully shared Bethmann's conviction that "such a new order in Europe promised far greater permanency than the outright annexation of foreign territory." Riezler also admitted, however, that *Mitteleuropa* "was the European disguise of our will to power." [16]

No one proposed to include the Ukraine in these particular schemes. It was the Polish problem that occupied a central position in the *Mitteleuropa* plans. Not only for Friedrich Naumann, the principal exponent of the concept, but for other *Mitteleuropa* advocates too, Poland was "a piece of genuine mid-European soil," and the Polish Proclamation of November, 1916, announced jointly by Berlin and Vienna more or less at the height of the *Mitteleuropa* agitation, was hailed by Naumann and his followers as an important step toward the realization of their goal.[17]

The German historian Hans Beyer is therefore correct in viewing the period from late 1914 through 1916 as the time when the Polish shadow dominated the entire "Berlin-Budapest-Vienna triangle." [18] The influence of the *Mitteleuropa* concept on German official thinking with regard to Poland might well have contributed to the fact that the Ukrainian problem did not figure prominently in German plans for the east during this period. It was only during the first months of the war that the German press as well as certain official circles devoted considerable attention to the Ukraine.

According to Naumann's project, only those parts of Ukrainian territory already under Austrian rule, such as East Galicia and North Bukovina, were to be included in his *Mitteleuropa*. Such caution concerning the Ukrainian problem on Naumann's part is understandable. After all, as long as Russia remained strong and there was some hope of coming to terms with her, Naumann could not have gone beyond Poland in his schemes. There are definite indications, however, that he sympathized with the national aspirations of other borderland peoples about whom he learned from his friend and collaborator, Paul Rohrbach. Hans Beyer even went so far as to credit Naumann with having contributed through his *Mitteleuropa* writings (read by hundreds of thousands in Germany and Austria as well as abroad) to the better understanding of, and greater interest in, the border peoples of the Russian Empire.[19]

It was not until the conclusion of the Ukrainian Treaty of Brest-Litovsk on February 9, 1918, that Naumann took a clear stand concerning the Ukrainian problem. He hailed the treaty as a positive step toward strengthening his *Mitteleuropa* (although he had primarily in mind food supplies that he expected from the Ukraine),[20] and soon afterward Walter Schotte, the editor of the weekly *Mittel-Europa*, referred to the Ukraine as "a constituent part of *Mitteleuropa*."[21] All this, however, was merely self-deception. The original *Mitteleuropa* concept of 1915 and 1916 was dead. Whereas some people stubbornly refused to recognize this fact, others quickly moved beyond it and transferred their *Mitteleuropa* interest to Ludendorff's *Drang nach Osten* or to Rohrbach's *Osteuropa*. Fritz Fischer, who unlike Meyer sees a close connection between *Mitteleuropa* plans and German official policy, believes that with Russia's collapse the *Mitteleuropa* idea gave way to a plan of "absolute domination in the east."[22]

An equally important role in the endless debates on the Reich's *Ostpolitik* was played by the *Osteuropa* movement. To refer to this school as Rohrbach's *Osteuropa* is far from an overstatement, for no other writer in wartime Germany did as much as Paul Rohrbach to develop and disseminate the ideas associated with the *Osteuropa* concept. He was not only the most prolific but also the best-known member of this school as well as its unchallenged leader from the beginning. Paul Rohrbach had already achieved an impressive publication record before World War I. As a Baltic German, he had firsthand knowledge of Russia, spoke the language well, and maintained an active interest in Russia's social, economic, and political developments after he left that country and settled in Germany, the land of his ancestors. One of the most widely traveled Germans of his time, Rohrbach made a name for himself as an expert on the colonial question and the German settlers, as a writer on Middle Eastern problems and as an advocate of German drive into this area, as a *Mitteleuropa* supporter, and finally as a student of Russia and its nationality problems.

Many other members of this school were also Baltic Germans.[23] Perhaps the most distinguished of them was Theodor Schiemann, who may be regarded as Rohrbach's teacher and the theoretical founder of the *Osteuropa* school. A highly respected university professor and scholar in the field of Russian history, Schiemann was first to advance the thesis that Imperial Russia was an artificial conglomeration of various nationalities that had the right to separate existence. By far the more influential of the two (he was Kaiser Wilhelm's friend and adviser both before and during the war), Schiemann took a considerably narrower approach to Germany's *Ostpolitik* than did Rohrbach and was primarily interested in the Reich's annexation of the Baltic area. Schiemann is believed by Fischer to have exerted considerable influence on the German Foreign Office as well as the Reich's military leaders, especially those engaged in the administration of the German-occupied areas in the east.[24] Schiemann might have had something to do with the ideas held by such individuals as Colonel (later General) Max Hoffmann or General Ludendorff, but there is no evidence that his views carried as much weight with the Foreign Office as Fischer claims.

With the outbreak of the war, Rohrbach and his co-workers began to stress the multinational character of the Russian Empire even more, and tried to make its dismemberment a specific war aim. One of the first and most important steps toward the realization of this goal was to be the restoration of the "old historical dividing line between Muscovy and the Ukraine," with the latter becoming a fully independent state. Needless to say, such a Ukrainian state was to have close economic and political ties with the Mid-European union led by Germany.[25]

Poland and Finland, too, were to become independent. As for the Baltic provinces, Rohrbach had a somewhat different plan for them. Not only Courland, Livonia, and Estonia but also Lithuania were to be detached from Russia and organized into the so-called *Baltikum,* which was to be Germanized by the German settlers from other parts of Russia. It is mainly because of his attitude toward the Baltic peoples that Rohrbach has often been called a Pan-German.[26] No doubt, Rohrbach did not appreciate the aspirations and desires of these small but nationally conscious ethnic groups; however, even here he was quick to warn the Germans not to take the haughty *Herrenvolk* attitude toward the Baltic peoples, but to grant them autonomy and make them partners in the common undertaking—a view for which he was violently criticized and denounced by the Pan-Germans.[27]

The *Osteuropa* school made a major contribution to the popularization of the Ukrainian question in wartime Germany. True, the Ukrainian question was discussed by many German writers, not so much with the intention of breaking up the Russian Empire and establishing a series of new, independent border states in the east as with the hope of bringing about the collapse, or at least a weakening, of the Russian army in order to facilitate the Central Powers' victory on the eastern front. But from the very beginning there were people like Rohrbach who drew a broad plan for a new order in the east and who never wavered in their advocacy of an independent Ukraine.

In addition to German writers advocating the establishment of an independent Ukraine, there were scores of Ukrainians from Galicia and émigrés from the East Ukraine carrying on their propaganda work independently, or with German financial support, as well as some pro-Ukrainian Austrian writers. Hans Beyer identifies "five basic Ukrainian theses," which are to be found in most of these writings:

1) The Ukrainians constitute a separate and distinct nationality and not a branch of Russiandom; Ukrainian is a separate language and not a Russian dialect.

2) The Ukrainian Renaissance can be traced back to Kotlyarevs'kyi's *Aeneid*, and the Ukrainian national movement is similar to national movements of the peoples of Central and Eastern Europe. Since 1798 (the date of the publication of the *Aeneid* in Ukrainian), the Ukrainian national movement has grown in depth and scope and has become a strong political force in the Dnieper region.

3) This national movement aims at separation from Russia and wishes to cooperate with the Central Powers.

4) Not only the Muscovites but the Poles, too, are the Ukraine's natural enemies. (This was the view of both the Galician Ukrainians and the émigré writers from the East Ukraine.)

5) Economically, the Ukraine is a key area of the east. Its separation from Moscow would greatly contribute to the victory of the Central Powers.[28]

These German efforts no doubt served as an important source of encouragement to the Ukrainians in Austria-Hungary, as well as to the émigré writers and political leaders from Russia who looked upon Rohrbach and others like him as individuals who exerted a strong influence on German officialdom. But because there was no communication between the Central Powers and Russia during the war, the influence of these German writings on the Ukrainian national movement was negligible.

The influence of the *Osteuropa* school on official German thinking and planning for the Ukraine cannot so easily be determined. According to Viet Valentin, German *Ostpolitik* was significantly and permanently influenced by Rohrbach's thinking. This influence, in Valentin's view, was especially important up to the time of the Treaty of Brest-Litovsk.[29] Henry Cord Meyer, who studied Rohrbach more thoroughly than Valentin did, arrived at a different conclusion. He felt that Rohrbach and his school enjoyed little support from German policy-makers prior to the Russian Revolution and that Rohrbach's influence on official German thinking had been greatly exaggerated.[30] Dmytro Doroshenko also concluded that whereas the German press, and to a lesser extent public opinion, favored an active policy in the east and advocated the exploitation of the Ukrainian movement as a force against Russia, the governing circles in Germany and Austria did not openly share this view. In fact, among influential political leaders of the Reich, only the former Chancellor, Prince Bernhard von Bülow, appreciated the significance of the Ukraine in German politics and did not hesitate to say so publicly.[31]

Although both German civilian and military leaders owed a great deal to Rohrbach's school of thought for their knowledge of the east, he seems to have had little success in exerting a direct influence on official German thinking. We know from his own account that in June, 1916, he had a conference with Bethmann Hollweg and that soon after that he tried also to win over Ludendorff to his view. Rohrbach met General Ludendorff and Colonel Hoffmann in Kovno and presented his thesis on the breakup of the Russian Empire. To this Ludendorff replied: "This is politics, which I as a soldier must not be concerned with. If I were to determine our policies, they would be simply—I hate England!" Rohrbach's request to see Marshal Paul von Hindenburg was turned down by Ludendorff in his typical soldierly way,[32] Rohr-

bach made a stronger impression on Hoffmann, of whom he
thought very highly.[33] Here, however, it was not so much the question of influence as similarity of views. Moreover, at the most critical stage of Germany's involvement in the Ukraine—during the
occupation of the country—neither of them was permitted to play
an active part in this development.

Rohrbach had closer contacts with the German Foreign Office
and cooperated with it through its Propaganda and Information
Bureau (Zentralstelle für Auslandsdienst) until the spring of
1917, when he found himself compelled to resign "because of the
Foreign Office's lack of objectivity with regard to Russia." [34] Rohrbach's visit to the Ukraine in May, 1918, undertaken at the suggestion of the German Foreign Office, did not bring him any
closer to official German circles.

Rohrbach's influence in wartime Germany was thus mainly
that of a prolific writer and a popular lecturer. His *Osteuropa*
school never succeeded in exerting a direct and permanent influence on any of the Reich's principal political and military figures.
The Brest-Litovsk negotiations and the subsequent development
of the Reich's Ukrainian policy during the occupation period
(March-November, 1918) were conducted without Rohrbach's
participation and counsel.

The Russian school (in which there were no Russians) probably played a more important role in the shaping of the Reich's
Ostpolitik during the war period than any other comparable
group. This school—identified with the "unity of Russia" concept
—had deep roots in German thinking and was closely associated
with Bismarck and his policies—a fact that considerably
strengthened the school's position. Professor Otto Hoetzsch, a well-
known German historian and a Reichstag deputy, was the most
influential member of this school and was also generally regarded
as its leader.[35] The Russian school did not publish as much as the
Osteuropa or the *Mitteleuropa* groups; its output was never even
remotely comparable to the flood of pamphlets and other writings
produced by the Pan-German circles. It had close contacts, however, with a number of important Reichstag leaders (for example,
Gustav Stresemann and Walther Rathenau) and, according to
Hans Beyer, was even more influential among the government
bureaucrats and military men "with whom the idea of unity of
Russia became virtually a dogma." [36]

A more specialized study of the role of university professors in wartime Germany, on the other hand, reveals a somewhat contradictory picture. Professor Hoetzsch's influence is reputed to have been as great as that of his colleague and rival, Theodor Schiemann. At the same time Hoetzsch is presented as a rather lonely figure among his peers in the Russian field because of his exclusive pro-Russian position.[37] Fischer went even further and concluded that Hoetzsch's Russian school "was overwhelmingly defeated" by its opponents.[38]

Of course, the influence of such informal groups cannot be measured with any degree of precision. Also, one cannot disregard the influence of habit and tradition, which were powerful allies of Hoetzsch's Russian school all along. Immanuel Birnbaum does well to remind us that there have always been pro-Russian as well as anti-Russian factions in all German parties.[39] One must, therefore, differentiate between Hoetzsch's influence in the early phase of the war, which admittedly was not very great, and three other factors: the role of the Russian school during the period of Russo-German attempts to conclude a separate peace (1915–1916); the eclipse that Hoetzsch's school suffered during the Brest-Litovsk days; and a slow, yet unmistakable resurgence of this political orientation in the summer of 1918.

Another group, the Polish school, was closely associated with the *Mitteleuropa* circles and can even be regarded as part of this larger movement. The Polish school's aim was the restoration of a unified Poland, in close association with the Central Powers. It must be considered here because of its impact on other solutions and orientations, especially the Russian school and the Central Powers' flirtation with the Ukrainian national movement. Like other schools, it is examined here primarily as a factor that influenced German official thinking with regard to the Ukraine in the period prior to the March, 1917, Revolution. The importance of this school becomes apparent when one bears in mind the fact that Austria-Hungary openly called for the restoration of Poland as early as August, 1914, and never entirely gave up the hope of realizing this goal. The plan, known as the Austro-Polish solution, aimed at organizing a Polish state within the framework of the Austro-Hungarian federation but under the joint protection of Berlin and Vienna.[40]

Moreover, some very highly placed and influential German civilian and military officials could always be counted among the supporters of the Polish school. Among them was Count Bogdan Franz Servatius von Hutten-Czapski, the Reich's principal eastern expert in the early stages of the war. This highly trusted Prussian nobleman of Polish descent, with close ties to the German Foreign Ministry, the Supreme Army Command, and the Kaiser himself, was an open advocate of the restoration of a "historical Poland" which was to include Lithuania and considerable portions of Byelorussia and the Ukraine.[41] General Hans Hartwig von Beseler, the Governor-General of German-occupied Poland, was called by a Polish historian "the most fervid advocate of Poland's independence in close connection with Germany." [42] Even though Germany failed to make any definite decision on the vital question of Poland's future, the Polish factor was most significant in the formulation and the conduct of the Reich's *Ostpolitik*. It became the object of almost constant negotiations between Berlin and Vienna, and no area was to be as deeply affected by the outcome of these talks as the Ukraine.

The German government never chose, clearly and definitively, to support any of the schools that competed on the German political scene during World War I. Military developments at the front and political changes abroad were more important in determining the Reich's *Ostpolitik* during the war years than the specific influence of any of the schools.

Strictly speaking, there was no Ukrainian school, although Rohrbach's *Osteuropa* most nearly fits that designation. There was, however, an important Ukrainian political organization in wartime Germany which, even though it cannot be compared to any of the above schools, played a certain role in the development of the Reich's *Ostpolitik*, especially its plans for the Ukraine, during World War I. This was the Union for the Liberation of the Ukraine (Soyuz Vyzvolennya Ukrayiny), and its activities provide an important index of German and Austrian planning for the Ukraine during this period. It was founded in Lviv (officially Lemberg), then a part of Austria-Hungary, on August 4, 1914, by a group of Ukrainian political émigrés from Russia, in close cooperation with Austrian Ukrainian leaders from Galicia. This represented a drastic departure from Vienna's traditional policy of cooperating with Russia against various revolutionary and subversive elements and organizations.[43]

From the beginning, the Union was determined to remain a political organization of East Ukrainian exiles (that is, former Russian citizens from the Central Ukraine), above all political parties. The main goal of this organization was the restoration of an independent Ukrainian state. In the view of most of the Union's leaders and supporters such a state was also to be socialist.[44] The leaders of the Union were from the very beginning irrevocably committed to a separatist course, whereas most of the Ukrainian leaders in the Central (Russian) Ukraine maintained an autonomist and federalist position. A good example of such a federalist-autonomist position, stemming from the awareness of the unpreparedness of the Ukrainian national movement for full independence, is the view expressed by one of the leaders of that movement, Symon Petlyura, in a letter dated December 21, 1914, to a West Ukrainian leader and the Union's representative in Sweden, Norway, and the United States, Osyp Nazaruk.[45]

The Union was soon recognized by both Austria-Hungary and Germany as a body representing the interests of the Ukrainians, not only on the territory of the Central Powers but in other European countries as well, especially neutral ones. Initially, a subordinate Austrian official, Consul Emanuel Urbas, served as Vienna's liaison with the Union, and the Austro-Hungarian authorities provided it with necessary funds as well as with telegraph, courier, and transportation services to facilitate its work.[46] The Reich's official assigned to work with the Union was the German Consul in Lviv, Karl Heinze.[47] However, during this early phase (August-November, 1914), the Ukrainian undertaking was almost exclusively an Austrian affair.

The Union began its work with an anonymous appeal, "To the Ukrainian People of Russia," issued in Lviv in early August, 1914, and a signed one, "To the Public Opinion of Europe," dated August 25, 1914. It bore the signatures of the following members of the Union: Dmytro Dontsov, Mykola Zaliznyak, Volodymyr Doroshenko, Andrii Zhuk, Oleksander Skoropys-Ioltukhovs'kyi, and Marian Melenevs'kyi (Basok).[48] The first two, Dontsov and Zaliznyak, left the organization shortly thereafter. Zaliznyak continued to cooperate with the Austrians independently and also played a certain role as a go-between during the Brest-Litovsk negotiations in 1918.

Then the Union leaders drafted another appeal that they proposed to have signed by the Austrian and German Emperors and issued as a manifesto to the Ukrainian people. This, of course, would have amounted to an open declaration of the two powers' support of the Ukrainian national movement and its programs. Vienna is reported to have rejected this plan (apparently without even consulting Berlin) and even the anonymous proclamation of early August, of which some half-million copies are supposed to have been printed in the meantime, was ordered to be destroyed.[49] All these appeals and proclamations seem to have been prepared on the Ukrainian initiative, inasmuch as extant Austrian documents do not contain any references to such plans. According to an official Austrian source, the following Russian pamphlets were among the Union's early publications: Parvus' (Dr. Alexander Helphand's) *Bor'ba protiv tsarizma* (The Struggle Against Tsarism)—3,000 copies; L. Martov's *Prostyya rechi* (Plain Talks) —3,000 copies; and an anonymous *Soldatam russkoi armii* (To the Soldiers of the Russian Army)—50,000 copies. The same source lists the number of the Union's employees—both full and part-time—as being forty-two.[50]

Meanwhile, in late August, 1914, the Union moved its headquarters to Vienna. East Galicia was then being overrun by the Russian armies, and soon Lviv itself fell into their hands. This made Vienna a natural refuge for the Union. This move and the fact that the organization came into existence on Austrian soil should not, however, be regarded as proof of the existence of some definite Austrian plan for the Ukraine or a firm commitment to support its national movement. True, several members of the Union had lived and worked in Austria long before the outbreak of the war, because there they could count on the support and cooperation of Galician Ukrainians. Moreover, it was Austria-Hungary, rather than Germany, that would occupy the Ukrainian territory in the event of the Central Powers' victory in the east. However, the Union soon became active in Germany also, where, if only in some private circles, it hoped to find more support for its ultimate goal—the liberation of the Ukraine. Galician Ukrainian leaders were again helpful in the establishment of relations between the Union and Berlin. Most of the credit for this must go to Kost' Levyts'kyi and Mykola Vasylko, both of whom were deputies in the Austrian Diet.[51]

The work of the Union was financed initially by the Dual Monarchy and then jointly by Vienna and Berlin, but openly neither government—neither German nor Austrian—would commit itself in any way to make the restoration of an independent Ukrainian state a part of its official program. According to Doroshenko, the Union accepted funds from the Germans and Austrians as a "loan" to the future Ukrainian government, of which it considered itself "the kernel." [52] The Union leaders, most of whom were socialists, found it embarrassing to accept financial support from the Central Powers, and pleaded with Vienna—the initial donor—for acceptance of the "loan principle." The Dual Monarchy, however, refused to go along with such a formula. The Union leaders, then, made an oral promise to return these funds to the Austrian government in the future.[53] There is no evidence in the German documents that the Union regarded itself as the nucleus of the future Ukrainian government. Certainly, neither Berlin nor Vienna ever considered granting it such status. The amount received from Austria during the initial period of cooperation—August-December, 1914—was 227,994.10 crowns. A substantial part of these funds was spent on the development of the library and the purchase of necessary office furnishings and equipment.[54]

Austria supported the activities of the Union first and foremost as a wartime measure. Anything that might weaken Russia, or perhaps even bring about her collapse, had to be encouraged so that at least one of the Allies could be eliminated and the encirclement of the Central Powers broken. Vienna had to be especially careful in this game. Being committed to the Austro-Polish solution and apprehensive of the growing political aspirations of its various national groups, Vienna, in the view of an influential Austrian diplomat, Count Ottokar von Czernin, simply could not afford to promote a movement aiming at the dismemberment of Russia, for this might strike a mortal blow to the system on which the Dual Monarchy itself was based.[55] Count Alexander von Hoyos, Permanent Secretary of the Austrian Foreign Office, also viewed Vienna's support of the Ukrainian movement as a risky enterprise, but was ready to promote it because he was convinced that only "internal troubles" in Russia could result in the weakening of the "eastern colossus." [56] Although the Ukrainian operation was an undertaking authorized by Vienna's Foreign Office, most Austrian officials were critical of it all along, and it remained Vienna's "unwanted child" till the very end.[57]

Germany's attitude toward the Ukrainian movement during this early phase (August-November, 1914) was even more cautious, in spite of the fact that Berlin did not have to face Vienna's dilemmas in these subtle and explosive national questions of the east. Count von Hutten-Czapski, in his capacity as eastern expert at the Great Headquarters, was instructed by the Emperor to follow national movements of the Poles, Jews, Ukrainians, and other ethnic groups in Russia with a view to their possible exploitation for the benefit of the German war effort. The fact that Hutten-Czapski was mainly interested in the restoration of a "historical Poland" left little room for the Reich's collaboration with other groups in the east, inasmuch as such a Poland was to include large portions of the Ukraine, Byelorussia, and Lithuania. Although Hutten-Czapski retired from the post of the Reich's chief nationality expert in September, 1914, he continued to have direct access to the Kaiser, and his influence on the German government is believed to have remained considerable until well after mid-1917.[58]

It was not until after Hutten-Czapski's resignation and Vienna's disillusionment with the Ukrainian movement toward the end of 1914, that Germany began closer cooperation with the Union. German officials directly responsible for the cooperation were General Emil Friedrich and Captain Walter von Lübers of the War Ministry, and Joseph Trautmann and Diego von Bergen of the Foreign Office. Of these, Bergen was probably most important, for he was the Foreign Office's principal "revolutionary expert." [59] Other Germans involved in the Union's work were Friedrich von Schwerin, a high-ranking Prussian official (Administrative President of the Frankfurt on the Oder District) and Under-Secretary of State Arthur Zimmermann's close friend, and his assistant, Dr. Erich Keup; both Schwerin and Keup were widely known in Germany for their promotion of annexationist plans calling for acquisition of new territories in the east.[60] Officially, the Union had no direct contact with the German Foreign Office. It received financial assistance from and remained under the general supervision of the Intermediary Agency of Frankfurt on the Oder, which Schwerin and Keup organized specifically for this purpose with General Friedrich's assistance.[61] The Reich's diplomatic representatives in neutral capitals, as for example Baron Hellmuth Lucius von Stödten in Stockholm, Baron Gisbert von Romberg in Bern, and Count Ulrich von Brockdorff-Rantzau in Copenhagen, also played an active role in Germany's attempt to revolutionize the east. They tried to accomplish this with the assistance of the Union for the Liberation of the Ukraine, the League of Non-Russian Peoples (Liga der Fremdvölker Russlands), and various Russian socialist groups. German Foreign Office archives contain literally hundreds of dispatches, memoranda, and other diplomatic communications attesting to the close cooperation between these German diplomats and the Union's representatives abroad. The most active and successful Ukrainian information centers were the ones in Bern and Lausanne and the Constantinople center. The German-inspired and financed League of Non-Russian Peoples carried out similar activities and differed from the Union mainly in its multinational character. The principal link between German official circles and Russian socialist groups abroad was the famous double agent, Alexander Helphand (Parvus).[62] Parvus is also believed to have been involved in various Ukrainian projects and to have served as a go-between in the Union's dealings with Russian socialists (for example, Vladimir I. Lenin, Khristian G. Rakovskii, and Karl B. Radek).[63]

Although Under-Secretary of State Zimmerman found it advisable to encourage privately the leaders of the Union by expressing his sympathy with their efforts,[64] officially Germany remained noncommittal and was determined to retain a free hand in the East. Bethmann Hollweg was especially careful in this game, and there is no evidence that he promised at any point, even privately, to support the Ukrainian movement. Of course, Zimmerman and other German officials who maintained a contact with the Union did so with his knowledge. This was, however, far from being a definite commitment on the Chancellor's part, as Fritz Fischer repeatedly asserts, to "roll Russia back" and to organize a chain of pro-German "buffer states" in the east with the Ukraine occupying a pivotal position in it.[65] Indeed, Friedrich von Meinecke's assertion that Bethmann Hollweg "did not wish to hear anything of the Ukrainians" even as late as May, 1918, because he was deeply convinced that Russia would recover,[66] is equally valid for the earlier period of Germany's *Ostpolitik*, and Bethmann's position was shared by an overwhelming majority of the high-ranking German officials.

In the spring of 1915 the Union transferred its headquarters from Vienna to Berlin. The transfer took place on Ukrainian initiative and came as no surprise to those familiar with the Union's activities. The most important factor behind this move was doubtless Austria's decision to abandon its plan to revolutionize the Ukraine. By early December, 1914, the Austro-Hungarian government had come to the conclusion that the Ukrainian movement could be of value only if Austrian troops marched into that area. The military situation was an important consideration in this decision, although nonmilitary factors also played a part in it. Vienna was disappointed with the accomplishments of Ukrainian organizations and feared the rise of Ukrainian nationalism in Galicia. Also, Vienna came to rely more and more on Polish support. Things came to a head on December 17, 1914, when the Union's annual allowance was reduced by 50 percent (from 200,000 to 100,000 crowns), serious restrictions were imposed by Vienna on its activities, and the Union was advised to transfer its headquarters to either Sofia or Constantinople. Another plan called for the transfer of the Union's headquarters to Switzerland.[67]

The Ukrainians, however, resisted these pressures for a hasty move to some secondary capital because they feared that this might weaken and disorient the entire movement. Also, they sensed correctly that the Austrians were not prepared to sever all ties with the Union. Protracted negotiations followed and by April, 1915, most of the Austro-Ukrainian differences were somehow ironed out. The Union was invited to remain in Vienna and was assured of a 100,000 crown allowance per annum, with Germany providing an equal sum.[68] Just the same, the Union's relations with Vienna remained strained, and it decided to move its headquarters to Berlin. There is no evidence of any Austro-German misunderstandings or rivalry over the Ukrainian question at this point. The choice of Berlin was an expression of the Union's hope of finding more understanding for its program in Germany as well as of its realization that it would be in Berlin rather than in Vienna that the future of the east would be decided.

The break with Vienna did not mean, however, that the Union completely abandoned its activities in Austro-Hungarian territory. On the whole, the Union was to benefit from its greater reliance on and closer cooperation with Berlin. New programs and projects were soon initiated with Germany's assistance, to which Austria-Hungary, too, felt compelled to give its belated and often grudging support.

The Union's activities can be divided conveniently into five categories: (1) information and political work in the Central Powers' camp and among the neutrals; (2) propaganda work on the eastern front directed primarily at the Ukrainians in the Czarist army: (3) work with Ukrainian prisoners of war in Germany and Austria: (4) intelligence work and "special projects" behind the front lines; (5) work in German- and Austrian-occupied territory inhabited by the Ukrainians (for example, the Kholm area).

Besides its headquarters in Vienna or Berlin, the Union maintained throughout the war period two information centers in Switzerland and at times also had offices in Sweden, Norway, Rumania, Italy, Bulgaria, Turkey, Great Britain, and the United States. Not only did it prepare materials in the languages of these countries; it also published in Hungarian, Czech, Croatian, and Russian. The Union's propaganda activities were most impressive among the Central Powers, however. In addition to drawing up the "Five Basic Ukrainian Theses," it produced publications that often served as bases for similar German and Austrian writings.[69] Its official organs were *Die Ukrainischen Nachrichten* and *Vistnyk Soyuza Vyzvolennya Ukrayiny* (The News of the Union for the Liberation of the Ukraine). According to a recent Austrian source, the Union, in the course of its four-year existence, published about 150 titles—books, pamphlets, and periodicals.[70]

The Union's contribution to German and Austrian intelligence work and special projects behind the front lines appears to have been very limited. The Austrians were first to experiment with propaganda teams to be sent into Russia to revolutionize the Ukrainian masses. By December, 1914, only three individuals were sent through the front lines. There is no record of the result of this experiment.[71] Vienna was also involved, during this early stage of the war, in what came to be known as the "Turkish Project." The plan called for the landing of a five-hundred-man force of Ukrainian volunteers on the northern shore of the Black Sea

(Kuban was one of the areas considered for this operation). The plan was cleared by both Constantinople and Vienna, but was never carried out.[72] The Union was not very enthusiastic about this plan, and it proved impossible to get such a force organized because of the lack of qualified volunteers. Equally important was the estrangement between Vienna and the Union that developed toward the end of 1914 and continued well into 1917.

In 1916 the Germans helped the Union send several Ukrainian propagandists through the front line; there is no evidence that other, similar missions were sponsored by the Germans at this stage. Thus, the Union had virtually no contacts with the Russian Ukraine. A reliable Union source speaks of only one individual who made two trips from the Ukraine to Germany in the course of the war period.[73] Shortly before the Russian Revolution the Germans tried again to enlist Ukrainian assistance for special duties behind the enemy lines. In January, 1917, the Reich's War Ministry began the recruitment of Ukrainian prisoners of war for special propaganda and sabotage missions. Some of these Czarist soldiers were to go back as escapees, invalids, or under some other guise.[74] It is not known whether such missions were actually carried out, or whether any other such projects were proposed by the Germans. It appears that the entire plan foundered because of lack of enthusiasm on the part of the Union leaders.

Propaganda work on the eastern front, directed at the Ukrainian soldiers in the Russian army, was launched as early as August, 1914, and continued in one form or another throughout the war.[75] Its effectiveness, however, appears to have been very limited.

Of considerable interest was the work, mainly cultural and educational, that the Union developed in the areas occupied by the German and Austrian forces during the 1915–1916 campaigns—Kholm, Pidlasha, and parts of western Volhynia. The Union took special interest in Kholm, viewing it as a part of Ukrainian territory and a testing ground for the determination of Germany's and Austria's aims toward the Ukraine as a whole.

The German attitude toward the Ukrainians in these occupied areas was clearly more sympathetic than that of Austria-Hungary. Vienna not only allowed but facilitated cultural and educational work conducted by the Union and Galician compatriots among the Ukrainians in Volhynia; however, it maintained a very different, clearly pro-Polish, position in Kholm and Pidlasha.[76]

The Union's work among the Ukrainian prisoners of war was not only one of its principal activities but the field in which it achieved the greatest success. In the first months of the war, the Union representatives were allowed to visit various prisoner-of-war camps in Austria-Hungary and Germany to determine the number of interned Ukrainians, and they used this opportunity to improve the prisoners' lot, though many did not possess a sufficiently high degree of national consciousness to be interested in the Union's programs. The number of these prisoners, according to a Ukrainian source, was approximately 500,000; an official German source put their number at 300,000, as of August, 1918.[77] Given the vagueness of the term "Ukrainian," and in light of the fact that in the spring of 1918 two divisions were formed out of these prisoners and dispatched to the east to fight against the Russian Bolsheviks, the two sources are not far apart. Whatever their exact number, it was the second largest national group among the prisoners captured by the Central Powers in the east, and the Union rightly viewed the work among them as its most important task.

In the spring of 1915 the Austrian authorities, at the Union's request, permitted the organization of two major special camps for Ukrainian prisoners; their number in these two camps eventually reached 30,000. Three similar camps, with approximately 50,000 inmates, were established in Germany later in that year. This happened only after the Union succeeded in removing a number of obstacles, the most important being the opposition of the German Foreign Office to any such separation.[78] It is interesting to note that soon thereafter the Germans also permitted the organization of special camps for Russia's Georgians and Mohammedans, but that the Poles and Finns had been separated even earlier.

The decision of Ukrainian and other non-Russian prisoners of war to join the special camps was a fateful one and could have resulted in far-reaching consequences for them and their families. In the event of a Russian victory or a separate Russo-German peace, their return home would have been completely out of the question.

Although initially, only a few of the Ukrainians who were voluntarily transferred to the special camps were nationally conscious to the point of supporting the Union's separatist position, they were potential backers of the Ukrainian national movement, and the Union leaders were confident that, given time, they could be won over. This expectation proved fully justified. However, the Union's task was not easy, despite the fact that it was given a free hand in its work, the only limitation being a ban on anti-German and anti-Austrian propaganda.[79]

In sum, the period from August to December, 1914, should be viewed as the most active phase in the Ukrainian cooperation with the Central Powers during the first three years of the war. The principal players in this undertaking were the Union for the Liberation of the Ukraine and the Austrian Foreign Office. In spite of numerous statements and writings sympathetic to the Ukrainian national movement that appeared in Germany during this period and Kaiser Wilhelm's eagerness to see the movement promoted ruthlessly and mercilessly," [80] it was initially almost exclusively an Austrian affair. The Kaiser knew very little about the east and even less about the Ukraine. As was the case with many other ideas and suggestions made by Wilhelm II in the course of the war, his urging that the Reich furnish full support to the Ukrainian "revolution" was not taken very seriously by the German Foreign Office—much less seriously than it was eventually to be taken by some later students of this period.[81]

By December, 1914, Vienna had become disillusioned with the Ukrainian movement. Nevertheless, it retained contact with the Union and continued to support it financially, even though at a greatly reduced rate. The Union's monthly allowance was usually about 25,000 marks, a very modest amount considering its educational work with some 80,000 Ukrainian prisoners of war, its publication projects, and its many other activities.[82] The Dual Monarchy continued to regard its limited support of the Union as a necessary wartime measure until the spring of 1917, when new developments in the east caused the Foreign Office to reestablish closer relations with the Union.

In the spring of 1915, following the transfer of its headquarters to Berlin, the Union stepped up its activities in Germany, the financing of its programs now being a joint Austro-German responsibility. The Union was financed secretly by a private German organization, the Intermediary Agency of Frankfurt on the Oder, headed by Schwerin. Like Vienna, Berlin was determined to retain a completely free hand in the east. The position of the Reich's Supreme Army Command with regard to the Ukraine before the March, 1917, Revolution was essentially the same.[83]

At the time of Russia's collapse, neither Berlin nor Vienna had any definite plans for the Ukraine, and there is no doubt that they would have abandoned the Union and the idea of supporting the Ukrainian movement in order to conclude a separate peace treaty with any Russian government ready to come to terms with the Central Powers. The Ukrainian "trump" was retained, however, so that it could be played if necessary, but this did not mean that official German and Austrian circles had much faith in its value.

CHAPTER III

German Plans in the East and the Russian Revolution

In the course of World War I, no event affected the general picture in the east more significantly than the March, 1917, Revolution in Russia. It was generally hailed as a development that would greatly contribute to bringing the war to an end, at least on the eastern front; and it served to stimulate various schools of thought that had been vocal on the German scene from the beginning of the conflict. All these groups felt that the revolution strengthened the chances of realizing their respective programs, and they used all available means to have their views adopted as official German policy. The Rohrbach school and the Ukrainians, organized around the Union for the Liberation of the Ukraine, also stepped up their activities in the hope of bringing the Reich's civilian and military leaders to their way of thinking.

German official spokesmen remained rather cautious, however, and continued to think more in terms of eliminating Russia from the war than in terms of effecting a permanent dismemberment of the Russian Empire. (Improvement of Germany's northeastern frontiers by detaching a part of the Baltic area was not viewed as conflicting with the second possible course of action.)

The establishment of a Central Ukrainian Council (Tsentral'na Rada) in Kiev in March of 1917 undoubtedly impressed the Germans, but they did not know how far the Ukrainians would go in their demands and how effective and popular this regional autonomous administration would be. After all, one of the first steps taken by the Rada leaders was a pledge of allegiance to the Provisional Government of Prince Georgii Ye. Lvov in Petrograd. All they asked at this juncture was acceptance of "the just demands of the Ukrainian people and its democratic intelligentsia for a cultural autonomy." [1] The fact that the Rada was headed by Mykhailo Hrushevsky, a noted Ukrainian historian and the most respected and best-known national leader, who in the prewar period held a chair in Ukrainian history in Lviv, the capital of West Ukraine (then part of Austria-Hungary), did not help matters much. Upon the outbreak of World War I, probably in order to destroy once and for all the accusation that he was an Austrophile, Professor Hrushevsky returned voluntarily to the Ukraine, only to be immediately arrested and deported by the Russian authorities. The Germans were also well aware of the fact that Hrushevsky, upon his return from Austria, publicly criticized the pro-German Union for the Liberation of the Ukraine. (He restated his negative view of the Union in May and then again in September of 1917 in his official capacity as the head of the Rada.) Thus, Hrushevsky's attitude and the fact that not a single important Rada leader could be regarded as being pro-German further increased the doubt, already present in the Reich's official circles, as to how much they could rely on the Ukrainian movement as a factor in eliminating Russia from the war. [2]

The developments in the Ukraine in the period following the March, 1917, Revolution made a greater impression on German journalistic and academic circles than on the German government. These developments were carefully studied and evaluated by various governmental agencies, but they had no immediate influence on official German thinking, and German plans for the Ukraine did not undergo any radical changes as a result of the March Revolution. The Polish problem continued to cast a long shadow on the eastern horizon, but even more important was the desire of Berlin and Vienna to come to terms with the new Russian government. Bethmann Hollweg and Czernin amply demonstrated this desire through the "peace program" they announced on March 27, 1917. [3] Austria-Hungary was especially anxious to end the war in the east as soon as possible. The food situation in the Dual Monarchy was already serious, and Czernin informed the Germans that the continuation of hostilities would result in a collapse of the Habsburg Empire—a view that was generally shared by other Austro-Hungarian leaders.[4] The German Supreme Army Command, while not openly opposing such peace moves, remained skeptical about the prospect of their success and counseled caution in dealing with the new forces in the east. "The outbreak of the Russian Revoluton," wrote General Ludendorff, "was a factor in the war upon which no general could dare to count with certainty." [5]

The endless discussions between the Reich's civilian and military leaders and their Austro-Hungarian counterparts concerning the Central Powers' aims in the east continued well into 1918. They are fully indicative of the uncertainty and lack of clearly formulated plans for that area during this period. A brief examination of the activities of the Union for the Liberation of the Ukraine in Germany and Austria-Hungary in the period following the March Revolution will further underscore the indecisiveness and confusion that accompanied the formulation of a definite program for the Ukraine by both Berlin and Vienna throughout 1917—that most crucial year of the war.

The collapse of the Czarist Empire was greeted with great enthusiasm in the Ukrainian prisoner-of-war camps in Germany and Austria, but the two powers were rather slow in exploiting this feeling. It was not until April, 1917, at the request of the Union, that the Germans agreed to organize a special military training camp for Ukrainian prisoner-of-war officers at Hannover-Münden. Two months later, in June, 1917, Vienna followed the German example, establishing a special camp for Ukrainian officers at Josephstadt, Austria.[6] (A Finnish volunteer battalion was organized by the Germans as early as 1915, and the Georgian Legion in 1916.)[7]

The Austrians were less enthusiastic about the prospect of organizing military units of Ukrainian prisoners of war than were the Germans. In August, 1917, the Austro-Hungarian Supreme Army Command was advised by the Foreign Office in Vienna to be especially careful in supervising the propaganda work of the Union in Ukrainian camps. According to these instructions, the Ukrainian movement was to be directed against Russia. References to Ukrainian-Polish differences were to be avoided, or at least played down.[8] The fact remains, however, that in spite of greater German interest in such a plan, it was not until after the conclusion of a separate treaty with the Rada in February, 1918, that Berlin and Vienna agreed to the transfer of some of these troops to the Ukraine.

There is no evidence whatsoever that the Germans played any role in the process of "Ukrainization" of the southern front and the organization of separate Ukrainian formations in the course of 1917. German military commanders reported regularly on these developments, but they did not seem to ascribe too much importance to them.[9]

Throughout 1917 the German Foreign Office carefully collected all available information on developments in the Ukraine —the activities of various parties and organizations and the aspirations of the Ukrainians in general. The Germans relied mainly on the following sources for this information: (1) reports from the eastern front and from German diplomatic representatives in Sweden, Denmark, and Switzerland; (2) materials forwarded by various German experts; (3) bulletins and other publications of the Ukrainian press bureau in Lausanne, as well as other Ukrainian information agencies.[10]

On the whole, the Germans preferred to remain in the background confining themselves to such innocuous measures as the publication of Ukrainian literature through which, in the words of Chancellor Georg Michaelis, they hoped "to further the process of disintegration inside Russia." Although some Ukrainian publications were sent in small quantities through the front lines by the Union in the earlier period, it was not until the fall of 1917 that the Germans decided to place special emphasis on the book publishing and propaganda effort. The project was taken rather seriously by responsible German officials; Chancellors Michaelis and Hertling both took a personal interest in it.[11] This project was under the general supervision of the German War Ministry. A Galician Jewish publisher and businessman, Jakob Orenstein, was offered a contract to publish these materials, and a sum of 250,-000 marks was set aside for this purpose. The project was initiated with the publication of 50,000 copies of selected poems of the Ukraine's foremost poet, Taras Shevchenko. General Emil Friedrich of the War Ministry signed the contract with Orenstein;

however, Rudolf Nadolny of the Foreign Office and Count Botho von Wedel, the German Ambassador to Vienna, also participated in launching the project.[12] The whole undertaking proved a success, and Mr. Orenstein's books are still found in many libraries.

Another measure designed to promote Ukrainian-German *rapprochement* at this point was the dispatch of a small Ukrainian military unit, organized in Germany with one Captain Cossack as its leader, to Brest-Litovsk with literature, pictures, and other propaganda material.[13]

The extent of somewhat increased financial assistance provided by Berlin and Vienna to the Union for the Liberation of the Ukraine in the period following the March, 1917, Revolution can be properly appreciated only by comparing the "steady flow of funds through various channels and under varying labels" (many times the amount given to the Union) that the Bolsheviks were receiving from the Germans in the spring and summer of 1917,[14] with even more generous assistance provided by the Allies to their supporters in the east during this period. At this point, official German circles continued to have serious doubts concerning the strength of the Ukrainian movement and were aware of a lack of enthusiasm among the Rada leaders for closer cooperation with the Central Powers. It is not surprising, therefore, that German financial assistance to the Union in 1917 amounted to a mere few hundred thousand marks and Austrian assistance to just 60,000 to 70,000 crowns.

The Orenstein book publishing project, for which 250,000 marks were earmarked, was mainly responsible for the increased German financial assistance to the Union. Its usual monthly allowance (to be spent mostly on educational work among the 80,000 Ukrainian prisoners of war in special camps in Germany and Austria) was about 25,000 marks. The total spent by the Union during the three-year period 1915–1917 was 743,295 marks.[15] The Germans also supported Ukrainian information centers in neutral countries; however, the sums allocated were never very large. The information bureau in Lausanne, for example, one of the most active German-sponsored Ukrainian propaganda centers abroad, had a monthly allowance of 5,000 Swiss francs.[16] It is of interest that the Germans continued their financial support of the Union's work among the Ukrainian prisoners of war throughout 1918. The Union's monthly allowance during this period was reduced to 12,000 marks.[17] (The two Ukrainian governments during the German occupation of the country in 1918 had nothing to do with the continued financing of the Union and, as far as can be ascertained, neither approved nor disapproved of these programs.) As for the Dual Monarchy, an Austrian study speaks of "several large sums" given to the Union during this period—38,000 crowns in October, 1917, and 12,000 in December of the same year! The Union received another 30,000 crowns from Vienna in April, 1918, and then was furnished a monthly allowance of 3,000 crowns for the subsequent months.[18]

In the meantime, millions were given to Parvus (Alexander Helphand) alone to provide Russian socialists, both in Russia and abroad, with necessary funds to carry on their work. The German Secretary of State for Foreign Affairs, Richard von Kühlmann, took a personal interest in these programs. Shortly before Lenin's take-over, in a message to the Supreme Army Command, Kühlmann stated flatly that "the Bolshevik movement could never have attained the scale or the influence which it has today without our continual support." [19] The Bolsheviks were thus clearly the principal beneficiaries of the Reich's financial support, and the estimates of the total amount Germany allocated for subversive efforts in Russia during the war period range from Edward Bernstein's 50 million marks to a sum of 30 million suggested by students who have studied this problem on the basis of new sources.[20]

There is no evidence of any direct financial assistance by Germany to the Ukrainian Rada or to any political groups active in the Ukraine at this time. Thus the prospect of cooperation with Kiev, through the Union for the Liberation of the Ukraine, did not improve, in spite of the Reich's increased support of that organization in the period following the Russian Revolution. The Rada continued to be wary of German plans for the east and did not abandon hope of solving the Ukrainian problem within the framework of an all-Russian federation. Even though as early as April 15, 1917, the Union publicly proclaimed its "official mandate" exhausted and promised to limit its future activities to the work among the Ukrainian prisoners of war and the defense of Ukrainian interests on the territory occupied by the German and Austrian forces, relations between the Union and the Rada did not improve.[21] The latter felt compelled to state repeatedly that it had "neither official nor any other ties with the Union for the Liberation of the Ukraine in Germany." [22] Even more important than the Rada's cautious position vis-à-vis Germany was the vagueness and uncertainty of Berlin's plans for the east. All this was reflected in the Reich's dealings with the Union and similar groups within Germany, from which the Reich could easily disassociate itself if its interests so required.

In the period between the March Revolution and the opening of peace negotiations at Brest-Litovsk in December of 1917, Germany and Austria-Hungary made a renewed effort to formulate and clarify their war aims. For obvious reasons, Germany played a far more important role than the Dual Monarchy in the development of the Central Powers' war program. Following the joint Austro-German Polish Proclamation of November 5, 1916, in which Bethmann Hollweg played a prominent role, the need for clarification of the Central Powers' war program became urgent. The pressures mounted as the powerful Supreme Command continued to demand a more precise formulation of Germany's war aims and President Woodrow Wilson made inquiries about them in January, 1917. Most important, of course, were the great changes in the east consequent on the Revolution.

From March to December German planning for the east proceeded simultaneously on three different planes: in exclusively German high-level conferences concerned with a general formulation of a German and Austrian war-aims program; in Austro-German conferences aimed at obtaining the Dual Monarchy's concurrence in a given program; and finally, in secondary meetings, lower-level consultations, written communications, memoranda, and so forth.

One of the important early conferences of this period was the so-called preliminary conference of March 26, 1917, held in Berlin, between the Austrian and German delegations headed respectively by Bethmann Hollweg and Czernin. As a result of this meeting, Bethmann Hollweg and Czernin agreed on a minimal program based largely on the *status quo ante bellum;* at the same time they declared that after the victorious conclusion of hostilities, Germany would be entitled to territorial extensions "principally in the east," and Austria-Hungary would be compensated with certain portions of Rumania.[23] The agreement of March 27, 1917, according to Klaus Epstein, "remained the fundamental basis of German-Austrian negotiations until the fall of Bethmann in July, 1917. It lost all importance thereafter." [24]

In the light of Bethmann Hollweg's modest aims in the east and his clearly negative attitude toward the Ukrainian question, it is not surprising that the problem of the future of the Ukraine was not dealt with at all at this conference. It was only during the later stages of the Austro-German war-aims talks in 1917 that the Ukraine and its territory became a factor in the negotiations.

The Bethmann-Czernin meeting of March 26, 1917, was followed by the four Kreuznach conferences (April, May, August, and December, 1917). The holding of these meetings at Kreuznach, the Great Headquarters of the Supreme Army Command in the Hindenburg-Ludendorff era, is indicative of the strong position that the Supreme Army Command enjoyed during that crucial stage of the war. Although officially Ludendorff was merely Hindenburg's assistant, power was concentrated in his hands. General Ludendorff thus played a major role in shaping Germany's *Ostpolitik* during the entire 1917–1918 period.

It may be well to note at this point that none of the principal characters of this unfolding drama had an intimate knowledge of the east and therefore none could be regarded as a Russian expert; nor did any one of them have a special interest in the Ukrainian problem. To all of them the east meant Russia, and the question of the Ukraine was a secondary issue that could be entrusted to subordinate officers such as Colonel (later General) Max Hoffmann and second-rank officials of the Foreign Office— Trautmann or Bergen. Chancellors Bethmann Hollweg, Michaelis, and Hertling and their Secretaries of State for Foreign Affairs, Jagow, Zimmermann, and Kühlmann, all had a very limited knowledge of the east and its manifold problems. Hindenburg and Ludendorff "knew" the east only from their wartime experience with the *Ober-Ost*—military administration of occupied areas in the northeast—an experiment which they hoped to extend to other areas of the east. [25]

General Hoffmann was one of the few German officials (not counting those born in the Baltic provinces) who possessed a good firsthand knowledge of the east and could speak Russian fluently. He traveled extensively in the Ukraine as a businessman prior to the war, became sympathetic toward the Ukrainians and their national aspirations, and kept up with Ukrainian developments with the help of such people as Paul Rohrbach and his writings. At first a trusted spokesman of the Supreme Army Command at Brest-Litovsk, Hoffmann soon came in conflict with Ludendorff and was never allowed to play a decisive role in the shaping of Germany's plans and policies for the east.[26]

The first Kreuznach conference was held on April 23, 1917, and was called at the insistence of the Supreme Army Command. A few days before, on April 20, in a letter to Bethmann Hollweg, Hindenburg had pressed the Chancellor for a definite war-aims program. Speaking in the name of the Supreme Army Command, Hindenburg emphatically rejected the idea of concluding a peace with Russia on the basis of the *status quo*. From his point of view it was imperative that Courland and Lithuania, at least, come under German control. If necessary, the Central Powers might compensate Russia with the Austrian provinces of East Galicia and Bukovina, whose population was predominantly Ukrainian.[27] On the same day Wilhelm II had asked Chancellor Bethmann Hollweg to work out a clear plan for the east in cooperation with Germany's allies. The Kaiser's telegram mentioned Poland and the Baltic provinces, but made no reference to the Ukraine.[28] In a telegram of April 22, 1917, Secretary of State for Foreign Affairs Zimmermann further developed Hindenburg's idea of compensating Russia with Austria's Ukrainian provinces. For the loss of East Galicia and Bukovina, Austria-Hungary was to receive a part of Rumania, but it was also to be asked to declare its *désintéressement* in the future of Poland.[29]

All these ideas were subjected to further elaboration at the first Kreuznach conference of April 23, at which Germany was ready to be even more generous with Ukrainian territory. Not only could East Galicia be taken over by Russia as a compensation for the loss of Courland and Lithuania; Poland, too, was to be offered more territory in the east, but not at the expense of the Baltic provinces.[30] (This meant clearly that the territorial deal between Germany and Poland was to be made at the expense of the Ukraine and Byelorussia.) One can, therefore, conclude that, despite German reports about "increased separatist tendencies in the east, and demands for a free Ukraine, free Lithuania," etc.,[31] and despite the talk about some kind of "greater undertaking" aimed at strengthening the Ukrainian movement,[32] the Germans had no positive plan for the Ukraine in late April 1917.

Austria-Hungary did not participate in the first Kreuznach conference, nor was Vienna immediately informed of its results. Responsible German officials, such as Secretary Zimmermann, were going to "work on" Vienna gradually to secure its acceptance of the Kreuznach program, and did not think that Austria would feel very strongly about the permanent loss of East Galicia. This feeling was further strengthened by the rather negative attitude of many Austrian officials toward the Ukrainians. General Arthur Arz von Straussenburg, for example, openly referred to them as "undesirable citizens." [33] As for Ludendorff, he had even less use and more contempt for the Ukrainians of Galicia and was rather impatient with Austria's reluctance to renounce its title to it. "In the autumn of 1914," said the general, "no one wanted to hear anything of the 'land of pigs' [*Sauland*]. No one is going today to sacrifice a single soldier to regain this territory." [34]

Of course, it would have been naïve to expect a diplomat of Czernin's caliber to yield at once without securing certain guarantees in return. Thus, on April 26 Zimmermann wrote to the Supreme Army Command that Czernin was giving the German Ambassador in Vienna, Count Wedel, a difficult time with his insistence that no territorial demands of any kind be made against Russia.[35] On May 5, 1917, Wedel reported again on Czernin's continued opposition to the idea of giving up East Galicia—not because of any sympathy for the Ukrainian cause, but simply because Austria's loss would look very bad in view of Germany's prospective territorial gains in the same general area.[36] Another reason for Czernin's reluctance to agree to a permanent transfer of East Galicia to Russia was his fear of the Polish opposition to such a move. Czernin, however, dropped his opposition on the following day and expressed readiness to consider the cession of East Galicia if the whole of Wallachia were guaranteed to Austria as compensation.[37]

The Imperial Chancellor, Bethmann Hollweg, while affixing his name to the official record of the April 23 Kreuznach conference, did not regard this program as binding on him; the program was nevertheless considered by both Germany and Austria as official.[38] Thus there is no basis for maintaining, as Fischer does, that the differences between Bethmann and the Supreme Command concerning Germany's war aims were minimal and involved chiefly questions of style and approach.[39]

During the three weeks between the first and second Kreuznach conferences, the German government did not make any important changes in its plans for the east. Reports on the growth of "separatist strivings" in the Ukraine and Ukrainian demands for a separate administration, more independent of the Provisional Government in Petrograd,[40] seem to have made no impression on German military and political leaders. On April 29, 1917, Ludendorff worked out a plan for an understanding with Russia which, in brief, contained the following points:

1) A three-weeks armistice with Russia.

2) Nonintervention in Russia's internal affairs.

3) German diplomatic support of Russia in Straits settlement.

4) Economic cooperation between the two countries; no reparations; German financial assistance in return for frontier corrections in Courland and Lithuania.

5) Russian recognition of Poland's independence.[41]

Ludendorff's "Bases for the Most Essential Peace Conditions" of May 12, 1917, were equally devoid of any recommendations or plans for the Ukraine.[42]

Of some interest, although of no practical significance, was the war-aims program prepared by Wilhelm II and forwarded to his Secretary of State for Foreign Affairs on May 13. It was a fantastically ambitious plan for territorial expansion, mainly in the form of colonies, and for the punishment of all those who dared to oppose Germany. The Kaiser, no doubt, assumed that Germany would achieve a complete victory over all its enemies everywhere. He would even force the United States to pay a $40 billion indemnity, in addition to delivering substantial quantities of cotton, copper, and nickel. Most interesting, however, for a discussion of Germany's plans for the east in 1917, was point 12 of the Kaiser's program, which read: "Poland free. Courland possibly autonomous, to be attached to us; a similar solution for Lithuania. *Ukraine*, Livonia, Estonia—autonomous, with an option of joining us at a later time." [43] There is no reason to think that this document, in itself evidence of the Kaiser's mental state at that time, had any immediate effect on German official thinking. Most of the ideas contained in it were politely disregarded at subsequent conferences, and apparently the Kaiser never made an effort to have his program adopted officially by his government. This was not surprising since, as one student of this period concluded, the Kaiser had come "to be almost a background figure, who rarely says the decisive word at any conference." [44]

The second Kreuznach conference, a joint Austro-German affair, was held on May 17 and 18, 1917. This time, however, the German officials did not have to worry about the Dual Monarchy's concurrence. As far as the east was concerned, the second conference largely reaffirmed the decisions that had been reached at the first. Most of Rumania (including its Black Sea coast) was to become an Austrian protectorate. The German plan for Poland, Courland, and Lithuania remained unchanged. The conference reiterated and made even more specific the Austrian *désintéressement* in Poland, significantly omitting all mention of the earlier plan to cede East Galicia and Bukovina to Russia.[45]

What was responsible for this important omission? Although, on the whole, the Kaiser's war-aims program of May 13 had not been taken very seriously, it may have encouraged some German leaders to take a fresh look at the Ukraine. An even more important factor may have been the rapid breakdown of the Russian army on the eastern front and the gradual "Ukrainization" of some of its sectors. Since the second conference was a joint Austro-German affair, it is not surprising that the Germans preferred not to bring the touchy problem of the Ukraine into the open. In the light of the above facts, it does not seem inappropriate to regard the second Kreuznach conference as a cautious resumption of official German planning for the Ukraine; although plans for its future remained vague, this question now became at long last a new and continuing factor in German *Ostpolitik*. As for the Dual Monarchy, both Czernin and Emperor Karl were well pleased with the results of the second Kreuznach conference. In mid-June Czernin officially informed the German Foreign Office that both Vienna and Budapest had accepted the Kreuznach program of May, 1917.[46]

There remained, however, some unresolved problems. The new German Chancellor, Michaelis, and the Austrian Foreign Secretary, Czernin, now tried to work them out jointly. Among these problems were the future of Poland and the question of Kholm and East Galicia, territories which the Ukrainians would inevitably demand as a reward for cooperating with the Central Powers. When the two leaders met in Vienna on August 1, 1917, Czernin opposed Michaelis' suggestion that these provinces be ceded to the Ukrainians, arguing that voluntary alienation of any part of its territory would weaken the entire structure of the Dual Monarchy. If Galicia were linked with Poland, however, Austria-Hungary, according to Czernin, would no longer care what happened to the eastern half of the province.[47]

In the meantime, other high-ranking German officials were beginning to take a greater interest in the growing strength of the Ukrainian national movement. Of special interest is a memorandum on the Ukrainian question prepared by the German Ambassador in Vienna, Wedel, and submitted to Michaelis shortly after the Chancellor's talks with Czernin.

"Here [in Austria] there is less interest for the Ukrainian movement than in Germany, partly because less importance is being attached to it, partly because people are less sympathetic toward it, fearing the development of irredentism among the Ukrainians in Austria and Hungary. . . . It should be of special interest for us [Germans] to promote the Ukrainian movement with full force, as it appears that the Russian working class is not strong enough to be able to gain the upper hand in the country. Perhaps national movements will prove to be stronger. Above all, we should support the Finnish and Ukrainian movements. I do not know whether we already have direct contacts with the Ukrainians; if not, the Austrian Ukrainians could serve as go-betweens." [48]

This renewed German interest in the Ukraine found a clear expression in the third Kreuznach conference, held on August 9, 1917. No Austro-Hungarian representatives were invited to this meeting. It was thus primarily an exchange of opinion between the Supreme Army Command and the Imperial Chancellery—the two principal German foreign policy-making bodies at the time. The first body, the Supreme Army Command, based its usurped prerogative on two myths—that of "irreplaceability" and that of being "the savior of the Fatherland." The second body, the Imperial Chancellery, was merely trying to carry out, even though often timidly and reluctantly, its rightful constitutional responsibilities, among which the conduct of foreign policy was the most important.

Above all, point 12 of the long report on the third Kreuznach conference deserves careful examination: "The aspirations of the Ukraine should be clarified. The movement should be directed toward a quiet and amicable union [*Anschluss*] with us. *Austria will have to be asked whether one can offer the Ukrainian East Galicia to the Ukrainians.*" Yet, the next paragraph of this document, which dealt with Poland, in effect again postponed decisive German action on the Ukrainian question. Its last point simply read, "we do not have a special interest at this time in Austrian renunciation of Galicia." [49]

The third Kreuznach conference recorded Chancellor Michaelis' complete surrender of the moderate program of war aims and his unqualified rallying to the Supreme Command's annexationist views. [50] His next assignment was to meet with Czernin in order to secure Austria's acceptance of the new German war aims. On the very eve of this meeting, which was held in Berlin on August 14 and 15, 1917, Ludendorff felt impelled to remind Michaelis of the war-aims program approved on August 9. In a special telegram to the Chancellor he repeated the principal points in that program, among them point 12, on the Ukraine. [51]

The record of the Czernin-Michaelis talks does not specifically mention the problem of the Ukraine as part of the agenda, but no doubt they dealt with it in their discussions about Poland. It was at about this time that Czernin, still under the spell of the Reichstag majority Peace Resolution of July, 1917, which seemed to have created a real basis for a peace of understanding, made an attempt to link the problem of Poland with that of a general peace. He suggested that Austria's cession of Galicia to Poland be matched with a German renunciation of Alsace-Lorraine—an offer that Michaelis found unacceptable. [52]

Generally speaking, Michaelis' eastern policy remained rather weak and vague. As far as the problem of border states was concerned, he merely recommended "the annexation [*Angliederung*] of former enemy territories, in the event they become autonomous and express a desire to join us, as independent commonwealths with merely military and economic links to us." [53]

The following months brought little change in Michaelis' *Ostpolitik.* Most of this time was taken up by the papal peace proposals and the German answers to them, as well as by the perennial question of the future of Belgium, which was basic to any general peace program. Not until late October, 1917, did some high-ranking German officials begin to point to the lack of sufficient appreciation of the Ukrainian questions in official circles. One of these critics was General Paul von Bartenwerffer, head of the Political Department of the German General Staff, who urged German support for Ukrainian national aspirations as the best way to weaken Russia: "Russia's drive toward the Straits and Constantinople would cease only if both fell into her hands, or if Russia were to be pushed back behind the Ukraine. Only after the formation of an independent Ukraine can one hope to establish permanent peace in the Balkans. Only then will the Balkan peoples be freed of the intrigues of the Russian protector, and only then will the Berlin-Bagdad route be secure. The Ukrainian independence movement is, therefore, just as important to Bulgaria and Turkey as it is to our own future policy in the Balkans." [54] An independent and strong Ukraine, General Bartenwerffer further argued in his memorandum, would also help keep Poland in check. (The idea of balancing the future Poland with the help of an independent Ukraine was not new, but it was rarely mentioned in official German documents. It was to play a much more important role in German thinking during and after the Brest-Litovsk negotiations in 1918.)

It is difficult to evaluate the influence that such ideas may have had at this time on the formulation of Germany's official plans for the east. At the Austro-German conference of November 6, 1917, called specifically for the purpose of revising the Kreuznach agreements, Czernin proposed a return to the Austro-Polish solution and made no reference to the Ukrainian problem.[55] However, the official German "Theses for the Negotiation of Separate Peace with Russia" stipulated that "Russia was to agree to the cession of the following regions: Poland, Lithuania, and Courland, which have already availed themselves of their right to self-determination. *Should other peoples of Russia express a wish of becoming autonomous or independent, both Russia and Germany would have to recognize their independence.*" [56] It is quite clear that "other peoples of Russia" meant above all the Finns and the Ukrainians. The German Ambassador in Vienna, Wedel, after discussing the above "Theses" with Czernin, sent Kühlmann, the new German Secretary of State for Foreign Affairs, the following report on November 16, 1917: "Czernin does not fail to appreciate the importance of supporting the Ukrainian movement and agrees in principle with Your Excellency's point of view. He feels, however, compelled at the moment to be reserved and cautious in his promises because of the necessity of having Polish support for the [Brest-Litovsk] delegations." [57]

In the light of the Reich's financial support of the Bolsheviks and other Russian socialist groups during the first three years of the war, German aid in Lenin's return to Russia one month after the collapse of the old regime, and continued German financing of his movement throughout 1917, it is very tempting to conclude that the Bolshevik take-over in November was greeted by the Germans with even greater enthusiasm than was the March Revolution. The fall of the Provisional Government in Petrograd no doubt represented a setback for the pro-Entente forces in Russia and brought that country closer to a complete military collapse, for which the Germans had worked so hard from the beginning of the war. Even so the chances for a peace in the east were still very uncertain, and it was probably for this reason that German financial assistance was increased substantially following the Bolshevik coup. On November 9, 1917, for example, the Reich's Treasury "allowed a further 15 million marks for political purposes in Russia," and an additional 2 million marks were transferred to the German Legation in Stockholm at about the same time "for known purposes." [58]

In the meantime, the Bolsheviks, while calling for a general peace, also made it clear from the beginning that it was to be based on the "no annexations, no indemnities" formula, and this the Germans simply could not accept. Moreover, the Bolshevik position was by no means secure, and their support in the country remained limited. This fact, general confusion behind the Russian lines, and doubts concerning the real strength of the Ukrainian and other national forces all contributed to the continuing vagueness in German plans for the east in the weeks before the opening of the Brest-Litovsk negotiations.

The indecision was especially noticeable in the German plans for the Ukraine. In his "Bases for Negotiations with Russia," drafted in early December, 1917, Ludendorff stressed the necessity for annexing Lithuania and Courland, and for creating an independent Poland "attached to the Central Powers." He further demanded that Russia evacuate Finland, Estonia, Livonia,

Moldavia, East Galicia, and Armenia, but made no reference to the Ukraine as a whole. In the same document the general advised the Foreign Office that in case the Russians should inquire about the possibility of concluding an alliance (*Bündniss*) with Germany, they were to be given an encouraging answer and were to be invited to enter into negotiations for such a treaty without delay.[59]

Kühlmann was even more clearly opposed than General Ludendorff to any active and open support of the Ukrainian movement by the Reich at this time. During the December 7 conference between the German military and civilian leaders at the Imperial Chancellery, Kühlmann was rather skeptical about the possibility of permanently detaching the Baltic provinces from Russia, and he also regarded the separation of the Ukraine from Russia as both impossible and undesirable. In no uncertain terms he warned the generals about the dangers that such a policy might generate: "If we were to press the creation of additional states in the east, it would be a political decision of most far-reaching consequences. A strong Russia would soon resume its drive to the west and move against these states." [60]

Other high-ranking German officials were just as cautious as Kühlmann about the possible exploitation of the Ukrainian movement as a means of bringing about a complete suspension of hostilities in the east, and even more so about any long-range plans for a "new order" in that part of Europe. Not all reports about the alignment of Ukrainian political forces were encouraging. A report on the movement among various peoples of the former Czarist Empire, prepared by a high-ranking official of the German Foreign Office (identified as "von R."; probably Friedrich Hans von Rosenberg) in mid-December, 1917, cast doubt on the real strength of the Ukrainian separatist movement and warned that Germany should not expect much from it. He foresaw that the non-Russians would play a very important role in the further development of events in Russia. Nevertheless, he also predicted that ultimately the unity of Russia would be preserved and urged that this prospect be taken into account in all future planning.[61]

At about the same time, the Foreign Office representative at the Supreme Army Command headquarters, Kurt von Lersner, prepared a rather detailed report on recent developments in the Ukraine, which he submitted to his superiors on December 16,

1917. In his report, Lersner discussed the "Ukrainization" of the southwestern front, the efforts of Entente agents to establish closer contacts with the Ukrainian Rada, and, finally, the growing conflict between Kiev and Petrograd.[62] Interestingly enough, he did not suggest that the Germans counter the Entente activities in the Ukraine or exploit the ever-widening rift between the Rada and the Bolsheviks. Indeed, there is no evidence that in the weeks prior to the opening of the Brest negotiations the makers of German policy were seriously exploring the possibility of concluding a separate peace with the Ukraine, or that they believed such a move desirable, although individual German officials had at various times proposed this.

On the eve of Kühlmann's departure for Brest-Litovsk, the Germans made a fresh attempt to work out a plan for the east. On December 18 another Crown Council was held at Kreuznach, with the Kaiser in the chair. The outcome of this meeting was likewise inconclusive. Germany's plans for Poland and the Baltic provinces remained unchanged. Toward other areas of the east it merely adopted a general and rather vague formula, stipulating that national groups that had not enjoyed independence before the war should be allowed to merge with one or another state or to proclaim their independence.[63]

Thus, Secretary of State for Foreign Affairs Kühlmann set off for Brest-Litovsk without a concrete plan for the Ukraine; and the separate treaty that was concluded with the Ukraine on February 9, 1918, was not the logical or inevitable result of a carefully formulated German scheme on which, as has so often been believed, the German leaders had been working since the outbreak of the war. The separate peace with the Ukraine was merely a hastily contrived improvisation; once adopted, it forced the German policy-makers, throughout the rest of 1918, to seek to define a concrete program that would be worthy of the name of the Reich's *Ostpolitik.*

CHAPTER IV

The Ukrainian Treaty
of Brest-Litovsk

An impressive body of specialized literature is now available on the Treaty of Brest-Litovsk, in addition to discussions in the many general works on World War I. It is, however, the German-Russian treaty, concluded on March 3, 1918, that is usually described at length. The Ukrainian treaty, which preceded the Russian by almost four weeks, is generally dismissed in a sentence or two or disregarded.[1]

The following discussion, therefore, concentrates on the Ukrainian treaty, concluded on February 9, 1918, which indeed deserves the appellation of "the forgotten peace." The negotiations leading to the conclusion of this treaty should be viewed as a process during which German plans for the east, slowly and hesitatingly, assumed a somewhat more concrete form.

Since the Crown Council of December 18, 1918, had failed to produce a definite program for the east, much less any special plans for the Ukraine, the German peace delegation, headed by Kühlmann, left for Brest-Litovsk on December 20 with a simple goal: the negotiation of a peace treaty with Russia as a whole. Two broad objectives were to be accomplished by a speedy conclusion of peace with Russia: (1) the transfer of additional troops to the west for the "final offensive," and (2) the procurement of food and necessary raw materials in the east to alleviate a serious situation caused by the tight Allied blockade.[2] Though not as desperate as in Austria, the food situation in Germany was, nevertheless, serious at this time. Interestingly enough, upon the conclusion of armistice in the east, on December 15, 1917, the Germans expressed a hope of obtaining one million tons of grain from the Soviet government and even sent a special commission to Petrograd to negotiate this transaction.[3] This was exactly the amount of grain that the Ukrainians promised to deliver to the Central Powers in their separate treaty.

The Germans, in the meantime, had kept an eye on the Ukrainian developments without getting involved in them in any way. On December 14, 1917, one day before the signing of the armistice in the east, Friedrich von Rosenberg, Kühlmann's principal assistant at Brest, informed the Foreign Office of an attempt by the Ukrainian Rada representatives to reach Brest-Litovsk in order to participate in the armistice talks. The Bolsheviks at first refused to let the Ukrainians cross the front line "because they would not have been able to reach Brest on time." [4]

Two days later the Soviet government announced that it would allow the Ukrainians to proceed to Brest, but this decision was in no way influenced by the Germans,[5] although once the Ukrainians did appear, the Reich representatives showed interest in them. General Hoffman did not agree to have the Ukrainians add their signatures to the armistice agreement, explaining that "it was good for the whole of Russia." Austrian pleas "not to 'flirt' with the Ukrainians, because of possible repercussions among the Poles and other nationalities of the Monarchy," were disregarded by the Germans. The Reich delegates at Brest, in private talks with the Ukranians, did not fail to express their sympathy with the Ukranian cause and stressed the many common interests of the two peoples.[6]

The fact that the Rada representatives were at Brest-Litovsk unofficially from December 16, and on December 19 participated in the Russo-German talks on war prisoners, "with the consent of the Russian delegation as representatives of an independent Ukrainian Republic," [7] made it imperative for the Germans to decide how to deal with this new factor in the impending peace talks. On December 17 General Ludendorff asked the Foreign Office for "guiding principles" for the handling of the Ukrainian problem. To satisfy this request, Under-Secretary of State Hilmar von dem Bussche-Haddenhausen prepared a rather detailed memorandum on the Ukrainian question. Bussche expressed his concern over the Rada's opposition to the Soviet government, fearing that this might endanger the chances for peace in the east and also imperil Ukrainian efforts to establish an independent state, "for it was doubtful whether any Russian government, other than the Bolshevik, would recognize the Ukraine's independence." Rosenberg was then instructed to convey the following message to the Ukrainians: "Germany has no intention of interfering in either Russian or Ukrainian internal affairs, but as soon as the two settle their differences, we shall be ready at any time to recognize officially the Ukraine's independence and request our allies to follow our example. Concerning the role of the Ukrainians in current peace negotiations, we have no objections, provided it will not offend the Russians, to dealing with them as representatives of an independent power equal to Russia, and allowing them to accede to the recently concluded armistice agreement." [8]

On January 1, 1918, an official Rada delegation appeared at Brest-Litovsk.[9] The decision of the Rada to send a separate delegation was arrived at on December 28, 1917, entirely on its own initiative after a long and heated debate.[10] The members of the delegation were Mykola Lyubyns'kyi, Mykola Levyts'kyi, Oleksander Sevryuk, M. Polozov, and Vsevolod Holubovych. They were all in their twenties; even the head of the delegation, Holubovych, who was then the Rada's Minister of Trade and Industry and subsequently assumed the post of Prime Minister, was only twenty-seven years old. The Rada's fateful decision was preceded by a "Peace Message to All Neutral and Belligerent Countries," broadcast on December 24, 1917, in which the Rada requested to be represented officially at Brest-Litovsk—a demand to which the Central Powers readily agreed two days later.[11] It was thus not some kind of German "trick" or intrigue, as it so often has been represented even in some serious works of western scholarship but the mistrust of the Bolsheviks that was chiefly responsible for the Rada's decision.

The undisguised Bolshevik hostility toward the "bourgeois nationalist" regime in the Ukraine had resulted in a complete break between Petrograd and Kiev and the first Bolshevik attempt to impose the Soviet will on the Ukraine through the use of military force. The swiftness of Bolshevik moves soon convinced the Rada that it too had to act swiftly and boldly. The Soviet ultimatum to the Rada was issued on December 17, 1917; Kiev rejected it formally on December 20, whereupon the Bolsheviks declared themselves to be at war with the "counterrevolutionary" Rada regime.[12]

In the meantime, the local Bolsheviks in the Ukraine, unable to master any meaningful opposition to the Rada in the Kiev Soviet, removed themselves to Kharkov (where they could establish a direct link with their northern Russian comrades), declared the Rada dissolved, and on December 26, 1917, proclaimed the establishment of the Ukrainian Soviet Republic. This, incidentally, was the first such Soviet move, and this technique was to be used by the Bolsheviks time and again both during the Civil War as well as in the post-World War II period.

No Rada leader could be regarded as a Germanophile or Austrophile, whereas several members of the Rada Secretariat (cabinet) were well known for their pro-Entente feelings. French and British agents were active in Kiev for many weeks prior to the Rada's decision to send a separate delegation to Brest-Litovsk, and Paris went so far as to furnish the Rada government with a 50-million-ruble grant in an effort to keep the Ukraine in the Allied camp. The Rada leader who did most to maintain the pro-Allied course during this period was the Ukrainian Foreign Secretary, Oleksander Shul'hyn (who even preferred the French spelling of his name—Choulguine).[13]

The German Foreign Office archives, as well as other sources, yield no evidence either of German agents being active on the Ukrainian scene or of the existence of direct contacts between the Rada and the German official or military representatives at this time. The Union for the Liberation of the Ukraine, which played such an important role in the earlier German planning for the Ukraine, proved to be both unable and unwilling to influence directly Ukrainian-German relations at this point. It continued to concentrate its activities among the Ukrainian prisoners of war in Germany and Austria-Hungary and took no part in the peace negotiations at Brest.

It is generally agreed that the Germans welcomed the Ukrainians at Brest mainly because they believed that their presence would enable them to put pressure on the Soviet delegation, and perhaps force it to accept the Central Powers' terms.[14] The arrival of the Ukrainians, however, added an element of complication not only for Count Czernin, who had good reason to fear irredentist claims of a most serious nature on the part of the Ukrainians, but for the Germans as well. Germany had to decide whether to support the idea of Russia, one and indivisible, or to cooperate with the non-Russian nationalities, which were organizing themselves into separate political entities by taking advantage of the general confusion following the March and November Revolutions. Either course had important and far-reaching advantages and disadvantages. A compromise between the two solutions could not be worked out.

On January 1, 1918, Ludendorff sent General Hoffmann "Suggestions and Instructions" in which he advised him not to allow the Ukraine to speak for Rumania, for the latter was an independent state with which Germany would deal separately. He further suggested that Ukrainian claims, insofar as they touched upon Austria-Hungary and Poland, should be met halfway. Finally, he asked Hoffmann whether he thought the Germans should deal with the Ukrainians separately or together with the Bolsheviks.[15] On the same day Kühlmann, at a meeting with Reichstag representatives, informed them that relations with autonomous regions of Russia had not been neglected and expressed confidence that the Germans would also be able to negotiate simultaneously with these "autonomous bodies," especially the largest and the most important of them all—the Ukraine.[16]

Despite Ludendorff's and Kühlmann's recommendation that the Ukrainian demands be satisfied at the expense of Austria-Hungary, the Crown Council of January 2, 1918, meeting at Bellevue Castle in Berlin, failed to produce a definite plan for the Ukraine. The problem of Poland continued to dominate the scene. As far as the general plan of action for the east was concerned, it was agreed that the border states, organized on the German side of the front line, were not to be returned to Russia.[17]

On January 4, 1918, Kühlmann returned to Brest-Litovsk from the inconclusive Bellevue Crown Council. Having learned that Rosenberg and Hoffmann had entered into preliminary talks with the Rada representatives, Kühlmann immediately asked the Chancellor for further instructions.[18] These preliminary talks with the Ukrainians had been opened with Czernin's approval, although without his participation.[19] It was only at this point that responsible high-ranking German officials began to consider seriously the possibility of concluding a separate peace with the Ukraine, although they were far from being certain whether the Ukrainians would be ready for such an offer. While Under-Secretary Bussche spoke of the possibility of concluding an alliance (*Bündniss*) with the Rada, Riezler, writing from Brest-Litovsk on the eve of the opening of separate negotiations with the Kiev delegation, stated somewhat pessimistically: "The uncertain situation makes further postponement [of peace talks] very dangerous. If only we could succeed in establishing contact with the Ukraine." [20]

After two days of preliminary talks with the official Ukrainian delegation (January 4–5, 1918), which the Germans referred to as "a friendly preparatory discussion of which no official use was to be made," [21] formal negotiations with the Rada representatives were opened on January 6, with all four delegations of the Central Powers participating.[22] Chancellor Hertling viewed it as an event of great importance, which would considerably strengthen Germany's position at Brest. Field Marshal von Hindenburg, however, merely noted that "the establishment of a state in the Ukraine may certainly reduce the Polish danger for Germany," but he did not think that the safety of the German Empire could rest upon this new factor.[23] Kühlmann agreed with the Chancellor that one should promote an understanding with the Ukrainians without delay. Kühlmann, however, regarded them as being "very cunning" and warned that it was necessary to proceed with great caution "for otherwise they might get the impression that we need them against the Petersburgers and proceed to make impossible demands upon us." [24] General Ludendorff also approved of a Ukrainian-German *rapprochement* and proposed that a special commission be sent to Kiev to deal directly with the Rada on various economic and financial problems.[25] But no one at this point went as far as Diego von Bergen of the Foreign Office, who had long been associated with the Ukrainian problem and had advocated the establishment of a separate Ukrainian state with German assistance. He urged coming to quick terms with the Ukraine and drawing it as close as possible to the German orbit.[26]

The Austrians in the meantime took a much more cautious

view of the prospect of closer cooperation between Kiev and Vienna. In general, the following line was to be pursued in the Dual Monarchy's propaganda offensive in the east: Austria sympathized with the Ukrainian efforts to establish an independent state but the form of its regime and its relations with Russia were an internal matter in which Vienna was not going to interfere. The Rada was referred to as a "temporary Ukrainian regime." The need for a general peace in the east was placed above all else.[27] Of course, Vienna's Foreign Minister, Count Czernin, who was soon to enter into direct negotiations with the Ukrainians, could not long adhere to such a neatly impartial formula.

Despite general agreement among the German military and civilian leaders on the desirability of coming to terms with the Ukraine, they remained reluctant to grant full recognition to the Rada delegation, although the Germans could have done this at the time of its arrival at Brest. It is ironic that Trotsky recognized the right of the Rada envoys to participate in these negotiations as a separate delegation of an independent state two days before a similar recognition had been granted by the Central Powers. Trotsky did so on January 10, 1918, at the plenary session of the peace conference. According to Wheeler-Bennett, it was Kühlmann who "headed Trotsky into recognizing the delegates of the Ukrainian Rada." [28] In the view of a member of the Ukrainian delegation, Oleksander Sevryuk, however, Trotsky granted this recognition in the hope of preserving a "united front" with the Ukrainians against the Central Powers.[29] This hope on Trotsky's part was not entirely unjustified. The Rada position at this time was not yet quite clear, and the Ukrainians and the Russians were conducting negotiations in an attempt to minimize the differences existing between them.[30] Official Soviet historiography, by the way, has been very critical of Trotsky's recognition of the Rada delegation, presenting him as an inept victim, or even a tool, of German imperialism.[31]

The Germans recognized the Ukrainian delegation only after it threatened to withdraw from Brest-Litovsk. The announcement granting the formal recognition was made by Count Czernin (who was most responsible for the delay) on behalf of all four Central Powers on January 12, 1918. The Central Powers went further than Trotsky in their official recognition of the Rada delegation by declaring that the Ukrainian state was a fully independent political entity.[32] (Formal recognition of the Ukrainian state was, nevertheless, to be granted only after the signing of the treaty.) Chancellor Hertling, discussing this German move a few months later, made it quite clear that it was German indecision, rather than any legal consideration, that was responsible for Berlin's reluctance to grant full recognition to the Ukrainian delegation.[33]

Although the official talks between the representatives of the Central Powers and the Rada delegates began as early as January 6, 1918, it was not until January 13, at a meeting to which the Soviet delegation was not invited, that the Ukrainians presented the Central Powers with an exact list of their demands. Their insistence on regarding the principle of self-determination as well as a general democratic peace without annexations and reparations as the basis for negotiations did not encounter any German opposition. It was, however, an entirely different story with other Ukrainian demands, namely the transfer of the Kholm area to the Ukrainian state, and self-determination for the Ukrainians in East Galicia, North Bukovina, and Carpatho-Ruthenia (later known as Carpatho-Ukraine). In effect, this meant that these Austro-Hungarian provinces, too, would go to the Ukraine.[34] Count Czernin flatly rejected all these territorial claims, terming them an interference in Austria's internal affairs. Germany took a similar position, although it was ready to satisfy the Ukrainian claim to the Kholm area.[35] More meetings with the Ukrainians followed, and both the Austrians and the Germans came to realize that the Rada delegates were tougher negotiators than originally anticipated. "Their cunning and peasant slyness," reported Rosenberg from Brest-Litovsk, "are not going to make things easy for us." Kühlmann also complained about the "immoderate demands" of the Ukrainians, and wrote to the Imperial Chancellor that even if one were to take the dimmest view of the possibility of making an agreement with the Bolsheviks, it was necessary to continue the talks with them, for otherwise the Ukrainians would increase their demands.[36] Kühlmann was quick to understand that at this stage the continued presence of the Russians at Brest was for him a necessity in order to pressure the Ukrainians and keep the Russians in check. It was mainly for these reasons that he and General Hoffmann did not follow Hindenburg's advice to present the Russians with an ultimatum; they were ready to do so only after they could positively count on an agreement with the Ukrainians.[37] As early as January 16, 1918, the Supreme Army Command received a secret report from a "reliable source" that Trotsky did not intend to conclude a peace treaty, but merely wanted to protract negotiations.[38]

In the meantime, separate and closed meetings between the Rada delegates and representatives of the Central Powers continued.[39] The Ukrainians were further aided by the news of the desperate food situation in Vienna, which reached Brest-Litovsk in mid-January. The Ukrainians also knew that Czernin would yield, for he had an express order from Emperor Karl to conclude any kind of peace in the east without delay. Baron Mykola Vasylko, a Ukrainian deputy in the Austrian Diet with close connections in the ruling circles in Vienna, deserves much credit for keeping the Ukrainians at Brest posted on all developments in the Dual Monarchy.[40]

The position of the Rada, however, had become more difficult, for it was now seriously threatened by Bolshevik invasion from the north directed by Vladimir Antonov-Ovseenko, and the need for peace with the Central Powers was pressing. Consequently, on January 18, the Rada dropped its insistence on the transfer of predominantly Ukrainian-populated East Galicia and North Bukovina to the Ukraine, and merely asked that these areas be organized into a separate province (crownland) under Vienna's rule. At the same time, however, the Rada advised its delegation that there was to be no change as far as the Ukrainian claim to the Kholm area was concerned. The Ukrainian demand that the "Hungarian" province of Carpatho-Ruthenia also become a part of the Ukrainian crownland within the Dual Monarchy was rejected by Czernin so emphatically that the Ukrainians did not dare to raise this question again.[41]

The new position of the Ukrainian government was communicated to German and Austrian representatives almost immediately, and at the next meeting (Saturday morning, January 19) Czernin agreed to the Ukrainian compromise formula, but demanded speedy conclusion of the treaty and insisted that a date be set for its signing. At first he suggested January 30, 1918, then February 15, as the deadline, but the Ukrainians were reluctant to commit themselves. It was agreed, however, at the afternoon meeting of the same day, to issue a joint "progress report" on peace negotiations. A semiofficial communiqué was released on January 20 by the Central Powers and the Ukraine, stating that an agreement had been reached on the fundamentals of a peace treaty between them, and that after a brief interval the negotiations would be resumed.[42] No one was better aware of the true nature of this agreement and the grave consequences that it could have for the Dual Monarchy than Count Czernin. He felt, however, that there was no alternative because, as Emperor Karl had stated in a note of January 17, 1918, "the whole fate of the Monarchy and of the dynasty depends on peace being concluded at Brest-Litovsk as soon as possible . . . if peace is not made at Brest, there will be revolution here." [43] It was at this point that Czernin complained bitterly about his difficult position. In his diary he wrote: "The Ukrainians no longer treat with us, they dictate!" [44]

Still, a separate treaty with the Ukraine was far from a certainty. Final approval had to be obtained from the individual governments, and it was with this in view that the delegations agreed upon a recess and on January 20 headed for their capitals.

Czernin's task was to overcome Polish and Hungarian opposition. Fortunately, the gravity of Austria's situation at home had greatly weakened his critics' arguments against the Ukrainian treaty, and at a special meeting in Vienna on January 22, under the chairmanship of Emperor Karl, Czernin was given the needed approval for the proposed agreement with the Ukrainians.[45]

The task of the Ukrainian delegation was not that of overcoming opposition within the Rada (which at this stage regarded the treaty with the Central Powers as an absolute necessity to save the Ukrainian Republic from being completely overrun by the Bolsheviks); it was a practical problem of reaching Kiev in time to find the Rada government still there, and then returning safely to Brest-Litovsk. In fact, the Ukrainian delegates were stopped by the Red Guards on their return trip from Kiev. Perhaps they would never have seen Brest-Litovsk again, had it not been for a slip of paper authorizing them to negotiate with the Ukrainian Soviet delegates from Kharkov, who were waiting with Trotsky at Brest for the resumption of negotiations.[46] After traveling for four days—a distance of some two hundred miles—and literally risking their lives, the Ukrainian delegates finally reached Brest on February 1. They were equipped with the authorization to con-

clude a separate peace with the Central Powers and also with
news of the declaration of the Ukraine's full independence, which
had been proclaimed in Kiev on January 22, 1918, in what came
to be known as the Fourth Universal.[47]

The Germans were not confronted with any major internal
problems stemming from the proposed Ukrainian treaty, as were
their partners in Vienna, but there were some important questions to be ironed out before the final decision could be made. It
was clear that a treaty with the Ukraine would significantly affect
the general situation in the east. Russia, Poland, and Rumania
were to be affected most deeply by this treaty; it was therefore
necessary to study the situation from both political and military
points of view. It was also necessary to make sure that the Austrians would not do anything that might expose their desperate
position even more, and so encourage the Ukrainians to increase
their demands. Accordingly, Rosenberg urged the Foreign Office to
advise Vienna not to send her Food Commission to Kiev at this
time, fearing that it might be interpreted by the Ukrainians as
additional evidence of the Central Powers' urgent need for food
supplies and make them "even more unreasonable than they had
been heretofore." [48]

On January 23, Marshal Hindenburg and General Ludendorff
met again with Chancellor Hertling to review the Reich's *Ostpolitik*. At this conference the annexation of Polish territory to Prussia was agreed upon; this represented a compromise between
Hoffmann's "minimal" and Ludendorff's "maximal" programs. It
is not unreasonable to maintain that the prospect of a separate
treaty with the Ukraine made it possible for the generals to accept
a "less extreme" position with respect to Poland. Already as early
as January 7, Marshal Hindenburg in a letter to the Emperor had
expressed the hope that the new Ukrainian factor might minimize
the "Polish danger." [49] As far as the general problem of the east
was concerned, the Imperial Chancellor and the generals agreed
on the following formula: "Gain clarity in the east as soon as possible. From the military point of view an early conclusion of peace
with Russia is desirable, so as to have at our disposal the troops
presently remaining in the area. In the event the negotiations
with Russia were to break down, a speedy settlement with the
Ukraine would have to be sought anyway." [50]

Although the Imperial Chancellor, following the January 23

meeting, was able to announce to the Reichstag that talks with the Ukrainians showed good progress and that a mutually advantageous treaty would be concluded as soon as the remaining differences were removed,[51] the Ukrainian treaty still could not be taken for granted, and the Germans acted with great caution in order not to harm the chances for its speedy conclusion. Thus, when Ludendorff suggested that an ultimatum be sent to Bucharest, he wanted to know what effect the possible resumption of hostilities against Rumania might have on the Ukraine and Russia. Hoffmann replied that he did not doubt the existence of some kind of understanding between the Rumanians and the Ukrainians, and warned that the resumption of hostilities against Rumania might seriously endanger peace talks with the Rada. General Hoffmann felt that by early February it should be possible to determine whether or not the Rada had enough power to conclude a separate peace. One could confront Rumania as well as Russia with an ultimatum only after the conclusion of such a treaty. Under-Secretary of State Bussche also advocated a firm stand vis-à-vis Petrograd, but thought that with the Ukrainians a "yielding attitude would be a more promising one." [52]

At this point the Germans decided to send a special commission to Kiev, similar to the one already in Petrograd. Having learned about this plan from Hoffmann, Ludendorff suggested that Rear Admiral Albert Hopman be appointed as head of the Kiev commission. Somehow, Baron Philip Alfons Mumm von Schwarzenstein, who later served as the Reich's Ambassador to the Ukraine, was chosen for the post instead. The Germans did approach the Ukrainians concerning this matter, but were advised that the commission might not be able to reach Kiev because of the Bolshevik advance and should, therefore, begin its work in Brest-Litovsk.[53] Foreign Secretary Kühlmann then suggested that the following tactics be used after the resumption of negotiations at Brest: "Continue to deal with the Bolsheviks and keep them in suspense until we can be certain of an agreement with Kiev, and then resort to the use of stronger language." By this time considerable portions of northern and eastern Ukraine were under Bolshevik control and Kiev itself was being threatened; however, Kühlmann viewed these troubles not as cause for reducing the Rada's demands but merely as complications that might force it to conclude the treaty without delay, and thus confront Trotsky with a *fait accompli*.[54] Repeated reports concerning the Bolshevik plan to terminate hostilities without concluding a treaty undoubtedly strengthened the Foreign Office's conviction of the correctness of its plan of action for the peace talks to be resumed at Brest on February 1. The first such report on Trotsky's famous "no war, no peace" formula reached the Supreme Army Command sometime in mid-January, and was rushed to the Foreign Office without delay. Two weeks later, on January 31, another such report was sent to Brest-Litovsk by Under-Secretary Bussche.[55] It is, therefore, difficult to understand why the Germans were so shocked by Trotsky's declaration of February 10, 1918. From reading the German archives of this period one gets the impression that the Germans at Brest-Litovsk (and this includes Secretary of State Kühlmann) did not take the reports on Trotsky's plan very seriously, mainly because of their conviction that the conclusion of the Ukrainian treaty would automatically force the Bolsheviks into immediate capitulation.[56]

Kühlmann's hesitancy to present Trotsky with an ultimatum was not the result either of his reluctance to offend the Bolsheviks or of any other scruples. It was simply the lack of firm agreement with the Ukrainians. "If I were to have my way," Kühlmann wrote on the eve of the resumption of peace negotiations, "I would break with Mr. Trotsky today rather than tomorrow. However, according to instructions from the Imperial Chancellor, which met the full approval of His Majesty, we should proceed cautiously with the Bolsheviks until we make an agreement with the Kievan Rada." [57]

Such was the situation when the delegations, all with fresh instructions, assembled for another plenary session on February 1. While Berlin, Vienna, and Kiev agreed in principle to conclude a treaty after the remaining minor differences had been ironed out, the prospect for an agreement between the Central Powers and Petrograd remained as dim as ever. The Soviet position, however, was strengthened considerably by the successful Bolshevik military advance against the Rada and the presence of two representatives of the Ukrainian Soviet government (organized in Kharkov on December 27, 1917) as part of the Russian delegation headed by Trotsky. As early as January 21, 1918, Rosenberg informed the Foreign Office of the arrival of two Ukrainian Bolshevik leaders, Vasyl Shakhrai and Ye. H. Medvedev, from

Kharkov. He emphasized that they did not claim to constitute a new group, but regarded themselves merely as Ukrainian members of the Russian delegation.[58] It is not so much for this as it is for his recognition of the Rada delegation on January 10, 1918, that Soviet historiography refers to Trotsky's stand as "treason." [59]

The status of these two gentlemen from Kharkov was most convenient for the Germans, who were quick to capitalize on Trotsky's mistake. Without being obliged to recognize them as representatives of the Ukraine, the Germans could allow them to remain at Brest in order to heighten the feeling of uncertainty in Kiev, and place the Ukrainian Rada under pressure to come to quick terms with the Central Powers. These tactics, however, were to be pursued with considerable caution to retain freedom of action and not to weaken the Rada.[60] This approach, however, had to be abandoned when the talks were resumed and Trotsky questioned the Rada's right to represent the Ukraine at Brest. At the heated and noisy plenary session of February 1, the representatives of the pro-Soviet Kharkov government were flatly denied the right to speak for the Ukraine, and on the insistence of the Rada delegation the Ukrainian People's Republic was immediately recognized by Czernin on behalf of the Central Powers as a free and sovereign state with full treaty powers.[61]

The Ukrainian treaty, however, was problematic even at this stage. The Rada's position was growing weaker every day, and both Hoffmann and Kühlmann began to think about the possibility of coming to its aid. General Hoffmann termed the Rada's difficulties "temporary" (even though it was then being driven out of the Ukraine by the Russian Red Guards) and was confident that the Germans would be able to support it with their arms and restore it to power. To Secretary Kühlmann, however, the prospect of German military assistance to the Ukraine at this point was not so simple a question as it appeared to Hoffmann. He was well aware of the possible consequences of such a move, especially the collapse of Soviet power; at the same time, believing as he did in the inevitability of a break with the Bolsheviks, Kühlmann thought that an alliance (*Bundesverhältnis*) with the Ukraine would make such a break more readily acceptable to both Germany and Austria-Hungary.[62] Nonetheless, the collapse of the Rada before the arrival of German reinforcements could not be ruled out.

Kühlmann wrote thus to the Imperial Chancellor on February 1, 1918: "I am inclined, in agreement with the Austrians and the Turks, to pursue the plan of reaching a settlement with the Ukrainians in any case, even though the authority of the Rada is supposed to be greatly weakened at this moment. For the Austrians such a treaty is necessary, for us and the Turks advantageous. One should not, however, deceive oneself as to the real value of the proposed settlement, because of the shaky position of the Rada." [63]

Count Czernin, while still clinging to the hope of making some kind of agreement with the Russians in spite of everything, was rather pessimistic concerning the prospect of coming to terms with the Ukrainians. "My plan," he wrote in his diary on February 1, "is to play the Petersburgers and the Ukrainians one against the other and manage at least to make peace with one of the two parties." [64]

The remaining political differences between the Austrians and the Ukrainians had to be settled before any definite agreement could be made. Despite the Rada's desperate position, its youthful delegates at Brest-Litovsk stood firm in their demands. Although Czernin had previously agreed to these demands in principle, and on January 22 secured his government's acceptance of the "compromise formula," the Rada's troubles caused him to question the validity of the whole arrangement. Kiev's difficult position, German impatience with the slow progress in the talks with the Ukrainians, and the uncertainty of Trotsky's next move were responsible for the decision of the Germans and Austrians to "toughen" their approach toward the Rada. An unofficial participant at these peace talks, Dr. Mykola Zaliznyak, reported that in the evening of February 1 (the day of official recognition of the Rada by the Central Powers) the Ukrainians were bluntly reminded of the critical position of their government in Kiev, and were presented with the "ultimatum"—sign the treaty on the following day or go home! The "draft treaty" handed to them by Czernin and Hoffmann contained the following points:

1) Termination of the state of war and resumption of diplomatic and consular relations between the signatories.

2) Delivery of 1 million tons of grain and other food products by the Ukraine.

3) Settlement of all other questions at a later period through special negotiations.[65]

Zaliznyak was an East Ukrainian political émigré in Austria who, with Czernin's approval, served as an unofficial mediator between the Central Powers and the Ukrainian delegation at Brest. He was one of the founders of the Union for the Liberation of the Ukraine, but broke away from that organization several weeks after its establishment and continued his collaboration with the Austrians independently. The Union itself, incidentally, was in no way involved in the Brest-Litovsk negotiations.

To convince the Ukrainians that the Central Powers meant business, upon the issuance of this "ultimatum" General Hoffmann advised them not to waste time, for if Kiev were to fall there would be no more talks.[66] Such tactics might have proved successful earlier in the day, before the question of the Ukraine's representation at Brest had been finally settled. Now this trump was no longer playable, and the Ukrainians knew it. The Ukrainian answer to the "Czernin-Hoffmann ultimatum," on which the Ukrainians worked feverishly all through the night, was an elaborate draft, which they presented to the Central Powers at a meeting on the following day (February 2). The Germans and the Austrians were impressed, and any allusion to the previous day's "ultimatum" was studiously avoided. Czernin, whom the Ukrainians found on that day even more worn out and nervous than usual, must have been greatly relieved by this turn of events. The Rada's counterdraft became the basis for the Ukrainian treaty concluded on February 9, 1918. It relied heavily on the general agreement reached with the Central Powers on January 19 but it also contained new features that were designed to make the whole draft more acceptable to the Austrians.

While insisting on the transfer of the Kholm area to the Ukraine, the Rada delegates were prepared to leave the door open for further negotiatons by proposing that the details of this transaction be worked out at a later date. An even greater concession was offered in the crownland question. The provision for the creation of an autonomous Ukrainian province of East Galicia and North Bukovina within the Dual Monarchy was to be contained in a special secret agreement rather than in the treaty itself. Similarly, the Ukrainian commitment to deliver grain and other foodstuffs was also to become a part of this secret agreement. Moreover, this delivery was to be matched with a German and Austrian promise to supply the Ukraine with various goods.[67]

German official records make no mention of the Austro-German "ultimatum," nor of the Rada's counterproposal; however, the treaty draft that Kühlmann sent to the Imperial Chancellor on February 2 was virtually identical with the one the Ukrainians claim to have prepared independently. It consisted of the following points:

1) Recognition of the Ukrainian People's Republic.

2) Delineation of its boundaries (the Kholm area to go to the Ukraine).

3) Delivery of 100,000 carloads of grain by the Ukraine before the end of June, 1918.

4) A secret agreement on Galicia.[68]

The Central Powers' agreement to continue negotiations on the basis of the Ukrainian draft did not, of course, constitute its immediate and unqualified acceptance. Czernin continued his efforts to secure more favorable terms for the Dual Monarchy, but the Ukrainians were equally determined not to yield the hard-won ground. Thus the talks were resumed on the following day (February 3). Although progress was slow at first—Kühlmann blamed this on Ukrainian "stubbornness and theorizing formalism"— more headway was made later in the day, and he was able to report to the Kaiser that "the work on the Ukrainian treaty was proceeding at full speed, and that within several days the final draft should be ready for signing." He also reassured the Emperor that immediately upon the conclusion ot the Ukrainian treaty, Trotsky would be presented with the alternative either to yield or to face the consequences of a complete break.[69]

On February 3, following the session in Brest, Kühlmann and Czernin took another break to attend an Austro-German conference that was to take place in Berlin on February 5 and 6. Despite further weakening of the Rada's position, Kühlmann was confident that the conclusion of the Ukrainian treaty was merely a question of a few days. He also felt that no new directives were necessary to iron out the remaining minor differences with the Ukrainians and that the final draft would be ready for signing upon his and Czernin's return from Berlin. Thus, as far as the Ukraine was concerned, Kühlmann did not ascribe much importance to the forthcoming Berlin conference. To him it was just another meeting between Czernin, the Imperial Chancellor, and General Ludendorff, convened mainly for the discussion of Austro-German differences on the vital question of war aims and general peace.[70]

The Berlin conference of February 5 and 6, 1918, restated the determination of the Central Powers to conclude a separate treaty with the Ukraine and thereby force Trotsky to show his cards. An agreement with the Bolsheviks was thought possible, but not absolutely necessary. In the event Trotsky remained unyielding, the armistice would be terminated and hostilities resumed. The possibility of the Rada's collapse before the final arrangement with the Ukrainians could be worked out did not disturb the Germans. Ludendorff's suggestion that military assistance might have to be furnished to the Ukrainians—but only at the express request of the Rada—met the general approval of the conference. Although Ludendorff stated that "no conquests were to be sought in Russia," because the Germans needed all available forces in the west, he thought that it was necessary to establish some kind of order in the east, since otherwise the Germans would have to maintain a strongly fortified frontier "against the ever-spreading poison of Bolshevism." [71] This was very likely the earliest expression of the *cordon sanitaire* idea.

On February 7, Czernin and Kühlmann returned to Brest-Litovsk with what might be called the "final and irrevocable decision" to conclude a separate peace with the Ukraine, and break with Trotsky if he still refused to yield. Kühlmann met with his staff and immediately reported to the Imperial Chancellor the great progress made on the final draft in his absence and assured Hertling that "barring some unforeseen complications, it was not impossible that the treaty with the Ukrainians might be signed the next day." [72]

Czernin did not seem to share Kühlmann's optimism even at this last stage. His last-minute attempt to come to terms with Trotsky can at least partly be explained by his pessimistic outlook. Czernin met Trotsky in a private conference in the evening of February 7, and then continued to negotiate with him through one of his advisors, Richard Schüller. Kühlmann preferred to deal with Trotsky through his assistant at Brest, Friedrich von Rosenberg.[73]

Czernin's efforts should not be interpreted as an indication that he seriously contemplated dropping the almost certain agreement with the Ukrainians—an agreement which at the time looked much more promising than it later proved to be. Czernin could not expect any bread from the Ukraine in the event that country should fall into Bolshevik hands; he knew how important Ukrainian supplies were to Russia and that Trotsky would not give them up voluntarily, especially at a time when the Red Guards were successful in their military operations against the Ukrainian Rada. The real reasons for Czernin's last-minute talks with Trotsky before the signing of the Ukrainian treaty and the resulting break with the Bolsheviks appear to have been: (1) a desire to weaken domestic opposition in Austria-Hungary to the proposed agreement with the Ukraine and thereby meet the criticism for inability to make a similar deal with Russia; (2) an effort to minimize adverse effects that these developments might have on the neutrals and the Allied powers; (3) an assurance that no chance had been wasted that might have resulted in Trotsky's acceptance of the Central Powers' terms.

Kühlmann, no doubt, was motivated by similar considerations when he decided to approach Trotsky through Rosenberg on February 8, just hours before the Ukrainian treaty became a reality. It may be added that Trotsky, too, was responsible for these last-minute talks, although he did not initiate them. By trying desperately to block somehow the imminent agreement with the Rada, Trotsky gave Kühlmann the impression of being ready for another discussion and the latter, therefore, acted accordingly.[74] Kühlmann must have felt strongly enough about this apparent last chance of coming to terms with Trotsky to threaten resignation if the Kaiser were to insist on issuing an ultimatum to the Bolsheviks before the conclusion of the Ukrainian treaty.[75] Thus it was not Kühlmann's wavering under the pressure of the Supreme Army Command, as so many Austrian sources maintain, but rather the German terms and Trotsky's refusal to accept them that were responsible for the failure of these last-minute talks.

These talks had no effect on the preparation of the final draft of the Ukrainian treaty; it was ready for signing in the early morning hours of February 9, 1918. The signing ceremony was conducted in a rather festive mood, and the treaty was regarded by official German circles as an event of great importance. Kaiser

Karl issued a manifesto on this occasion; the German Kaiser, too, addressed his people in a solemn talk, in which he emphasized that peace between the Central Powers and the Ukraine was achieved "in a friendly fashion," [76] a fact that cannot be disputed.

The representatives of the Central Powers, including Count Czernin (even though he felt humiliated on being forced to deal with the "young men" from the Ukraine), took the Ukrainian delegates quite seriously and acted as though they were dealing with equal partners. Both Kühlmann and Hoffmann had genuine admiration for the young Rada negotiators at Brest. In Kühlmann's words "they behaved bravely, and in their stubbornness forced Czernin to agree to everything that was important from their national point of view." [77] Even Trotsky, much as he despised the Rada delegates, met them in informal talks and admitted that they had to be taken seriously.[78]

Much has been said and written about the rivalry between the German Imperial Chancellery, especially its Foreign Secretary Kühlmann, and the Supreme Army Command, or more correctly General Ludendorff, during the Brest-Litovsk negotiations.[79] Undoubtedly, some differences existed between the two at various times. As far as the east is concerned, they were mainly differences of opinion on the German plan for territorial aggrandizement in the Baltic provinces and Poland—a problem that lies beyond the scope of this study. Although it is true that Ludendorff was critical of some of Kühlmann's moves and pronouncements at Brest and was rather impatient with the slow progress of peace negotiations, in general no real differences existed between the two as far as the Ukraine was concerned. A good example of such criticism was Ludendorff's reaction to the Central Powers' answer to Petrograd delegate Adolf Abramovich Joffe's "Bases for Peace Negotiations," which Czernin read at the December 25, 1917, meeting, and which amounted to an agreement in principle to the Bolshevik "no annexations, no reparations" formula. Ludendorff vigorously protested this move and, as a result of this reaction, General Hoffmann, with Kühlmann's approval, had to tell Joffe privately, at one of their meals, that Poland, Lithuania, and Courland were not to be affected by that formula because they had already availed themselves of their right of self-determination.[80]

Obviously, no important decision could be taken at Brest without the express approval of the Supreme Army Command; but there is no basis for maintaining that the treaty was dictated by the generals, as is so often claimed.

True, General Hoffmann did play an important role at Brest; however, this was due less to his official position as the Supreme Command's representative than to his unrivaled knowledge of the east. The two principal German spokesmen at Brest-Litovsk, Secretary Kühlmann and General Hoffmann, remained on friendly terms and cooperated closely and smoothly with one another throughout the period of negotiations.[81] It was with Ludendorff that Hoffmann developed a serious difference of opinion, mainly over Poland, at the Crown Council in Berlin on January 2, 1918, and if it had not been for the Kaiser's high regard for General Hoffmann's ability and dedication, Ludendorff, no doubt, would have succeeded in his attempt to remove him from Brest-Litovsk to some remote point at the front in the capacity of a divisional commander.[82]

The relations between Count Czernin, the head of the Austro-Hungarian delegation at Brest, and his German colleagues, though interesting, will not be treated here for lack of space. One may point out, however, that Austria's position at this time was so weak that Czernin had to content himself with playing a secondary role at the conference, although it was the Dual Monarchy that had to pay for the Ukrainian treaty. The mere acceptance in principle of the Rada's demands concerning Ukranians in East Galicia, North Bukovina, and Kholm completely destroyed the Austro-Polish solution, which had been the cornerstone of Vienna's eastern policy from the beginning of the war. These Austrian concessions brought about permanent alienation, if not hostility, of Poles everywhere. Polish disillusionment with Austria continued in spite of the fact that Vienna's commitments with regard to its Ukrainian-populated provinces and the Kholm area were never fulfilled, nor did Austria ever exchange the ratification of the treaty with the Ukraine, in spite of the fact that other signatories did so in the summer of 1918.

The other German allies, Turkey and Bulgaria, while maintaining a sympathetic attitude toward the Rada, played practically no role in the negotiations with the Ukrainians at Brest; nor were they in the position to influence in any significant way subsequent developments in the German-dominated east.

Some writers maintain that the Ukrainian treaty of Brest-Litovsk did not bring any positive results for that country.[83] Others go even further and brand it as an "act of treason" on the part of the Ukrainians. Such is as a rule the thesis in Soviet as well as in some western writings. This is also the burden of John W. Wheeler-Bennett's well-known study of the treaty, in which he discusses it completely from the Allied point of view. Still other writers claim that the Ukrainians owed their short-lived independence to the Germans, who moved into the area just in time to prevent complete domination of the country by the Bolsheviks. Consequently, they view the treaty as "one of the high points of Ukrainian history." [84] Although it may be justifiable to maintain that had it not been for German intervention, the Ukraine, with the exception of Austria's Ukrainian provinces and the areas already under the Central Powers' occupation, would have fallen into Bolshevik hands, one cannot be certain concerning the consequences of such a development. It can be safely assumed that anti-Bolshevik Ukrainian forces would have continued their struggle after the Rada's collapse; that the Ukrainian peasant would have opposed arbitrary confiscations of grain for shipment to Moscow and Petrograd as much as he opposed such measures undertaken by the Germans and the Austrians; and, finally, that many other elements in the Ukraine would also have remained in opposition to the Bolsheviks. It is therefore difficult to accept the view that Petrograd's rule in the Ukraine would have been firm from that time on, that the idea of Ukrainian statehood would have been destroyed, and that the Ukrainian national revolution would have been arrested at that point.

In the light of all this (and one may add that the final outcome of World War I was then still in doubt), the Ukraine's acceptance of a separate treaty with the Central Powers—a treaty which, despite some obvious dangers, was rather advantageous for Kiev—can only be viewed as making the best of a bad situation. Because of the chaotic conditions in the country and the Allies' inability to come to its aid, the Rada was in no position to continue the war against the Central Powers and was faced with a possible Austro-

German occupation. At the same time the newly established Ukrainian republic was being overrun by the Bolshevik forces from the north. Rather than surrender to Petrograd, the Rada decided to make a deal with a friendly although not entirely disinterested German Reich. As a result of the treaty, the Ukraine emerged as a formally independent and neutral state—a status which the Ukrainians hoped to strengthen in the future. That the Ukraine was soon to become a German satellite cannot be denied; however, it is not entirely correct to maintain, as does a noted student of the Ukrainian revolution, John S. Reshetar, that it became a satellite by reason of the treaty alone.[85]

The conclusion of a separate Ukrainian treaty also had far-reaching repercussions for Soviet Russia, which it will suffice to summarize at this point. One of them was the loss of food supplies and raw materials that were badly needed in Russia at the time. Moreover, the treaty facilitated a new German advance in the east, which soon forced Petrograd to accept German terms unconditionally, and resulted in strengthening other border areas and their national movements (for example, the Caucasus, the Crimea, Byelorussia).

Irrespective of its negative aspects and the serious consequences to the Ukrainian national movement and the idea of Ukrainian statehood, the treaty may be considered a victory, a rather costly one, to be sure, but nevertheless a victory, of the Ukrainian national forces—a fact that Soviet Russia could not and did not ignore. Ukrainian participation in the Brest-Litovsk negotiations and the subsequent conclusion of a separate treaty demonstrated rather dramatically to the Bolsheviks the need for a federal solution for the non-Russian border areas of the former Czarist Empire; otherwise, the national movements could become an even more serious source of opposition to the new regime in Petrograd.

The German Foreign Office documents used for this study show rather convincingly that in the beginning Germany had no definite plans for a treaty with the Ukraine and that separate talks with the Rada delegation were initially undertaken in the hope of strengthening the Reich's position vis-à-vis the Bolsheviks to force them into a speedy acceptance of Germany's terms. Berlin's decision to make a separate agreement with the Ukrainians was ar-

THE UKRAINIAN STATE IN 1918

BALTIC SEA

FINLAND

L. Ladoga

Narva

Petrograd

Vologda

Pskov

Riga

BYELORUSSIA

Vitebsk

Moscow

Minsk

Mogilev

RUSSIA

Brest-
Litovsk

Kholm

Kursk

Lviv

U K R A I N E

Kiev

R. Dnieper

Kharkov

R. Don

R. Volga

Chernivtsi

R. Dniester

BESSARABIA

Ekaterinoslav

Tsaritsin

Iuzovka

Taganrog

Novocherkassk

RUMANIA

Odessa

Rostov

AZOV
S.

KUBAN

R. Danube

Constanta

CRIMEA

Simferopol

Sevastopol

Novorossiisk

B L A C K

S E A

GEORGIA

Batum

Tiflis

—— Eastern Front, December 1917
—•—• German advance in the East in 1918
---- Boundaries of the Ukrainian State in 1918

rived at in mid-January, 1918, but it did not crystallize fully until after the Berlin talks between German and Austrian civilian and military leaders held on February 5 and 6.

In the initial stage of the Brest-Litovsk negotiations the Bolsheviks could have made peace with the Germans in the name of the entire former Czarist Empire, as was the case with the armistice. It is likely that the Bolsheviks still could have done so even after the appearance of the Rada delegation, although they might have had to make additional concessions. But once the Germans became convinced that the Bolsheviks would not accept the proposed conditions and became aware of their plan to checkmate the Central Powers with a rather ingenious "no war, no peace" formula, the Ukrainian peace, despite some remaining differences between Vienna and Kiev, was a virtual certainty. Additional considerations in the German decision to make a separate peace with the Rada were the following: (1) the release of as many of their eastern troops as possible for a decisive battle in the west; (2) the prevention of the reopening of the eastern front; (3) the procurement of food supplies and raw materials necessary for the continued conduct of war; (4) the strengthening of German morale at home and at the front; (5) the checking of the spread of Bolshevik propaganda; (6) and finally, and to a large extent a by-product of the above considerations, the organization of a system of border states in the east, with the Ukraine occupying a pivotal position in it.

It is not easy to establish the relative significance of the above considerations. According to Hans J. Beyer, the military considerations were paramount in the German behavior at Brest.[86] Volkwart John, on the other hand, feels that the question of morale was more important. Indeed, the Germans became greatly concerned about the deteriorating morale, both at home and at the front, as early as mid-1917. "Our greatest anxiety at the moment, however, is the decline in the national spirit," wrote Hindenburg to the Kaiser on June 27, 1917. "It must be revived, or we shall lose the war." [87] Of course, later in the year, in the wake of the failure of the unrestricted submarine warfare, United States entrance into the war, the worsening food situation, industrial strikes, mutinies, and so forth, the problem of bolstering German morale became even more compelling. Still other writers, as for example, Erwin Hölzle and Erich Volkmann, stress the concern of the German military with the threat of the Bolshevik revolutionary propaganda. One of the best ways, in their view, to check its spread was through the encouragement and support of separatist movements among the non-Russian peoples of the east.[88]

The Ukrainian treaty was thus not a corollary of a long and clearly discernible process of German political planning and scheming but merely a product of a series of military and economic considerations produced by a long period of ceaseless warfare, and of the determination to bring the hostilities to a victorious end, or at least an "honorable and equitable" settlement. The often-dramatized difference of opinion between the Supreme Army Command and the Imperial Chancellery, especially in the person of Secretary of State for Foreign Affairs Kühlmann, had much less bearing on the Ukraine than on other areas, notably Poland and the Baltic provinces. It should also be remembered, as Karl Helfferich put it, that "it was not the Treaty of Brest-Litovsk that broke up the Russian giant; on the contrary, the treaty was the result of such a breakup. The territorial questions decided at Brest came into existence with the disintegration of the Russian Empire." [89] Moreover, the process of disintegration of the Russian Empire and the growth of various national movements on its territory were not directly and significantly influenced by the Germans during the period prior to the opening of peace negotiations at Brest-Litovsk.

The Ukrainian treaty of Brest should, therefore, be viewed as the beginning of an experiment, undertaken somewhat reluctantly by the Germans, aimed at extending the Reich's influence and power into the vast areas of Eastern Europe. The treaty itself provided only a framework, and not a very elaborate one at that, for the development of some kind of German policy for the Ukraine and its neighbors for the future.

The Austrians stressed, almost exclusively, the economic advantages that they hoped to derive from the Ukrainian treaty. It was Czernin who named it the "bread peace." And Austrian Prime Minister Ernst von Seidler spoke in a similar vein in his address to the nation on the occasion of the conclusion of the treaty.[90] The German Emperor and the Supreme Army Command, on the other hand, were more appreciative of the military benefits that they expected. Speaking of the Treaty of Brest-Litovsk in general several years later, Wilhelm II defended it by saying that "at the time it was made it was necessary to give preference to military requirements," and that the treaty "had to include conditions that would guarantee our safety until the end of the war." Hindenburg argued similarly: "The separation of the border states from the old Empire as a result of the peace conditions was in my view mainly a military advantage." [91]

It was left to German political spokesmen to evaluate the treaty with the Ukraine in terms of long-range political objectives. They too stressed the economic value of the treaty; at the same time, however, they emphasized their conviction that the Ukraine would prove to be a permanent and important factor in the east with which Germany would have to reckon. Prince Max von Baden, for example, said in a public interview that the foundation of the Ukraine would prove "a factor of lasting pacification in European history." Kühlmann expressed a similar view by stating that the Ukrainian state idea would always remain an influential factor in Russia and an important force in the east.[92] The prevailing view among the Germans, however, was the feeling that the Ukrainian treaty was but a temporary arrangement which, in Helfferich's view, would have to be considerably modified, and in Rathenau's opinion, should have been abandoned altogether as a wartime "provisionality." The man who succeeded Kühlmann as Germany's Foreign Minister, Admiral Paul von Hintze, also held a very critical view of the Treaty of Brest-Litovsk.[93]

At the time of the conclusion of the Ukrainian treaty the Rada was no longer in Kiev; not only the Ukraine but the entire east was in chaos. The possibilities stemming from the treaty were numerous. Various processes and reactions were set in motion by it, but the treaty did not provide any clear guidance for their further development. The true nature of the treaty, especially its vagueness and its temporary character, can be fully appreciated only after a thorough examination of German plans and policies in the east in the preceding period, 1914–1917. Similarly, the importance of the Ukrainian "peace" in the further development of German *Ostpolitik* during the last year of the war can be understood only in the context of the entire German experiment in the southeast, of which the treaty with the Rada was but the beginning.

CHAPTER V

The Occupation of
the Ukraine

The German occupation of the Ukraine in February of 1918, following the conclusion of a separate treaty between the Central Powers and the Rada, is usually viewed as the "next step" in the development of the Reich's expansionist plans and policies in the east. And yet, it was a difficult decision which the Germans arrived at after considerable debate. True, the Germans were well aware of the Rada's difficult position long before the conclusion of the treaty on February 9, 1918 (the day the Rada was forced by the Bolsheviks to leave Kiev), but it was not until February 1 that Kühlmann and Hoffmann seriously considered the need to come to the assistance of their new ally in the east.[1] This eventuality was further discussed at the Berlin conference on February 5–6. General Ludendorff suggested that military assistance be given to the Rada, but only on its express request, a view that seems to have been shared by those present. The scope of such assistance and other details were not dealt with at this point.[2] It is of some interest that the Bulgarians, through their representative at Brest, Andrea Toshev, urged Czernin to furnish the Rada with military assistance as early as January 29.[3]

Even at the moment of the signing of the Ukrainian treaty, however, the extent and exact form of German intervention in the

Ukraine were not yet decided upon. Extending German domination over an area larger than the Reich itself, at a time when every available able-bodied German was badly needed in the west, was a difficult decision. A special conference was called, therefore, in Homburg on February 13, to work out a plan for further German involvement in the east. The meeting took place under the Kaiser's chairmanship, and can be viewed as one of the high points in Ludendorff's brief career of political overlordship in wartime Germany. It was not so much military assistance to the Ukraine that disturbed the Foreign Office at this point as it was the resumption of hostilities against Russia in the north, with which Germany was still at war. Whereas Chancellor Hertling was apprehensive of repercussions at home as a result of the proposed march against Russia, Foreign Secretary Kühlmann was more concerned with the effect that this move might produce in Austria-Hungary—a fear that proved more justified than Hertling's.[4] Consequently, Kühlmann opposed even a limited operation in the north, rightly suspecting that it would not be as "limited" as General Ludendorff promised. However, with the Emperor siding with the military, and Imperial Chancellor Hertling and Vice-Chancellor Friedrich von Payer also accepting this view, Kühlmann's opposition collapsed. The Homburg conference thus paved the way for the proposed advance against Russia in the north, as well as for intervention in the Ukraine.[5]

The occupation of the Ukraine was viewed by the German military as part of a larger operation in the east and not as a separate problem that could be solved independently. Although the drive in the north was to be localized in the region of Dünaburg, in the form of "a brief but hard push," [6] plans for the military penetration of the Ukraine were initially less clear. Kühlmann (then on his way to Bucharest) even expressed the hope that a limited operation in the north against Russia might make direct intervention in the Ukraine unnecessary, as if echoing the sentiment expressed to him by the Reichstag leaders several days earlier.[7] Soon, however, he accepted the Chancellor's view that the Ukraine would receive German military assistance provided the Ukrainians specifically requested it.[8] On February 15 General Hoffmann advised the Ukrainian delegation at Brest to make an appeal to the German people on behalf of the Rada, and on the following day General Ludendorff informed the Foreign Office that the Ukraine would be given "active military assistance." [9] It is therefore clear that the German decision to move into the Ukraine was primarily a military one, to which the Foreign Office merely gave its tacit consent.[10]

These military considerations were closely linked to economic factors. General Wilhelm Groener went even so far as to maintain that in the occupation of the Ukraine (as of Serbia in 1915) economic considerations were important enough to dictate specific military and political moves. For him the penetration of the Ukraine by German armed forces was above all an attempt to weaken the effect of the Allied blockade. This could be accomplished only by making Ukrainian food supplies and raw materials accessible to the German and Austrian economies.[11] It may be added that the resumption of the German advance into Russia and penetration of the Ukraine, coupled with the promise to replenish the dwindling German stocks of bread and butter, were to prove for a period of time rather beneficial to German morale, both at home and at the front. As to the so-called Bolshevik danger, General Ludendorff referred to it on various occasions, and the Kaiser echoed his argument at the Homburg meeting when he spoke of the necessity of destroying Bolshevism "which is attempting to bring revolution into Germany." [12]

The Ukrainian treaty of Brest-Litovsk did not provide for direct German military assistance to the Rada government against the Bolsheviks. A treaty of alliance was mentioned as a possibility during the negotiations, and the Germans returned to this subject on other occasions, but at the moment German military intervention in the Ukraine was being considered, there was no time to work toward such an alliance. So desperate was the Rada's position, there were fears that the Ukrainian government might collapse before the Germans could come to its aid. Unable to establish contact with the Rada (then no longer in Kiev), the Germans approached Mykola Lyubyns'kyi, the only member of the Ukrainian peace delegation still at Brest, and advised him to make a formal appeal to Germany for military assistance against the Bolsheviks in order to save the Rada from complete destruction. To "simplify and expedite" matters, General Hoffmann is supposed to have presented Lyubyns'kyi on February 15 with the script on an "Appeal to the German People" (which was being printed in Berlin) and to have requested him to sign it in the name of the

Rada government.[13] The correctness of this Ukrainian version of the origin of the appeal for assistance could not be verified on the basis of German archival materials; they did not yield any documents dealing specifically with this problem. According to an official Austrian source, two nearly identical appeals, one addressed to the German and the other to the Austrian people, were drafted by the Rada delegates Sevryuk, Levyts'kyi and Lyubyns'kyi.[14] The Rada was by then in such straits that need for the military assistance of the Central Powers was no longer in question. What mainly disturbed the Ukrainian delegates at Brest was the problem of personal responsibility for such a fateful decision. Lyubyns'kyi's position was especially difficult. He, too, lost contact with the Rada and was presumably the only remaining Ukrainian representative at Brest; yet there was no time for waiting and reflection. Finally, he managed to arrange a telephone conversation with Sevryuk, the head of the Ukrainian peace delegation then in Vienna, and the two decided that there was no choice but to accept Hoffmann's suggestion.[15] The Supreme Army Command received the appeal on the same day and immediately notified the Emperor and the Foreign Office that German military assistance would be furnished without delay, and that two German detachments had already been ordered to Pinsk and Rovno.[16]

In view of German eagerness to transfer as many troops as possible to the west, and the fact that the Bolshevik forces in the Ukraine were mostly irregular and loosely organized Red Guards from the north (not more than two or three divisions in strength),[17] Ukrainian attempts to have the Galician Legion Sichovi Stril'tsi, certain predominantly Ukrainian units of the Austrian army stationed on the Italian front, and Ukrainian prisoners of war in Germany and Austria transferred to the east to fight against the Red Guards may not have been as "naïve" as some later students of the period asserted.[18]

Most of the Galician Ukrainians who served in the Austrian army during World War I were stationed on the Italian front and were often organized into predominantly Ukrainian units. Their exact number is not known, but several divisions could have been organized and sent to the Ukraine had the Austrians been willing to give serious consideration to such a plan. The idea was rejected because of alleged transportation problems.

There was also a Ukrainian plan to have limited German forces dispatched to the Ukrainian-Russian border in the north, where they would operate against the Bolsheviks, and a plan of putting certain German detachments in Ukrainian uniforms and having them fight the Reds along with the remaining Ukrainian troops loyal to the Rada.[19]

Interestingly enough, the German military leaders took some of these Ukrainian suggestions quite seriously. General Hoffmann, for example, did not at first regard the Ukrainian plan to have German soldiers in Ukrainian uniforms fight alongside the Ukrainians as unacceptable. He believed that a small force could rid the Ukraine of the Bolsheviks, and that direct and undisguised German intervention would further weaken the Rada's position in the country. General Ludendorff, too, was ready to consider some of the Ukrainian suggestions, and on February 16 ordered a Ukrainian detachment of nearly 1,000 men, composed mainly of former Ukrainian prisoners of war and reinforced with German officers and other personnel, clothed in Ukrainian uniforms, and headed by a Ukrainian general, to proceed to Kovel in Volhynia to join the Rada forces.[20]

But even after the decision in favor of a direct and open German thrust into the Ukraine, the Germans preferred to present their advance as a joint undertaking and did not object to Lyubyns'kyi's "order" to the Ukrainian prisoners of war in Germany and Austria "in the name of the Rada" exhorting them to join the Ukrainian forces in their struggle against the Bolsheviks. Those unwilling to comply with the "order" were warned in advance that they would be regarded as traitors and refused repatriation following the liberation of the Ukraine.[21] Almost simultaneously the Germans proceeded with the formation of two Ukrainian prisoner-of-war divisions; the Austrians followed suit, though after some delay. None of these forces was to be dispatched to the Ukraine until two or three months later.

The German march into the Ukraine began on February 18, concurrently with the resumption of hostilities against Russia in the north. Army Group Linsingen began its operations in Volhynia (where the remnants of the Rada forces were still fighting the Bolsheviks), advancing mainly along the railroad lines. Its goal was Kiev, and it entered that city on March 1.[22] The pattern of advancing along the railroads was followed throughout the operation. Such tactics allowed the Germans to move forward rapidly and to carry out the occupation of a vast area with limited forces and minimum losses.

The trains were hurriedly equipped with guns mounted on open lorries and stocked with plenty of ammunition—a combination with which the Bolsheviks could not cope. The mop-up operations against the remnants of the Red Guards were often entrusted to the Ukrainians, although the Bolshevik forces usually either managed to escape or to lose themselves in the general chaos and confusion. Of decisive importance to the whole undertaking was the role of the Ukrainian railroad workers. The Germans gave them full credit for their cooperation and frankly admitted that without the benevolent attitude of Ukrainian railroad personnel their occupation of so vast an area could not have been carried out within such a short time.[23]

General Field Marshal Hermann von Eichhorn soon replaced General Alexander von Linsingen as commander of the main German force advancing along the Kiev-Kharkov line. By early May, Army Group Eichhorn (not counting the smaller army group headed by General Field Marshal August von Mackensen, which moved into the southern Ukraine with the Austrians) was composed of twenty weak divisions, among them eight reserve (*Landwehr*) and three cavalry divisions.[24] By German standards, this was a second-rate army, with the exception of the cavalry divisions, but under conditions of general chaos it was a formidable force and was to prove a decisive factor in the Ukraine throughout the period of occupation.

It was one thing to rid the central and northern Ukrainian provinces of the Red Guards, but an entirely different thing to reestablish and maintain law and order in an area larger than Germany itself, and this after a full year of revolutionary ferment which had resulted in almost complete political, social, and economic disintegration of the area. The Germans were quick to realize that both Austrian military cooperation and the participation of Ukrainian forces, however weak and ill-equipped, were also necessary to accomplish the task of pacifying the country.

Although the Germans may have somewhat overestimated the strength of the Rada force, they had no illusions about its real military value. They estimated the Rada forces at 30,000–40,000, as of mid-February 1918, a rather high figure even if it included various independent units and guerrilla formations fighting on the Rada's side.[25] A reliable and sympathetic Ukrainian source put the number of Ukrainian troops loyal to the Rada at the time of the opening of the German campaign in the Ukraine at 12,000–13,000, with a very high percentage of officers, professional people, and students.[26] Unquestionably this is a more realistic estimate. Whatever its size, the Germans did not think much of the Rada force. Although the Rada troops gave a good account of themselves during the brief anti-Bolshevik campaign in February and March of 1918, these ill-clad, tired soldiers, some of whom were only in their late teens, could have hardly impressed the Germans, and this was reflected in the critical reports prepared by the Reich's political officers in the east.[27]

It was mainly for political reasons that the Germans allowed the small Ukrainian force to play such an important role in the occupation. Following a specific request by Lyubyns'kyi, who remained at Brest-Litovsk after other members of the Rada delegation had departed, General Hoffmann arranged for these Ukrainian troops to enter Kiev ahead of the German army. This was intended to strengthen the Rada's authority and thereby to create the impression that the liberation of the Ukraine was a joint undertaking in which the Rada forces played an important role.[28] This pattern was repeated in many other places. It should be added, however, that the Ukrainians, supported by the German artillery, engaged the retreating Bolshevik forces in numerous brief but fierce skirmishes, and in many instances their priority in entering a given city or town was well deserved.[29]

It was only after the return of the Rada to Kiev, in early March, 1918, that the Ukrainian and German military commanders agreed that the Ukrainian force was to remain independent, both administratively and operationally, under direct supervision of the Rada Ministry of War, although in their joint action against the Bolsheviks the two armies agreed upon close cooperation. In practice, however, the Ukrainians preferred to operate on their own, to make certain that they would stay ahead of the Germans and be looked upon as the liberators of the country.[30]

The opening of the German advance into the Ukraine on February 18 had been accompanied by a "marching order" which described the operation as "military assistance to a state with which

we have a treaty against our common enemy, the Bolsheviks." [31]
The Germans were fully aware of the weak legal basis of their
Ukrainian undertaking (Lyubyns'kyi's appeal for assistance on
behalf of the Rada), and showed great interest in reassembling
the Rada prior to the launching of the campaign. They wanted
the Ukrainian government to reaffirm its delegate's action and
thereby clarify the legal status of the German forces in the
Ukraine.[32] On February 19 (one day after the opening of the campaign), Richard Schüler again reminded the Foreign Office of the
necessity of reestablishing the Rada administration in the newly
liberated areas, in order to convince the Ukrainian peasant that he
was faced, not with simple military occupation, but with the return of a legitimate Ukrainian government that he should support. On the following day Schüler urged an immediate meeting
of the Rada in Rovno (Volhynia) to restate unequivocally the
Ukraine's request for German military assistance.[33]

Hoffmann and Schüler, who remained at Brest-Litovsk as political directors of the Ukrainian undertaking, received unqualified
support from Berlin. While the Lithuanians, Latvians, and Esto-
nians were promised by Imperial Chancellor Hertling on February 19, "a free *Baltikum* in close relationship with Germany and
under our military, political, intellectual, and cultural protection," [34] Foreign Secretary von Kühlmann, discussing German
plans for the Ukraine at the Reichstag on the following day, said:
"We are interested in maintaining the railroads [in the Ukraine]
in good condition in order to be able to ship grain and other food
items in accordance with the peace agreement. This much we
admit. But, as we have already indicated, we shall not go beyond
this, and shall refrain from all political involvement in that country." [35] Kühlmann returned to this question later in the day. He
denied the existence of an alliance between Germany and the
Ukraine and assured the Reichstag that nothing of the sort was being considered. He then went on to declare again that he would
recommend the seizure and control of Ukrainian railways, with
the consent and approval of the Ukrainian government, as a necessary security measure—an arrangement that a noted German
student of the period rightly regarded as an important prerequisite for the Reich's economic preponderance in that area in the
future.[36]

The German military in the Ukraine were eager to reassure the

Ukrainian peasants, who were growing apprehensive lest land and other property they had seized from the landlords would have to be returned. According to Ukrainian sources, the Germans tried to present themselves as "friendly guests," and promised noninterference in the Ukraine's internal affairs.[37] Imperial Chancellor Hertling is also reported to have made a pledge to this effect by declaring that German troops would be withdrawn as soon as the Ukrainians, seeing their mission fulfilled, requested it.[38] It was, thus, the reestablishment of law and order in the country (by ridding it of the Bolsheviks), and not some kind of cultural tutelage (*Kulturträgertum*) or political overlordship, that was stressed openly by the Germans in this early stage of their Ukrainian undertaking—the theme to which they were to return time and again throughout the period of occupation.

Not until February 23, 1918, did the Rada cabinet, while on its way to Zhytomyr where it was to remain temporarily until it could return to Kiev, issue a statement in which it explained the role of the German army in the Ukraine. It referred to the German troops as "friendly forces which were invited to help us against our enemies, forces which had no evil intentions of any kind, and which were fighting along with our Cossacks under the command of our military staff [*sic*]." [39] On March 7 the Rada, after its return to Kiev, issued another statement, asserting that the Germans had come to the Ukraine "for a limited period of time as friends and supporters to help us at a difficult moment of our life," and that they had "no intention of either altering our laws and regulations or limiting the independence and sovereignty of our Republic." [40] On the basis of subsequent developments in the Ukraine the Rada statement may be termed "unbelievable," as John S. Reshetar terms it; however, a limited occupation or military assistance without a serious curtailment of national sovereignty on the part of the helping power, although not very common, is not without precedent in world history. Not only German promises and assurances but also objective circumstances of the war at that particular stage may have lent a certain credence to the Rada's announcements and protestations.

The effect of these German and Ukrainian declarations was generally reassuring; and one can say that the Ukrainian people accepted the Germans with relief but without enthusiasm. A witness to the German occupation of the Ukraine and one of the foremost Ukrainian students of the period, Dmytro Doroshenko, gives us an interesting description of the reaction of various groups in the Ukraine to the appearance of German troops in the country after a brief Bolshevik rule: "The population responded to the appearance of the advancing German troops with complete calm. In the country they were met with neither fear nor joy. In the cities the bourgeoisie rejoiced at being delivered from the Bolshevik terror; the working class, however, the bulk of which was sympathetic to the Bolsheviks, remained passive and generally adopted a wait-and-see attitude. Nationally conscious Ukrainians were happy to see the reestablishment of Ukrainian authority in the country." [41]

German actions in the early stages of the occupation were nonetheless more important than their declarations. The troops were directed to be friendly with the local population, and the requisitioning of food and fodder was expressly forbidden in an order issued by Ludendorff himself.[42] Even critics of the German intervention, such as the former Secretary of the Rada, Volodymyr Vynnychenko, described the German advance in the Ukraine as "quiet and unobtrusive." [43] This, no doubt, aided their rapid advance and promoted the ready acceptance of German presence in the country. There were, of course, other factors that gave the Ukrainians reason to tolerate German intervention on such a large scale. The Rada supporters, and most other nationally conscious Ukrainians, regarded the German troops as allies against the Red Guards from the north, and their assistance was viewed as the Rada's "second chance" to organize the young Ukrainian state into a viable political structure.

Although the Germans continued to show interest in strengthening the Rada's authority by facilitating its return to Kiev as soon as possible,[44] they also wished to strengthen it internationally by gaining recognition for it. In early March, 1918, they tried to approach Switzerland, but their ambassador did not think that such a move would be successful, and the matter was soon abandoned. The only foreign power that could be compelled to recognize the Rada was Soviet Russia, and the Germans insisted on this point in the Russo-German treaty which they forced on Petrograd on March 3.[45] The initiative for this came from the Ukrainian representative at Brest, Mykola Lyubyns'kyi, and the Germans readily agreed to defend the Rada's interests in their talks with the Bolsheviks.[46]

When the German troops began their march into the Ukraine on February 18, the Austrians did not join them. Despite repeated attempts on the part of the Rada representatives to secure Austria's military assistance, beginning shortly after the signing of the treaty at Brest, Vienna had remained firm in its refusal to commit its armed forces to any new involvement in the east.[47] Ukrainian interest in Austria's participation was based not only on military considerations but also on the hope that the presence of two different armies on its soil might prove beneficial in the future by offering an opportunity for balancing the two forces against each other.

The Germans had made no definite arrangements with Vienna concerning Austria's participation in the occupation of the Ukraine, assuming that the movement of the Austro-Hungarian forces eastward would follow automatically upon the German advance. The Austrian refusal to join the advancing German armies presented the German military with a serious problem. Ludendorff found Vienna's position "incomprehensible." "At first it was announced that the State [Austria] had to conclude an unfavorable peace treaty in order to survive," Ludendorff wrote in his war memoirs, "and now it does not want to act in order to secure, on the basis of that treaty, things necessary for life." General Hoffmann was annoyed, and Kaiser Wilhelm anxious.[48] The latter's personal appeal to Emperor Karl produced no results. The Austrian Emperor explained his refusal to join the German forces by declaring that it was not a military operation, but merely a police action.[49]

The real reasons behind Austria's reluctance to move into the Ukraine were the well-known "external considerations." Austria had a genuine desire to refrain from doing anything that might destroy the chances for a general peace by agreement, which she rightly viewed as her only hope for survival as an empire. Equally important was her fear of further internal complications in the Dual Monarchy stemming from the opposition to the Ukrainian treaty and its implementation by Austrian Social Democrats, as well as Poles, Czechs, and South Slavs.[50] Austrian official circles also knew that the Dual Monarchy's participation in the occupation of the Ukraine would greatly excite and embolden the Ukrainian population in Galicia, Bukovina, and Carpatho-Ruthenia, which in turn could affect other nationalities of the Empire and bring about a serious weakening of its entire structure.

Austria's Foreign Minister, Czernin, one of the architects of the Ukrainian treaty, urged his country's participation in the occupation, although he did not mind some delay, hoping that it would help him to obtain concessions from the Ukrainians in the Kholm area and the Galician crownland question. Czernin did obtain Ukrainian concessions in the Kholm area in favor of Poland on February 18, and on the following day Austrian Prime Minister Ernst von Seidler, speaking in the parliament, openly reassured the Poles on this question.[51]

Vienna's demands, however, were opposed by Germany and this further contributed to the delay. Thus, when on February 19, the Austrian Ambassador in Berlin reported to the German Foreign Office the Rada's acceptance of Vienna's demand for the formation of a joint commission to delineate the Ukrainian-Polish boundary in return for the promise of Austrian military assistance, Ludendorff immediately declared that he would not accept any changes of the Ukrainian boundary in favor of Poland.[52] One week later Ludendorff again advised General Hoffmann to "oppose with all sharpness" any attempts on Austria's part to force the Rada into renouncing its claim to the Kholm area. Hoffmann replied that he had already taken the opportunity of strengthening the Ukrainian stand and would not let them down.[53]

Vienna thus faced a serious dilemma as the Germans advanced deeper and deeper into the rich steppes of the Ukraine without encountering serious opposition from the Bolsheviks. More and more people in Austria were beginning to realize that in order to obtain bread from the Ukraine they would have to go after it.[54] Opposition to Austria's military involvement in the Ukraine had not subsided, despite the real threat of famine in Vienna and other urban centers of the Dual Monarchy. Ultimately, the exigencies of physical survival of the Monarchy proved stronger than special political interests, even those of such influential national groups in Austria as the Poles, especially now that some of their demands could be met more than halfway. Austrian intransigence gave way to anxiety lest "in the absence of Austro-Hungarian troops [in the Ukraine] the entire wealth of the Russian grain treasury fall solely into German hands and Austria-Hungary be rendered even more dependent than heretofore upon her ally for food supplies." [55]

Austria's food emergency undoubtedly played a most important part in her decision to intervene actively in the Ukraine. Hardly less important was the fact that by deciding to intervene Vienna secured the Radas consent to revision of a secret agreement on East Galicia and Kholm, amounting in practice to the revocation of all the concessions won by the Ukrainians at Brest. (Nevertheless, most of the Austrian students of the problem, as well as some of those who were involved in the Dual Monarchy's operation in the Ukraine, felt that Czernin should have obtained further concesssions from the Rada, such as compensation for the occupation costs or greater freedom in the economic exploitation of the country.) [56] Finally, the ease with which the Germans advanced in the vast area of the Ukraine—in a "victorious march" entailing almost no casualties—induced Austria to participate in the occupation.

The Austrian decision to join Germany in its Ukrainian campaign was made reluctantly and was regarded in many quarters as another of those operations into which the Dual Monarchy was drawn by its ally against its wish. The fact that the Austrian High Command ordered preparations for the march into the Ukraine on February 21 and that another week elapsed before the advance began shows that Vienna had not originally planned to furnish military assistance to the Rada.[57]

The Rada representatives at Brest were informed by the Dual Monarchy's diplomats that the advance of Austro-Hungarian troops aimed above all at the creation of "peaceful conditions" in the country. Emperor Karl followed with a formal statement terming the operation "a peaceful penetration into a friendly land." [58] The Austrian military command in the east issued a proclamation in which it reaffirmed its friendship for the Ukrainian people and its sympathy with their efforts to rebuild their state and economy.[59]

The German Army Group Mackensen, moving along the advancing Austro-Hungarian forces in the direction of Odessa, gave the belated Austrian intervention the appearance of a joint undertaking and helped to conceal initially the cleavages and friction that were soon to develop into open rivalry between the two allies. The Austrian task proved even easier than that of the Germans. Their advance was greatly facilitated by the fact that the main Bolshevik forces were concentrated in the north and had been dispersed by the Germans by the time the Austrians decided to intervene. They imitated the German pattern of advancing along the railroad lines. Small Ukrainian detachments of "Free Cossacks" moved with the Austrians, eagerly engaging the fleeing Red Guards wherever and whenever they could catch up with them. As was the case in Kiev, Ukrainian units were first to enter Ekaterinoslav (now Dnepropetrovsk); it is not clear whether or not this was done in accordance with some kind of agreement with the Austro-Hungarian command.[60]

Austro-German differences in dealing with the Ukrainian question can be traced to the pre-World War I period, and they became more pronounced at various stages of the wartime cooperation in the east, especially during the Brest-Litovsk negotiations. It was not, however, until the Austrians moved into the Ukraine that these differences manifested themselves in open rivalry that seriously strained relations between Berlin and Vienna.

After the initial Austrian refusal to march into the Ukraine the Germans began to explore the possibility of freeing the country from the Bolsheviks single-handedly, thereby becoming the sole "protector" of the recently organized Ukrainian state. On February 19, 1918, Ludendorff advised the Foreign Office that he did not care whether the Austrian troops would cooperate or not. One week later, however, General Hoffmann notified the Supreme Army Command that although he had informed the Ukrainians that German military assistance would not go beyond Kiev, he was convinced that the Rada would need additional help to gain control of Odessa and the Black Sea coast in general, as well as the Donets Basin with its rich coal deposits. Hoffmann urged that the Germans, not the Austrians, furnish this additional military assistance, asked the Foreign Office to approach the Rada concerning this matter, and requested permission to begin working in this direction.[61] The Foreign Office went along with this plan and urged that economic concessions be obtained from Kiev in the Donbas in return for further military assistance.[62]

The Germans, however, did not have sufficient forces in the

GERMAN RULE IN THE EAST
IN 1918

L. Onega

FINLAND

Helsinki

L. Ladoga

BALTIC SEA

Reval   Petrograd
ESTONIA   Narva

Dorpat

Dvina R.

Riga

LITHUANIA   LATVIA

Dvinsk

Volga R.

GERMANY   Polotsk   Vitebsk

Vilna   BYELORUSSIA   ⊙ Moscow

Lake
Vyhonovske   Mogilev   • Tula   RUSSIA

Warsaw   Zhlobin

POLAND   Pruzhany

Kholm   Brest-   POLISSYA   Chernyhiv   Rylsk
Litovsk   • Kursk   • Voronezh
           Kiev   Belgorod

Lviv   UKRAINE   *Dnieper R.*   Kharkov
GALICIA   1918   • Poltava   *Don R.*

AUSTRIA-HUNGARY

BESSARABIA   • Kryvyi Rih   DON   • Tsaritsin

Odessa   Mariupol
RUMANIA   TAURIDA   • Rostov   Astrakhan

Bucharest   *SEA OF
AZOV*

DOBRUJA   CRIMEA   KUBAN   CASPIAN
SEA

BULGARIA   Novorossiisk

BLACK   CAUCASUS

Constantinople   SEA   GEORGIA • Tiflis

MEDITERRANEAN   Batum   Baku
                AZERBAIDZHAN

TURKEY   ARMENIA

PERSIA

▨   Areas under indirect German influence
▤   Areas under the Austro-German occupation
---   Line of German advance in the East in 1918

east to do the whole job alone and were greatly relieved when the Austrians finally decided to join them. Ludendorff frankly admitted later that Austrian cooperation was necessary to accomplish the task at hand.[63] Nonetheless, the Germans had no intention of giving Austria a free hand in her zone of occupation. When the Austrians began to move into the Ukraine, there was only a general understanding that they would confine their operations to the southern portion of the country. The Germans were quick to exploit the lack of precise agreement with Vienna on the territorial division of the Ukraine and proceeded to establish a strong foothold in the Austrian sector as well.

From the very beginning of their involvement in the Ukraine, the Germans consistently tried to prevent Austro-Ukrainian bilateral talks and agreements from taking place. Berlin was determined that nothing of importance should happen in the Ukraine without direct German participation or express approval, although the Germans did not consider themselves bound by similar restrictions.[64]

It was the German thrust southward in the direction of the Black Sea coast and the Donbas (planned before the Austrian advance had begun), as well as the Germans' undisguised and arrogant assertion of their primacy over the entire region that led to open rivalry, which at times was to become so acute as to endanger the continued existence of the Austro-German alliance.

The most serious incident between the two allies occurred in Odessa when both German and Austrian forces tried to "liberate" the city. "Endless trouble with the Austrians in the Ukraine," General Hoffmann wrote in his diary on February 23, 1918. "They want to enter Odessa alone, and are behaving with their usual meanness. . . ." General Wilhelm Groener was also greatly annoyed with the Austrians because he saw that the Rada was quick to exploit the misunderstandings between the two occupying powers. According to Groener, to deal with the Austrians proved more difficult than to free the Ukraine from the Bolsheviks.[65]

The question of selecting a supreme commander for the Central Powers' forces in the Ukraine, a position for which Ludendorff proposed General Linsingen, led to further complications between Berlin and Vienna. Emperor Karl greatly resented Ludendorff's "dictatorial tone," and whereas most Austrians recognized the need for a unified Austro-German command in the

Ukraine, the young Austrian ruler preferred to have two clearly separated spheres of influence there. The advance of Austrian and German troops continued independently.[66]

Although the Germans and the Austrians repeatedly tried to agree on the exact delineation of their respective spheres of influence, it was not until March 28 that the division of the Ukraine into two zones took place. Berlin's determination to establish a position of dominance over the whole country and Vienna's resistance to the German bullying tactics were mainly responsible for this delay. The fact that the Rada, too, had to be taken into consideration and that its wishes could not be ignored completely added further to the Austro-German difficulty in dividing the "spoils." [67]

The Austro-German agreement on the division of the Ukraine, concluded on March 28, 1918, was an arrangement between the two Supreme Army Commands reached without direct participation of the German and Austrian Foreign Offices. According to this agreement, the Germans received a larger share of Ukrainian territory than the Austrians. In addition to the northeastern half of Volhynia, which they occupied first, the Germans also claimed the following provinces: Kiev, Chernigov, Poltava, Kharkov, Novocherkassk, and Taurida, with the Crimea. The Austrians obtained the other half of Volhynia and the provinces of Podolia, Kherson, and Ekaterinoslav. Moreover, the Germans, who controlled the Ukraine's two principal cities—Kiev and Kharkov— obtained Austria's agreement to the joint occupation of Nikolaev, Rostov, and Mariupol. (The first two ports were to be under German command, and Mariupol was to be under Austrian.) Two additional Black Sea ports, Taganrog and Novorossiisk, were to be exclusively in German hands.[68]

As a result of this agreement, the Dual Monarchy was relegated to a secondary position as an occupying power. By establishing several stategically located strongholds along the Black Sea coast, reaching as far eastward as Novorossiisk, Germany prepared the ground for further extension of its power in this area—into the Crimea and the Donets River Basin, and later on into the Don region and the Caucasus.

This agreement, one-sided as it was, did not last long and, according to General Ludendorff, "as conditions changed, the agreement lost its value. It soon became necessary that Germany alone be entrusted with the collection and distribution of foodstuffs and other materials." [69] Marshal von Hindenburg may have been sincere in saying that political considerations played no part in the Supreme Army Command's participation in the Ukrainian undertaking, and that its actions were primarily motivated by military and economic factors.[70]

To sum up: At first the Germans did not plan to go beyond Kiev. Then, they decided to move as far eastward as Kharkov. Soon afterward the knowledge that the coal of the Donets Basin was absolutely necessary for the operation of Ukrainian industries and transportation convinced the Germans that they had to move into this area, too, to make the coal region safe from the Bolsheviks.[71] Finally, the Germans extended their domination still farther eastward by occupying roughly one-third of the Don region, and eventually they established themselves in Georgia.[72] The fear of the reopening of the second front by the Allies (regarded by the Germans as a real possibility at the time) and the desire to keep the Bolsheviks off balance also played a part in the German decision to increase the area of occupation in the east. Thus, the extension of German domination in the Ukraine was not the result of a well-developed political plan but merely the Reich's military response to the deteriorating economic situation at home and recognition of the fact that the Rada would have to be offered further military assistance if it was ever to fulfill its promise to supply the Central Powers with the agreed quantity of food and raw materials. While political and legal arrangements in the Ukraine remained unclear, one thing was beyond dispute: Germany was deeply committed to intensify its exploitation of the Ukrainian economy. This was bound to deepen the Reich's political involvement not only in the Ukraine but in the east as a whole.

CHAPTER VI

The Aftermath:
The Development of
Occupation Policies

It may be best to begin an examination of the development of German occupation policies in the Ukraine with a brief discussion of the Reich's military and civilian officials who were entrusted with "guiding the destinies" of the young Ukrainian state. There were no personnel changes within either the Supreme Army Command or the Imperial Chancellery and its Foreign Office during the period of the peace talks and the resumption of the German advance in the east. Ludendorff remained the dominant personality on the German political scene. The Foreign Office, unable to develop a positive policy of its own, tacitly accepted Ludendorff's overlordship and acquiesced in the German occupation of areas in the southeast that had not been encompassed in the initial plan.[1] It is not surprising, therefore, that the diplomatic representatives in Kiev were destined to play a secondary role in Germany's Ukrainian undertaking throughout the period of the occupation.

Although there were among the Germans in the Ukraine such experienced diplomats as Ambassador Philip Alfons Mumm von Schwarzenstein, and such gifted military experts as General Wilhelm Groener, none of the principal German officers or diplomats in Kiev had any real knowledge of the Ukraine and its problems.

Groener frankly admitted that he and his colleagues knew nothing about the country and the people in whose destinies they were to play such an important role.[2]

Prior to his appointment, first as head of the Reich's Ukrainian Delegation and then as its Ambassador Extraordinary and Plenipotentiary in Kiev, Mumm had served as Ambassador in Washington, Peking, and Tokyo. From the outbreak of the war until his Ukrainian assignment, Mumm was in charge of Germany's Central Propaganda Agency in Berlin.

Before going to the Ukraine, General Groener had made a name for himself by his brilliant performance as chief of the Transportation Division of the Supreme Army Command and as head of the War Production Office (Kriegsamt) in Berlin. At the close of the war, Groener succeeded Ludendorff as Quartermaster General and then served as a member of the cabinet in the Weimar Republic.

General Hoffmann, who was fluent in Russian, was the only high-ranking German officer in the east with real knowledge of the area; however, after the transfer of the Supreme Command East, of which he remained Chief of Staff, to Kovno on May 1, 1918, his influence on Ukrainian developments ceased completely. It had already been greatly reduced in March with the appointment of General Groener to his post in the Ukraine.

General Field Marshal Hermann von Eichhorn, Commander in Chief of the German forces in the Ukraine from March, 1918, until his assassination in Kiev in July of the same year, is usually regarded as the key German figure in the east during the crucial first half of the occupation period. Although it is true that most of the orders and directives were issued in his name, the real director of the whole undertaking was his Chief of Staff, General Groener, who from the very beginning was given a free hand in dealing with the Ukrainian problem. (General Linsingen, who was initially slated for the post of Supreme Commander in the Ukraine, was given a different assignment by General Ludendorff, not so much because of Vienna's objections as to satisfy General Groener, who could not get along very well with Linsingen but had no objection to the appointment of Eichhorn to the commanding post in Kiev.)[3]

Although the task of composing the Reich's Ukrainian Delegation had been undertaken in late February, 1918, it was not until mid-March that the Rada government was requested to prepare hotel lodgings for Mumm and his staff, "naturally, at the expense of the delegation." [4] Mumm's nomination to his Ukrainian post (he was selected over the Supreme Command's candidate, Rear Admiral Albert Hopman) spurred Ludendorff to double his efforts to establish the primacy of the military in Germany's Ukrainian undertaking. As early as February 27, Rosenberg, then at Brest, was told confidentially by General Hoffmann that Colonel von Stolzenberg had been appointed military attaché in the Ukraine and ordered to proceed to the Rada headquarters. [5]

Stolzenberg's assignment to Kiev did not fully satisfy Ludendorff, however. A much more able and energetic individual was needed to make certain that the fruits of German victory in the east would not be dissipated. The choice of General Groener was by far the best that could be made at the time, and Ludendorff acted with deliberate haste in dispatching him to the Ukraine. Ludendorff was motivated by his desire to seize the Ukrainian stocks of grain before the arrival of the Austrians on the scene. Thus, on February 27, General Ludendorff directed Hoffmann at Brest to demand from the Rada that it deliver all the food supplies at its disposal to Kiev for immediate shipment to Germany. Only after that could certain supplies be given to the Austrians. [6] Also, the general was determined to grasp the initiative and have his men well established in Kiev before the arrival of the Foreign Office representatives. Groener received his new assignment on February 25, was given his instructions and powers at a special meeting with Ludendorff and Hindenburg at Kreuznach on February 28, arrived in the Ukraine on March 4 to assume command of the First Army Corps, and was named the Chief of Staff of the Army Group Eichhorn on March 28, that is, immediately upon its formation. [7]

It was thus clear from the beginning that General Groener's task in the Ukraine would not be merely a military one, so his official title at a given time had no particular significance. His real tasks were in the realm of war economy and politics. In his own words, he was to accomplish the following in the Ukraine: "to put the Ukrainian government back into the saddle, to lend it the support of the German armed might, and, above all, to extract from it grain and other foodstuffs—the more, the better!" [8]

General Groener's new assignment was not an easy one. The

weakness of the Rada, chaotic economic conditions in the country, the unpopularity of the Germans (a factor from the outset), social and political ferment generally, and uncertainty about the future—all contributed to the complexity of his mission. Although Groener found in Ambassador Mumm a close collaborator (in spite of the many differences and frictions between the two bodies which they were representing in the Ukraine), and could also count on the full and willing cooperation of a strong German economic commission in Kiev headed by Krupp director Otto Wiedfeldt, his mission failed. The general soon found himself deeply involved in a Ukrainian political crisis that was to result in the removal of the Rada and the establishment of a new government in Kiev.

Privy Councillor Wiedfeldt, on leave from Krupp for the duration of the war, was assisted in his task by an equally respected financial leader, Karl Melchior, of the Warburg banking firm in Hamburg. They represented the Ministry of the National Economy (Reichswirtschaftsamt) and the Department of the Treasury (Reichsschatzamt), respectively.

General Groener's political advisers in the Ukraine were Majors Hasse and Jarosch, both Russian-speaking intelligence experts. The two officers were destined to play a much more important role in Ukrainian affairs than their rank and titles would suggest.

Even before he assumed his post in Kiev, Mumm conceded that during the initial period of the occupation, while military operations were still in progress, only the German army was in a position to obtain supplies from the Ukraine. Mumm, in fact, advocated the acceptance of a military plan for the procurement of food, although he fully appreciated the political complications that could result from it, and insisted that the diplomats had an important role to play.[9] Nevertheless, General Ludendorff remained critical of the Foreign Office's "mingling" in Ukrainian affairs. A successful exploitation of the country, the general rightly suspected, "could not always be carried out in a gracious manner . . . and in case of dire necessity, methods unbecoming to the highest diplomatic representative of the German state might have to be employed."[10] What Ludendorff had in mind was the establishment of a "real hegemony" in the country. To achieve this, Ludendorff demanded that General Groener be given a free hand in the Ukraine and suggested that Privy Councillor Schüler or "an even younger Foreign Officer" be sent to Kiev to assist Groener in his task. Count Johann Forgách von Ghymes und Gacs, who was to serve as the Dual Monarchy's Ambassador in Kiev, also urged that a diplomat of a lesser rank be assigned to the Ukraine.[11]

The German Foreign Office, however, stood firm on its position and succeeded in obtaining the Emperor's confirmation of Mumm's appointment. To the Foreign Office the Ukrainian problem was more than just the collection of food. It rejected Ludendorff's proposal that the military alone be given this task and reminded him that Germany had recognized the Ukraine as a state and had concluded a treaty with it; it was therefore necessary to deal with it in the usual diplomatic manner. The Foreign Office further declared that the economic and political tasks in the Ukraine could not very well be separated and that Ambassador Mumm's presence in the country was necessary for the solution of outstanding political problems.[12] The Foreign Office spokesmen in the east were even more disturbed by their military colleagues' approach to the Ukrainian problem during this early stage and urged that Mumm be dispatched to Kiev "without delay," to cool off the military hotheads, who were beginning to develop some rather fantastic notions about the Ukraine and their role in it.[13] Although the Supreme Army Command abandoned its attempts to bar Mumm from the Ukraine, it continued its efforts to limit the scope of his activities. On March 21, Marshal von Hindenburg made another appeal to Imperial Chancellor Hertling and demanded that Mumm be ordered to refrain from interfering in German economic policies in the country.[14]

Such was the alignment of German forces in the Ukraine at the time of the reestablishment of the Rada. The Emperor played practically no role at this time in the shaping and conduct of Germany's Ukrainian policy. The same can be said of the Reichstag. The various ministries—War, Navy, Treasury, Economy, Colonies—were also occasionally involved in Germany's Ukrainian undertaking, but their role was always secondary. The story of the development and implementation of German plans and policies in the Ukraine during the occupation is therefore to a large extent the story of rivalry and cooperation between the Imperial Chancellery and its Foreign Office, on the one hand, and the Supreme Army Command, or more correctly General Ludendorff, on the other.

As the Germans were laying the groundwork for a systematic economic exploitation of the Ukraine, the question of the Rada's status arose again. Now, following its return to Kiev, the Rada reconstituted itself as the legitimate civilian government in the country, and the issue could no longer be evaded.

Continued Austro-German misunderstandings and the inability of the Supreme Army Command and the German Foreign Office to agree on a definite policy for the Ukraine greatly contributed to the difficulty of solving this basic problem; so did the weakness of the Rada and its inability to organize an effective administration in the country. The Germans thus found themselves in an impossible situation. While strengthening the government with which they had made a treaty and which they had promised to support militarily and politically, they were at the same time weakening and undermining it through their extreme demands. Immediate procurement of food from the Ukraine and its speedy shipment to Germany were foremost in the thinking of all the Germans. Yet, few could see that a weak Rada could not, and a strong one would not, keep its promise of food deliveries unless the Germans clarified their future plans for the east as a whole, established a clear relationship with the Ukrainian administration, and revealed their position on the problems that concerned the Ukrainian peasant most—notably the land question.

The struggle between the Supreme Army Command and the Foreign Office reached a critical stage following the return of the Rada to Kiev in early March. It was further intensified after the initial implementation of German economic policies in the Ukraine—policies on which the Germans placed rather high hopes and which they, especially the military, were determined to carry out at all costs. Many of the military, both in Berlin and in the Ukraine, maintained from the beginning of the occupation either that a new government must be established—"since it was utterly hopeless to deal with the Rada, that bunch of Social Revolutionaries"—or that the country should be ruled martially "as if it were a German Governor-Generalship (*Generalgouvernement*)," [15] that is, a colony or a conquered province. Few Germans in Kiev took the Rada seriously. A German intelligence officer in the Ukraine, Colin Ross, referred to the Rada as a "club of political adventurers," and General Groener's adjutant, Richard Merton, called the Ukrainian state *"Operettenstaat."* [16] General Groener at first attempted to pursue Germany's aims in the country with the cooperation of the Rada.[17] Soon, however, he, too, became disillusioned with it and began to seek new ways of accomplishing his task in the Ukraine.

Austrian reports from the Ukraine were equally critical and pessimistic. A report from Kiev, dated March 10, for example, noted the weakness of the Rada and a general hostility toward the Austrian forces in the country; the Austrian Consul in Kiev, Hoffinger, went further and questioned the wisdom of cooperating with the Rada.[18] The Austrian Supreme Command's answer to all this was its "Directives for the Support of the Ukrainian Government in Administrative Matters." It recommended that a friendly and correct attitude toward Ukrainian authorities be maintained by the Dual Monarchy's occupation forces in the country at all times.[19]

The Germans, in the meantime, continued to explore other approaches to establishing a clearer relationship with the Rada. To the alternatives of establishing a new government in the Ukraine or subjecting the country to direct military administration, a third was added by Colin Ross, namely, "permeation of the Ukrainian government apparatus and armed forces by German elements." A milder version of this idea, coming from a German diplomat in Brest-Litovsk, recommended the assignment of a German expert to each Rada ministry or agency.[20]

That the Rada was weak and had difficulty coping with the chaotic conditions in the country cannot be denied. Indeed, it would have been surprising had it been otherwise. After three difficult years of war, followed by a year of revolutionary ferment, Bolshevik occupation and, finally, German and Austrian intervention, it was unrealistic to expect immediate restoration of normal economic and social conditions in the Ukraine. Moreover, under those conditions the Ukrainian national movement could hardly have reached maturity; nor had the social revolution in the country been completed. The Rada's contact with the rest of the country was poor, but this was also true of the Soviet government in Petrograd and, indeed, all other governments in Russia during the revolutionary period. Since few Germans appreciated the situation, they tried to measure the Rada by the standard they were accustomed to find in Germany and other well-organized European countries. Many of them, especially people like General Groener who had had some experience with the exploitation of Belgium (which fell into German hands practically untouched), could see no reason why the Belgian experience could not, at least to some extent, be repeated in the Ukraine.

General Hoffmann (then still at Brest-Litovsk), who had been aware of the Rada's weak position all along, continued to advocate its strengthening so that it could survive as a government. His recommendation was based on a long-range view of Germany's policy in the east. Hoffmann saw two distinct alternatives for Russia in the future: (1) further development and completion of the process of decentralization, which would vindicate Germany's conclusion of a separate treaty with the Ukraine; and (2) the reemergence of Russia as a unified state, which would prove Germany's Brest-Litovsk policy wrong. To prevent the latter possibility, the Rada had to be supported and maintained.[21]

After Hoffmann was transferred, together with the Army Headquarters East, to Kovno, Ambassador Mumm had to struggle alone for the maintenance of Germany's original approach to its Ukrainian undertaking. Mumm had to defend it against all those who were prepared to forget diplomatic niceties and international agreements and who urged that Germany simply "help herself to whatever she needs to be able to survive and wage war, through the use of naked force if necessary, and irrespective of the wishes of the Ukrainian government, which could always be replaced by another one, or simply done away with." [22]

Ambassador Mumm's efforts to direct Germany's Ukrainian undertaking along the lines recommended by General Hoffmann called for further strengthening of the Rada and for making it into a government that would voluntarily deliver to the Central Powers the promised foodstuffs in return for the diplomatic and military support furnished to it earlier. All this was to be accomplished in a manner that would not violate the existing agreements, or call for the employment of undiplomatic methods. Mumm began expounding this view prior to his arrival in Kiev. The first opportunity to do so presented itself at Brest-Litovsk, where he stopped overnight on his way to his new post of duty in the Ukraine and where he met various German military and diplomatic officers. Mumm told them bluntly that any other approach to German's Ukrainian policy would antagonize the population and destroy all chances of accomplishing the Reich's aims in that country.[23] Mumm continued to insist upon this approach following his arrival in Kiev in mid-March where a number of "solutions" to the Ukrainian problem were presented to him.

Mumm's Ukrainian assignment might have been facilitated by the fact that the Germans had not yet developed a clear-cut occupation policy in the country. "There is absolutely no common political watchword [*Parole*] in the Ukraine," a German political officer reported in early March, 1918. "One might say that each staff officer, each commander, is making policy decisions of his own, and yet this is the only way things can be handled here." [24] On the other hand, his mission was greatly complicated by the Foreign Office's continued failure to develop a definite policy for the Ukraine, which alone would have enabled him to seize the initiative and to bring a certain uniformity to the conduct of German relations with the Rada. While Kühlmann was busy in Bucharest with his "Rumanian affairs," General Ludendorff set forth his "General Directives of the Administration and Exploitation of the Occupied Eastern Regions after the Conclusion of the Peace Treaty." The entire part "B" of this memorandum, dated March 18, was devoted to the Ukraine. Ludendorff termed the German involvement in the Ukraine a "relief expedition into a friendly land," and noted that the exact agreement with the Rada concerning the cost of this military assistance was yet to be agreed upon. Then, the general went on to say that the military commanders were empowered to issue orders and decrees and to take necessary measures in order to insure the safety of troops and to achieve pacification of the country. Although all such measures were to be adopted in cooperation with the local authorities, the occupation forces were to carry them out if local agencies refused or proved unable to do so. Again, although the military commanders were not allowed to issue orders or otherwise interfere in matters of general interest to the local population (for example, commodity price control), any action against the Germany army or its personnel was to be handled by the military courts according to Royal Decree No. II of December 28, 1899. Finally, Ludendorff recommended "far-reaching" support of the Rada authorities in the reestablishment of regular administration and in the rehabilitation of the country. To clarify this last point, the general ordered that an immediate and most extensive cultivation of the land be carried out "in the German interest." [25] One can readily see that General Ludendorff, while advocating support of the Rada and maintenance of its authority in the land, was trying to strengthen the position of the German military in the Ukraine and prepare them for all possible contingencies.

Ludendorff's "General Directives" must have been welcomed by the military for bringing more clarity to the role they were to play in the Ukrainian undertaking. The memorandum could not, however, be regarded as a definite political program to be pursued in the Ukraine and did little to improve the situation there. In the meantime, General Groener became highly critical of the Rada and concluded that "its administrative apparatus was completely shattered, unreliable, and totally incapable of any serious effort." He also reported to Ludendorff the existence of widespread anti-German feeling in the Ukraine and warned that additional forces would be necessary to maintain German authority in so vast an area. Groener, however, reserved his strongest criticism for the German Foreign Office for its treatment of the Ukraine "as though it were a normal and equal partner." He had at the same time high praise for the Austrians and their "practical approach" (introduction of death penalty in the province of Podolia and forcible requisition of grain), and thought that the Germans, too, should follow such tactics.[26]

In his talks with the Austrian Ambassador, Count Forgách, Groener did not hide his astonishment and annoyance that such an enormous operation as the occupation of the Ukraine had been undertaken with so little previous planning, and the two agreed that the Rada would accomplish little unless it accepted Austro-German guidance and leadership.[27]

It is not surprising, therefore, that a few days later, Mumm was approached by Stolzenberg and asked what the position of German occupation forces should be in the event of a monarchist reaction in the country. In the absence of specific directives from the Foreign Office, Mumm had to confine himself to his "personal opinion," declaring that any radical change within the country could take place only with the express approval of the occupation authorities. Mumm also stated that the fundamental prerequisite for the success of Germany's Ukrainian undertaking was the maintenance of law and order in the country, and that it could best be secured, at least for the time being, by preserving the *status quo*. Following the same line of thinking, Mumm denounced the German and Austrian practice of arresting Ukrainian civilians and warned that such measures would change the German position in the Ukraine from that of an ally to that of an occupier.[28]

It was not until late March, 1918, that Foreign Secretary Kühlmann, writing from Bucharest, decided to come to Mumm's support. In a memorandum which he prepared for the Foreign Office in response to repeated requests for further directives, Kühlmann again discussed the nature of German military intervention in the Ukraine and declared that it was based solely on an appeal for help made by the government that Germany had recognized and with which it had concluded a treaty. The conduct of German policy in the Ukraine was to be guided by these facts; otherwise it would lose its base. He acknowledged that the main purpose of German intervention in the Ukraine was the procurement of grain and added that the Foreign Office's representatives were to aid in carrying out this vital task. They were to make sure at the same time that it would not result in a political upheaval. The Rada was to be supported and strengthened, but it was also to be reminded that it was the promise of Ukrainian food that had induced Germany to come to its aid and that Germany was determined to insist on the exact fulfillment of the Ukrainian commitment. He reiterated Germany's desire not to interfere in the Ukraine's internal affairs and did not challenge the Rada's right to carry out its economic and social reforms; however, he emphasized very strongly the necessity of putting all available land into cultivation, pending eventual settlement of the ownership question, "even if it were to mean temporary postponement of some of the Rada's programs." [29]

Kühlmann's program for the Ukraine was based on two assumptions: (1) the expectation that the Rada would heed German advice, and (2) the conviction that it was both able and willing to fulfill the commitments undertaken at Brest. It is thus clear that both Ludendorff, in his "General Directives" of March 18, and Kühlmann, in the above memorandum, failed to provide guidelines for the development of alternative policies should the assumptions on which their approach to Germany's Ukrainian undertaking was based prove false. Nevertheless, both documents contained the seeds of Germany's future "hard approach" to the Ukrainian problem, which people like Field Marshal Eichhorn and General Groener embraced quickly and gladly without qualms, but which the Foreign Office and its spokesman in Kiev, Ambassador Mumm, required considerably more time to accept.

Since economic factors were the key to Germany's Ukrainian undertaking, a full understanding of the Ukrainian crisis, which reached its high point with the overthrow of the Rada toward the end of April, can be gained only after an examination of initial German plans for the economic exploitation of the Ukraine and the methods and techniques employed to this end.

While the final touches were being added to the general Ukrainian Peace Treaty (signed on February 9, 1918), the Minister Plenipotentiary of Austria-Hungary, Baron von Wiesner, representing the Central Powers, and his Ukrainian counterpart, Lyubyns'kyi signed a "Protocol" dated February 7, 1918, which estimated the amount of surplus breadstuffs in the Ukraine to be "at least one million tons." These supplies were to be delivered promptly and paid for by "an equivalent value in wares." The Ukrainians accepted the Austrian insistence on "promptness," although they said that this would greatly depend "on the cooperation of the Central Powers with the Ukraine, both in the work of dispatch and in the improvement of the transport organization." [30] This, in fact, was an invitation to direct German and Austrian intervention in the Ukraine's economic affairs—a move the Ukrainians soon came to regret. It is not surprising, therefore, that German Foreign Secretary von Kühlmann recommended the seizure and control of Ukrainian railroads as early as February 20, and that the Germans soon felt justified in ordering much sterner measures to insure the fulfillment of the Ukraine's economic commitments.

The general principles regulating economic and commercial relations between the signatories of the Ukrainian peace were contained in Article VII of the treaty of February 9, 1918, and the "Supplementary Treaty" concluded on February 12.[31] Without going into details, it is worth noting that all the economic provisions were based on complete equality and reciprocity between the signatories, and might thus be viewed as quite fair to the newly established Ukrainian state.[32] In the early German-Ukrainian economic talks, the Rada officials presented the Germans with a long list of articles to be delivered in return for Ukrainian foodstuffs. At the head of the list were such items as agricultural machinery, tools, implements, paints, and chemicals. The Ukrainians were greatly surprised by the German readiness to supply so many of the requested articles. Austrian deliveries were to consist of scythes and sickles; it was generally felt that the Dual Monarchy was in no position to supply more.[33] The Central Powers waived all claims to compensation for war costs and reparations. The problem of state debts was dropped for all practical purposes, mainly because of Vienna's fear that it might set a precedent and prompt the Allies to advance similar claims against Austria-Hungary in the future. Various commercial and tariff arrangements were based mostly on the old Russian treaties and agreements. The provision for most-favored-nation treatment was also revived. The treaty with the Ukraine was to remain in force until the conclusion of a separate commercial agreement. In the event such a commercial agreement did not materialize, the treaty was to remain in effect for six months after the conclusion of general peace.[34]

It was not until April, that the Ukraine, in a special agreement concluded in Kiev, accepted a specific commitment to deliver cereals, grains, and oilseeds. The Rada government promised to supply Germany and Austria-Hungary with one million tons of these products. They were to be delivered at fixed prices—6 rubles per pood (36.11 pounds) for wheat, and 5 rubles per pood for rye. Exact quotas were set for April, May, June, and July. The products were to be received from the Ukrainian Commercial Agency. An Austro-German mercantile office was to be established in Kiev, to which Ukrainian officials (deputy commissioners) were to be attached to facilitate the task of storing and shipping the food supplies.[35] Some Germans considered these prices rather high. Matthias Erzberger, an influential Reichstag leader was especially unhappy and urged that the prices of German goods to be delivered to the Ukraine be adjusted accordingly.[36] It may be interesting to note that the Central Powers ascribed a rather high value to Ukrainian paper currency, despite the fact that the economic foundations of the young Ukrainian state were not very firm. At this time (April, 1918) 1 karbovanets (the

Ukrainian ruble) was worth 2 Austrian crowns or 1.33 German marks.[37]

Two weeks later, on April 23, 1918, a much more detailed economic convention, consisting of several separate agreements, was signed in Kiev. The most important agreement dealt with the delivery of grains, podded grains, fodder, and seeds, and largely repeated a similar agreement made on April 9. Other special agreements regulated the purchase of eggs, cattle, bacon, and sugar. There was also a separate protocol providing for "free purchase" of potatoes, onions, and other vegetables, as well as a special agreement for the delivery of various raw materials, such as timber, wool, iron and manganese ore, scrap iron, and rags. The Central Powers in turn pledged themselves to supply the Ukraine with agricultural machinery and tools, coal, chemicals, and mineral oil. They further undertook to supply 105,000 metric tons of coal per month, 101,500 plows before July 31, 1918, and 350,000 scythes "to be delivered at once." [38]

This convention, according to an official German source, was "reached after protracted negotiations accompanied by the application of constant pressure on the Ukrainians." [39] Since it was concluded several days prior to the Rada's overthrow, it was to play a very important part in the development of German economic policies in the Ukraine in the period of the Hetmanate.

While the economic talks were in progress, Ukrainian Prime Minister Vsevolod Holubovych had to promise Mumm that no state would be permitted to purchase (or otherwise acquire) Ukrainian grain until the Rada's obligations to the Central Powers had been fulfilled—a commitment that the Ukrainian government reaffirmed in a special declaration made public on April 16.[40] This action formalized the existing Austro-German monopoly in the economic exploitation of the Ukraine.

Berlin and Vienna began working out the arrangement for joint exploitation of the country even prior to the formal conclusion of the Ukrainian treaty. It was agreed in Berlin on February 4, 1918, that Ukrainian grain was to be divided equally between the two partners. On February 21, a series of additional agreements was concluded on the division of other foodstuffs and raw materials, as well as a financial agreement between Germany and Austria-Hungary concerning payment for them. The details of these agreements (comprising more than forty pages) need not be discussed here, especially since so few of the provisions were to be realized, but it may be noted that the tasks of purchasing and shipping were entrusted either to the Austro-German economic agencies created in the course of the war or to syndicates especially organized for this purpose. Even more interesting is the ratio between the Austrian and German shares: wool, 38:62; flax, 45:55; silk, 1:2; cotton products, 5:8; minerals, 1:2; hides, 4:7; leather and furs, 2:3; manganese, 1:2, and so forth. Austria-Hungary was to pay five-twelfths of the total and Germany, seven-twelfths.[41]

In practice, however, the Germans tried from the beginning to relegate Austria to a clearly subordinate position in the economic exploitation of the Ukraine, and the Rada government was naturally aware of the true relationship between the two occupying powers. For example, shortly after Austria's advance into the Ukraine in late February, 1918, Ludendorff instructed General Hoffmann (then still in Brest) to direct the Rada to forward all available foodstuffs to Kiev as soon as possible, for immediate shipment to Germany. Austria-Hungary's needs were to be met later.[42]

Faced with the Rada's inability as well as unwillingness to cooperate in the fulfillment of its economic commitments, and confronted with German determination to run things in the Ukraine without regard for Austrian needs and wishes, the Austrian occupation forces in the Ukraine soon found it necessary to resort to rather harsh methods to make certain that they would not end up empty-handed. For example, they resorted to forced requisitioning of foodstuffs and compulsory restitution of land and other property seized by the peasants from the landlords.[43] Such tactics met with the full approval of the Austrian Supreme Army Command in Baden. In an order of March 19, it advised the Austrian food collection centers in the Ukraine to obtain necessary supplies "regardless of the political conditions in the country." [44] Ambassador Forgách concluded that the Rada could not be taken seriously "either politically or economically." He believed that the Rada officials should be disregarded (and if necessary forcibly prevented from interfering in the collection and shipment of foodstuffs), and recommended that the task of obtaining supplies from the Ukraine be entrusted to the Austrian military.[45] This approach was in full accord with the views of other Austrian leaders, such

as Count Czernin and Prince Gottfried zu Hohenlohe-Schillingsfürst. They all remained very hostile to the Ukraine. The country
was to be exploited economically and then abandoned, possibly to
be reincorporated into Russia.[46] Finally, as the critical food situation in Austria continued and the large-scale deliveries from the
east failed to materialize, Emperor Karl on April 1 gave a completely free hand to the commander of the Austrian Second Army
in the Ukraine instructing him to act quickly, for otherwise the
continuation of the war might become impossible.[47]

In the meantime, Bülow of the German Foreign Office as early
as March 10 urged that Germany, too, should resort to forced requisition of food, confiscation of the available stocks, and reestablishment of large landownership.[48] Even Ambassador Mumm, not
to speak of his military colleagues in Kiev, was beginning to wonder whether the Germans should not imitate "tough" Austrian
methods, and perhaps confront the Rada with an ultimatum.[49]
General Ludendorff, however, at this point strongly disapproved
of Austrian tactics and wrote "an energetic letter" to General Arthur Arz von Straussenburg in the Ukraine, reminding him that
forced requisitions by Austrian forces in their zone of occupation
were in flagrant violation of all existing agreements.[50] This ad-
monition, of course, had little effect on the Austrians, especially
since the Germans were rapidly moving toward the introduction
of the same methods. Initially, the Germans and Austrians carried out the economic exploitation of their respective zones in the
Ukraine independently. Then, shortly before the overthrow of the
Rada, in late April, 1918, they agreed on the "militarization" of
the grain trade in the whole occupied area, and even worked out a
joint plan for carrying out this project. To save the Rada's face, it
was declared officially that this was to be done in the areas where
the Ukrainian authorities "were not in a position to collect
grain." [51]

Thus, the actions of the German and Austrian military forces
in the Ukraine counted for more than all the written agreements
and other solemnly undertaken commitments put together, although most of them were never openly repudiated. The territorial extension of the German occupation, which continued well
into May, 1918, was unquestionably designed to strengthen Germany's over-all position in the Black Sea region, and it constituted
an important step in the development of her long-range objectives

in the southeast of Europe and the Near East. It also strengthened Germany's position vis-à-vis her junior partner, the Dual Monarchy, as well as enabled her to press the Ukrainian government for more concessions, describing them as "compensation for additional military aid against the Bolsheviks."

Furthermore, the Germans managed to free themselves of their commitment to supply the Ukraine with coal. Originally, the Germans undertook to deliver 100,000 tons of coal per month to the Ukraine, and viewed this both as a convenient pressure device on the Rada government and a rather advantageous economic agreement. (The price of German coal was from 4.5 to 5 rubles per ton.) [52] When this commitment, too, proved somewhat burdensome to the German economy and transportation, and the Ukrainian demand for coal increased, the Germans decided to extend their occupation to the Donbas coal fields (which the Ukraine claimed anyhow), and thus solved all these problems in one stroke.[53] Obviously, economic considerations played an important part in all this, but one cannot speak here of the unfolding of a previously agreed upon program of "making the east safe for German economic interests," as does Fischer in his well-known book. In his view, German industrial circles reserved for themselves the mineral resources of the Ukraine as early as December, 1917, before the opening of peace negotiations at Brest.[54] German documents of the period, however, clearly suggest that the extension of their domination to the Don and Donets regions was as much an improvisation as was the Reich's entire *Ostpolitik* of this period.

German control of the Ukraine's transportation network was regarded from the beginning as an absolute prerequisite for the success of the Ukrainian undertaking. Consequently, one of the first actions of the Germans was to take over the Ukrainian railroads—the plan Kühlmann announced as early as February 20. Although no special agreement was concluded to justify such action, the Rada government did not openly oppose it and had, in fact, encouraged German and Austrian participation in the maintenance and operation of the railroads. The assignment of General Groener to the Ukraine is further indicative of the importance that the Germans ascribed to the effective control and smooth running of the Ukraine's transportation system.

Joint Austro-German control of this system was provided for in the agreement on the division of spheres of influence in the

Ukraine that was concluded between Berlin and Vienna on March 29, 1918.[55] The railways as well as the waterways of the Ukraine were placed under the control of the Central Railroad Administration (Eisenbahnzentralstelle), with headquarters in Kiev. This office was headed by a German railroad official with an Austrian official serving as his deputy. Although the maintenance and repair of the railways were to be carried out jointly, traffic control in each zone was the concern of the chief of the respective field service, with the exception of the Kharkov-Crimea line, which was to remain in German hands despite the fact that it ran through the Austrian zone.

Also, a special Black Sea Bureau (Schwarzmeer-Stelle) was organized, with its main office in Berlin. The task of this Austro-German agency was not only to organize Black Sea and Danube traffic but also to regulate the transportation on the lower Dnieper. Whereas the Bug River was left under Austrian control, the regulation of the upper Dnieper was assigned to the Central Railroad Administration.[56] As a result the Ukrainian railways operated smoothly most of the time. The Black Sea and the river traffic was also very well organized and was able to handle a considerably greater shipping load than it was called upon to do. In Odessa alone more than a hundred transport vessels were seized as war booty and put immediately into service.[57]

As to war booty generally, valuable military and industrial supplies fell into the hands of the Germans and Austrians after their advance into the Ukraine. Although the formal agreement with the Ukrainian government on the division of the spoils was not concluded until the middle of August, 1918, the Germans and Austrians encountered little difficulty in dispatching home the most valuable items, such as tires, airplanes, and copper.[58]

Labor recruitment in the Ukraine was seriously considered by the Germans even before the conclusion of the Ukrainian treaty. The Germans also insisted on keeping all Russian prisoners of war, including the Ukrainians, "for to do otherwise," according to General Ludendorff, "would have meant wrecking the German economy." Consequently, some 1,200,000 Russian prisoners had to remain in Germany until the end of the war.[59] The Germans tried at Brest-Litovsk to obtain the Ukraine's permission to recruit additional agricultural workers; however, when the Rada representatives showed no enthusiasm for this proposal and declared that no surplus labor was available at the time in the Ukraine,[60] the plan was dropped, but not forgotten. It was General Ludendorff who returned to this question in the summer of 1918. He urged the recruiting of German colonists in the Ukraine to serve in the Reich's armed forces, and hoped to obtain more recruits from other groups in the area. He also planned large-scale recruitment of labor in the east to replace German workers at home, so that new reserves for the German army could be obtained. General Ludendorff blamed the failure of all these schemes on the "refusal of the War Ministry to cooperate." [61] Although some Soviet sources claim that the Germans deported Ukrainian and Byelorussian workers and peasants for work in the Reich in this period, German archives and other sources examined by this writer did not produce any evidence of such deportations.[62]

The lack of cooperation on the Rada's part in the economic field and growing German dissatisfaction with the over-all results of the Ukrainian venture are not entirely explained by the weakness of the Rada and a greatly exaggerated estimate of surplus grain stocks in the Ukraine. These two facts played an important part in the German-Ukrainian conflict, but there were other points of disagreement which precluded a compromise settlement. While meeting many of the Central Powers' demands, the Rada was determined to preserve at least some of its prerogatives as a government. It must also be remembered that there were serious ideological differences between the socialist Rada and the representatives of Imperial Germany and Austria-Hungary. Nevertheless, it can be assumed that had the Rada been merely weak, and had it given the Germans a free hand in organizing the country so as to enable them to satisfy their economic needs, it would have been allowed to continue as a territorial administrative body throughout the period of the occupation. The Austrians, who were generally more critical of and less patient with the Rada, did not hide their annoyance over the fact that "a Social Revolutionary regime, weak and incompetent, enjoyed so much support from the Germans." While remaining cynically indifferent as to what would happen to the Ukraine in the future, they too had to deal with the Rada because they needed Ukrainian bread.[63]

The differences between the Germans and the Rada arose very

early on agrarian policies. From the beginning of the occupation the Germans showed concern not only for the collection of the available grain surplus but for future grain production as well. This meant taking a long-range view of the economic exploitation of the Ukraine by insuring the cultivation of all available land, regardless of ownership. As early as March 18, 1918, General Ludendorff tried to impress on the military in Kiev the necessity for "immediate and most extensive cultivation of the land." [64] A few days later the Rada was requested by the Germans to issue two orders: one dealing with the restitution of landlords' lands and property and compensation for their unlawful seizure, and the other prescribing the cultivation of all arable land and providing heavy penalties for noncompliance with the orders.[65] The Rada refused to carry out these German recommendations. Anyone who cares to compare these two orders with Field Marshal Eichhorn's famous cultivation order of April 6, 1918,[66] will immediately see that what the Germans tried to induce the Rada to do in late March, the German Supreme Commander in the Ukraine did himself two weeks later. In the meantime, the German Foreign Office supported the policy of compulsory cultivation of all arable land just as strongly.[67] The slight delay in issuing Field Marshal Eichhorn's order was not the result of any difference of opinion between the Foreign Office and the military. It should rather be attributed to the German expectation that the Rada would cooperate, and that it would satisfy the Reich's economic demands while "preserving its state socialist mask." [68]

One should not imagine, however, that the Germans had any sympathy with the Rada's socialist programs. On the contrary, they had always been very critical of them, even though they were ready to tolerate all that "socialist nonsense" as long as it did not seriously interfere with their political and economic designs for the country. General Hoffman, for example, declared that "on the land question the more moderate Social Democrats who compose the Rada are just as idiotic as the Bolsheviks." [69] Ambassador Mumm, too, spoke of the Rada as a "pseudo-government" and sneered at its "Communist experiments." [70] The German military and the Austrians expressed their criticism of the Rada at an even earlier date.

The Rada desired more than mere tolerance. It insisted on implementing an agrarian policy based on the nationalization of large estates for the benefit of the peasants; however, the Germans, convinced that it was easier to get supplies from the large landowners than from the peasants, began opposing the Rada on the land question with increasing determination and boldness.[71] The German practice of requisitioning grain and fodder was resented just as much, and quickly aroused armed resistance from the peasants. As early as March 9, Colonel von Stolzenberg, writing to the Supreme Army Command from Kiev, reported growing dissatisfaction among the peasants and increased guerrilla activities against the Germans in rural areas. Two weeks later General Groener complained to his wife: "The so-called 'eastern peace' is the most problematic thing; the war goes on here, too, although in a different form, to be sure." [72] The Germans met the peasant resistance with arrests and punitive expeditions. A German divisional commander at Kremianets, in Podolia, warned the local population: "For the death of each German or Polish soldier, ten Russian [*sic*] soldiers or civilians, chosen at random, will be immediately executed by the firing squad." [73] Although this writer did not come across any similar notices by other local commanders at this early stage of the occupation, in practice such retaliation was not uncommon.

On March 23 the Rada Minister of Justice, Mykhailo Tkachenko, in an attempt to stop these executions and to strengthen the position of the Ukrainian judiciary, issued a circular denying the right of military courts of the occupying powers to take punitive action against the local population.[74] This move accomplished little except to deepen the German-Ukrainian conflict. One month later, Eichhorn decreed that all criminal offenses as well as actions that might disturb the public order would henceforth be punished by German military courts.[75] Eichhorn's order thus limited the jurisdiction of Ukrainian courts to civil cases, and without openly stating so, introduced martial law throughout the country (with Kiev being most significantly affected by it).

Although questions about the duration and the nature of the occupation arose frequently in the German-Ukrainian talks during the early stages of the campaign, they remained open throughout the Rada administration. Imperial Chancellor Hertling, in a special message sent to Rada Prime Minister Vsevolod Holubovych in early March, 1918, promised that German troops in the Ukraine would be recalled whenever the Ukrainian government declared their mission fulfilled. Ludendorff endorsed the Chancellor's action and recommended that the Ukrainians be re-assured on this point;[76] however, no agreement on the duration of German military involvement in the Ukraine was concluded.

The Rada returned to this delicate issue in late March; more or less at the same time the Germans perceived that their involve-ment in the Ukraine could no longer be regarded as "a temporary mission." [77] Curiously enough, the Germans themselves contrib-uted to the Rada's decision to reopen the matter precisely at this moment. On March 22, acting on orders from the Supreme Army Headquarters, Colonel Stolzenberg encouraged the Rada to press for Austrian withdrawal from the Ukraine. The Germans had al-ways been suspicious of Austrian plans in the east, and, like the Ukrainians, resented the presence of so many Polish and Bo-hemian troops in the Austrian occupation army.[78]

Once the question of Austrian withdrawal from the Ukraine was allowed to come up, Rada Foreign Secretary Lyubyns'kyi also decided to raise with the Germans the question of the duration of their stay in the country. Whereas Ambassador Mumm's answer was simply that he would refer this matter to Berlin, his Austro-Hungarian colleague, Count Forgách, was so disturbed by the Ukrainian move that he phoned the Austrian Foreign Office in the middle of the night. Mumm took the Ukrainian inquiry less seri-ously and advised Forgách not to reject it outright, for fear that such action might further complicate their relations with the Ukrainians.[79] Kühlmann's advice to Mumm was to avoid discuss-ing the question with the Rada, until it had been settled with General Ludendorff.[80] The Rada, in the meantime, worked out a detailed draft of a convention designed to regulate the activities of German troops in the Ukraine and submitted it to Mumm on March 27. The proposed convention was meant not only to clarify the extent of the German occupation, the relations between the occupying forces and local authorities, the location of their gar-risons, their over-all strength, and the duration of their stay in the country but also to define German relations with the Rada and other troops on Ukrainian soil, clarify the status of foreign na-tionals in the Ukraine, determine ways and means of exporting various goods from the country, and finally, reaffirm once again the promise of German noninterference in the Ukraine's internal affairs.[81]

Both Mumm and Stolzenberg, who were presented with identical drafts, favored the conclusion of the proposed convention. They felt that it could not hamper the Germans and Austrians in any serious way, and regarded the Ukrainian government's move as a necessary action "to save its face vis-à-vis the Great Rada and the people," rather than as an attempt to embarrass the Germans and present them with additional demands.[82] (The Great Rada was the Ukraine's legislative body.) The Austrians, in the meantime, continued to rage. Forgách ascribed German "softness" to General Hoffmann's influence, and again called for replacement of the Rada by more "responsible" people.[83]

It was not until two weeks later that Mumm bluntly told the Rada leaders that "without German military assistance none of them would be in power and that the withdrawal of German forces from the Ukraine would result in immediate expulsion of the Rada and return to chaos and lawlessness."[84] Although the Ukrainian lawmakers continued to demand the withdrawal of German troops, especially in the debates following various German orders and actions in violation of earlier assurances and guarantees of noninterference in the country's internal affairs, the Rada government was not to press the Germans and the Austrians on this point again.

The question of organizing an effective Ukrainian army after the reestablishment of the Rada represented another difficulty in the growing German-Ukrainian conflict. The Germans were determined from the beginning to maintain military preponderance in Kiev, the Ukraine's capital. At first, only German troops were stationed there. After Kiev was freed from the Bolsheviks on March 1, most of the Ukrainian units continued their march eastward along with the Germans. However, when on March 26, part of a Ukrainian division organized from Ukrainian prisoners of war in Germany was brought to Kiev to participate in a parade, General Groener strongly disapproved, calling it "a most unnecessary undertaking," and expressed apprehension lest these troops turn against the Germans.[85] Austrian presence in Kiev was also to be limited. According to an agreement between Berlin and Vienna, Austro-Hungarian troops in that city were not to exceed two battalions.[86]

Ambassador Mumm seems to have shared Groener's suspicion of the Ukrainian troops. On April 12, for example, he advised the

Foreign Office that "the strengthening of the Ukrainian army was absolutely undesirable," and then went on to urge his superiors in Berlin to reject "by means of delaying tactics" the Georgian plan (already approved by the Rada), which recommended the employment by the Georgian government of Ukrainian veterans of the former Czarist army in the Caucasus and the transfer of an equal number of Georgian prisoners of war from Germany to serve the Rada in the Ukraine.[87] Questions of the feasibility and practicability of this plan aside, it is evident that the Germans were determined to keep the Rada militarily weak, but to do it in a manner that would not unduly antagonize the Ukrainians and their friends in the east.

As to the fate of the military forces organized in Germany from among the Ukrainian prisoners of war, the first German-sponsored Ukrainian division—the so-called Blue Division (Syn'ozhupannyky)—arrived in the Ukraine in mid-March, 1918; the second division followed approximately a month later. (The Austrians, too, began organizing a Ukrainian division in mid-February 1918, but it was not until August that it arrived in the Ukraine.) [88] These units were to be dissolved by the Rada according to an agreement with the Germans concluded on April 13 as part of a general military convention;[89] however, as a result of worsening Ukrainian-German relations, and in preparation for the Rada's removal, the Germans decided to take matters into their own hands and in a sudden move, during the night of April 26–27, disarmed both the Blue Division, already stationed in Kiev, and the second division, then on its way to the Ukraine.[90]

It is true that the Germans did not like the idea of a strong Ukrainian army, but it is equally true that the Rada was not able, or perhaps did not try hard enough, to strengthen its military position vis-à-vis the occupying powers while the opportunity existed. Although not a basic reason for the difficulties between Berlin and Kiev, the hindrance to organizing an effective Ukrainian military force—and the dissolution of the units that the Germans themselves helped to create—did contribute to deepening the German-Ukrainian conflict.

The foreign relations of the Ukraine during this period were mainly with the Central Powers, the newly organized East European and Transcaucasian states (such as Finland and Georgia), and finally, with some of the European neutrals, notably Sweden and Switzerland. Limited as they were, Ukrainian diplomatic and informal foreign relations with other states offer another clue to an understanding of Germany's long-range objectives in the east and the ripening of the Ukrainian-German conflict.

No formal restrictions were imposed on the Rada's foreign relations, and there is no evidence of direct and open interference on Germany's part with the work of the Rada Foreign Office or with the selection of its diplomatic representatives abroad. There were, however, several factors that tended to narrow the scope of the Ukraine's foreign relations, so that the Germans had little need to worry about exerting a controlling influence. Among these were the following: (1) the Rada's preoccupation with manifold domestic problems resulting from the brief Bolshevik occupation and the Austro-German military intervention; (2) its general weakness and the almost complete absence of trained and experienced diplomats; (3) further need for German military support; (4) the limitations imposed on Ukrainian diplomacy by the hostile attitude of the Allies and the continuing struggle in the West.

First, the Germans saw to it that no bilateral Austro-Ukrainian talks and agreements took place. They were, however, even more interested in seeing to it that all ties were severed between the Rada and Allied officers and other personnel who remained in the Ukraine after the German advance. The first request for the ouster of Allied personnel from Ukrainian territory, made by German military representatives in Kiev around the middle of March, was rejected by the Rada; however, the two sides shortly thereafter agreed on a special formula. The Germans were to renew the request, which the Rada would again reject. Thereupon, the Germans would remove the Allied representatives from the theater of operations—a move which the Rada was to oppose by lodging a *pro forma* protest.[91] Since this was a matter of practical importance for the Germans, the way they handled it is indicative of the delicate relations between them and the Rada during this early period.

German reaction to a Rada plan of mid-April to approach all belligerents with a general peace proposal is also of interest. Having learned of the plan, the Supreme Army Command promptly advised the German military attaché in Kiev, Colonel Stolzenberg, to dissuade the Rada Prime Minister from taking this step.[92] The

Germans were just as determined to prevent the Rada from serving as a third party in the dispute between Turkey and the Transcaucasian republics. In this case, it was Foreign Secretary von Kühlmann who ordered the rejection, "in the friendliest manner possible," of the Rada's suggestion that it do so. This decision met with the complete approval of General Ludendorff, who believed in the necessity for Germany to "retain in her own hand the solution of the Caucasian question." [93]

Of much greater importance to the Ukrainians was the German attitude toward the Rada's territorial claims. By comparison with its successor, the Hetmanate, the Rada was rather modest in its demands. In the beginning it was only the Kholm area that the Rada claimed specifically as part of its territory. Neither the Crimea nor Bessarabia was sought by the Ukrainians at Brest-Litovsk, although on Bulgaria's repeated request, the Ukrainians finally agreed to add a sentence to the treaty expressing the desirability of a common frontier between them. (To make this possible the Ukraine would have to receive Bessarabia, and Bulgaria to obtain Dobruja.)

The Rada's strict adherence to the principle of self-determination called for giving the Crimean Tartars a completely free hand in their struggle for independent national existence (even though they constituted a definite minority on the island). In the case of Bessarabia, since it was Kiev's earlier decision to regard it as a separate republic, the Ukrainians could not lay claim to it at Brest. Upon examination of the record of German-Ukrainian negotiations at Brest, however, one can readily agree with a Ukrainian observer at these talks, Mykola Zaliznyak, that if the Rada representatives had asked for these two territories then, such a request would have been given serious consideration.[94]

Several weeks later the Ukrainians asked for a voice in the solution of the Bessarabian question. German Foreign Office spokesmen in Brest were at first sympathetic toward the Ukrainian claim. Kühlmann, however, ruled in favor of incorporating a substantial part of Bessarabia into Rumania. He felt that the Ukraine's military and political position did not warrant consideration of her claim, but his main concern was to prevent Bulgaria from establishing a common frontier with the Ukraine should Sofia obtain Dobruja.[95] Officially, the Germans did not immediately reveal their position and even allowed the Rada to open direct negotiations with Rumania concerning the future of Bessa-rabia. Berlin wished to avoid antagonizing the Ukrainians and to facilitate at the same time a German-Rumanian understanding, which was then being negotiated, by exerting pressure on Bucha-rest. Not until toward the end of March was Kühlmann ready to give Bucharest a free hand in Bessarabia—a move that received the full approval of the Emperor and General Ludendorff.[96]

The question of the future of the Crimea and other areas in the east with a substantial Ukrainian minority came to the fore only after they were subjected to complete German occupation and domination, which was after the replacement of the Rada.

The Kholm question, on the other hand, was one of the most pressing issues confronting the Rada after the conclusion of a separate treaty with the Central Powers. The Poles felt equally strongly about this area, viewing its acquisition as the first step toward the restoration of the so-called historical Poland. This ac-counts for the violent Polish reaction to the Austro-German com-mitment at Brest-Litovsk to cede the Kholm area to the Ukraine, and for the subsequent wrangling over its future. (The Polish leaders expressed the desire to go to Brest-Litovsk even before the appearance of the Ukrainians at the conference.) [97]

It is not surprising, therefore, that the Austrians did not lose any time in trying to revise the Ukrainian treaty to meet Polish objections with regard to Kholm and East Galicia. As early as February 19, 1918, the Austrian Prime Minister, Seidler, openly reassured the Poles in the Diet that their interests in Kholm would not be disregarded, and informed them about the concessions made by the Ukraine on the previous day.[98] Although defending, in principle, the previous Austro-German commitment to cede Kholm to the Ukraine, German Foreign Secretary Kühlmann fully supported the Austrian view by declaring in the Reichstag that the Kholm area would not be handed over immediately to the Ukraine, and that the Ukraine's western boundary would be de-lineated by a special commission to be composed of representa-tives of the signatories of the Ukrainian peace treaty and Poland.[99]

Two weeks later, on March 4, another protocol was signed at Brest-Litovsk between the Central Powers and the Ukraine re-affirming this new formula for the solution of the Kholm prob-lem. These protocols radically altered the original (February 9) settlement of the Kholm question by empowering the proposed commission to move the Ukrainian-Polish boundary eastward.[100]

General Ludendorff's determination not to allow Poland "to be enlarged at the expense of the Ukraine," was mainly responsible for the fact that the question of Kholm was to remain unsettled, although in mid-January, 1918, the general suggested that the Poles and Ukrainians meet to talk things over among themselves.[101] In the meantime, not only the Austrians but also the German Foreign Office continued to bar Ukrainian official representatives from the Kholm area, and it was not until late April that the Rada was allowed, largely as a result of Ludendorff's efforts, to take measures aimed at countering Polish propaganda there.[102]

In sum, although German interference in the Rada's external affairs and lack of support for the Ukraine's territorial claims may not have played a major part in the growing Ukrainian-German conflict, they nevertheless contributed to it by strengthening Ukrainian resentment of the German overlordship.

CHAPTER VII

The Turning Point:
General Skoropadsky's
Coup d'Etat

The overthrow of the Rada, following General Pavlo Skorapadsky's coup d'état, and the establishment of a new government in Kiev under his leadership in the capacity of a Hetman (the title of the old Ukrainian Cossack leaders) constituted the most critical stage in the Ukrainian revolution. During this period German interference in the Ukraine's internal affairs reached a high point; moreover, Germany departed radically from the arrangements encompassed in the Ukrainian treaty of Brest-Litovsk and subsequent agreements made with the Rada government. The fall of the Rada and, indeed, the entire period of the Hetmanate present the most controversial problems of modern Ukrainian history. From the German point of view, not only were the Reich's relations with the Ukraine at their most critical stage, but the establishment of the Hetmanate was the most important and consequential single event during the Central Powers' occupation of the country.

German reservations about the future of the Rada, expressed privately even before the occupation began, arose initially from doubts about the Rada's ability to reestablish its rule in the Ukraine rather than from anticipation of serious German-Ukrainian differences and difficulties. Kühlmann's statement of

Febrary 18 (the day the German army began moving into the Ukraine) had, nevertheless, a prophetic ring: "I am not a prophet and cannot tell the future. Nor can I undertake any commitments with regard to the form of government of the Central Rada in the future. Also, I do not know whether the individuals who occupy leading positions in the Ukraine today will remain in their places in the days to come." [1]

In the latter part of March, two or three weeks after the German military in Kiev began advocating the replacement of the Rada or even conversion of the Ukraine into an Austro-German "Governor-Generalship," Ambassador Mumm, too, began to wonder whether it would not become necessary soon to look for a new Ukrainian government to improve the German economic position in the country.[2] However, it was not until late April that an irrevocable German decision to remove the Rada was reached. There was, thus, a considerable interval between the expression of German dissatisfaction with the Rada and its replacement by a Right-oriented and more cooperative Ukrainian government headed by the Hetman.

Ambassador Mumm was fully aware of the adverse consequences that replacing the Rada could have on further development of the idea of Ukrainian statehood.[3] The Austrians, on the other hand, were more concerned with the military aspects of the plan and hastened to make a concrete offer of five additional divisions to facilitate the coup. By early April, if not earlier, the Austrians were fully committed to the removal of the Rada; however, the Germans had yet to be convinced of the desirability of such a course of action.[4] The German military plenipotentiary in Kiev, Colonel Stolzenberg, also thought largely in terms of a power move but preferred an approach that would merely compel this existing Rada government to follow the German dictates.[5] Confronted with a specific question about the most likely German reaction in the event of an anti-Rada coup, Stolzenberg gave an evasive answer and stressed German interest in preserving law and order in the country. His answer could be interpreted as German discouragement rather than support of the anti-Rada forces at this stage of the game. Stolzenberg was approached on this matter by Count Grigorii Golovkin-Khvoshchinskii, a not too well-known landowner from the district of Poltava and one Lieutenant Weber, a former Czarist officer who was at that time in Ukrainian service.[6] It is not clear whether the two gentlemen even knew each other; nor could it be ascertained whether they were spokesmen for some organized groups or simply acted on their own. Mumm, who was in full accord with Stolzenberg, urged that a well-known friend of the Ukrainians, Paul Rohrbach, be sent to Kiev in the hope that he might exert a "sobering influence" on the Rada and change its orientation toward the Right. Mumm also recommended the inclusion of Dr. Eduard David, a Reichstag deputy, in the proposed mission, because of his Jewish background. He was less enthusiastic about Albert Südekum, another socialist deputy known for his pro-Ukrainian sympathies, because of his reputation as a *Kavaliersozialist* (parlor socialist).[7]

Stolzenberg's military colleagues in Kiev were openly critical of his "softness and undue indulgence" toward the Ukrainians. Eichhorn and Groener, while agreeing that no public disorders of any sort would be tolerated, had no objections to a quiet and bloodless coup, hoping that German "neutrality" would be sufficient to insure its success.[8] Mumm, too, was fast becoming more critical of the Rada and even went so far as to question the correctness of Germany's original policy—support of the idea of Ukrainian statehood. He was wary of the danger that German backing of a socialist government of "an extreme Communist brand" in the Ukraine could produce for Germany's domestic politics,[9] a fear that existed in the minds of other German leaders.

Ambassador Mumm's impatience with the Rada became more pronounced as the days passed, and he did not hesitate to show it to the Ukrainians when opportunity arose. He did so rather bluntly and with little regard for the diplomatic niceties in which he, a seasoned diplomat, was so well versed. On April 13, in the course of a two-hour conference with the Rada leaders (headed by President Mykhailo Hrushevsky)—a meeting arranged pursuant to the Ukrainian request to discuss the crisis resulting from Eichhorn's notorious order on the cultivation of land—Mumm defended the Reich's policy and reminded the Ukranians that without German military support they could not have returned to Kiev, nor would they remain in power if this support were to cease. As a result of this meeting, Mumm became fully convinced that further cooperation with the Rada was impossible. Nevertheless, the Rada was to be tolerated for the time being, pending the conclusion of a commercial treaty with the Ukraine. At this point neither Mumm, nor the German military, nor the Austrian representatives in the Ukraine knew who or what could replace the Rada, although they all agreed that the successor was to come from Right-oriented circles, with which the Germans had yet to establish contact.[10]

Mumm defended Eichhorn's cultivation order not only against Ukrainian criticism (explainable by his desire to present the appearance of a "united German front") but also in a secret communication to the Foreign Office. He viewed the move as both necessary and reasonable, and declared that German military and civilian representatives in Kiev had to work closely together at all times to avoid weakening the German position vis-à-vis the Ukrainian government. He again expressed concern over the lack of suitable successors to replace the Rada, and wondered whether German forces were adequate to maintain law and order in the country in the event the proposed change of government resulted in strife and disorders. Already at this time there was virtually complete harmony and understanding between Mumm and Groener,[11] and this was to continue for the remainder of their stay in Kiev.

The reluctant German toleration of the Rada can best be explained by the absence of a clearly defined policy for the Ukraine and the east as a whole. General Ludendorff's recommendation that the Ukraine be kept in "permanent and sharp opposition" to Poland did little to remedy the situation.[12] The German military in Kiev were just as vague on the Reich's policy for the Ukraine. Although even more critical of the Rada than Mumm by mid-April, they still thought cooperation with a "reformed Rada" possible, provided the latter would keep in closer touch with them. General Groener also felt that the Rada could be permitted to continue as a local government, but should it ever interfere seriously with effective German exploitation of the country, one should simply "send it to devil." [13] Several days later, on April 18, he and Mumm definitely decided that the Rada had to be replaced and agreed on specific measures to prepare the ground for it. While the search for a successor went on, the Germans even set the time for the proposed change of government—April 28, the date of a previously announced landowners' congress.[14]

The general atmosphere was tense and there was no need for any psychological preparation of the public for the forthcoming developments. A month or so before the coup, Kiev was full of rumors of an impending change of government in the Ukraine. The Austrians did much to feed these rumors through their negative, even openly hostile, attitude toward the Rada officials in their zone of occupation. General Arz, for example, referred to the idea of the Ukrainian state as a "phantom," and Czernin, while urging the general to refrain from criticizing the Rada openly, had no objections to the Austrian occupation forces' maintaining close ties with various local organizations or authorities which openly and defiantly opposed the Rada and all it stood for (for example, the City of Odessa Duma).[15]

Since the Rightist parties did not act on General Groener's offer to form a new government in the Ukraine, he made his first attempt to get in touch with the so-called Hetman party. Ambassador Mumm counseled caution in order not to jeopardize chances for a quick settlement of the German-Ukrainian trade agreement that was then being negotiated, but at the same time he advised the Foreign Office to forewarn German socialists about the imminent showdown in the Ukraine.[16]

The preparations for the overthrow of the Rada, however, made slow progress. The lack of suitable successors continued to be one of the principal difficulties. On April 21 (one week before the coup) General Groener wrote to his wife: "We must have a new government [in the Ukraine], but what kind of government?" And then he went on to complain about the absence of a party capable of governing the country and the lack of "right people," whom the Germans could trust.[17] Confronted with this situation, General Ludendorff advised immediate and unconditional subordination of the existing Ukrainian government to the dictates of the joint Austro-German military command. In the event the Ukrainians refused to accept this "solution," the Rada leaders were to be arrested and the country was to be subjected to a direct Austro-German military rule.[18] General Groener, however, opposed this plan. He argued that German forces in the Ukraine were inadequate to establish an effective military administration in so vast an area, and he recommended the maintenance of an independent Ukrainian state—which he viewed as a mere cloak to facilitate the continuation of German control and exploitation of the country.[19]

Ambassador Mumm and his Austro-Hungarian colleague,

Count Forgách, also favored the retention of what they called the "Ukrainian theatrics" (*Kulisse*), a position which they defended at a joint Austro-German conference in Kiev on April 23, on the very day the long-awaited commercial agreement with the Rada was concluded. The German and Austrian documents leave no doubt that the timing of the overthrow of the Rada was closely tied to the conclusion of this commercial treaty, which, of course, was to be binding on the Rada's successor. Several days before this meeting Mumm "begged" his military colleagues to wait a few more days before taking the proposed "tough measures" against the Rada so as not to delay the conclusion of the commercial treaty.[20]

General Groener and the German and Austrian military plenipotentiaries also took part in the conference of April 23. The result, according to Mumm, was "an agreement on the aims, but not the method." [21] On the same day Groener received a note from Ludendorff that gave him a free hand in dealing with the Ukrainian problem. "The Russian [*sic*]," wrote General Ludendorff, "still wants to feel the knout. So go ahead, be firm, and rest assured that you can always count on my support." [22]

The Austro-German talks in Kiev continued on the following day (April 24), and it was at this time that the final touches were added to the plan of doing away with the Rada. Complete agreement was reached on the following points:

1) Cooperation with the Rada was no longer possible.

2) The creation of a "Governor-Generalship" in the Ukraine was not to be attempted.

3) A Ukrainian government was to be maintained as long as possible, but subject to the dictates of German and Austrian military commands; it had to promise noninterference in the necessary military and economic measures of the Central Powers.[23]

The following additional restrictions were to be imposed on the new Ukrainian government:

1) No Ukrainian army was to be organized as long as the German and Austrian troops remained in the country; the size of the Ukrainian police force was also to be regulated by the occupying powers.

2) German and Austro-Hungarian military courts were to handle all offenses committed against the Central Powers' military personnel stationed in the country.

3) The Ukrainian state administration was to be purged of all the "unclean elements." Land committees and other similar bodies were to be dissolved.

4) Since the Ukraine did not have war production laws (*Kriegsleistungsgesetze*), German, Austrian, and Hungarian laws were to be followed.

5) All restrictions imposed by the Rada government on trade in foodstuffs and raw materials were to be declared null and void. Free trade was to be allowed, subject to joint German-Austro-Ukrainian control. Ukrainian export restrictions and railway control were also to be removed. Frontier checks were to be administered jointly.

6) The agrarian question was to be solved through the reestablishment of the principle of private property. The peasants were to pay for the land which came into their possession. Large estates were to be maintained for the time being until legal limitations on their size were promulgated.

7) Financial and monetary problems were to be solved along similar lines. Other conditions and limitations were reserved for military and economic agreements to be concluded in the near future.[24]

How did the Germans select General Skoropadsky to head the new Ukrainian government? On whose initiative did they meet and what exactly was their or his role in the overthrow of the Rada? Unfortunately, it is not possible to provide fully satisfactory answers to these basic questions. There are certain gaps in the German and Austrian documentation; Ukrainian sources are even more disappointing. The Hetman's personal papers have not yet been opened to researchers, and only carefully edited "fragments" of his memoirs are available in print. They cover the period from March, 1917, through April, 1918.[25]

It would be all too simple to maintain that in the spring of 1918 Skoropadsky just happened to be in Kiev and that the Germans, in the absence of other suitable candidates to replace the Rada, decided to use this ambitious former Czarist general (who happened to be of Ukrainian descent) as a convenient figurehead to mask the tightening of their control over the Ukraine through the continued maintenance of a seemingly independent Ukrainian state. General Skoropadsky was well known in the Ukraine long before the German occupation of the country.

Pavlo Skoropadsky (1873–1945) was a descendant of an old Ukrainian Cossack family, one of the wealthiest in the Ukraine, with the bulk of its landed estates in the province of Poltava. Skoropadsky differed little from the scions of other aristocratic families of Czarist Russia; in fact, his distinguished military career could have been the envy of any true Russian. He served as Nicholas II's aide-de-camp, and at the outbreak of the March Revolution was in command of an army corps and held the rank of lieutenant general. By the autumn of 1917, he was the most respected and best-known Ukrainian general, a distinction that no one dared to contest. He won a name for himself as the organizer of a Ukrainian corps on Russia's southwestern front and as one of the leaders of the Ukrainian Free Cossacks, a military organization which sprang up spontaneously about the same time in several parts of the country.[26] Skoropadsky remained active on the turbulent Ukrainian scene throughout 1917, going into hiding during the brief Bolshevik rule in the Ukraine in January and February, 1918, to reemerge in Kiev, the center of the Ukrainian revolution after the arrival of the Germans. Although he did not play an active part in Ukrainian political life during the early period of the German occupation, he was far from being merely an observer, and is believed to have considered a possible alliance with Germany even before Brest-Litovsk. (Such was the impression that Skoropadsky made on his old friend and colleague, General Cantacuzène.)[27] General Skoropadsky, while admitting that in late 1917 some of his supporters in the Ukraine thought that he should assume power as a Hetman of the country, maintained that as late as early March, 1918, he did not seriously consider such a possibility.[28]

The Austrians were first to establish contact with Skoropadsky. This happened sometime in early April, 1918. On April 8, the Austro-Hungarian military plenipotentiary in the Ukraine, Major Fleischmann, reported to Baden that General Skoropadsky was preparing for him a memorandum on the Ukrainian problem. Fleischmann thought that the general enjoyed considerable support throughout the country and that he could be won over to the Austrian side.[29] For some reason, however, this contact was not maintained, for shortly after the coup an authoritative Austrian source made it very clear that initially the Germans alone conducted negotiations with the Skoropadsky camp.[30]

The first official contact between General Skoropadsky and the Germans took place on April 11 or 12, 1918. According to Skoropadsky's memoirs, the meeting was arranged at Major Hasse's request. At subsequent meetings, held on April 13 and 15, Hasse was joined by Major Jarosch.[31] (Hasse was the chief of German military intelligence in Kiev; Jarosch was one of General Groener's Russian-speaking assistants.) German official sources make no mention of these preliminary conferences. While these meetings were taking place, both Groener and Mumm continued to complain about the lack of suitable people to take over the government in the Ukraine. Either General Groener's assistants, Hasse and Jarosch, approached Skoropadsky on their own initiative, without informing their superior, or, pending further investigation of the future Hetman and his circle, Groener did not want to report on these meetings, since he did not know whether Skoropadsky would really be suitable and available for the post. It thus appears that the Germans took the initiative in establishing official contact with the Hetman, but only after some of his supporters had unofficially approached both Ambassador Mumm and the German Military Command in Kiev to ascertain whether the two sides might join forces against the Rada. Mumm does mention the unofficial feelers made by certain members of the Hetman organization, the League of Landowners, in a special report to Chancellor Hertling, dated April 29, 1918, without, however, giving any details on these meetings.[32]

One may well agree with those who knew Skoropadsky personally that his part in the matter was important;[33] however, it is difficult to accept the thesis advanced by the general himself (and supported by certain German students of the period) that the Germans played but a minor role in the overthrow of the Rada and that he acted fully on his own initiative and simply "confronted them with a *fait accompli.*"[34] In the beginning, what took place can be described as independent preparations for the removal of the Rada by both General Skoropadsky and the Germans. It was logical, if not inevitable, that sooner or later the two parties would be drawn together and agree on close cooperation. Skoropadsky was no doubt as eager to secure German support for his schemes as the Germans were to enlist his collaboration. Austrian sources tend to support this thesis. In his special report on the Ukrainian situation following the coup, the Austrian Ambassador in Kiev, Count Forgách, spoke of General Skoropadsky's "quest for power," which coincided with the German search for a suitable successor to the Rada. He regretted only that Skoropadsky's submission to the Germans was so immediate and complete.[35] Ideological affinity, naturally, did much to facilitate the understanding between them. Although the two parties did have some reservations about each other in the beginning, the alliance proved to be a lasting one, for it survived the remainder of the occupation period.

The agreement between General Skoropadsky and the Germans was reached in the evening of April 28, 1918, following the joint Austro-German conference. Final arrangements were made at a special Groener-Skoropadsky meeting, at which time the future Hetman was assured of German "benevolent neutrality" and was also told that although he could count on German support only after he had assumed power with his own forces, no public disorders of any kind would be tolerated. This meant in effect that the Germans were ready to intervene on Skoropadsky's behalf, if need be.[36]

The presence of German troops in Kiev and other key points in the Ukraine was unquestionably the most important single factor in insuring the success of General Skoropadsky's coup d'état, although he, too, had to do his share. The operation had to be quick and smooth to impress the Germans and, thus, to secure their permanent support. Although both Mumm and Groener were determined that the seizure of power would be carried out as a "truly Ukrainian political undertaking," [37] their behind-the-scenes activities were not always conducted as discreetly as diplomatic practice would ordinarily require.

Indeed, preparations for the Rada's overthrow were made by the Germans long before the coup. Already in March, 1918, arrests of Ukrainian citizens and various repressive and punitive actions undertaken in connection with food requisitioning did much to undermine the Rada's position. The cultivation order issued by Eichhorn on April 6 did even more damage. Several days after the Germans approached General Skoropadsky, additional measures were taken which further weakened the Rada. To insure a smooth and quiet change of government in the Ukraine the German garrison in Kiev was strengthened in mid-April—a move

against which Rada Prime Minister Holubovych vainly protested.[38]

The "Dobry affair" offered the Germans a convenient pretext
for taking other steps to facilitate the planned change of government in Kiev. On April 24 a wealthy Ukrainian banker of Jewish
origin, Abraham Dobry—an open critic of the Rada and its policies, who, nonetheless, at this time served as a member of the
Rada commission engaged in economic negotiations with the
Germans—disappeared under mysterious circumstances. Even
though certain Ukrainian officials were implicated in this strange
affair, it was just the same a strictly internal Ukrainian matter.
The Germans, nevertheless, chose to consider it as a direct challenge to their position in the Ukraine. They ordered Dobry's release and decreed that all disturbances of public order and all
criminal acts would henceforth be handled by German military
courts. As it turned out later, Dobry was arrested on direct orders
from the Ukrainian Minister of Internal Affairs, Mykhailo
Tkachenko, and deported to Kharkov. This action by a member of
the Rada cabinet was taken on his own initiative to break up the
anti-Rada conspiracy in which Dobry, supported by the Germans,
is supposed to have played a leading role.[39] That Dobry was close
to the Germans cannot be denied; however, his part in the anti-
Rada movement was not as significant as most Ukrainian sources
claim. Dobry was soon released unharmed, and eventually several
Rada officials, including the deposed Prime Minister Holubovych,
were tried by the Germans for their involvement in the Dobry
affair.[40]

Finally, on April 25, General Field Marshal Eichhorn promulgated an order on the jurisdiction of German military courts in
the Ukraine. Groener was ready to go even further and to proclaim martial law in Kiev, but on Mumm's advice postponed such
a drastic measure, agreeing that it might create a bad impression
both in Germany and in neutral countries.[41] On the following day
(April 26) came the disarming of the Blue Division, composed of
former Ukrainian prisoners of war in Germany.[42] It is therefore
either naïve or downright cynical to claim, as did General
Skoropadsky and Ambassador Mumm, that the raid on the Rada
Chamber on April 28 by German troops and the arrest of several
Rada ministers were not "directly connected" with the impending

coup.[43] Such "independent" action by a group of German soldiers against a "friendly government of which they were guests," although undertaken without Mumm's and Groener's knowledge, caused irreparable damage to the Rada's prestige and broke its will to resist. The raid was the German response to Dobry's abduction, but it is not clear who issued orders for such a humiliating intrusion into the Rada's headquarters. Eichhorn felt compelled to send an apology to the Rada.[44] This move on Eichhorn's part did not affect the plans for the Rada's overthrow. He made it probably in order to mask the planned coup and also to minimize the appearance of direct German intervention in Ukrainian internal affairs.

Naturally, following all these bizarre happenings, General Skoropadsky's task proved easier than was at first thought possible. The congress of the League of Landowners convened, as scheduled, on April 29, very appropriately in the local circus. Some 6,500 delegates representing substantial landowners from eight Ukrainian provinces did not need any prompting to stage an ovation when General Skoropadsky was presented on the podium. At the suggestion of the presiding officer of the congress, Mykhailo M. Voronovych, who prior to the Revolution had served as Czarist governor of Bessarabia, the gathering conferred upon General Skoropadsky the title of Hetman, with dictatorial powers "to save the country from chaos and lawlessness," and all these arrangements were restated by Skoropadsky in a festive "manifesto" to the Ukrainian people which he issued on the same day.[45] The country, in the meantime, remained calm and accepted the change quietly, more in resignation than in approval. Only in Kiev did a few minor skirmishes occur on the night of April 29, in which three of the Hetman's officers perished. Otherwise, the whole operation was virtually bloodless. Thus, the Germans had no difficulty remaining "neutral," although the Hetman himself admitted later that they were ready to intervene in the event pro-Rada forces proved too strong.[46]

Few people in the Ukraine failed to see the real force behind the coup, but it mattered little, since the Germans had already lost whatever popularity they had enjoyed in the country, and it had never been great. Peasant risings increased in scope and intensity, and soon entire districts were taken over by independent guerrilla forces determined to keep the Germans and the Austrians, as well as the Hetman police detachments, away from their territory. Punitive expeditions and other strong measures resulted only in heightening these popular guerrilla activities. Ultimately even major cities of the Ukraine that had strong German or Austrian garrisons, ceased to be islands of safety and tranquillity. It is of interest that the Bolsheviks have always claimed that they were the organizers of these anti-German peasant uprisings and have produced over the years an impressive body of literature on this question. The fact remains, however, that their party organization in the Ukraine's villages was then virtually nonexistent and most of the uprisings were spontaneous, loosely organized, and almost completely uncoordinated local guerrilla actions. Some of the former Rada supporters and officials were involved in organizing the anti-Hetman forces, and some of the guerrilla leaders eventually joined the Bolsheviks; however, most of the bands were simple anarchists.

Rumors about the impending change of government in the Ukraine circulated in Germany long before the coup. Various measures taken by Eichhorn during the last days of the Rada gave these rumors credibility. As a result, certain Reichstag deputies decided to look into the matter. In a special letter to Vice-Chancellor Friedrich von Payer, socialist deputy Philip Scheidemann warned the German government in no uncertain terms that the destruction of the Rada might result in bringing to power people with no following among the Ukrainians whatsoever. He was also seriously apprehensive lest this policy play into the hands of the Bolsheviks.[47] Two days later the Emperor, greatly disturbed over the arrest of several Rada ministers, wired the Supreme Army Command and the Commander in Chief in the east urging immediate release of Ukrainian leaders.[48]

The change of government in the Ukraine produced a strong reaction in the Reichstag. General Field Marshal Eichhorn was the principal target of these attacks, but since everything that happened in the Ukraine at this time was "the result of most careful consultation between the Chancellor, the Foreign Office, and the General Headquarters,"[49] the Reichstag debates on the Ukrainian crisis proved of little practical value.

The German military, who were most responsible for the change of government in the Ukraine, did not conceal their satisfaction with the liquidation of the Rada. Even General Hoffmann, who did not always see eye to eye with Ludendorff on Germany's eastern plans and policies and who had more sympathy with Ukrainian efforts to reconstruct their national state than any other German official, welcomed Skoropadsky's assumption of power in the Ukraine and termed this change "advantageous." [50] German Foreign Office spokesmen, both in Berlin and Kiev, accepted the change with relief rather than with enthusiasm. An embarrassing political crisis in the Ukraine was over, and one could now turn to more pressing practical problems, such as food collection and speedy shipment to the Central Powers, or the establishment of law and order in the country. As it turned out, however, the change of government in Kiev made it even more difficult for the Germans to attain these basic goals of their Ukrainian undertaking.

The conditions on which Skoropadsky agreed to assume power in the Ukraine were essentially the same as those on which he was to rule the country after the successful coup d'état. The country was to remain independent of Russia, with close political and economic ties to the Central Powers, on the basis of the Treaty of Brest-Litovsk and subsequent agreements. [51] According to an earlier Austro-German decision, no Ukrainian army was to be organized as long as the troops of the Central Powers remained in the country. [52] Although now the Hetman was to be permitted to raise an army, this "concession" could hardly be taken seriously since the German military reserved the right to determine its size and the Hetman never succeeded in organizing an effective force of his own.

The Hetman also had to agree to hold new elections after the pacification of the country had been completed. This, too, was subject to the High Command's approval. German military courts were to continue handling all crimes committed against the German personnel in the country. By the same token, German war production laws (*Kriegsleistungsgesetze*) were to remain in force in the Ukraine. Various "undesirable" individuals in the former Rada civil service were to be dismissed, and the so-called land committees were to be abolished. [53] (These were local agencies charged with the implementation of agrarian reforms enacted by the Rada.) Other obligations and restrictions imposed on the new Ukrainian government were of an economic and financial nature.

The overthrow of the Rada resulted in the tightening of German control in the Ukraine and also in strengthening the position of the German military in the country. The Supreme Army Command had had an important say in Ukrainian matters all along; after the coup, however, the influence of the German military in eastern affairs became more complete. General Groener noted this development when he said: "The change of government [in the Ukraine] must be held firmly under control by the High Command. So far everything has developed according to plan. In the Foreign Office in Berlin one can see the usual alarm and dismay, as the Chancellor [Hertling] is really quite a senile old man. This, however, does not disturb us, since the Supreme Army Command stands firmly behind us." [54]

Ambassador Mumm did not find it hard to accept further strengthening of the position of the military in Kiev. In fact, he was quite happy with the relations that existed between him and Field Marshal Eichhorn and General Groener, which he termed "very good." True, Mumm admitted that the way things worked in the Ukraine, political considerations in most cases had to give way to military requirements. He did not really object to this arguing that he had always been given the opportunity to discuss these matters and to express his view of them. He also pointed to the futility of all criticism of Germany's eastern policy in the Reichstag, since, as he put it, the power in the Ukraine was now completely in the hands of the military. Such was the situation there, and one had to "make the best of it." Things might have been worse, had the command of German forces in the Ukraine been entrusted to Linsingen or Mackensen rather than to people like Groener and the "good Eichhorn." [55]

Austro-Hungarian representatives in Kiev, who did not have very much to do with the preparations for the Rada's overthrow, merely gave their approval to the German plan and were kept informed about all developments. The coup, therefore, was largely a German-Ukrainian affair, and the Hetman entourage clearly showed that it preferred to deal with the stronger occupying power rather than with both partners, as before. On May 4, for example, Mumm reported that the new Ukrainian Prime Minister, Fedir A. Lyzohub, was ready to cooperate closely with the Germans, but that "the Ukrainians did not want to hear anything of Austria-Hungary." [56] The Austrians reciprocated with a cool and halting attitude toward the new Ukrainian regime. The Germans were unabashedly pleased with the fact that the change of government in Kiev had occurred without direct Austrian participation, and did not pay much attention to their complaints.[57]

The first month following the coup of April 29 was a period of transition and uncertainty for the Germans as well as the Hetman. Although the Germans were greatly relieved to find at last a suitable successor to the Rada, and appeared to have stood solidly behind General Skoropadsky from the beginning, they remained rather pessimistic in their view of the future. Their early dealings with the Hetman were somewhat cautious. Although most of the Germans felt that for the time being there was no alternative but to support the new regime, they hinted repeatedly at the temporary character of the arrangement. Discussing General Skoropadsky's future, the Army Group Eichhorn said the following in one of its reports: "The duration of Skoropadsky's rule cannot be foreseen at this point. A great deal will depend on him. Even more crucial will be the ability of the new government to carry out its responsibilities and the matter of whether Skoropadsky will remain under the German influence." [58]

The Germans withheld full recognition of the Hetman government until June 2, although shortly after the coup they made it quite clear that the return to power of Ukrainian Social Revolutionaries (the majority party in the Rada) was out of the question. Groener even went so far as to tell a delegation of Ukrainian socialist parties that the new regime had already been "recognized" by Berlin.[59]

Despite continued vagueness in the Reich's plans for the Ukraine in the initial period of the Hetmanate, there was agreement on the following points: (1) The Rada was definitely out, but the participation of certain Ukrainian socialist leaders (especially the Socialist Federalists, who resigned from the Rada cabinet of Holubovych several days before the coup) was to be sought. (2) The new government was to be built on a clearly Ukrainian platform, and the Ukrainian state was to remain completely independent of Russia, with close political and economic ties to the Central Powers.[60]

Mumm at first reported that Groener worked closely with him to realize this program. For example, the two met with Skoropadsky in order to impress on him the necessity of forming a national Ukrainian government and eliminating all Russian tendencies from it.[61] The German and Austrian Foreign Offices, too, continued to regard the existence of an independent Ukraine as an absolute necessity.[62] All of a sudden, however, the Army Group Eichhorn declared on May 4 that the maintenance of such a separate state was neither possible nor desirable and suggested that the fiction of the Ukraine as a "friendly state" be abandoned. In subsequent messages, the Army Group Eichhorn urged that the Foreign Office in Berlin adopt a similar approach to the Ukrainian problem.[63] The Foreign Office, surprised and somewhat disturbed, asked Mumm whether it meant that in the future the Ukraine should be dealt with as an occupied area rather than as a "friendly state" living in peace with Germany.[64] Eichhorn and Groener, however, again pressed for the adoption of their policy for the Ukraine, arguing as follows: "It is a gross error to believe, as does the Imperial Chancellor, that German troops in the Ukraine were received as an ally in a friendly country. This fiction is to be done away with once and for all. The Germans were received in the Ukraine worse than in a hostile country. Practically nowhere did the Ukrainian authorities show an interest and desire in cooperating on the procurement of food and shelter for our soldiers. . . . We should like to suggest to the Imperial Chancellor that he listen to those individuals who have visited the Ukraine in recent weeks. They all will support the view that in an extraordinary situation extraordinary means must be employed, rather than the techniques worked out so nicely at the green table in Berlin." [65]

General Hoffmann, although no longer in the Ukraine, continued to follow the developments in the country and showed concern lest the Germans completely abandon their original plans for it. "The efforts of the Supreme Army Command and Eichhorn," noted the general in his diary on May 6, 1918, "are, though they do not know it, driving the Ukraine back into the arms of Great Russia. At the moment this does not matter, but for the future purposes I should have thought it useful to have preserved the Ukraine as an independent entity." On the following day he added: "Dr. Rohrbach, the well-known writer, came to see me yesterday on his way to Kiev. He shares my anxieties about the Ukraine. . . ." [66]

The Foreign Office, in the meantime, remained firm in its support of the idea of an independent Ukraine, and the Hetman and his cabinet were warned that they could expect German backing only as long as they upheld the Ukrainian national banner. Mumm's advocacy of this policy was based on the following considerations: (1) his concern for German public opinion and the attitude of neutral and friendly countries; (2) his disinclination to treat the new Ukrainian government as a puppet so as not to destroy its authority and prestige in the country; (3) his interest in developing good political and economic relations with the Ukraine for the future.[67]

General Groener was soon brought around to Mumm's view, although he remained rather pessimistic concerning the future. "What will become of the Ukraine eventually cannot be foreseen clearly at this point. For the time being we are still supporting the idea of an independent Ukraine." [68] There is no evidence that Eichhorn disapproved of his chief assistant's adoption of the Foreign Office's line. Colonel Stolzenberg, however, was reported to have agitated among the Austrians as well as among the visiting German journalists against the new Ukrainian government;[69] but he was soon recalled from his Kiev post in order not to embarrass the Hetman and his German supporters.

In a special edict (*hramota*), which the Hetman issued with German approval on April 29, 1918 (immediately upon the fall of the Rada), he proclaimed himself the "supreme authority" in the country and proposed to rule as a dictator, with the assistance of a personally appointed cabinet, until the convocation of the Ukrainian Diet.[70] Although Ukrainian socialists had little liking for the idea of a military chieftain being chosen to serve as head of state, there is no denying that the tradition of the Hetmanate had a special place in many people's memories, especially among the Ukrainian peasantry and some members of the intelligentsia. "Hetman" was the traditional title of the leaders of the Ukrainian Cossacks in the seventeenth and eighteenth centuries. The term is most likely of German origin—*Hauptmann*, meaning headman or captain—and was probably brought to the Ukraine in its corrupted Slavicized form through Poland. This title was used by both Bohdan Khmelnytsky and Ivan Mazepa, the most illustrious Ukrainian leaders of the Cossack period, and also by General Skoropadsky's ancestor, Ivan Skoropadsky, who is remembered in history as a Cossack leader who refused to support Mazepa in his struggle with Peter the Great.

Despite his high-sounding title of "Hetman of all the Ukraine," Skoropadsky was seldom free to initiate his own policies, and all his appointments, too, were subject to German approval. In this respect there was a marked difference between him and the Rada, which came into being and was reorganized without any German pressure or influence whatsoever.

The first man whom the Hetman charged with the task of forming the cabinet was a little-known landowner and horse breeder, Mykola Ustymovych. Following German directives, the Hetman advised him to get in touch with some of the Ukrainian socialists, since the new government was to be both "Ukrainian in character and Left-oriented." Ustymovych's failure to persuade the Socialist Federalists to participate in the Hetman cabinet resulted in his resignation on April 30, allegedly on German insistence.[71] Although his successor, Mykola Vasylenko, a law professor at the University of Kiev, had just as little luck in persuading Ukrainian socialists to cooperate with the Hetman, a cabinet was composed without them, and the Germans, convinced that Socialist Federalists would soon join the Hetman camp anyhow, gave it their prompt recognition. On May 2, only hours after the cabinet had finally been constituted, Mumm, in a note to the Hetman whom he addressed as "Herr General," took official cognizance of this fact and declared that he, German Ambassador to the Ukraine, was ready to establish formal relations with the new Ukrainian government![72] An official German spokesman described this act as *de facto* recognition of the new Kiev regime.[73] (*De jure* recognition of the Hetman government was not granted until one month later.)

Mumm and the German military, both in Kiev and at the Supreme Army Command, soon had nothing but praise for General Skoropadsky, although they wondered at times whether the Hetman would remain so cooperative in the future, and also whether all of his assistants would be equally responsive to German wishes.[74] The Germans, though, were less enthusiastic about certain members of his cabinet, notably his Foreign Minister, Dmytro Doroshenko. A former Socialist Federalist who left the party to join the new government, Doroshenko was regarded as the only "real Ukrainian nationalist" in the Hetman's May cabinet, and the Germans would certainly have welcomed his participation in it, had it not been for his reputation as a confirmed Austrophile. The German military in Kiev were determined to block his candidacy "at all costs." [75] Mumm, too, at first opposed Doroshenko, but was ready to accept him because in his view there were no other suitable candidates for the post. Mumm had another reason, however, and that was General Groener's rejection of Doroshenko, an act which Mumm described as "impermissible interference in the performance of my duties." To reassert his position as Germany's principal diplomatic representative in the Ukraine, Mumm announced the acceptance of Doroshenko's candidacy, but only if the latter would call on him and personally request this favor.[76] Doroshenko did this, both in person and in writing, and was finally allowed to head the Foreign Office of the new Ukrainian government, first as Acting Foreign Secretary, and several weeks later as a full-fledged minister in the Hetman cabinet.[77]

The Doroshenko case is indicative of the relationship that existed between the German representatives in Kiev and the newly established Ukrainian government. This relationship was to last almost to the end of the Hetmanate. It also reflects the continued rivalry between the Reich's military and civilian officials in Kiev as well as perennial German suspicion of Austrian aims in the Ukraine.

But it was not enough for the Germans to have a cooperative administration in the Ukraine to satisfy their immediate aims in the country. They wanted the new government to be popular and to have a broad national base as well. It was mainly with this in view that the German Foreign Office arranged a visit of two distinguished authors and journalists, Paul Rohrbach and Axel Schmidt, to Kiev in early May.[78] Both men enjoyed the reputation of being trusted and devoted friends of the Ukrainians.

The whole affair is representative of the half measures and vague improvisations so characteristic of Germany's Ukrainian undertaking and can hardly be called a failure, since no one really thought it would accomplish much. The idea was conceived during the Rada crisis, but by the time the two gentlemen arrived in the Ukraine, the Rada no longer existed and the Hetman was firmly in the saddle. Instead of making the Hetman regime more acceptable to the Ukrainian nationalists, the visit of the two gentlemen from Berlin exposed the pro-Russian leanings within the circles close to the Hetman. Rohrbach and Schmidt became even more outspoken in their criticism of the Hetmanate and Germany's Ukrainian policy after they had had an opportunity to observe it close at hand. The visit lasted only about a week, and Mumm, who had much to do with arranging it, soon made it clear that he was thoroughly bored and was looking forward to the end of the Rohrbach-Schmidt mission.[79]

Having confirmed his suspicion that the Hetman, "at the bottom of his heart was more Russian than Ukrainian," and that he "had always looked with an eye to Moscow," Rohrbach also concluded that Ambassador Mumm knew nothing about the Ukraine and just as little about the eastern problem as a whole.[80] It is not surprising, therefore, that the main thesis of the twenty-three-page "Rohrbach Report," prepared on May 13, 1918, and submitted by Mumm to Imperial Chancellor Hertling a few days later, contained the following statement: "The present [Hetman] cabinet is of Great Russian orientation and is endeavoring to lead the Ukraine back to Moscow. It simply cannot be trusted, since it is composed mainly of the Cadets. These people have clearly shown themselves as enemies of the Ukraine not only during the Czarist regime but since the Revolution as well." [81]

The report did not disturb Mumm, and he agreed that "politically most of the [Hetman] ministers were close to the Great Russian camp." Mumm further argued, however, that with his and his military colleagues' control of these people the situation was not at all serious. Moreover, the Hetman cabinet was above all a "working administration" (*Arbeitsministerium*), since other suitable ministers were unavailable.[82]

Mumm did not, however, let things rest at that. In a confidential report on Rohrbach's visit, prepared for Chancellor Hertling, Mumm wrote: "As far as Dr. Rohrbach's practical proposals are concerned, they are essentially identical with the position I have already adopted. In a few days, I expect to have the opportunity of stating officially that the German government will continue its support of the idea of an independent, democratic Ukrainian state. I shall urge the new Ukrainian government to carry out an immediate and thoroughgoing agrarian reform as well as the establishment of a national Ukrainian educational system." [83]

Ambassador Mumm then declared openly that the Hetman regime could expect German support only as long as it would honestly support this program.[84] Kühlmann also reassured the Ukrainians privately of continuing German support of the idea of independent Ukrainian statehood. This he did at a meeting in Berlin with Kost' Levyts'kyi and Yevhen Petrushevych, the leaders of the Ukrainian faction in the Austrian Parliament.[85] The Austrians likewise restated their continued support of the Ukrainian national idea,[86] although their diplomatic spokesmen in Kiev privately remained as anti-Ukrainian as ever and the behavior of their occupation forces in the country made it difficult to take these Austrian protestations seriously.

All this, therefore, failed to satisfy Ukrainian and German critics of the Hetmanate. On May 23 General Hoffmann again expressed his concern over Ukrainian developments: "The Ukraine still causes me anxiety. The men at present in control there are steering straight for union with Great Russia." [87] Ukrainian national circles in Kiev reacted to the pro-Russian tendencies of the Hetmanate with increased activities in the Ukrainian National State Union (Ukrayins'kyi Natsional'no-Derzhavnyi Soyuz), where most former Rada elements had gathered. In the meantime, the peasant uprisings, mostly of a local and spontaneous character, were becoming more and more serious and causing the Germans and the Hetman much anxiety.[88]

Others criticized Germany's Ukrainian policy because they felt it lacked clarity and purpose. Friedrich Naumann, for example, while finding some consolation in the fact that such "prudent individuals" as General Groener had engineered the change of government in Kiev, nevertheless concluded rather pessimistically: "Everything is in flux, nothing is predictable, a great deal is unknown; our policy is nothing but an experiment." [89] Another Reichstag leader, Matthias Erzberger, was even more outspoken in his criticism of German *Ostpolitik* at this point. Although several weeks earlier he had strongly criticized Eichhorn for his part in the destruction of the Rada, now he predicted an inevitable fiasco for an eastern policy based on the support of an independent Ukraine; in a lengthy memorandum he tried to impress upon Kühlmann the necessity of establishing a basis for friendly relations between Germany and Russia in the future.[90]

Although few people appeared happy with Germany's *Ostpolitik* at this point, no major changes were contemplated for the Ukraine. Skoropadsky was to continue as head of the new government in Kiev, in spite of criticism at home and abroad. Nevertheless, the status of the Hetman administration and its obligations toward the occupation authorities had to be clarified. This was done in an order signed by Field Marshal Eichhorn and directed to all army groups in the Ukraine. The order bears the date of May 22, 1918, and greatly resembles the minutes of the historic joint Austro-German meeting held in Kiev on April 24, which sealed the fate of the Rada. The two documents resemble each other even in wording, although the second document is somewhat longer and more elaborate than the first. It called for drastic measures against all those who created disturbances, agitated against the new Ukrainian regime, or interfered with German activities in the country, especially food collection. Also, local military commanders were given a free hand to take the necessary steps to quell all armed insurrection in the country. It was stated that Germany's principal commitment was military and economic aid [*sic*] to the new Ukrainian regime. The Reich was to be compensated fully for this assistance on the basis of a separate convention to be agreed upon in the near future. In the meantime, all remaining obstacles to the fulfillment of the Ukraine's economic obligations toward Germany, notably grain deliveries, were to be removed, and no new hindrances in this area were to be tolerated. The military *Oberkommando* in Kiev also reserved for itself extensive control powers over Ukrainian internal affairs. For example, the first point of the order stipulated that new elections might be held only after complete pacification of the country and with the approval of the *Oberkommando*. Similarly, the size and tasks of the future Ukrainian army were to be determined "in cooperation with German authorities." [91]

The Austrians, feeling more and more left out or bypassed, also resorted to various measures designed to strengthen the control in their zone of occupation. In mid-May General Alfred Krauss was appointed commander of the Dual Monarchy's forces in the east and was given unlimited powers in order to defend Austria's interests in that area. This arrangement aimed above all at a more effective economic exploitation of the Ukraine. To insure the success of General Krauss's mission, the Austrian Supreme Army Command created a special Ukrainian Department, headed by Colonel Kreneis. [92] The Austrians continued to show concern over the fact that their relations with the Hetman remained cool and that he preferred to deal with the Germans alone. Although the

Austrians maintained that the agreements the Germans had concluded with General Skoropadsky had no treaty power, they did regard them as valid for the entire Ukraine, including the Austrian sector; and to insure closer cooperation between the new Ukrainian government and the Austrian occupation authorities they proposed that a special agency of the Hetmanate be established in Odessa.[93]

While the German military were dictating the conditions on which the new Ukrainian government was to collaborate with them in the administration of the country, Ambassador Mumm had to confine himself to tasks of a "diplomatic" nature, such as the supervision of the Hetman's appointments. On June 1, Mumm had his assistant, Count Hans von Berchem, call the Hetman's attention to the fact that some of his recent appointments (especially those to provincial governorships) were "rather unfortunate," and that "real Ukrainians" should have been offered these positions. The Hetman accepted the German criticism and promised to be more careful in the future.[94] The Austrians became concerned over the Hetman's appointments at an even earlier date. They were especially unhappy with the new governor of Kiev, Count Czartoryski, the former governor of Tarnopol and an avowed opponent of the Ukrainian national idea.[95]

More important was the problem of full recognition of the Hetman regime. It was not, however, on the initiative of Ambassador Mumm, but rather on that of the Hetman that this question was reopened.[96] Kaiser Wilhelm, too, became interested in it, raised the issue at one of his meetings with Hindenburg, and was informed that Vienna had already been approached but had refused to cooperate because General Skoropadsky was considered "too friendly to the Germans." [97] Whereupon the Kaiser found it advisable to express astonishment to the Foreign Office over the fact that the Hetman had not yet been recognized. The result was immediate *de jure* recognition of the Hetman, by both Germany and Austria-Hungary, on June 2, 1918.[98]

German and Austrian withholding of *de jure* recognition of the Hetman regime had little practical significance. It merely reflected the confusion and improvisation that characterized the Reich's Ukrainian undertaking and the even more confused and uncertain policy of the Dual Monarchy. Full recognition, nevertheless, signified the irrevocable decision on the part of the two

Central Powers to give the Hetman their permanent and unqualified support.

The Austrians, having opposed the Rada long before the Germans decided to move against it, and now finding themselves confronted with a completely pro-German and equally noncooperative new Ukrainian regime, considered the possibility of assisting the former Premier, Vsevolod Holubovych, the former President, Professor Hrushevsky, and other Rada leaders threatened with German arrest in fleeing to Switzerland; and at the same time they expected to be invited to send a special economic adviser to Kiev to help the Hetman government with its budgetary problems! [99] The Austrians questioned the legal status of the Hetmanate and argued that the Ukraine was in reality an "unrecognized protectorate" (*stillschweigendes Protektorat*); yet they insisted that the Hetman send a special representative to Odessa to insure closer contact with the Austrian occupation authorities in the south of the Ukraine.[100] Then, the Austrians made an issue of General Skoropadsky's official title, "Hetman of all the Ukraine" (they did not like the *all*), fearing that it would strengthen Ukrainian irredentist claims vis-à-vis Austria-Hungary. On similar grounds they refused to change from the old ethnic term "Ruthenian" to the new, and obviously more political, designation "Ukrainian." [101] Finally, determined though they were to pursue a policy of nonrecognition of the Ukraine, the Austrians were compelled to abandon it to avoid the risk of further weakening their position in the Ukraine in the event of its unilateral *de jure* recognition by Germany, and seeing this fabulously rich area become the Reich's exclusive satellite in the east.

CHAPTER VIII

The Hetmanate:
Return to "Normalcy"

De jure recognition of the Hetman government by Berlin and Vienna had more than formal significance. By this act the two powers sought to provide the Hetmanate with a greater degree of stability and to assure Skoropadsky a more consistent support.

At this point Kiev was again full of rumors predicting yet another change in the Ukraine. Some people spoke of the establishment of an Austro-Hungarian "regency"; others speculated about a complete take-over of the entire country by the Germans.[1] Perhaps in order to counter such rumors, but above all to bolster the Hetman regime, the Army Group Eichhorn took the initiative in promoting a more uniform approach to the Reich's policy in the east by declaring: "Any fluctuation in our policy [in the Ukraine] would be damaging, since it might result in weakening the confidence which is being placed in us. The more taste the Hetman develops for power, the more likely he is to promote the strengthening of the idea of a national Ukrainian state and turn his inner eye away from Great Russia."[2]

Ambassador Mumm likewise tried to steer the Hetman away from extreme Right orientation in order to strengthen the Ukrainian national idea and eliminate the Russian influence—a program that the Hetman gladly promised to follow. Mumm and his military colleagues in Kiev also urged the Hetman to enact a number of agrarian reforms to counter the more reactionary Austrian policy in the south, which favored big landowners, many of whom were Polish.[3]

General Groener's meeting with representatives of the moderate Ukrainian national organizations headed by Mykola Mikhnovs'kyi, on June 10, reflects a more consistent policy adopted by the Germans in Kiev. In response to the delegation's complaint about the anti-Ukrainian policies of some of the Hetman's ministers and its plea for the establishment of a genuine Ukrainian government under Skoropadsky's leadership, Groener made the following observations concerning the Reich's Ukrainian policy: Ukrainians, notably Socialist Federalists, had been offered several posts in the Hetman cabinet. Had they agreed to cooperate, they would now be in a position to exert more influence in the new government. As to the dismissal of the present cabinet, as suggested by the delegation, General Groener declared that the *Oberkommando* had no authority to decide such questions. Moreover, one could not have a new government every few weeks, since such changes might adversely affect current Ukrainian-German military and financial negotiations. The general also tried to convince the delegation that a solid fiscal system and an effective armed force were more essential for the continued existence of an independent Ukraine than certain personnel changes on the cabinet level. While promising "to bring to the attention of Ambassador Mumm and the Hetman" [note the order] the alleged abuses of Ukrainian ministers, especially dismissals of Ukrainian officials on grounds other than professional incompetence, Groener came to the defense of the Hetman cabinet, maintaining that its members, too, subscribed to the idea of an independent Ukraine, and that one could not hold it against them if they held a different view in the days of the old regime. Groener's argument in support of the current Hetman regime, however, was also based on a rather pessimistic view of the possibility of permanent separation of the Ukraine from Russia (a thought he acknowledged to have shared with some of the Hetman ministers) and recognition of the lack of nationally conscious Ukrainians with sufficient training and experience to occupy important administrative positions. The general then gave the Ukrainian another piece of advice, namely, to undertake an intensive propaganda campaign in all strata of the Ukrainian population in support of the idea of an independent Ukrainian state, and especially to make a concerted effort to win over to the Ukrainian cause business, industrial, and religious circles, whose support was essential though they were Russian-oriented. All this, ran General Groener's argument, was infinitely more significant than the replacement of this or that cabinet minister in the present Ukrainian government.[4]

It is, indeed, ironic that precisely at the moment when the Germans in Kiev were beginning to work out a more consistent occupation policy, based on unwavering support of the Hetman and his idea of a Ukrainian state, General Ludendorff, who only a few weeks earlier had declared himself in favor of a merger between the Don and Donets [*sic*] Cossacks, on the one hand, and the Ukraine, on the other, viewing the latter as "the only state in the east capable of survival," [5] came to the conclusion that the Ukraine was but an ephemeral phenomenon and that in the near future it would turn back to Russia. To meet such a contingency, Ludendorff suggested the creation of an "anti-Slav federation" (*antislavischer Bund*) to be organized around Georgia, which was to be "automatically" joined by the Don, Kuban, Terek, and Volga Cossacks.[6]

Without mentioning the fact that most of the Cossacks, notably those of the Don and Kuban, were also of Slavic descent, Mumm and Groener argued against such a plan, terming it "utopian," and blamed the Secretary for the Colonies, Friedrich von Lindequist, for putting such ideas into Ludendorff's head. Reporting to the Foreign Office on the plan, Mumm exposed its unrealistic nature and stressed the absence of the unifying factors most essential to such a federation. He then submitted to the Foreign Office the following recommendation: "Irrespective of any possible developments in the future, our present policy, based on the Treaty of Brest-Litovsk, is to aim without any 'zigzags' at the consolidation of a strong, independent Ukraine closely allied to us." Mumm concluded his report with a warning that the implementation of the Ludendorff plan would not only seriously complicate German-Turkish relations but might also discredit Germany's policy in the eyes of the Ukrainian government and drive it completely into the arms of Russia.[7]

While refusing to support General Ludendorff at this point in his rather fantastic plan, Groener was also critical of the Foreign

Office and its spokesmen in Berlin. This criticism was not the result of Germany's Ukrainian policy, with which Groener had more to do than Kühlmann, but of the Foreign Office's insistence that Germany's best interests demanded continued cooperation with the Bolsheviks.[8]

German relations with the Russian Right also presented certain problems. From the first days of the Hetmanate, the German military in Kiev maintained close contacts with the Russian political circles in the Ukraine and allowed them a considerable degree of freedom in organizing their political and even their military forces in this area.[9] Now the Germans became uneasy over the growth of Russian influence in the Ukraine and expressed the hope that the Hetman's "pro-Ukrainian position" would be sufficient to preserve the idea of Ukrainian statehood.[10]

The Austrians, too, were becoming more alert to the Russian surge in the Ukraine and decided to take steps in order to arrest this trend and dissociate themselves from it and thus gain the good will of Ukrainian national circles. It was with this in view, for example, that the Dual Monarchy opposed the selection of Archbishop Antonii Khrapovyts'kyi, a notorious Ukrainophobe, as the Metropolitan of Kiev. After the Austrian Embassy in Berlin learned that Antonii was mainly responsible for the Russification and anti-Uniate drive in East Galicia during the 1914–1917 period, Vienna opposed the choice of such an individual for the highest post in the Orthodox Church in the Ukraine. Austria's Foreign Secretary, Baron Stephan Burián von Rajecz, recommended that the Hetman government be requested to cancel, or at least to postpone, the confirmation of the selection of Archbishop Antonii for this post. Consequently, Forgách was advised to look into this matter jointly with General Groener and Ambassador Mumm.[11] Similarly, he was instructed by Vienna not to participate in the memorial service for Czar Nicholas II, who had just been murdered by the Bolsheviks, since such an observance would undoubtedly be conducted in the "Great Russian spirit," which was hostile to the Ukrainian idea. Forgách was to take part in the service only if the Hetman himself decided to attend.[12]

Despite the loss of faith in many official circles in Germany's Ukrainian undertaking and a great deal of local anti-Hetman opposition, the Army Group Eichhorn and Ambassador Mumm continued to support their plan for a "new Ukraine" headed by a Hetman of their choice. In a lengthy memorandum dated June 17, 1918, devoted mainly to the problems of the east, Eichhorn remarked: "I believe it is of utmost importance to us that the Ukraine really become an independent state. I do not say this simply in anticipation of various economic advantages that we shall obtain from a Ukraine closely allied with Germany. It is not just increased security vis-à-vis Russia that makes me feel that way. . . . A Ukrainian state, on which we shall border or to which we should have an access through Lithuania, constitutes a bridge for us to the Caucasus, Asia, and in the final analysis India—a better bridge than Turkey, from which we shall always remain separated. . . . Many, if not most, people doubt if such a state is possible. Since its existence would be advantageous to us, one should do all one can to make it possible. One must, therefore, believe in it. I also feel that the Ukrainian state's existence is closely bound to the person of the Hetman, and shall stand or fall with him. One should not, therefore, hesitate to give up some of the advantages, which would be easily attainable now, in order to strengthen the Hetman's position in the country and make the Ukraine into a state capable of survival. . . . The longer chaotic conditions continue in Russia, the more favorable will be the prospects for a Ukrainian state. The more the Ukraine differentiates itself from Russia by establishing order, the sooner will the elements that lean toward Great Russia develop Ukrainian national consciousness." [13]

To translate his words into action, Eichhorn issued an order directing German officers to refrain from showing sympathy for the Russian monarchist circles in the Ukraine. He declared that Germany continued to support the Hetman, who was "the mainstay" of the Ukrainian idea. "The fact that the question of the Ukraine's independence is a difficult problem and will require further clarification and development cannot be denied," the Field Marshal stated further. "This, however, will in no way alter our policy in the country." [14]

At this point Ambassador Mumm appeared even more optimistic regarding the Ukraine's future. "The Ukrainian government and its people are very friendly toward us at the present time," noted Mumm in his report to Imperial Chancellor. He then pleaded with Berlin to take a long-range view of Germany's Ukrainian policy: "There are two possible approaches that we can follow in our policy toward the Ukraine. One of them is a ruthless exploitation of the country, regardless of ultimate consequences. The other approach is the creation of a viable political organism which, in close association with Germany, would become an important political, military, and economic factor in our eastern policy in the future." [15]

The Austrians did not share at this time the German optimism concerning the Ukraine and did not think that they were in the position to pursue an independent long-range program comparable to the Reich's plans as outlined by its Kiev representatives. The Dual Monarchy's key man in the Ukraine, General Alfred Krauss, merely hoped that Austria-Hungary would not be completely pushed aside but would be allowed, along with Germany, to pursue its modest aims in the east.[16]

Berlin and the Supreme Army Command were clearly less optimistic concerning the general picture in the east than were the German representatives in Kiev, and made a renewed effort to agree on a more positive and consistent policy; however, the results of the imperial conference held in Spa, July 2–3, 1918, under the Kaiser's chairmanship were just as disappointing as those produced by other such meetings. Although there was a great deal of agreement in the review of the general situation in the east, the German leaders failed to come up with clearly defined concrete recommendations for the conduct of the Reich's policies in various occupied areas of the region, such as the Ukraine, the Don, and the Crimea. The decisions concerning Germany's future relations with the Bolsheviks and the Russian monarchist elements (then becoming increasingly active in the south) were just as vague, despite the rather pretentious title of the official summary of the conclusions reached at the conference: "New Orientation in Russia." The following passage contains one of the basic conclusions reached at the Spa conference: "The overthrow of the Bolshevik government should not be sought now; at the same time, however, closer ties should be established with the monarchists in order to be prepared for any eventuality. The condition for this [close cooperation with the Russian monarchists] is their acceptance of the Treaty of Brest-Litovsk. They should not be deprived of their hope for the eventual reestablishment of Great Russia. His Majesty, the Kaiser, recommends the rallying of [Russia's] orderly elements in Kiev." [17]

In the border states, especially the Ukraine, the situation was viewed as serious, almost hopeless. "A viable Ukrainian state will not come into being. A Ukrainian national idea is entirely dependent on the presence of our forces in the country. We have to prepare ourselves for all possible contingencies." [18] Such was General Ludendorff's view of the Ukrainian situation at this point, although only a few weeks earlier he had been convinced that the Ukraine was the only viable political entity created on the ruins of the Russian Empire. [19]

Ludendorff was not alone in holding such a pessimistic view of the Ukraine's future at the Spa conference. The Prussian Secretary of War, Lieutenant General Hermann von Stein, also concluded that while the monarchists might agree to a permanent loss of the Baltic provinces, they would insist on retention of the Ukraine. [20] Kaiser Wilhelm, too, forgetting his earlier schemes in which the Ukraine had figured rather prominently, declared: "We went to the Ukraine in order to secure necessary food supplies. It is there that we want to create an island of order in the sea of Russian chaos, but we should not succumb to the illusion that the Ukraine could be permanently separated from Great Russia. The Ukraine is Slavic, so is Great Russia. The two will get together again. All Russian forces of order should assemble around Kiev and from there continue their struggle for the rebirth of Russia." [21]

While Berlin groped for a new approach to Germany's Ukrainian policy, Mumm and Groener continued to press the Hetman and his Prime Minister, Fedir A. Lyzohub, for further Ukrainization of the cabinet. The Germans had expressed such a wish on other occasions, but now the need to add "couleur locale" to the Hetman government became much more pressing in order to forestall the possibility that the entire cabinet might move into the Russian camp. [22] Kaiser Wilhelm took direct interest in this matter by writing a personal letter to Hetman Skoropadsky. The original plan, worked out in close cooperation with Mumm through his assistant, Count Berchem, called for the resignation of almost the entire cabinet, with the exception of Dmytro Doroshenko, Mykola Vasylenko, and Anton Rzhepetsky; then such prominent Ukrainian leaders as Dmytro Dontsov, Serhii Yefremov, and Mykola Porsh were to be offered ministerial portfolios. [23] These efforts continued through the month of July, but instead of insisting on complete reorganization of the cabinet, Mumm now advised the Hetman to replace individual ministers. Replacements, however, were to be made only in close cooperation with the German Ambassador. On July 25, Baron Mumm, before going away on a business trip, reminded the Hetman that no changes were to be made in the Ukrainian cabinet during his absence from Kiev.[24] At about this time the Hetman planned several important changes in his government, including the appointment of a new Prime Minister. One of the men seriously considered for this post was a well-known Ukrainian patriot, uncle of the Foreign Minister and a close friend of General Skoropadsky, Dr. Petro Doroshenko.[25]

In the final analysis, even though the Hetman was always ready to accept German recommendations, nothing came of the efforts to broaden the base of his cabinet. Most nationally conscious Ukrainians refused to have any dealings with either the Germans or the Hetman. Constant reprisals against the restless Ukrainian peasantry and arrests of individual Ukrainian leaders did little to make these circles more receptive to repeated German overtures. The most prominent victim was, without doubt, Symon Petlyura, who was arrested on July 27. (He had served as the Rada's Secretary of Military Affairs and was later to become the dominant political personality in the Ukrainian national movement.)[26]

It is clear that neither the Spa conference nor Hintze's appointment replacing Kühlmann as Foreign Secretary shortly thereafter produced any important changes in Germany's Ukrainian policy. Rear Admiral Paul von Hintze had served in the prewar period as a naval attaché in St. Petersburg and was at one point closer to Czar Nicholas II than to his own Emperor. Although he knew Russia fairly well and could be regarded as her friend, there was not much difference between him and Kühlmann with regard to Germany's eastern policy; consequently, no immediate change in Germany's Ukrainian policy took place.

The general feeling of uncertainty and futility continued to prevail among the Germans in the east. "It is none too pleasant to conduct politics here at this time," the Reich's Consul General, Erich von Thiel, reported from Kiev on July 26. "But in spite of conditions we are still trying to keep our original lines of action, that is, to establish an independent Ukraine with the aid of our military power." Thiel, however, was far from optimistic about the possibility of realizing this goal, despite his sincere desire to help the Ukrainian cause. His dim view of the Ukraine's future as an ally of the Reich was based on the conviction that, politically, the Ukrainians were "hopelessly impractical" and that the semi-occupied status of the country was making it difficult to establish normal political relations there.[27]

On July 30, 1918, Field Marshal Eichhorn was assassinated in Kiev by Russian Social Revolutionaries (the same group that had carried out a successful attempt on the life of Count Wilhelm von Mirbach-Harff, the German Ambassador in Moscow earlier in the month). Viewed by the Germans as an isolated incident in which the Ukrainians were not implicated, Eichhorn's assassination did not produce any changes in the Reich's policy in the Ukraine. After the assassination, according to an eye-witness account, the Germans in Kiev remained on the alert, but otherwise acted so as not to stir up the people.[28] Eichhorn was succeeded by Count Günther von Kirchbach, a general who had been in command of the Eighth Army. General Groener was quite pleased with Kirchbach, whom he described later as "an easy-to-get-along-with superior" who, like Eichhorn, gave him a free hand in running the *Oberkommando* in Kiev.[29]

Despite General Groener's and Ambassador Mumm's repeated recommendations that Ukrainian interests be openly supported by the Reich, Berlin continued its rather cautious policy of half measures and procrastination. The Supreme Army Command, in the meantime, seemed to lose interest in Germany's Ukrainian undertaking. It adopted a view that, once a decisive victory in the west had been achieved, the *Ostproblem* would easily be settled in the way most advantageous to German interests.[30] The result was that the German representatives in Kiev, left to themselves, could now pursue a more consistent "pro-Ukrainian" line such as they had advocated earlier, although, ironically, the conditions for a closer German-Ukrainian cooperation no longer existed.

All told, the measures designed to placate Ukrainian national circles and to strengthen the Hetman's position in the country did not go beyond mere diplomatic gestures, such as a visit to Berlin by a Ukrainian delegation headed by Prime Minister Lyzohub, a meeting between the Hetman and the Kaiser, and the awarding of medals and orders to various officials of the Hetman government.

Whatever these measures were worth, Ambassador Mumm deserves most credit for having initiated them.

It was on his suggestion that Prime Minister Lyzohub, accompanied by other high-ranking Hetman officials, went to Berlin in mid-August on a good-will visit.[31] The purpose of the trip was to establish direct contact with German authorities in the hope of achieving a favorable settlement of the Black Sea problems, especially the future status of the Crimean Peninsula. No definite concessions were obtained in Berlin; moreover, Lyzohub's statement to the German press in an interview on August 18, 1918, in which he reportedly declared himself in favor of the eventual reunion of the Ukraine with Russia, although soon disavowed by him and the Hetman, introduced further complications into the already confused Ukrainian picture.[32]

Ambassador Mumm, continuing his efforts to improve Ukrainian-German relations suggested to the Foreign Office in Berlin that "Your Excellency" be replaced by the more dignified title of "Your Highness" (*Durchlaucht*) in addressing the Hetman.[33] At first the Germans employed a rather cumbersome title, "General Skoropadsky, Excellency, Hetman of all the Ukraine." Then, the term "excellency" was eliminated from this long title, after it had been discovered that the Hetman did not particularly like it. The Austro-Hungarian government was careful to refrain from using this title, lest it be interpreted as Vienna's acceptance of the Ukraine's irredentist claims, especially in East Galicia and the Kholm region. It was also Mumm's suggestion to award medals and decorations to various Ukrainian officials. By mid-September, 1918, more than a dozen such awards had been made; among the recipients were Hetman Skoropadsky and his Prime Minister Lyzohub.[34]

The high point in Mumm's efforts to improve Ukrainian-German relations was reached when the Hetman went to Germany to meet the Kaiser and the Reich's war lords, Hindenburg and Ludendorff. The German Foreign Office was approached concerning this matter by the Ukrainian Under-Secretary for Foreign Affairs, Oleksander Paltov, during his stay in Berlin. It responded with remarkable promptness and advised Mumm to arrange the Hetman's visit for the following week. The haste was explained by the Kaiser's "disposition" (which apparently was subject to frequent and unexpected fluctuations). On Mumm's recommendation the planning of the visit and the trip itself were to be kept secret to preclude possible sabotage or an attempt on the Hetman's life.[35]

The Hetman arrived in Berlin on September 4. The visit was not only hastily arranged but ill-prepared. In spite of the fact that the Hetman spent almost two weeks in Germany, he returned home empty-handed, and Ukrainian-German relations remained as ill-defined and vague as before. The Germans on the whole took the Hetman's visit quite seriously. Foreign Secretary Hintze furnished the Kaiser beforehand with "guiding principles" for his talks with Skoropadsky, including the questions the guest was most likely to raise and the answers to them. The Kaiser was to remind his guest of German assistance given to the Ukraine at a critical moment, and of the commitments that the Ukrainian government had undertaken to repay Germany for this military support. The Hetman was then to be praised for his loyalty and cooperation and congratulated for his tireless efforts to establish order in the newly formed Ukrainian state, despite various difficulties and complications. He was further to be commended for the agrarian reforms enacted by his government and encouraged to continue his efforts in that direction. The Hetman was to be assured of continued German support, and he was to be promised assistance in the establishment of a Ukrainian army; at the same time, however, the Kaiser was to request manpower from the Ukraine to help Germany overcome its labor shortage. Finally, the problem of German colonists in the Ukraine was to be dealt with, "if possible," and Ukrainian cooperation in the settlement of this matter requested. Among the questions that Hintze expected the Hetman to raise were the problem of the Crimea, the future of Kholm and Bessarabia, and recognition of the Don by Germany. To all these questions, except that of Kholm, carefully worded evasive answers were to be given and no commitments made.[36] (These questions are discussed in the subsequent sections of this chapter.)

Although the Hetman was well received by the Kaiser and the members of the government,[37] Ludendorff showed little interest in meeting the Ukrainian leader. True, Ludendorff agreed to receive the Hetman, but asked that no such visit be planned unless the visitor himself specifically requested it. Skoropadsky did express a wish to pay a visit to the Great Headquarters at Spa, but it was not until September 12 that it could be arranged. He was met at the station by both Hindenburg and Ludendorff, although most of the talking was done by the latter.[38] The questions discussed at the meeting were almost identical with those dealt with in the earlier talks with the Kaiser, and Ludendorff's answers were just as evasive and disappointing. Although the fate of the Black Sea fleet and the progress of Soviet-Ukrainian peace talks were discussed, it was only on the maintenance of ties between the Hetman and General Mikhail V. Alexeev, commander of the Russian Volunteer Army, and the barring of the young Austrian Archduke Wilhelm from the Ukraine that the three found themselves in full agreement.[39] (Archduke Wilhelm, known among the Ukrainians as Basil the Embroidered (Vasyl' Vyshyvanyi), was fluent in Ukrainian and had close ties with Ukrainian pro-Austrian circles. His presence in the Ukraine, in the capacity of an officer of the Galician Ukrainian Volunteer Legion, Sichovi Stril'tsi, greatly added to Austro-German rivalry in the country and was also the cause of constant irritation to the Hetman as well as to the Germans.) [40]

Having thrown in its lot with the Central Powers at Brest, the Ukraine had greatly narrowed the scope of its foreign relations. Although Kiev insisted on Ukrainian neutrality and did not assume any military obligations to the Central Powers, the Ukraine, by the very act of concluding a separate treaty, shut the doors to the Allied as well as most of the neutral capitals. Ukrainian foreign policy-makers recognized this fact but hoped, with the Reich's assistance, to strengthen their state's international position and regain the necessary freedom of initiative to become an independent factor in the making of a new order in the east. Emancipation from German "tutelage" was supposedly the principal goal of Ukrainian foreign policy in the period of the Hetmanate.[41]

Although the Ukraine as an occupied satellite of the Reich was in no position to establish close ties with many countries, the Germans (as much aware of this as they were of the potential significance of Kiev's connections with other powers) manifested a high degree of sensitivity and wariness in all foreign policy matters that had some bearing on the Ukraine. This had been the case in the Rada period, but became even more noticeable after the coup of April 29.

On May 21, General Ludendorff set the line of German advance in the east (a decision that was officially communicated to the Soviet government), and declared that it was the Ukraine's responsibility to decide how far east its forces were to advance.[42] Several days later, however, Kühlmann advised Ambassador Mumm in Kiev that His Majesty's decision was that "the liberation of the Ukraine from the Bolsheviks had been completed, and that it was now Kiev's responsibility to come to terms with Soviet Russia." The Ukrainians were then informed that any operations against Russia beyond the line of German advance would receive neither military nor diplomatic support from the Reich.[43]

On May 31 Mumm was again advised by the Foreign Office to use all his influence to prevent the Ukraine's territorial extension beyond its "national boundaries." This concern was voiced by Berlin in connection with a reception given for the representatives of the provinces of Kursk, Voronezh, and Chernigov by the Hetman's chief delegate to the Ukrainian-Soviet talks, Serhii Shelukhin. The representatives from these border provinces used this occasion to express their wish to be incorporated into the Hetman state rather than remain under Bolshevik rule.[44]

In the opinion of a member of the Hetman's cabinet, Sergei M. Gutnik, the Germans were rather indifferent to, and at times even actively opposed, Kiev's territorial claims.[45] This was generally as true of the Ukrainian-Don boundary dispute, Kiev's claim to Bessarabia, and its desire to annex the Crimea, as it was of the Ukraine's irredenta, such as East Galicia and Kholm, which the Ukrainians could claim with greater justification than others.

Like so many other problems with which the Hetman had to deal, the problem of Bessarabia had its beginning in the Rada period. Although not regarded by the new Ukrainian regime as one of its most pressing foreign policy tasks, the Bessarabian question was used by the Hetman administration to try to determine the German attitude concerning Ukrainian territorial claims in general.

Anticipating hopefully German neutrality in the event of a re-opening of the Ukrainian-Rumanian dispute over Bessarabia, the Hetman government, in one of its first foreign policy moves, in early May, 1918, broke off diplomatic relations with Bucharest (they had been established by the Rada in April, despite Rumania's annexation of Bessarabia a month earlier), and on May 11

imposed a commercial embargo on all goods destined for Rumania and Bessarabia.[46] Ukrainian expectation of German neutrality
was not completely baseless. On June 19, 1918, at a meeting with
the Reichstag committee, Kühlmann reaffirmed German neutrality on this question, adding, however, that Germany was not interested in forcing Rumania out of Bessarabia.[47]

Following the severing of diplomatic and commercial relations
with Bucharest, other measures were resorted to by the Ukrainians, such as continued payment of pensions and subsidies to
various officials who resigned from service rather than cooperate
with the Rumanians and the sale of low-priced sugar and other
food products to Bessarabian cooperatives. The most serious
measure was the closing of the Dniester River traffic, since it imposed further hardships on the already badly strained Rumanian
economy. Such economic measures were soon abandoned, however, partly because of Rumanian complaints in Berlin and Vienna (both capitals officially maintained a hands-off attitude and
merely advised the Hetman about these protests), but principally
because of Kiev's desire to have direct contact with a country in
which Allied representatives were still active. Thus, in the
summer of 1918, diplomatic and economic ties between the
Ukraine and Rumania were reestablished and negotiations for the
conclusion of a commercial treaty initiated.[48]

Nevertheless, in August, 1918, during Prime Minister Lyzohub's visit to Berlin, German support of the Ukraine's claim to "a
substantial part of Bessarabia" was sought again. The Under-
Secretary of State, Baron von dem Bussche, evaded a direct answer by pointing to the Ukrainian-Rumanian negotiations then in
progress.[49] Although Ukrainian-Rumanian relations further improved upon the conclusion of a broad commercial agreement between the two states on October 26, 1918,[50] the future of Bessarabia was left undecided. All available evidence indicates, however,
that if it had come to a showdown, Germany as well as Austria-
Hungary would have supported Rumania in its claim to the entire
province.

The Ukrainian-Rumanian dispute over Bessarabia contributed
to the growth of Ukrainian-Bulgarian friendship, for which a solid
foundation had been established during the peace negotiations at
Brest-Litovsk. It was quite natural that Bulgaria, the only Slav
state among the Central Powers, and the Ukraine should be

drawn closer together. Indeed, one can say that few countries in the east during this period were as friendly as Bulgaria and the Ukraine. This friendship was manifested in various ways—from Sofia's generous diplomatic support of the newly founded Ukrainian state and a popular collection to aid the victims of munitions dump explosions in Kiev in June, 1918, to the continued, though secretly held desire to establish a common frontier between them, and thus construct a solid Slavic wall along most of the northern and western Black sea shore. Bulgaria's friendly attitude toward the Ukraine was expressed in her early ratification of the Ukrainian Treaty of Brest-Litovsk, on July 15, 1918, ahead of Germany and Turkey and despite Vienna's strong opposition. The Germans, fully aware of the friendly relations between Kiev and Sofia, kept a watchful eye on their development but did not really try to weaken the tie.[51] The development of close relations between the two countries was also aided by Sofia's choice of its Ambassador to the Ukraine—Ivan Shishmanov, Mykhailo Drahomanov's son-in-law.

The irredenta about which the Ukrainians felt much more strongly than Bessarabia were East Galicia and Kholm. The two provinces figured prominently in the Brest negotiations between the Central Powers and Kiev in January and February, 1918, and continued in the foreground of East European diplomacy throughout the year. Not only the Ukraine and Poland but Austria-Hungary and Germany, too, were vitally interested in the future of these areas.

On the basis of a "secret" agreement concluded at Brest-Litovsk, East Galicia, an area with a Ukrainian majority, strong and well-organized Polish islands in urban centers, and a large Jewish minority, was to be organized together with northern Bukovina into a distinct Ukrainian crownland within the Dual Monarchy. This commitment and the transfer of Kholm to the Ukraine were not to be carried out pending the Ukraine's fulfillment of its obligations toward the Central Powers (mainly food deliveries), a prospect about which most people were openly skeptical. Czernin expressed skepticism about the Ukraine's ability to make all deliveries on time several days before the signing of the Ukrainian treaty. This was the beginning of the Austrian plan to cancel all the concessions they made at Brest.[52] However, it was not enough for the Austrians, who had not yet forgotten their humiliation at Brest, to confine themselves merely to post-poning fulfillment of their promises.

Even before the Poles were openly reassured about Vienna's determination not to honor the concessions granted to the Ukrainians at Brest (the Austrians did this literally days after the signing of the Ukrainian treaty),[53] the Austrian Foreign Office approached the Germans with a request to assist it in the destruction of the secret agreement on East Galicia, of which there were only two copies—one in Austrian and the other in Ukrainian possession. Vienna's request, made about February 15, was favorably received by German Foreign Secretary Kühlmann, and a week or so later his representative at Brest, Friedrich H. Rosenberg, persuaded the Ukrainians to give him their copy of the document "for safekeeping" in Berlin.[54]

Matters could not be left at that, however, especially in view of the well-known anti-Austrian attitude of the new Ukrainian government and the approaching deadline (July 20, 1918) for the formation of a distinct Ukrainian crownland. Moreover, powerful Hungarian and Polish parliamentary circles, which had an important say in foreign affairs of the Dual Monarchy, continued their criticism of the promises Vienna had made to the Ukrainians at Brest-Litovsk.

The new Foreign Secretary, Baron Burián, therefore, did not find it very difficult to bring to a close this unhappy episode in Vienna's foreign policy. As it happened, the Ukrainian government reinforced Vienna's determination to have the Galician problem settled once and for all by repeatedly requesting ratification of the Ukrainian treaty of Brest-Litovsk by all the Central Powers following *de jure* recognition of the Hetman on June 2.[55] The Austrians, on the other hand, pressed for annulment of the secret agreement on Galicia and made this a *sine qua non* for the ratification of the treaty. Having been assured of Berlin's "benevolent neutrality" (that is, full cooperation), and knowing that not only Germany but Bulgaria and Turkey, too, were eager to ratify the Ukrainian treaty, Vienna decided to act quickly and force the Hetman to accept the annulment. On July 1 Count Forgách, the Austro-Hungarian envoy in Kiev, was instructed to approach the Hetman personally, and in a friendly yet firm manner advise him confidentially of Vienna's decision. He was to justify it to the Hetman by pointing out the Ukraine's failure to meet its obligations and also a radical change in the conditions under which the secret agreement had been made. Rather than conclude a new convention in order to declare the old agreement void, Forgách was to ask the Hetman for an oral acceptance of his government's demand, a procedure designed to spare the Ukrainians unnecessary embarrassment.[56] According to German records, the Hetman agreed to the Austrian demand without much resistance. The Ukrainian Foreign Minister, Doroshenko, however, claimed that Skoropadsky accepted the Austrian demand under protest and instructed his envoy in Vienna, Vyacheslav Lypyns'kyi, to continue a defense of the Ukrainian case before the Austro-Hungarian authorities, hoping in the meantime to secure German support against Vienna's pressure.[57] However, the Ukrainian note of protest was presented to Count Burián only on July 24, 1918 (more than a week after the burning of the Ukrainian copy of the secret document), and it was rejected by the Austro-Hungarian Foreign Office "because the entire case had already been settled in Kiev"! The second note, dated July 28, sent by Ambassador Lypyns'kyi, to Count Burián by mail, proved just as futile as the first one.[58] The document had been burned on July 16 by the German Under-Secretary of State, von dem Bussche, in the presence of the Austrian Ambassador in Berlin, Prince Hohenlohe.[59] The Germans, who had as much to do with this "diplomatic move" as did the Austrians, also maintained that it was a closed issue and refused to be drawn into further discussion of this matter.

The destruction of the secret Austro-Ukrainian agreement on Galicia did not bring Vienna any closer to ratifying the Ukrainian treaty. That Austria did not intend to ratify it, at least not at this point, can clearly be seen from its reaction to Bulgaria's and Germany's decision to complete the ratification of the treaty, which they did in Vienna on July 15 and 24, respectively. Exchange of ratification notes was announced in each case by the local press. Austria's expression of unhappiness over Sofia's action was immediate and strong.[60] Berlin, too, confronted Vienna with a *fait accompli*. Count Burián was officially advised of the exchange of ratification notes between Germany and the Ukraine by the Reich's chargé d'affaires in Vienna, Prince Stolberg-Wernigerode, two days later. Burián immediately protested against such a *post factum* notification in a special note to the German Foreign Office.[61]

A somewhat belated exchange of instruments of ratification between the Ukraine and Turkey in Vienna on August 22 also failed to change Austria's position in this matter.[62] (The delay was probably caused by the Ukrainian-Crimean dispute in which Turkey was indirectly involved.) Austria came closest to ratifying in early October, 1918, when Burián, realizing at long last that the policy of nonratification had lost its usefulness, went so far as to draft the ratification document and present it to the Emperor for signing.[63] Polish influence in Vienna, however, proved stronger than Burián's desire to bring about at least a partial improvement in relations between Austria-Hungary and the Ukraine. Consequently, the treaty concluded between the two countries at Brest-Litovsk was never ratified.

The problem of Kholm figured just as prominently in the strained Austro-Ukrainian relations throughout 1918 as did the future of East Galicia. The Ukrainians again took the initiative in reopening the Kholm question. Encouraged by the *de jure* recognition of the Hetman by the Central Powers, in early June, the Ukrainian government sent a note to Vienna in which it reaffirmed its adherence to the March 4, 1918, "Protocol" (consent to accept a new frontier in the Kholm area); at the same time, however, it protested the continued Polonization of the Austrian zone, Vienna's refusal to admit Ukrainian officials into the area, as well as a series of other acts regarded as injurious to Ukrainian interests in the Kholm region.[64] The Austrian government, no doubt annoyed by Kiev's "impertinence," ignored the note.

In the meantime, German Foreign Secretary Kühlmann concluded that Germany could not afford to become a disinterested party in the Kholm area; consequently, Austria was not to be allowed to act as if she had a free hand there. Mumm, too, felt quite strongly about the abandonment of Kholm to Poland, arguing that such action would seriously weaken the Hetman's position and inevitably produce strong criticism, from both the Ukrainian and the German Left.[65]

Although the Austrians and the Poles were well aware of Berlin's position,[66] they continued to demand that the Ukraine renounce its claims to Kholm. In mid-August the Poles were invited to Spa for a conference with the Kaiser, General Ludendorff, Chancellor Hertling, and Foreign Secretary Hintze. In response to the German offer of a "candidate solution" (a German Catholic prince to be chosen for the Polish throne), the Poles stated that they could consider it only upon the granting of the following demands: (1) "minimal" boundary rectifications [in the west]; (2) transfer of the entire Kholm province to Poland; (3) conclusion of a German-Polish military convention.[67]

At this point Mumm reported increased Austrian pressure on the Hetman to give up the Ukraine's claims to Kholm, which Mumm described as "a purely Ukrainian region." [68] The Germans, however, remained firm. General Ludendorff was ready to acquiesce to the strengthening of Poland, provided it would remain under German influence, but he rejected the Austrian demand that the entire Kholm area (up to the Bug River line) be given to Poland, arguing that this would completely destroy the Ukraine's confidence in Germany and also greatly complicate the fulfillment of the Reich's military and economic tasks, so important for the winning of the war.[69] The German Foreign Office held essentially the same view on the Kholm question, trying to achieve an agreement that "would leave neither the Ukrainians nor the Poles entirely dissatisfied." [70] This formula was faithfully adhered to during both Lyzohub's and Skoropadsky's visits to Berlin in August and September, 1918. In each case the Ukrainians were promised an early solution of the Kholm problem, although they were asked to grant certain concessions to the Austro-Polish point of view.[71]

Finally, in late September, Foreign Secretary Hintze prepared a new plan for the settlement of the Polish question, in which he advocated German annexation of the considerably reduced districts of Bendzin, Thorn, Lomza, and Ossowiec, in return for Polish territorial aggrandizement in the Kholm area and Byelorussia. Nothing came of this plan, and in late October, 1918, when General Hans Hartwick von Beseler requested the Foreign Office to allow the Poles to move into Kholm, the new German Secretary of State, Wilhelm Solf, opposed it very strongly.[72] Moreover, on November 9 a special agreement was concluded in Berlin between the Ukraine and Germany providing for the dispatch of two German divisions into Kholm so that Ukrainian administration could, at long last, be established there.[73] The agreement proved to be merely a friendly, though futile, gesture on the part of the last imperial cabinet headed by Prince Max von Baden, and the Poles moved into the area virtually unopposed; nevertheless, it offers an interesting contrast to the Austrian stand at this point, which remained as anti-Ukrainian as ever.

The desire to normalize Ukrainian-Soviet relations constituted one of the most pressing foreign policy tasks of the young Ukrainian state. The Germans, too, viewed it as an important problem that could be solved only with their assistance. Thus it was by Article 6 of the Russian treaty of Brest-Litovsk, concluded on March 3, 1918, that the Bolsheviks were forced to open negotiations with the Ukrainian government. Although the Ukrainian-Soviet peace talks extended over a period of more than five months, they failed to bring about a settlement of the most fundamental problem, that of the long frontier separating the two countries, and were finally broken off by the Bolsheviks in early November, 1918, when they reopened hostilities against the Ukraine.

Among the issues agreed upon by the Ukraine and Soviet Russia, in a preliminary convention concluded on June 12, 1918, were the termination of hostilities between the two countries, establishment of consular offices in a number of cities by both parties to facilitate the exchange of population and repatriation of their nationals, and a series of arrangements concerning communication between the two states.[74]

A draft of the proposed peace treaty between the Rada and the Bolsheviks had been prepared by the Ukrainians even before Soviet acceptance of the Russo-German treaty of Brest-Litovsk and presented to the Germans for approval.[75] The Rada took the initiative in preparing the ground for these talks. It was not until May 10, 1918, however, that the Soviet delegation arrived in Kiev, and the first meeting of this prolonged peace conference opened two weeks later.[76] The Soviet-Ukrainian talks, therefore, belong entirely to the period of the Hetmanate.

The Germans, no doubt, exerted a considerable direct influence on the Ukrainians in these talks, but the Soviets, too, had to take German wishes into consideration, at least to some extent. The Bolshevik government, for example, accepted at the outset the German claim to be regarded as an interested party in Ukrainian-Soviet talks, raised no objections to the presence of German representatives at the negotiations, and occasionally used the Germans to transmit certain requests or conditions to Kiev.[77] Of great interest to the Germans politically, the Soviet-Ukrainian talks were even more important to their economic considerations, at least as long as the war lasted. Ludendorff, for example, gave specific instructions that the natural resources of such states as the Ukraine and Georgia were to be reserved primarily for the use of the German war economy; Russian needs were to be satisfied only in the last instance, that is, after all other claims and requirements had been satisfied.[78]

Austria-Hungary, too, was determined to see to it that no economic agreements would be concluded that might prove injurious to its interests. Yet, while the Germans delegated two official representatives, Major Friedrich Brinckmann of the Supreme Command East and Count Hans von Berchem of the German Embassy in Kiev, to sit in on these talks, and also assigned their top economic and financial experts, Otto Wiedfeldt and Karl Melchior, to keep an eye on the negotiations,[79] the Austrians maintained from the very beginning that direct German and Austrian participation in these talks would be of no practical value and was politically inadvisable. The Germans at first did not appreciate Vienna's position, but soon accepted this view and abandoned the practice of sending their own official representatives to Soviet-Ukrainian peace negotiations.[80]

Naturally, both the Germans and the Austrians continued to follow the development of the talks very closely so that they could intervene immediately through the Ukrainian government whenever their interests should so require, but Germany played a far more important part in these behind-the-scenes *démarches* designed to "guide" the Ukraine in its talks with Soviet Russia than did Austria-Hungary. On May 30, for example, Ambassador Mumm told the Ukrainians that "a delay in the negotiations was not in their interest," meaning, of course, that the Germans wanted the Ukrainians to do all they could to achieve an early settlement with the Soviets.[81] At about the same time the Foreign Office instructed Mumm to warn the Ukrainians not to extend their control beyond their "national boundaries." (This was Berlin's reaction to the expressed wish of the delegations from the provinces of Kursk and Veronezh to be incorporated into the Hetman state.)[82] Of an even greater importance was a lengthy memorandum prepared by the Reich's chief economic adviser in the Ukraine, Otto Wiedfeldt, and submitted to the Ukrainian government on June 1. Through this communication the Germans sought to impose specific restrictions on economic commitments that Kiev might undertake toward Soviet Russia, to make certain that they would not interfere with the Austro-German exploitation of the Ukraine. Moreover, Wiedfeldt demanded a share, for both Germany and Austria-Hungary, of everything that the Ukraine might obtain from Russia on the basis of the peace treaty or some other agreement. The Germans had in mind platinum and other strategically important raw materials, compensation for war damages, and other financial settlements.[83]

Nevertheless, at the beginning of the negotiations between the Ukrainians and the Soviets the Germans maintained a more or less consistent pro-Ukrainian line, provided that the Ukrainians behaved so as not to jeopardize German interests. Later, in the summer of 1918, the German position in these talks was less clear and may be regarded as an example of the vagueness and confusion so characteristic of Germany's entire *Ostpolitik* of this period. Indeed, by early June some Germans began to wonder whether the pressure on Kiev had not been excessive. Both Ludendorff and Kühlmann urged that the Germans involved in the talks avoid giving the impression that they were ready to help the Bolsheviks at the expense of the Ukraine. At the same time, however, German official spokesmen opposed the transfer of the Crimea to the Ukraine prior to the conclusion of the Ukrainian-Soviet peace treaty, refused to back Skoropadsky's plan to dispatch a Ukrainian force to Kuban to strengthen Ukrainian elements there, and took an equally negative stand on the Ukrainian-Don *rapprochement*.[84]

The German military, especially General Ludendorff, even though they approved of German-Soviet cooperation, were actually strongly anti-Bolshevik, and only after the "Black Day" in the west (the breakthrough of Allied tanks on the Albert-Moreuil sector on August 8, 1918) gave a reluctant consent to Germany's conclusion of a supplementary agreement with Soviet Russia.[85] And yet, only a few weeks earlier Ludendorff had gone so far as to prepare a detailed plan for an anti-Bolshevik campaign, and on August 5, while the final touches were being added to the German-Soviet supplementary agreement, he again assured Hintze that "the German army could advance into Russia and establish a new government there, which would have the people behind it." [86]

The German Foreign Office, under both Kühlmann and Hintze,

consistently pressed for continued cooperation with the Soviet regime. Although it may be correct to emphasize Kühlmann's "western orientation" and Hintze's greater familiarity with the east, German Foreign Office archives did not reveal any significant changes in Germany's *Ostpolitik* with Hintze's replacement of Kühlmann in July, 1918.

Ludendorff's endless oscillation between a militantly anti-Soviet position and a grudging and halfhearted coexistence with Moscow was just as characteristic, even though it was less clearly expressed, of his Ukrainian "policy." This confused and inconsistent approach to the problem of the east found its full reflection in Kaiser Wilhelm's views and was greatly responsible for the general confusion surrounding the Reich's *Ostpolitik* throughout 1918. Fritz Fischer, in his study of Germany's policy during World War I, does a masterful job of revealing this duality and contradiction (he calls it *Zwiespältigkeit*) in Ludendorff's and the Kaiser's thinking; however, Fischer's conclusions are often more sweeping and definitive than these oscillations warrant.[87]

Thus, it was the weakening of Germany's over-all position, which could also be perceived in the east, rather than a shift in its Ukrainian policy that was really responsible for the shelving of Ludendorff's plans to move against Soviet Russia. With things in the west going from bad to worse, Germany had to make certain that no new trouble in the east developed at this time. That German-Soviet relations improved somewhat in late August cannot be denied, but a new agreement made between the two states did not affect the Soviet-Ukrainian talks, then still in progress. Germany continued its role of a "neutral," though not an uninterested, observer. As late as October 25, Ludendorff requested that the Hetman be advised not to do anything that might be regarded as a provocation against the Bolsheviks.[88] Of course, the Soviets did not need any provocation to break off peace negotiations with Kiev and renew their drive into the Ukraine. This, however, came after the fall of the Hetmanate, and it was up to the new Ukrainian government, the Directory, to cope with the renewed challenge from the north.

As for Kiev's other territorial claims, the future of the Crimea presented a most important and difficult foreign policy task for the Hetmanate. Because of its close connection with Germany's long-range objectives in the east, especially the Black Sea question, this subject is dealt with in a separate chapter devoted to the broad aspects of Germany's *Ostpolitik* in this period.

Polissya presented a somewhat different problem than did other areas in which the Ukraine showed an interest. This region, lying directly north of the pivotal Kievan area, was claimed by the Ukraine mainly on strategic grounds. Even those who were directly responsible for insisting on the inclusion of Polissya in the Ukrainian state (for example, Ukrainian Foreign Minister Dmytro Doroshenko) admitted that Byelorussian claims to it were well founded, even though they argued at the same time that the question could not be solved pending the establishment of a genuinely independent Byelorussian state.[89]

The Polissya region was made up of three districts of the former Minsk province (Pinsk, Mozyr, and Richytsya) into which the Rada had extended its administrative network in the early days of the revolution. Shortly after the Hetman's coup, this area was enlarged to include the purely Byelorussian district of Gomel.[90] The Germans did not oppose this move, regarding it as a necessary strengthening of the Ukraine's defensive line against the Bolsheviks. Although the bulk of the Polissya region (the three districts annexed by the Rada) was regarded as Ukrainian by the Germans at Brest-Litovsk, and although subsequent annexation of the Gomel district by the Hetman was not opposed by Berlin, these attitudes were probably more indicative of Germany's lack of interest in the Byelorussian national movement at this point than of the Reich's readiness to support the Ukraine's territorial claims in the east. In spite of the fact that the Germans refused to recognize the Byelorussian Rada as a government of that area and remained rather indifferent to the strivings of the Byelorussian national movement, they left Kiev free to deal with its northern neighbor and raised no objections to the presence of Byelorussian "envoys" on Ukrainian territory.

The Germans were likewise cautious in controlling the Hetman's contacts with Allied representatives, both in the Ukraine and in neighboring countries in order to preserve, at least in theory, the Ukraine's status as an independent state. The problem of controlling or removing Allied consuls and other "hostile elements" from the Ukraine first arose in the Rada days. The Germans originally proposed to remove them "on security grounds," suggesting also that the Rada should launch an official "protest" against such action of the German occupation forces.[91] In late June, however, the problem was still unsolved, and the German Army Command East again suggested to the Hetman government that Allied representatives be removed from the Ukraine.[92] The German Foreign Office's position concerning this matter was the following: "Since on the basis of the Hague Convention on the conduct of land warfare the Ukraine cannot be regarded as an occupied area, and, moreover, since the German troops went into that country on the Ukrainian government's invitation and remained there with its consent, as far as the international law is concerned the Military Command in Kiev has no right to demand from the Ukrainian government that it oust Allied representatives, as long as these confine themselves to the defense of interests of their respective nationals. On the other hand, Germany is to be regarded at this moment as a protector [*Schutzmacht*] of the Ukraine and will not, therefore, tolerate any political activities of enemy consuls which may undermine the Reich's position in this area. Necessary measures would have to be taken by the German Army Command East in the Ukraine in the event of the Hetman regime's failure to control political activities of Allied consuls on its territory." [93]

The Austrians followed the German example in this delicate matter, and soon the ban on Allied personnel was extended to include everybody possessing Allied citizenship.[94] It was not until October, 1918, that the Germans openly stated that they had no objection to the Ukraine's establishing diplomatic ties with the Allies.

Germany placed no restrictions on the Ukraine's relations with neutral states. Besides the Central Powers, Spain and Holland recognized the Ukraine. Switzerland did not go so far as to recognize the Ukrainian state but had no objection to Kiev's opening consular offices in Geneva and Zurich. Persia and Denmark opened negotiations with Kiev concerning the establishment of normal diplomatic relations, and Sweden promised to review the problem following the conclusion of a general peace treaty. The four Central Powers had a number of consular offices throughout the Ukraine, and so did the following countries (mostly in Kiev and Odessa): Sweden, Switzerland, Norway, Italy, Denmark, Greece, and Estonia. Also, the Ukraine maintained limited diplomatic and consular ties with the Don, Byelorussia, the Caucasus, Rumania, and the Soviet Russian Republic.[95]

On balance, all these ties provided little advantage to Kiev but had a potential value for the development of Ukrainian statehood in the future. The presence of the German and Austrian troops in the country and the Reich's political hegemony in the east as a whole remained the decisive factors in both foreign and domestic affairs of the Ukraine throughout the year 1918.

CHAPTER IX

Economic Exploitation of the Ukraine:
A Balance Sheet

The establishment of the Hetmanate did not produce any immediate basic changes in Berlin's economic policies for the Ukraine. The new Ukrainian government solemnly promised to honor all economic commitments undertaken by its predecessor, enormous though they were, and the Germans did not press for additional concessions; they merely expected the new Kiev regime to be more cooperative and more obedient than the Rada.

Although the Germans and the Austrians resumed economic talks with the Ukrainians immediately after the coup,[1] the economic exploitation of the country was to proceed according to previous agreements, among which the economic convention of April 23, 1918, was most important. True, one of the conditions to which General Skoropadsky agreed before taking over the government was that it grant Germany a free hand in trade and raw materials procurement as well as control over the Ukraine's finances;[2] however, such had been the practice in the Rada period and its continuation was not to bring about any real improvement in Germany's economic position in the Ukraine.

It was mainly through various direct measures and the initiative of their local military commanders that the Germans were able to continue the collection of food and other materials in the

Ukraine. Although additional economic restrictions were eventually imposed on the Hetman government, in most cases they proved either unnecessary or ineffectual and are of interest mainly as indices of German intentions and plans. Among these restrictions was one curtailing the activities of Ukrainian grain cooperatives, to guard against undermining the position of the Central Powers' grain purchasing centers in the Ukraine.[3] In addition, the Germans forbade the export of grain and other foodstuffs to neutral countries, and imposed a similar restriction on Ukrainian-Soviet, and even Ukrainian-Georgian, trade relations.[4] The Germans, no doubt, might have imposed similar restrictions on the Rada, but in neither case were such measures really needed, since Kühlmann himself pointed out that the Germans had such complete control over the Ukraine's transportation system that it would have been impossible for the Kiev government to undertake any independent economic action detrimental to the Reich's interests.[5] The Germans were determined to maintain this control at all costs and, anticipating a strike of railroad workers following the Hetman's coup, prepared a special order to cope with such a contingency. By this order the Germans declared the destruction of railroad installations to be punishable by death, and they threatened to invoke other severe measures to insure the smooth operation of the railroads.[6] Again, it is reasonably certain that the Germans would have taken similar measures during the Rada period had there been need for such action.

The strengthening of German control over the Ukraine's finances also had its beginnings during the Rada period. On April 26, virtually in the last hours of the Rada's existence, a special agreement was concluded providing for the printing of Ukrainian currency in Germany.[7] Two weeks later another financial agreement was signed in Kiev with Germany and Austria-Hungary establishing the ratios between the Ukrainian currency and the German and Austrian currencies (1.33 marks or 2 crowns for 1 karbovanets), and providing for a 400-million karbovanets loan to the Ukrainian government, one-half to be furnished in marks and the other half in crowns, in order to facilitate Kiev's business transactions with the two Central Powers.[8] The Ukrainian currency, although it theoretically had a rather high value, was really a worthless paper money. The old rubles continued to be popular, but they were hard to get, and German marks and Austrian crowns were viewed locally with great suspicion; hence, these financial agreements did little to stimulate healthy trade relations in the country.

The Germans and the Austrians continued to rely on direct requisitioning for food procurement, although this technique was recognized to be rather ineffective and resulted in the burning of grain and open armed resistance by the Ukrainian peasantry.[9] Another widely used device, employed by both Germany and Austria-Hungary, was the seizure of military supply centers and depots, as well as warehouses, plants, and drydocks, and even the dismantling of certain rail lines on the excuse of confiscating war booty. Although it was not until mid-May that Field Marshal Eichhorn officially declared such property to be German war booty, and not until mid-August that a special agreement was signed between the Ukrainian government and the two occupying powers on the division of such materials, the Germans and Austrians helped themelves freely to whatever supplies they could lay their hands on from the moment they moved into the country.[10]

The establishment of the Hetmanate revived German hopes for obtaining manpower from the Ukraine, although several months earlier, during the Brest-Litovsk negotiations, the Rada representatives had made it clear that there was no Ukrainian labor surplus. Shortly after the coup Ludendorff declared: "I need men for the army and the home front to bring relief to our war economy. Until now Germany has worked for others, now others will have to work for it. I have in mind the occupied areas, above all the Ukraine." [11] Such hopes, however, proved as illusory as the expectation of relieving the Reich's manpower shortage by drafting German colonists in the east.

Food procurement in the Ukraine continued to dominate German economic thinking. The Germans were constantly torn between satisfying their immediate economic requirements, which, in their view, were being only partially fulfilled, and pursuing long-range plans, which were being thwarted because of the ruthless methods they employed in food collection. The result was failure on both counts, and this was reflected in the constantly rising peasant unrest, disorganization and strikes, in both industry and transportation, and a growing general hostility toward the Germans and Austrians as well as the Hetman government, which they continued to support.

According to a Ukrainian source, some 30,000 German and Austrian soldiers died in the Ukraine during the occupation period in the struggle against local guerrillas; Ukrainian losses, both killed in action and executed, are put at 50,000.[12] The losses of the occupying troops were serious enough to prompt the Austrian Command of the *Ostarmee* to suggest at one point to the German Supreme Command that the Ukrainian government [sic] be fined for all the individual killings of the Central Powers' personnel stationed in the country at the following rate: 200,000 rubles for a general; 150,000 for a staff officer; 100,000 for an officer; and 50,000 for a common soldier. The German Consul General in Kiev, Erich von Thiel, urged the rejection of such a plan on political and legal grounds.[13]

Both the Germans and the Austrians failed to utilize Ukrainian industrial potential for war purposes, except for outright confiscation and the dismantling of certain plants for shipment home. Thus, many factories remained closed, and those that did operate, did so on a limited basis only. According to a reliable Ukrainian source, the number of unemployed during the Rada period was about 200,000.[14] This is probably a rather conservative estimate because of incomplete reporting; the plight of the industrial workers in the Ukraine was a desperate one and no doubt further contributed to the widespread anti-German feeling in the country.

The transport workers, especially the railroadmen, were much better off, since throughout the occupation period the Germans in their own interest did all they could to insure efficient operation of trains and were therefore ready to meet the workers' economic demands. Nevertheless, in mid-July, the same people who several months earlier had done so much to facilitate the movement of German troops against the Bolsheviks in the Ukraine, declared a countrywide strike. The strike, more political than economic in nature, was a fiasco. The Germans anticipated it for weeks and were well prepared for it. Consequently, enough trains remained running to make the strike ineffectual. Arrests and other repressive measures soon broke the back of this anti-German movement, although sabotage and other hostile acts were frequent, and additional troops were needed to prevent the Ukraine's rail lines from being cut.

The failure of the Central Powers to obtain the amount of food they expected from the Ukraine cost the Rada its life. After the establishment of the Hetmanate Ludendorff urged a "new approach": "In the face of our deteriorating food situation [at home] we must quickly bring more order in the Black Sea area. Immediate relief can be obtained only by force of arms. Negotiations mean only more lost time. . . ."[15] This was essentially what the Austrians and the Germans had been striving for some time in the Ukraine. In mid-May, Austria-Hungary made an effort to militarize the economic exploitation in its zone. General Krauss was appointed "dictator of the Ukraine," but this, too, failed to improve the situation and the experiment was abandoned almost as soon as it had been launched. The Germans, always rather suspicious of Austria's aims in the Ukraine, had a great deal to do with Vienna's abandonment of this experiment.[16]

By mid-June, according to official German estimates, a total of only about 90,000 metric tons of various food products had been shipped from the Ukraine to the Central Powers. (This was equivalent to roughly 4,500 carloads, estimated at 20 tons per car.) Of the 50,000 tons of food supplies shipped via frontier points and the port of Braila, 13,000 tons went to Germany, and Austria-Hungary received 37,000 tons.[17] According to an authoritative Austrian source, the amount of food obtained from the Ukraine up to the middle of April, that is, during the entire Rada period, was approximately 1,600 carloads, or about 32,000 tons.[18] There was thus a marked improvement in the collection and shipment of food from the Ukraine following the installation of the Skoropadsky regime. Also, substantial quantities of food were shipped without any official supervision, but such figures are unavailable.

In subsequent months the situation improved but little. It was not until July, 1918, that the Ukrainian Foodstuffs and Ukrainian Provisions councils were organized, composed of German, Austro-Hungarian, and Ukrainian officials. The two central councils had offices in most of the large cities and district centers. The policy was to employ purchasing and barter methods; but in the event these failed to produce the desired results, harsher methods were to be resorted to with the assistance of the occupation forces. This new organization began in late August, but because of insufficient cooperation on the part of Ukrainian officials and the necessity of satisfying the most important local needs (for example, feeding the occupation armies and sending at least minimal supplies to the Ukrainian cities and industrial centers), very little food was available for shipment to Germany and Austria, and the new arrangements proved almost as ineffective as the earlier ones.[19]

The German failure to organize an effective food collection system in the Ukraine soon became apparent both at home and abroad. Thus, when the Soviet representative in Berlin, Adolf Joffe, proposed in early July that his government be entrusted with the procurement of grain from the Ukraine for both Germany and Russia, such responsible German spokesmen as Gustav Stresemann thought that a suggestion of this nature merited serious consideration.[20] Discussing the Reich's propaganda program in mid-August, 1918, the Permanent Secretary of State, Erhard Deutelmoser, concluded that no one at home would any longer believe in the German propaganda. "The population," said he, "has been disappointed in the following expectations: (1) the submarine warfare; (2) the western offensive; (3) promise of additional food from the Ukraine and other benefits of the so-called eastern peace." [21]

Another important factor in the Austro-German failure to obtain food from the Ukraine was the inability of the occupying countries to reciprocate with manufactured goods. The Central Powers could deliver farming machinery and tools. Textiles, leather goods, paper, and a number of other items promised to the Ukrainians earlier were unavailable. At first the occupation forces were given agricultural tools and other small items of everyday use, with the order to exchange them for foodstuffs. Since the troops had many other duties and were not numerous enough to reach every village, this device produced but meager results. It was not until early September that the manufactured goods were transferred to the Ukrainian-German-Austrian-Hungarian Food Purchasing commissions. Independent private merchants were more successful in such transactions. Those who brought their own manufactured goods into the Ukraine had no difficulty persuading the Ukrainian peasant to sell his surplus grain stocks.[22] At this stage, the Austrians were especially successful in utilizing individual tradesmen, mostly Jewish grain dealers, in such direct trading. The Germans preferred to rely on requisitioning and compulsory delivery quotas as their principal procurement methods.[23]

It is not easy to arrive at an exact figure of the total Ukrainian food deliveries to Germany and Austria-Hungary for the entire occupation period (March-November 1918). Whereas certain figures are likely to be fairly accurate, others are only rough estimates; still others are not available. According to an authoritative Austrian source, total food deliveries from the Ukraine amounted to 42,000 carloads. This was roughly equivalent to 840,000 metric tons, at 20 tons per car. Of the total 42,000 carloads, 30,757 were handled officially; the rest were smuggled. The smuggled supplies included 4,622 cars of grain and meal.[24] Czernin, who had a great deal to do with making the deliveries possible, cites somewhat higher figures: 113,421 tons of grain, flour, and other products (Austria's share being 57,382 tons); 30,757 carloads of cattle, meat, fats, sugar, etc. (Austria's share being 13,037 carloads); 15,000 carloads of various food items smuggled without official permission (Austria's share not given).[25] By Czernin's calculations, the total was about 51,428 carloads, or 1,028,560 tons.

As to smuggling, unreported stealing, and unauthorized confiscations, for which no exact figures exist, quantities of food were sent home in individual parcels. So widespread was this practice among both German and Austrian occupation forces that, according to an Austrian source, special sawmills and carpenter shops had to be set up in the Ukraine to manufacture "countless boxes" for military personnel who sent food parcels home. The same source estimated that from June until the end of the occupation in November approximately ten carloads of such packages were dispatched to Austria-Hungary every day.[26] This implies a total of 1,800 cars, or something like 36,000 tons of food. If the number of parcels sent in the earlier period of the occupation (February-May) could be calculated in the same manner, the grand total for the Austrians would, indeed, be impressive. Comparable German figures are not available, but it can safely be assumed that they greatly exceeded the Austrian figure of perhaps as many as 2,500 carloads (or 50,000 tons) of miscellaneous food items sent home on the soldiers' private initiative.

In any event, the total amount of food taken out of the Ukraine must have been even higher than the figure supplied by Count Czernin (although one could suspect him of an upward bias in order to justify his "bread peace"). Possibly as many as 75,000 carloads (or approximately 1.5 million tons) of various food-stuffs were taken out of the country by official and unofficial means during the entire period of Austro-German occupation.

Although the Germans were constantly suspicious of the Dual Monarchy's intentions in the Ukraine and General Krauss was advised to establish the basis for close Austro-Ukrainian economic relations in the future,[27] Austria-Hungary never went beyond the procurement of food supplies from its zone and was in no position to establish a permanent economic foothold in the country. Granted that there were Austrians who toyed with the idea of putting a member of the Habsburg House on the Ukrainian throne, the responsible officials, as for example General Krauss, were quick to admit Austria's weak position in the Ukraine and to reconcile themselves to the fact that the Dual Monarchy had no choice but to follow the German leadership and accede in all the Reich's undertakings in the east.[28]

The Germans, on the other hand, while also stressing immediate economic exploitation of the Ukraine for war purposes, displayed great interest in the prospect of developing permanent close economic relations between the two countries. This was especially true of various nonmilitary agencies, and the overthrow of the Rada regime seems to have stimulated such thinking. Take, for example, the message sent by Under-Secretary of State von dem Bussche to Ambassador Mumm on April 30, 1918, only hours after General Skoropadsky's coup d'état. In his view not only was the Ukraine to fulfill the economic obligations to Germany that it had undertaken at Brest-Litovsk and in subsequent economic talks, but its economy was to be closely associated with that of the Reich in the future. Bussche visualized an important role for German capital and skilled labor in the Ukraine's economic growth, such growth to be marked by the establishment of a dense transportation network, further development of the industrial potential, and, last but not least, modernization and intensification of agricultural production. All, however, was to have the appearance of a purely Ukrainian national undertaking.[29] Mumm, too, urged the taking of a long-range view of Germany's economic position in the Ukraine: "I presume that we do not plan a one-time 'stripping' of the Ukraine like that of Belgium, but instead will want to develop a permanent German economic influence in the country. In order to accomplish this, we must replace military methods by civilian methods in our economic relations with the Ukrainians." [30]

General Ludendorff also advocated the promotion of German economic domination over the Ukraine, to include the exploitation of its manpower;[31] but whereas he thought primarily in terms of winning the war, Secretary of State for Foreign Affairs Kühlmann, who held a similar view, maintained that such domination should be extended into the postwar period. Kühlmann, therefore, extracted from the Ukraine a promise not to make any food deliveries to the neutrals until its commitments to the Central Powers had been met. Moreover, he instructed Mumm to extract from the Ukrainian government a promise to abide by such restrictions in the future. An even more burdensome restriction was imposed on the Ukraine in its economic relations with Soviet Russia. Kiev was not to export anything to Russia without German approval, and any imports from the Soviet state were to be shared with the Reich.[32]

An even more important role in the development of the Reich's long-range economic plans in the Ukraine was played by the two top German economic and financial experts in Kiev, Wiedfeldt and Melchior. Other high-ranking German officials who worked toward permanent German economic domination in the Ukraine were the Minister of the National Economy, Baron von Stein, the Prussian War Minister, Hermann von Stein, and Under-Secretary of State for Foreign Affairs von dem Bussche. That Otto Wiedfeldt was the principal architect of these programs cannot be denied. Fischer, however, who has studied them more thoroughly than any other student of the period, seems to ascribe too much importance to the plans that this German industrialist and others like him drew for the Ukraine and the east as a whole.[33] These plans never fully crystallized and had a limited bearing on the Reich's economic policies in the Ukraine during the period of the occupation.

The most serious German effort aiming at the establishment of a permanent economic preponderance in the Ukraine was made in the field of transportation, especially the railways. In other fields the gains were not very impressive. On April 18, shortly before the overthrow of the Rada, a German-Ukrainian iron ore syndicate (*Eisenertzgesellschaft*) was organized on Wiedfeldt's recommendation;[34] and following General Skoropadsky's take-over, a month or so later, fifteen leading industrial magnates of Germany met at Stahlhoff near Düsseldorf to discuss ways and means of establishing economic and financial domination of the east, especially the Ukraine and Russia.[35] Then on June 4, a high-level conference of German government officials and representatives of such leading industrial and financial firms as Krupp, Stinnes, Warburg, and Die Deutsche Bank took place in Berlin, chaired by Baron von Stein, Secretary of State for Economic Affairs. The outcome was a decision to organize two financial syndicates, one for the Ukraine and one for Russia.[36] Somewhat later, toward the end of August, the Germans explored the possibility of developing machine tool industries in the Ukraine;[37] and at one point they planned to establish air lines between Germany and Turkey via Odessa and were determined to prevent the Ukrainians from competing with them in this enterprise.[38] Nothing came of these schemes, and German economic policies in the Ukraine continued to concentrate on the task of alleviating the serious food situation at home. Yet, later on, people like General Ludendorff, who gave full backing to all these designs, quite unjustly accused the Ministry of National Economy of having followed a long-range peace economy policy instead of a short-range war economy policy in the Ukraine.[39]

In fact, it was nothing but a war economy policy until the very end, and this the Germans planned to continue well into 1919, as is evident from the September 10, 1918 economic agreement—the last one to be concluded between Germany and Austria-Hungary on the one hand and the Ukraine on the other. According to this agreement, 35 percent of the available grain supplies was to be exported to the two Central Powers and the remaining 65 percent was designated for home consumption. Collection was to be left exclusively in the hands of a Ukrainian Grain Control Office, and requisitioning of food by the troops of the Central Powers was to cease. To insure sufficient German and Austrian voice in this operation, German and Austro-Hungarian officials were to be permanently seated on a Ukrainian Food Control Council. In addition to the commitment to supply the Central Powers with more than one-third of its grain, the Ukraine granted Germany and Austria the right to "free export" of other foodstuffs and raw materials. (These included 11,200 carloads of timber,

620 carloads (750,000 poods) of hemp, 300,000 hides, 700,000 calfskins and sheepskins, and 205 carloads (250,000 poods) of tobacco.[40] The Central Powers were also to be free to purchase sugar, alcohol, and many other items in the Ukraine. In return for all this, Germany promised to supply 2,545 carloads (3 million poods) of coal per month, and Austria-Hungary "certain quantities of fuel oil." [41] Even though these fuels were to be used in large measure for the shipment of Ukrainian supplies to the Central Powers, the promises were soon forgotten and Ukrainian economic relations with the two countries came to resemble more and more those between a colonial power and its dependency.

Along with the economic agreement of September 10, a new financial arrangement was concluded between the two Central Powers and the Ukraine. The ratios between the Ukrainian currency and the German and Austrian currencies remained unchanged. The Ukrainians were promised assistance in carrying out a monetary reform. In the meantime, however, the Germans were to print an additional 5.75 million karbovanets in the government printing press in Berlin; of this sum 1.6 million karbovanets were to remain in German hands. The Germans promised to furnish the Ukrainian government with a corresponding supply of marks and crowns, but this money could not be used by Kiev to purchase German and Austrian goods until one year after the conclusion of a general peace.[42] Although these September, 1918, agreements did not specifically provide for implementation of the various long-range plans so carefully developed by Wiedfeldt with the assistance of the Reich's leading industrial and financial circles, they went a long way toward assuring Germany of a commanding economic position in the Ukraine, at least in the immediate postwar period, provided that the Reich's power should remain the dominant political factor in the east.

CHAPTER X

German Plans and Policies in the Crimea and the Black Sea Basin

Apart from the Ukraine's economic significance for Germany's war effort and postwar reconstruction—especially in view of the almost certain loss of German colonies—its central location on the Black Sea coast afforded the Reich a gateway to the Near and Middle East. Even though officially no comprehensive and clearly formulated program for Germany's long-range involvement in the east had ever been drawn, powerful industrial and financial groups of the Reich drew grandiose paper plans for the economic penetration and domination of the Ukraine and other areas of the east. Some German writers in 1918 went so far as to suggest exploitation of all Russian Asia, including Siberia and the Far East;[1] however, the more realistic or moderate ones among them thought rather in terms of the Near East and India.[2]

Most official German spokesmen were inclined to the second school of thought. With the outbreak of World War I, the Germans studied and supported national and revolutionary movements of the Caucasus with almost the same degree of interest they had displayed in the Ukraine. In late 1917 the German Foreign Office expressed its happiness over the growth of national movements among the Mohammedans of the Caucasus, referring to it as a "useful development." [3] The German military were more explicit in their advocacy of a thrust into the Persian Gulf area and then into India. Ludendorff devoted some attention to such schemes shortly after the conclusion of the Treaty of Brest-Litovsk.[4] Groener and Eichhorn are also reported to have regarded the Ukraine as a road to the Near East and India.[5]

Such schemes were by no means confined to mere planning. In June, 1918, shortly after Georgia proclaimed its independence, a German expeditionary force landed in Batum in order to prevent the extension of Turkish domination into Russian Transcaucasia. German policy in the Crimea, which aimed at eliminating both Turkish and Austrian influence, Berlin's refusal to agree to the transfer of this area to the Ukraine, and the Reich's treatment of the entire Black Sea question are all suggestive of Germany's long-range objectives in the Near and Middle East.

Unlike the Ukraine, the Crimea was a "mixed territory" with a rather complex national composition. According to the all-Russian census of 1897, the total population of the Crimea in that year was 564,592, of which 35.1 percent were Tatars.[6] In 1916 the Germans prepared their own figures based on earlier Russian data. They placed the total population at 713,370. Tatars constituted 35.1 percent (250,240); Russians 32.8 percent (233,990); Ukrainians 11.7 percent (83,835); Germans 6.0 percent (42,990); others 14.4 percent (102,315).[7] These figures are fairly accurate, except for an almost certain inflation of the number of Russians at the expense of the Ukrainians and other Slavs.

Like virtually every other part of the former Russian Empire, the Crimea was drawn into the revolutionary whirlwind of 1917; however, its small size, the heterogeneous character of its population, and its somewhat isolated position (a peninsula behind the front lines, removed from revolutionary centers of the north, and separated from other Tatar territories by the Ukraine) all contributed to its being left out of the mainstream of revolutionary and political developments in the east. The Crimea had no representation at Brest-Litovsk and, indeed, the future of this area was not dealt with at this conference as a separate problem, in spite of the fact that the conclusion of a peace treaty between the Central Powers and the Ukraine on February 9, 1918, cut off the Crimean Peninsula from the rest of the former Russian Empire.

It may be noted at this point that from late January almost to the end of April, 1918, the Crimea was under Bolshevik rule. It must have been at least partly owing to this fact that the future status of the Peninsula was not discussed with the Ukrainians during the peace negotiations at Brest. Even more significant, however, was the Rada's strict interpretation of the principle of self-determination; Hrushevsky and other Rada leaders felt that only "purely Ukrainian territories" should be included in the Ukrainian state. Ukrainian-Tatar relations were thus quite friendly during the first revolutionary year and could be expected to grow even friendlier in the future.[8]

German Foreign Office archives did not yield any evidence of concrete German plans for the Crimea in the period of the Brest-Litovsk negotiations. The Turks, although vitally interested in all Black Sea questions, especially the fate of the Russian fleet, did not at first regard the Crimea as an important separate problem; nor did they advocate any specific solution for it.[9]

In one of his earliest pronouncements on the general Black Sea problem, made in the Main Committee of the Reichstag in his second appearance before it on February 20, 1918, Foreign Secretary Kühlmann voiced the hope for a favorable solution of the Straits question "from the German point of view." He was convinced that in the future the Black Sea policy would be "predominantly Ukrainian," and that the Dardanelles question would definitely be settled between Turkey and the newly founded Ukrainian state.[10] General Ludendorff, too, dealt with the over-all Black Sea problem about this time. While omitting a direct reference to the Crimea, the general made it clear that Turkish territorial ambitions should be directed to the east and that their influence might be extended as far as Central Asia.[11] Thus, Ludendorff implied that the Porte should not be encouraged to strengthen its position in the Balkans and on the northern Black Sea coast.

The Foreign Office, on the whole, was rather ill-prepared to deal with the Crimean question and showed little imagination in developing a positive German policy for that area. Consequently, the German Ambassador in Kiev, Baron Mumm, instead of receiving specific instructions concerning German plans for the Peninsula, was advised by the Foreign Office on March 25 of the Turkish press campaign demanding the right of self-determination for the Crimean Tatars in order to pave the way for eventual union with Turkey. Mumm was asked to determine whether such was the wish of the Crimean Tatars, since, according to the latest information received from that area, the sentiment was, supposedly, for a federal tie with the Ukraine.[12] Kühlmann, then still in Rumania, was just as vague concerning Germany's plans for the strategically important Peninsula. In his view, there was no basis for German opposition to the formation of an independent Crimean state, provided this was the express wish of its population. A Ukrainian-Crimean boundary line was to be agreed upon by the two interested parties. At the same time, however, Kühlmann did not preclude the possibility of extending German occupation into this area, regarding it as a purely military problem to be solved by the Supreme Army Command.[13]

The German military plenipotentiary in Kiev, Colonel Stolzenberg, nevertheless believed his country to have far-reaching political aims in the Crimea. One of these aims was supposedly the establishment of a new link with Persia. Mumm, in reporting this to the Foreign Office, voiced no opposition to such a plan for German hegemony in the Black Sea with the Crimea as its principal base. On the contrary, he was quick to remind the Foreign Office that the Ukraine could have no objection to such schemes, since its representatives at Brest openly declared their *désintéressement* in the Peninsula.[14]

The German decision to extend military domination to the Crimea was arrived at as early as March 21, 1918, and General Kosch was ordered to prepare his corps for an advance into the Peninsula. The Austrian Supreme Command promptly gave its approval to the plan, since it involved an area essentially within the Dual Monarchy's sphere of influence in the east. Mumm and Stolzenberg were asked to inform the Ukrainian government above the move, so that there would be no interference. At the same time General Ludendorff requested the Foreign Office to make necessary preparations to facilitate the task.[15] The entire venture, however, remained politically ill-prepared.

Initially, the Turks, responding to the Tatar appeal for assistance, suggested that one of their divisions be allowed to participate in the occupation of the Crimea. The German Ambassador to Constantinople, Count Johann von Bernstorff, who was asked to convey this wish to his government, was quick to warn Berlin that this would greatly strengthen the Turkish position in the Peninsula and the Black Sea area as a whole.[16] Several days later the Turks volunteered to cut the size of the expeditionary force to be dispatched to the Crimea to "a regiment and some officers." Ambassador Bernstorff opposed this, too, and warned his government that Turkish participation in the occupation of the Crimea, regardless of the size of the expeditionary force might result in a union between the Crimea and the Ottoman Empire.[17]

In the view of the German Foreign Office, a Bolshevik-controlled Crimea simply could not be tolerated after the decision to support an independent Ukraine had been made. Turkish annexation of the Peninsula, on the other hand, would also create complications. Under-Secretary of State von dem Bussche, therefore, favored the establishment of an independent or autonomous Crimea with close ties to the Ukraine. Such a solution, he argued, would facilitate the extension of German rule into the Crimea without openly violating the Russian Treaty of Brest-Litovsk. To avoid an open breach with the Bolsheviks, Bussche advocated the employment of Moslem troops (former Czarist soldiers mostly of Tatar nationality) who were also to be supported by certain Ukrainian units. It was his contention that direct German participation in the occupation of the Peninsula would be possible only after German recognition of the Tatar state.[18]

General Ludendorff took a different view of the situation and on April 5 declared the German occupation of the Crimea to be a military as well as a political and economic necessity. He saw no legal complications in the plan, arguing that since the pro-Bolshevik naval forces stationed in Sevastopol had attacked German troops in Kherson, the Central Powers should feel free to take the necessary measures to prevent repetition of such attacks in the future. Ludendorff also felt it was essential to seize various supplies stored in the Crimea, to gain control of its ports, and, finally, to furnish the necessary protection to German colonists residing in the area (even though they constituted but 6 percent of the Crimea's population). The job was to be done by German troops under the command of General Kosch. A Moslem corps commanded by former Czarist General Suleiman Sulkevich was also to take part in this operation; Austrian and Ukrainian consent to its free transfer to the Crimea had been secured beforehand.[19] Sulkevich, who was eventually to play the role of "the Crimean Skoropadsky," was born near Minsk in Byelorussia and was the descendant of Lithuanian Tatars. Having attained the rank of lieutenant general in the Russian Imperial Army during World

War I, he commanded the Thirty-Third Infantry Division, and after the March Revolution headed a Moslem corps which he helped to organize on the Rumanian front.

Ludendorff was even willing to allow Turkey to join in the anti-Bolshevik campaign in the Crimea. He seemed unconcerned at this point about the ultimate fate of the Peninsula, that is, whether it would become a Turkish province or develop into an independent Tatar republic; he did not even mention the possibility of a union with the Ukraine. He was inclined to support the Turkish solution, suggesting that in the event of Turkey's loss of Mesopotamia and Palestine, a development which he termed a "likely possibility," the Crimea would be the most convenient area to compensate the Porte for such territorial losses.[20]

German Foreign Office spokesmen, however, continued to oppose Turkish involvement in the Crimea, fearing the development of a Ukrainian-Turkish conflict. They again argued that neither a Soviet nor a White Russian Crimea could be tolerated and, by urging Ukrainian participation in the occupation of the Peninsula, made it clear that they would rather see it in close association or even in union with Kiev.[21] General Ludendorff reserved the right to return to the question of the political future of the Crimea later and viewed the proposed extension of German control to the Peninsula as primarily a military measure. At the same time, however, he was brought closer to the Foreign Office's thinking concerning Turkish participation in the occupation, agreeing that a Turkish force might be employed more usefully in the Caucasus and recommending that the Porte's ambitions in this area be clearly ascertained.[22]

A few days later, on April 19, the German advance into the Crimea began, with the participation of a Ukrainian brigade under the command of General Natiev.[23] It was not until early May that General Sulkevich was permitted to bring the remnants of the Moslem corps to the Crimea, too late to take part in its liberation.[24] Neither did Turkish troops participate in this undertaking. Moreover, General Ludendorff asked the Porte for the assurance that it would not pursue any political designs in the Peninsula.[25]

Ukrainian participation in the occupation of the Crimea did not, however, mean that Berlin and Kiev had arrived at an agreement concerning the future of the Peninsula. Being aware of the confusion and uncertainty in the Reich's plans for the Crimea and having learned of the German decision to occupy it, the Ukrainians simply decided to take advantage of the situation and to move into this area, too, in order to establish a better claim to the Black Sea fleet stationed in the Crimean ports and to seize at least some of the valuable military supplies there.[26] It was not until after several days of "joint" German-Ukrainian operations in the Crimea and a Ukrainian attempt to enter Sevastopol (before the Germans could do so) that General Natiev's brigade was ordered to halt its advance.[27] A week later this Ukrainian force was recalled from the Crimea. It is interesting to note that the German Foreign Office and Ambassador Mumm had nothing to do with this decision. The withdrawal of the Ukrainian brigade from the Crimea was ordered by the Rada War Ministry as a result of repeated and vehement protests made by the German military plenipotentiary in the Ukraine, Colonel Stolzenberg.[28]

The German Foreign Office, in the meantime, became panicky and went so far as to attempt to halt the advance of German troops into the Crimea by enlisting the cooperation of the naval headquarters. The Foreign Office feared further straining of German-Soviet relations and the growth of anti-German feeling in Russia. Perceiving, however, that General Ludendorff could not be deterred from going through with his plan, and admitting that his aim was to secure routes into Central Asia so as to gain control over this area's raw materials, the Foreign Office, although it referred to these plans as "Napoleonic," agreed that such sweeping designs would be fully justified in the event of a prolonged conflict with Great Britain.

As far as Soviet Russia was concerned, Germany could grant it a "share" in oil and metals from the Caucasus and cotton from Turkestan.[29] This, of course, did not satisfy Moscow, and Georgii V. Chicherin, the Soviet Commissar for Foreign Affairs, continued to voice strong protests against the German occupation of the Crimea; these the Germans simply ignored.[30]

The elimination of Turkey and the Ukraine as partners in Germany's Crimean undertaking did not mean that the Reich had decided to support the Tatar national movement. True, this movement was not to be interfered with, but the final solution of the Crimean question was to be worked out in cooperation with both Russia and the Ukraine. This view was held by Ludendorff as well as Kühlmann.[31] At this point the Turks became rather alarmed at the thought of the Crimea being united with the Ukraine and requested that it be made into an independent state.[32] Although animated by different considerations, both Ludendorff and Kühlmann agreed on "some kind of an independent Tatar state now," [33] which meant that no one would be allowed to interfere with German control of this strategically significant Black Sea peninsula.

In the meantime, the new Ukrainian government, now headed by General Skoropadsky, reopened its drive to annex the Peninsula. The claim was based on the "economic and maritime necessities" of the Ukrainian state. Mumm, to whom the request had been made, was inclined to recommend the support of Ukrainian aspirations, maintaining that a German promise to transfer the Crimea to the Ukraine would greatly facilitate Berlin's dealings with Kiev in the future. Mumm apparently felt rather strongly about his recommendation and hastened to add further arguments in its support. He pointed out that German demands for further economic concessions in the Ukraine were "most far-reaching" and that they could be won only through further application of force. To avoid this, Mumm urged the establishment of German "credit" with the Ukrainians by granting them concessions in the Crimea.[34]

Although the commander of the German forces in the Crimea, General Kosch, maintained friendly contacts with the Crimean Tatars in the early days of the occupation and even attended the reopening of the Tatar National Assembly, the Kurultai, on May 8, 1918, to declare German support of its efforts to establish an administration in the Crimea,[35] this did not mean that Berlin was ready to allow the Porte to play a more active political role in the Peninsula. The German position was made abundantly clear when Djemal Pasha, Turkish Secretary of the Navy, planned to visit the principal Crimean port of Sevastopol on a Turkish man-of-war in early May, 1918. Fearing that he might be welcomed by the Crimean Tatars as their "victor-liberator"—which would have embarrassed the Germans and could have generated unwarranted hopes among the local nationalists—orders were given to receive this Turkish dignitary "as if he were in a German port" and thus prevent his interference in Crimean affairs.[36] A brief detention of the Tatar leader, Dzhafer Seidahmet, by the Germans upon his return from Turkey in mid-May[37] was also occasioned by their suspicion of Turkish designs for the Crimea. His quick release was to underscore the fact that the Germans had, as yet, no definite plans for the Peninsula, and would merely confine themselves to keeping others out of it.

The Spa conference of May 11 between Germany's top military and civilian leaders did little to bring more clarity into the Reich's Crimean venture. It was merely agreed that the future of the Peninsula would be determined at a later time, and that in the meantime "purely German interests should guide the Reich's policies in the Crimea." [38] Ludendorff, however, seemed most determined in his opposition to the Ukraine's claim to the Crimea, pointing out that originally no such claim had been made by Kiev. He then urged the Foreign Office to instruct Ambassador Mumm to advise the Ukrainians that the annexation of the Crimea was "out of the question." [39] In the meantime, Mumm continued to oppose the idea of a German protectorate over an "independent" Crimea, even after Major Brinckmann's assurance that this was to be only a temporary arrangement. General Groener, too, favored an early transfer of the Peninsula to the Ukraine, but, like Mumm, would not openly fight for it.[40]

General Ludendorff, however, was to modify his anti-Ukrainian stand in the Crimean question after he had been convinced that the Crimea could not survive unless it established close ties with one of the larger states in the area. Ruling out Great Russia, Ludendorff felt that the Crimea should in the future be linked to the Ukraine. The general made this contingent upon the cooperation of the Ukrainian government in meeting various German demands, both in the Ukraine and the Crimea, especially in the economic sphere and in problems concerning the safety and well-being of German settlers in the east.[41]

The German Foreign Office was in full accord with this plan[42] (which in effect echoed its previous recommendations), and this approach continued to dominate its thinking during the remainder of the occupation period. General Ludendorff and certain colonial circles, in the meantime, developed new ideas and again urged the establishment of a German stronghold in the Crimea.

The future of the Germans settlers or colonists in the Black Sea area constituted an important aspect of Germany's Crimean policy as well as of its over-all long-range plans in the east during

World War I. According to an official German source, there were approximately 1.5 million German colonists on the territory of the former Russian Empire (not counting Poland and the Baltic provinces). Most were farmers residing in prosperous agricultural settlements, of which there were roughly 2,000. There were approximately 450,000 Volga Germans (Saratov and Samara provinces); 650,000 Black Sea Germans (provinces of Bessarabia, Kherson, Ekaterinoslav, Kharkov, Taurida with the Crimea, and the regions of the Don, Kuban, and Terek); 250,000 German settlers in Volhynia (this figure is definitely exaggerated); and 150,000 Germans in the Urals, Siberia, and Central Asia.[43] It is interesting to note that the Black Sea Germans lived in widely scattered settlements stretching from the Terek to the Danube. Moreover, German colonists in the Crimea, constituting only 6 percent of the Peninsula's population (the exact figure being 42,990),[44] represented less than 3 percent of the total number of Germans residing in the east as a whole. German settlers began to move into the Crimea following its annexation by Russia in 1783; at the outbreak of World War I they and their descendants were well established in that area but still retained their ethnic identity. The same can be said of other Germans in the east. The majority of them had been born in the areas in which they resided and they had few ties with the land of their forefathers. Nor did the Reich Germans care much about the fate of their brethren in Russia. On the whole, Germany was more interested in its overseas colonies than in settlers of German origin in the east.

The problem of organizing German settlers in the Ukraine and other areas of the east was never discussed during the Brest-Litovsk peace negotiations, an omission that produced widespread disappointment among the settlers themselves.[45] Neither did the question arise during the early period of the German occupation of the Ukraine. Even Germany's decision to extend its domination to the Crimea—the area that was soon to figure prominently in plans to organize a German colony (*Kolonialstaat*) on the northern shores of the Black Sea—was not specifically linked to the Reich's desire to protect and organize German settlers in the east. It was not until April 5, 1918, that General Ludendorff, while arguing in support of the extension of German occupation to the Crimean Peninsula, mentioned the necessity of protecting German colonists residing in that area.[46] Moreover, this was just one of the several arguments employed by General Ludendorff.

The two individuals most responsible for promoting the idea of a German colony on the Black Sea were Friedrich von Lindequist, the Reich's former Colonial Secretary, and the Reverend I. Winkler, a German Protestant minister from Bessarabia, who represented German settlers.[47] From the beginning, efforts were made to obtain General Ludendorff's support for such a plan. While preparations for German occupation of the Crimea were being made, Lindequist presented to Ludendorff a glowing picture of the possibility of enlisting German settlers "in the service of the Fatherland." He spoke of great quantities of food possessed by German colonists in Kherson and their willingness to cooperate with the occupation forces, on condition that they be given additional military protection. Hinting at the possibility of exploiting their manpower for military service, Lindequist mentioned "self-defense units" organized by the colonists and praised them for their "excellent horse and human material." [48]

The idea of organizing German settlers in the east into a distinct colonial state closely associated with the Reich as well as the later plan for their mass repatriation seem to have originated with the colonists themselves. On April 10, 1918, a congress of German settlers of Kherson province, held in Odessa, made an appeal to the Kaiser and the German government. Although their settlements were in the Austrian zone of occupation, they requested German military protection, and in turn promised full cooperation with German authorities, including service in the armed forces. The colonists further suggested that "the east Germans" who had been forced to serve in the Russian army and had become prisoners of war of the Central Powers be immediately released and organized into special military units to protect German settlements in the east. The most important point in the resolution, however, was a request to establish a German "sphere of influence" in the Black Sea Basin, or, if this proved impossible, to facilitate the return of German settlers to the Reich.[49]

In the plan of Reverend Winkler the Black Sea colony was to stretch from Odessa to the mouth of the Danube and be closely linked to the Reich. Those Germans of the east who either could not or would not settle in the *Baltikum* (German resettlement area on the shores of the Baltic) were to be directed to this southern center. Winkler further maintained that sooner or later the

Ukraine would be reunited with Russia and, therefore, the German colonial state on the shores of the Black Sea should be completely independent of Kiev. Such an attitude on Reverend Winkler's part is understandable, for this state could serve as Germany's springboard for further "peaceful penetration of the east." [50]

General Ludendorff in his memoirs admitted that he favored the concentration of German settlers of the east into one area of the occupation zone but denied that he ever went as far as to advocate the creation of a colonial state on the Black Sea; he dismissed the whole idea as fantastic.[51] However, official German documents of this period leave no doubt that for a certain time Ludendorff gave full backing to the Winkler-Lindequist plan. In a special memorandum devoted to this problem and submitted to the German Foreign Office sometime in mid-April, General Ludendorff referred to the Crimea as an area "best suited for the establishment of a stronghold of German colonists in the east." The Crimean colony was to be closely linked to the Ukraine, and yet Sevastopol was to be made into a "German Gibraltar" of the Black Sea. This was not a completely impossible arrangement, for, according to Ludendorff's plan, the German Crimea, the Ukraine, and Georgia were to be organized eventually into some kind of South Russian Federation under the German aegis.[52]

It was thus only natural that in late May, following the German occupation of the Crimea, the settlers in the east came to regard the establishment of a German colony on the Black Sea as a virtual certainty.[53] The Foreign Office was not of the same mind. Although it instructed Mumm to appoint a special minister or commissar to the Hetman government to safeguard the interests of German settlers in the Ukraine, it remained strongly opposed to the idea of founding a German colony in the east. Ambassador Mumm, General Groener, and Prince Heinrich Reuss (German representative in the Crimea) shared the Foreign Office's opposition to such a plan. Mumm was especially disturbed by the activities of Winkler and Lindequist, fearing that their efforts might be viewed as Germany's official policy and thus further complicate Ukrainian-German relations. Mumm also saw the danger in stimulating such hopes among the colonists and was concerned about the consequences if they were thwarted.[54] The Foreign Office continued to regard the granting of local autonomy to various German settlements in the east as the most feasible solution of the problem, and tried to obtain the cooperation of the Supreme Army Command and the Secretary of the Interior in restraining Lindequist from further activities among the German colonists.[55]

Lindequist, however, was not to be so easily discouraged. On June 8, he again conferred with Ludendorff in an effort to secure the general's support for his schemes, and also tried to obtain the backing of the Imperial Chancellor. When the latter repeated that there was no prospect whatsoever of pursuing his plan for a separate German colonial state in the east, Lindequist quickly presented the Chancellor with a new plan. Since the Crimea was eventually to be linked to the Ukraine, certain conditions could now be imposed on Kiev as a price for such a concession. Permission could be secured from the Ukrainian government to allow German colonists from other parts of Russia to settle in the Crimea and the adjoining province of Taurida. This, Lindequist argued, was the only way to save the "Germandom" of the east from denationalization and destruction. Oskar Paul Trautmann of the Information Division of the Foreign Office, who participated in the conference between Lindequist and Imperial Chancellor Hertling, warned Lindequist that such a plan would encounter opposition from the Ukrainians; he maintained that it would be sufficient to secure guarantees from Kiev concerning the rights of the German settlers in the area under its control. Trautmann, nevertheless, promised that the new plan would be studied further by the Foreign Office.[56]

General Ludendorff, however, held a more sympathetic view of Lindequist's plan. True, he also concluded that a German colony on the Black Sea shore could not be established, because it would be indefensible in the event of war; but he agreed with Lindequist that the Germans from various regions of the east should be gathered in the Crimea and neighboring Taurida, and recommended that this new political creation be associated with the Ukraine. The nature of this association was not clearly defined. Ludendorff spoke of an "independent Crimea-Taurida" through which German political and economic preponderance on the Black Sea was to be assured, and again mentioned the necessity of converting the port of Sevastopol into a stronghold of German naval forces. In a lengthy memorandum on German colonists in the east, Ludendorff also presented a detailed program for their resettlement

in the Crimea and other areas to be opened to German colonization (Lorraine, the Baltic provinces, and certain regions to be
taken away from Poland). He urged the Imperial Chancellor to
give prompt consideration to this plan so that Eichhorn could
have a clear answer to the repeated inquiries of German settlers
in the east concerning the Reich's plans for their future.[57]

Ambassador Mumm, who learned about Ludendorff's new plan
for the creation of a German protectorate in the Crimea from Major Brinckmann, promptly concluded that it was but a "slight
modification" of the original Winkler-Lindequist project, and expressed his skepticism concerning its feasibility.[58] This was, however, more than just a rehash of an older plan; General Ludendorff was clearly ready to go further than either Winkler or
Lindequist, although he was careful not to reveal fully his plan at
this point. He knew full well that there was widespread opposition
to the extension of German commitments in the east, and that not
only the Foreign Office spokesmen in Berlin but also General
Groener and Ambassador Mumm in Kiev favored an early transfer of the Crimea to the Ukraine, with no conditions to be attached to such a transaction.[59]

Judging from General Ludendorff's plan for the creation of an
"anti-Slav federation [*Bund*] centered around Georgia, which
was to be automatically joined by the Don, Kuban, Terek, and
Volga Cossacks," it is quite apparent that he could not be sincere
in his advocacy of the eventual union of the Crimea with the
Ukraine. Both Mumm and General Groener were quick to point
out that the bases for the creation of such an anti-Slav *Bund* were
lacking, and dismissed the plan as "utopian." Noting that this
plan and Ludendorff's formula for the solution of the Crimean
problem were closely connected, Mumm and Groener urged continuation of the policy aiming at strengthening the idea of independent Ukrainian statehood and again recommended an immediate transfer of the Crimea to the Ukraine.[60] Austro-Hungarian
observers in the Ukraine were, therefore, right in maintaining
that the Germans (and by this they meant the powerful Supreme
Army Command) were determined to retain the Crimea under
their exclusive control and that this was a part of the general plan
to extend German economic and political influence to Persia,
Mesopotamia, and other areas of the Near East.[61]

The new Lindequist plan for the Crimea, which General Ludendorff fortified with his blessings, continued to create concern in the Foreign Office as well as among the Germans in Kiev. The Supreme Army Command was again approached with a request to support the Foreign Office's view, and various guarantees were offered to convince General Ludendorff that the interests of German settlers in the east would be fully safeguarded.[62] In the meantime, Lindequist, encouraged by General Ludendorff's continued support of his plan, in mid-June made a bid to obtain the Kaiser's backing for it by suggesting that the autonomous *Kolonialstaat* be ruled by a German regent. The Kaiser, however, reluctant to be drawn into such schemes, announced his support of the Foreign Office's view that the formation of a German colonial state in the east was an impossibility.[63]

Despite the Kaiser's decision, the problem of German colonists in the east remained unsettled. Faced with Ludendorff's continued support of the Lindequist plan, the Foreign Office tried to work out a more acceptable solution. It was to be based on the transfer of German settlers from the Ukraine to Bessarabia, and the Ukrainians from that province to the Ukraine. This, according to Bussche, was to insure the Germans, both in Bessarabia and the Ukraine, of more adequate protection and fuller cultural autonomy, and was also expected to find strong Rumanian backing, inasmuch as it would remove the Ukrainian irredenta from the province to which the Ukraine still held a claim.[64] Evidently there was little enthusiasm for the plan, for it was quickly dropped and never heard of again.

General Ludendorff, in the meantime, continued to think of a Southeastern Union (*Südostverband*) to be composed of the Caucasus and the areas around it. This was another version of his earlier plan to establish an anti-Slav federation in the east.[65] On the very eve of the imperial conference at Spa on July 2–3, 1918, he reiterated his unwavering support for the plan to create a German *Kolonialstaat* in the Crimea: "Ethnographically, the Crimea is not Ukrainian, and we have not promised to transfer the province to the Ukraine. The Ukraine is, thus, in no position to object to our plan to concentrate German settlers in the Peninsula. The Ukraine will certainly accept such a plan, because a Crimea left in Great Russian hands would be more painful to Kiev than a German-populated Crimea closely associated with the Ukraine. It is difficult to understand why such a concentration of Germans in one area should be more unpleasant to the Ukraine than the present existence of various German settlements scattered all over the country. Moreover, the interest of German state should be paramount, and it is in our interest to organize a political entity on the shores of the Black Sea in which the German element would predominate, and which would serve as a base for our further economic involvement in the Orient." [66]

The Spa conference of July 2–3, held under the Kaiser's chairmanship, although it did not specifically endorse General Ludendorff's ideas on the Crimea and German colonists in the east, greatly strengthened his position.[67] True, Ludendorff did not dare to unveil his plan in its entirety, but it was equally true that the German Chancellery was rather timid in presenting its formula for the solution of the problem of German settlers in the east, with which the general Crimean question was so closely linked. Indeed, the Chancellery showed little initiative and imagination, and allowed General Ludendorff to dominate most of the deliberations at the conference. Having declared categorically, "a viable Ukrainian state will not come into being," [68] the general managed to convince others that, at least for the time being, the Crimea should be maintained as a distinct and separate area under German domination. It was further agreed at the conference that the Sulkevich administration would best serve German interests. The German government did not grant it formal recognition; however, the German military command in the Crimea was instructed to treat it as a *de facto* local administration, though making certain that the Tatar national movement would not be unduly strengthened.[69]

General Ludendorff then turned to the problem of recruitment of Black Sea German settlers, especially those residing in the Crimea, into service in the Reich's armed forces. On his recommendation it was decided to make a concerted effort to induce the settlers to volunteer for military service. Legal aspects of the problem were to be worked out by the Foreign Office and it was agreed that German citizenship would be conferred on those who would contribute to the Reich's war effort.[70] Ludendorff was quick to perceive that, once substantial numbers of Germans residing in the east were drafted, the plan for the creation of a *Kolonialstaat* in the Crimea, or some other Black Sea region, would have a better chance of adoption.

It may be argued that the imperial conference at Spa on July 2 and 3 failed to produce a clear-cut decision for the solution of the Crimean problem; nevertheless, it went a long way toward preparing the ground for converting the Crimea into a German military stronghold in the Black Sea area as well as a haven for the German colonists of the east.

Although General Ludendorff warned that the recruitment of the Germans in the Crimea could be successful only after a clear decision about the area's political future had been made,[71] he was apparently quite pleased with the results of this meeting and immediately ordered preparations for a mass induction of the settlers into the German armed forces. They were to undergo a three month training program before being dispatched to the western front. The number of German settlers in the areas under the German control was put at 600,000, but, in the opinion of local German observers, their response to an official appeal to serve in the German armed forces was not likely to be very enthusiastic.[72] This prediction soon proved correct, and the plan was abandoned.

In the meantime, the Foreign Office, now headed by Admiral Paul von Hintze, decided to reassert its position on the still unsettled question of German colonists in the east. In a lengthy memorandum to the Imperial Chancellor on July 5 it flatly rejected the assertion of the Supreme Army Command and the War Ministry that the settlers had the right to demand protection from the Reich, since, technically, they were Russian citizens. It restated the objections to the creation of a *Kolonialstaat* in the Black Sea area and cited the following supporting points: (1) technical difficulties that might be encountered in implementing such a plan; (2) political difficulties that were bound to arise regardless of whether the Ukraine remained independent or was reunited with Russia; (3) difficulties with Turkey, especially after the rejection of a plan for a Turkish colony in the Crimea; (4) rejection of the claim that the concentration of German colonists in the Black Sea area would provide them with maximum protection; (5) conviction that the distribution of a large number of German settlers throughout the area would result in greater German influence over larger areas of the east; (6) conviction that a successful repatriation of German settlers could be arranged, and that the Ukrainians and others would cooperate in this matter. Finally, the Foreign Office offered a number of specific recommendations designed to guarantee complete protection of the interests of German colonists in the east. Among them were suggestions to organize local and district administrative units headed by German officials; to secure guarantees for religious and educational freedom; to send German representatives to legislative bodies of the countries in which they resided; to have a special minister or representative in the central governments of various countries in the east; and to secure the right of the German government to defend the interests of German colonists.[73] This was to be the Foreign Office's last word concerning the problem of German settlers in the east; and General Ludendorff did not openly contest it.

The leaders of the settlers, however, refused to accept this ruling as final and continued to promote the plan calling for the formation of a German colonial state in the east. On August 22, 1918, the Confidential Council of German Colonists in the Black Sea Basin, headed by the Reverend Winkler, presented Foreign Secretary Hintze with a lengthy memorandum containing a plan for the creation of a "settlement area on the Black Sea under complete German protection." They predicted that what they called somewhat innocently "a settlement area" (which, incidentally, was to comprise not only the Crimea but also the adjoining Taurida, the southern portion of the province of Ekaterinoslav, and southern Bessarabia, including the mouth of the Danube) would sooner or later become an integral part of the Reich. In addition, they rejected a suggestion to link the proposed colonial state to the Ukraine, and instead urged the establishment of a German sphere of influence over the entire length of the northern Black Sea coast, including the Don region, so that an effective German-controlled land route to Persia, Afghanistan, and India could be maintained.[74]

The German Foreign Office was in no hurry to reply to the memorandum. It did so only in mid-September in a brief note to the chairman of the Society for German Settlement and Migration, in which it again cited grounds of "impracticability" in rejecting the plan to concentrate German colonists of the east in the Black Sea area.[75]

In fact, little was done to initiate the establishment of a German *Kolonialstaat* in the Crimea and the adjoining area, in spite of the fact that until the middle of July or so General Ludendorff gave strong support to the plan. Although some Russian sources claim that the Germans went so far as to examine various possible resettlement sites in the Crimea[76] and to develop plans for the construction of additional railways and seaports, and even began purchasing real estate,[77] German official documents give no support to such contentions.

The representatives of the settlers nonetheless continued to work on their plan and scheduled a general congress of the colonists of the Crimea and Southern Ukraine for November 5, 1918.[78]

For all practical purposes the Ottoman Empire was eliminated as an active contender in the struggle for the domination of the Crimea about mid-April, 1918, prior to the German occupation of the Peninsula. Kiev, too, somewhat belatedly, was ordered to keep its hands off the Crimea, and the Ukrainian force, commanded by General Natiev, was forced to withdraw from the Peninsula. This, however, by no means settled the problem and was to mark the beginning rather than the end of a sustained Ukrainian effort to establish its domination over the Crimea.

Although Tatar sources trace Ukrainian "aggression" against the Crimea back to April 19,[79] when a Ukrainian force entered the Peninsula to assist the German army in its cleanup operations against the Bolsheviks, it was not until after the Hetman's takeover in the Ukraine that Kiev was to begin working actively toward the incorporation of the Crimea into the Ukrainian state. The Hetman personally discussed this with Mumm on May 7, and in subsequent weeks his Foreign Minister, Dmytro Doroshenko, continued these efforts in his diplomatic contacts with the Germans in Kiev.[80] The result was that Ambassador Mumm, General Groener, Under-Secretary of State von dem Bussche, and other German diplomats were quite sympathetic to the Ukraine's claim to the Crimea.

Thus, during the months of May and June, while the Hetman concentrated on consolidating his power in the Ukraine, and the situation in the Crimea was still in a state of flux, the Ukrainian government, confident that the Germans would support its claim, adopted specific measures to strengthen the Ukrainian national movement in the Peninsula. A Committee of the Steppe Ukraine (Komitet Stepovoyi Ukrayiny) and Ukrainian clubs (*hromady*) were organized in the Crimea for this purpose. These organizations and three Ukrainian newspapers published in the Peninsula were under the direct supervision of the Ukrainian Foreign Ministry in Kiev and enjoyed its financial support.[81]

This was the period in which the Winkler-Lindequist group made its most sustained effort to secure the Reich's support for a German *Kolonialstaat* in the Crimea, and this may partly account for the fact that the Ukrainians promoted their Crimean claim with considerable caution and restraint. Not until late June and early July did the Ukrainian-Crimean dispute break fully into the open. The eruption of the conflict was closely linked to two significant developments that took place at about the same time: (1) the formation of the Sulkevich government in the Crimea, in which the Russians played a dominant role (Dzhafer Seidahmet may, indeed, be viewed as the only Tatar nationalist in the cabinet);[82] and (2) the German Foreign Office's decision not to support the plan for the creation of a German colony on the Black Sea—of which the Ukrainians were fully informed.

The conflict manifested itself mainly in an economic war waged by the Ukraine against the Crimea from early July, 1918, and a diplomatic duel between the Crimean and Ukrainian missions in Berlin in August of the same year. It was, however, General Sulkevich rather than the Hetman who ordered the suspension of all communications and transactions between the Crimea and the Ukraine. The Hetman immediately complained to Count Berchem, German chargé d'affaires in Kiev, who promised to exercise a restraining influence on Sulkevich through Major Brinckmann. Berchem also sought to quiet Ukrainian fears by pointing out that the Sulkevich government would not be granted full recognition, and that the general's actions would not prejudice the final solution of the Crimean question.[83]

At this point General Ludendorff still hoped to organize a German *Kolonialstaat* on the shores of the Black Sea, preferably in the Crimea. While ordering Army Command 52 (General Kosch) to establish official contact with the Sulkevich administration, Ludendorff advised it to remind Sulkevich that the legal status of the Crimea, vis-à-vis the Ukraine and Russia, was yet to be determined and that in the meantime he was to maintain friendly relations with Kiev. Ludendorff further recommended that Sulkevich make an official announcement along these lines and also order the suspension of various "vexatious" measures against the Ukraine.[84] General Kosch immediately conveyed the wishes of his superiors to Sulkevich. At the same time, however, Major Brinck-mann, just back from a brief visit to the Crimea, reported to the Army Group Eichhorn that a federal union of the Peninsula with the Ukraine was not possible and that "the Crimean leaders" were not prepared to go beyond the linking of their railways and postal and telegraph services with those of their northern neighbor.[85]

Several days later, Brinckmann prepared another, more de-tailed report on the Crimean situation. General Ludendorff liked it so much that he immediately forwarded it to Imperial Chancel-lor Hertling. The report began with a restatement of Brinck-mann's conviction that a federal union between the Crimea and the Ukraine would be rejected by the political circles of the Penin-sula. Some link with Germany—either a protectorate or a colony —was recommended by Brinckmann. He further spoke of the de-sirability of merging Taurida with the Crimea into one political unit, but he saw little hope for the realization of such a plan be-cause of anticipated Ukrainian opposition. His opinion of the Tatars and their ability to organize a good administration was very low. Brinckmann also felt that there was no chance of sepa-rating the Crimea from Russia by a popular vote or referendum and concluded that the Sulkevich administration would best serve German interests in that area.[86]

German interest in the Crimea was based mainly on political, strategic, and military considerations. Economically, the Crimea was not important; the economic exploitation of this area during the period of German occupation was very limited, and the Ger-man authorities went so far as to assure the Sulkevich adminis-tration that, unlike the Ukraine, the Crimea would not have to make any food deliveries to the Central Powers.[87] True, having occupied the Crimean ports, the Germans helped themselves to the supplies and provisions that had been amassed there in great quantities by the Czarist government, but as far as local products were concerned (such as tobacco, wine, and fruits), they were purchased by the Germans and shipped home. Yet, the Germans brought necessary food supplies into the Crimea from the Ukraine. This practice continued even during the period of badly strained relations between Skoropadsky and Sulkevich.[88]

In the meantime, economic difficulties in the Peninsula and continued German refusal to grant full recognition to the Sulke-vich regime gave rise to fears that it would fall. The German military command in the Crimea was especially disturbed by such a prospect. It recommended that the two leading members of the Sulkevich cabinet, Tatishchev and Seidahmet, be allowed to proceed to Berlin to confer with German officials. Such a diplomatic mission, the military in the Crimea argued, could be regarded, for the time being, as "silent recognition" of the Sulkevich regime.[89] General Ludendorff fully endorsed this recommendation. "Otherwise," said the general, "I do not see how I can bear the responsibility for maintaining law and order in the Crimea. . . ."[90] The Foreign Office countered by advising Ambassador Mumm "to try to prevent Seidahmet and Tatischev from going to Berlin." Mumm did not think he could do much, and replied that the proposed trip could be postponed or canceled only through direct intervention of the Supreme Army Command.[91]

In many cases problems pertaining to the Crimea were handled through Kiev rather than directly through the Reich's military and civilian representatives in the Peninsula. Although both Mumm and Groener had to follow the directives they received from their superiors, their views—and both could be classified as pro-Ukrainian in the Crimean question—carried a great deal of weight. It is thus not surprising that Field Marshal von Eichhorn and Ambassador Mumm ignored the Sulkevich government completely and refused to meet with its members while traveling through the Crimea in late July, 1918.[92] The Supreme Army Command, nevertheless, continued to advocate support of this regime, and in early August the Tatishchev-Seidahmet mission appeared in Berlin.[93] This was the Crimean government's answer to Ukrainian pressure designed to bring about the fall of General Sulkevich.

The Hetman, greatly disturbed by the proposed trip of the Crimean mission to Berlin, decided to counter it by sending a Ukrainian delegation, headed by Prime Minister Lyzohub, to the Reich's capital at precisely the same time. Although Ambassador Mumm tried at first to dissuade General Skoropadsky from going through with this plan, the Ukrainians were finally allowed to proceed to Berlin.[94] This and the Soviet protest against the presence of Tatishchev and Seidahmet in Berlin,[95] as well as continued German suspicion of Turkish intentions in the Peninsula, were more than enough to insure the failure of the Crimean mission to Germany.

General Ludendorff was especially concerned about the Turkish influence in the Crimea. The presence of two Turkish officers there in July worried the general so much that he ordered them to be followed by German agents and was very disappointed that, "despite all efforts, no basis for their removal could be found." [96] Similarly, in August, the Crimean delegation in Berlin was forbidden to make contact with the Turkish ambassador there and was refused permission to return to the Crimea via Constantinople.[97]

The Ukrainians had already decided to put economic pressure on the Crimea to make it more cooperative. To prove that the Crimea could not exist as a separate political entity and that its future lay in a close association with the Ukraine, a tight economic "blockade" (complete suspension of Ukrainian-Crimean trade) was ordered by the Hetman government in early July.[98] German occupation troops in the Peninsula were not affected, but the Crimean economy, greatly dependent upon Ukrainian imports, markets, and transportation, could be seriously hurt by such a drastic measure. Even though there is some disagreement about the effectiveness of the "blockade," [99] it must have produced sufficient economic dislocation to bring about German intervention on behalf of the Crimea. On July 20 General Groener, probably acting on the orders of the Supreme Army Command, requested Ambassador Mumm to exert all his influence on the Hetman to halt Kiev's economic war against the Crimea.[100] There is no basis for maintaining that General Skoropadsky would not have blockaded the Crimea without German permission and support, as Tatar authors seem to believe;[101] however, it cannot be said that Mumm acted with speed and determination in approaching the Ukrainians on this matter. Mumm met Doroshenko, the Ukrainian Foreign Minister, one week later, and, having discussed the food shortage in the Crimea, tried to convince him that continuation of the blockade was not in the best interest of either Germany or the Ukraine. The German government, according to Mumm, favored an amicable solution of the differences existing between the two governments and had already impressed upon General Sulkevich the necessity of cooperating in this matter.[102] Several days later, however, Mumm reported the worsening of the Ukrainian-Crimean dispute and spoke of continued German efforts to persuade the Hetman to lift the blockade.[103] These efforts were apparently never taken very seriously by the

Germans in Kiev. The Ukrainians continued their economic war against the Crimea, and soon General Groener and Ambassador Mumm began to espouse openly the handing over of the Crimean Peninsula to the Ukraine.[104]

General Ludendorff, although he continued to insist that the fate of the Crimea should be decided in future negotiations with the Ukraine and Russia, advised the exertion of diplomatic pressure on the Ukrainian government to convince it that its economic war against the Crimea was not best calculated to bring about annexation of the Peninsula and that Kiev should concentrate instead on drawing the Crimea into its economic orbit.[105] A week or so later, the German Foreign Office echoed Ludendorff's view and again asked Mumm to convey it to the Hetman. Berlin also expressed the hope that Tatishchev's threatened resignation could be used as a pretext for the dismissal of the entire Sulkevich administration and the formation of a new Crimean government more sympathetic to the idea of union with the Ukraine. This plan was soon formally presented to General Ludendorff by Foreign Secretary Hintze. In Hintze's view the only permanent solution for the Crimea was its union with the Ukraine.[106]

In an attempt to strengthen the Foreign Office's argument in support of the above solution, Ambassador Mumm warned against the rise of Pan-Islamism, both in the Crimea and in the Caucasus. In order to dramatize the gravity of this danger, he pointed out that General Groener and the Hetman shared his uneasiness. He put the blame for the growth of Pan-Islamism in the Crimea squarely at the door of the Supreme Army Command and the Kosch corps headquarters because of their backing of Sulkevich and Seidahmet.[107]

The first round in the Ukrainian-Crimean diplomatic duel in Berlin ended in early September in a draw. The Germans succeeded in persuading the two parties to open direct negotiations, but this can hardly be interpreted as recognition of the Crimea's independence, or as an achievement of the Crimean diplomatic mission in Berlin, as was concluded by Tatar sources. Nor is there any basis for maintaining that at this point "there was a shift in the Reich's policy that was favorable to the Crimea and detrimental to the Ukraine." [108]

The second round in the Ukrainian-Crimean diplomatic struggle took place in Berlin between the Hetman and the Crimean Foreign Minister, Seidahmet. The latter was backed by the Turkish Foreign Minister, Mehmed Talat Pasha. The Hetman arrived in Berlin on September 4 and Talat Pasha on the 7th. The presence of the two in Berlin at the same time was obviously not purely accidental. Neither the Hetman nor Talat Pasha went to Berlin solely for the purpose of securing German support for their solution of the Crimean problem, and yet this problem was high on the list of questions that they raised in their talks with German spokesmen.[109]

The result of this second diplomatic encounter was likewise inconclusive. Although a Tatar student of this period not only claims that Talat Pasha went so far as to threaten an open break between Turkey and Germany unless the interests of the Crimea were safeguarded but credits this Turkish diplomat with having won "a great diplomatic victory," [110] official German records present us with a very different picture. At a meeting with Foreign Secretary Hintze, Talat Pasha was told that German interests in the Crimea were primarily military and that Germany was not interested either in keeping the Crimea permanently or in maintaining its forces in that area. Implying that Germany continued to favor a union between the Ukraine and the Crimea, Hintze praised the Ukrainians for their offer of far-reaching autonomy and economic assistance to the Peninsula. Talat Pasha, in turn, explained the problems of the Moslems in the Crimea, expressed his satisfaction with the German approach to the solution of this question, and concluded by stating that the Ottoman Empire would continue to follow closely further developments there.[111] Talat Pasha was equally unsuccessful in his talks with the Supreme Army Command, which remained suspicious of Turkish intentions in the Crimea. The Supreme Command continued to press for the removal of Turkish propaganda officers still active in the Peninsula and advised General Hans von Seeckt to inform his Turkish colleagues, "without unnecessarily hurting their feelings," that the establishment of an independent Tatar state was out of the question.[112]

Hetman Skoropadsky did not fare much better in his efforts to secure German backing for his plan to annex the Crimea, although the answers given him concerning this matter were cautious and evasive, rather than directly negative. The Kaiser was advised to call the Hetman's attention to the fact that in the

"Third Universal" of the Rada, proclaimed on November 20, 1917, following the Bolshevik coup in Petrograd, no claim to the Crimea had been made. He also stressed the complexity of the problem and the effect that it might have on current German-Russian relations.[113] General Ludendorff, too, confronted with the Hetman's request to support Ukrainian efforts to organize "a new and a more cooperative regime in the Crimea," refused to commit himself one way or another and replied that what the Germans needed was an administration capable of maintaining law and order in the area, and that it mattered little whether this job was done by the existing Sulkevich administration or some other local government.[114]

German representatives, both in Kiev and in the Crimea, continued to work toward the union of the Crimea and the Ukraine. On September 6 General Sulkevich was told bluntly by General Kosch that Berlin would not recognize the Crimea's independence and that its union with the Ukraine was unavoidable. Ambassador Mumm, on his part, tried to convince the Crimean government that it had no choice but to seek a political and economic settlement with Kiev.[115] Indeed, Mumm was the principal force behind this policy and was prepared to go to any length in his efforts to impose it on the Crimea. This did not mean that Kiev was to be given a free hand in dealing with the Crimea. Mumm made it clear that in the forthcoming negotiations between the two the Germans were going to play a conciliatory as well as a controlling role.[116]

At this point Ambassador Mumm gave up his Kiev post and returned to Germany. His resignation, according to General Groener, was caused by the Foreign Office's "impossible Russian policy." [117] It does not seem to have been directly occasioned by developments in the Crimea, for exactly at this point the Sulkevich cabinet was reorganized, having accepted new conditions for its cooperation with the German authorities.

The reorganization of the Sulkevich cabinet took place September 14–18, and, according to a Tatar student of the period, included both Seidahmet and Tatishchev, Ministers of Foreign Affairs and Finance, respectively.[118] Although officially Seidahmet did not resign his post until after his return from Berlin, on October 11, in the light of earlier German demands that the Crimean Foreign Ministry be abolished and Seidahmet dropped from the cabinet, and Sulkevich's acceptance of these terms, it can be concluded that Seidahmet ceased to be a member of the Crimean administration as of its reorganization in mid-September, 1918. Nor is Tatishchev's position in the second Sulkevich administration very clear. He, too, remained abroad during the period of reorganization, and A. Nikiforov, a member of the Crimean delegation that went to Kiev to negotiate with the Ukrainians, was officially listed as Sulkevich's Minister of Finance—the post originally held by Tatishchev. German official records nowhere mention the possibility of Tatishchev's becoming General Sulkevich's successor, as some Ukrainian and German informants thought at the time.

The Crimean government was now to be called a "provincial administration" (*Landesverwaltung* or *krayevoye pravitel'stvo*) and not a "government" (*Reichsregierung* or *gosudarstvennoye pravitel'stvo*), and its Foreign Ministry had been abolished. This meant that the Crimea was not to resume its diplomatic relations with other powers, and that Seidahmet would have to resign. The second condition imposed by the Germans was political union with the Ukraine, the Crimea to retain an administrative autonomy. The third condition was that the new Sulkevich regime return to a coalition government composed of Russians, Tatars, and Germans.[119]

The Germans felt quite strongly that the union of the Crimea and the Ukraine should be achieved promptly and decided that in the event of Sulkevich's refusal to follow this course a member of his first cabinet, V. Nalbandov, was to be entrusted with the formation of a new administration. They also believed that those Crimean leaders who in the earlier period had categorically rejected the idea of a Crimean-Ukrainian union were greatly responsible for the various punitive economic measures to which Kiev had subjected the Peninsula. To end the economic war and to reach agreement on the specifics of their political union, Ukrainian and Crimean representatives were to meet in Kiev, with the Germans serving as a third party at the conference.[120]

Although he formally accepted all the German conditions, General Sulkevich sought ways to preserve the ties that the Crimea had managed to establish with the outside world. Accordingly, having agreed to political union with the Ukraine, the general requested the creation of a "joint Foreign Ministry" and the appointment of Crimeans to diplomatic posts abroad.[121] While a four-man

Crimean delegation was being chosen for the forthcoming Kiev conference, the Ukrainian government decided to "suspend temporarily" its economic war against the Crimea, and expressed its readiness to open immediate negotiations with Crimean representatives. The Crimean delegation was empowered to discuss the following problems with the Ukraine: customs and tariffs, trade, railways, postal and telegraph services, finances, justice, refugees, ports, and canals.[122] Both the German military in Kiev and the Reich's special representative in the Crimea, Prince Reuss, were instructed to give close attention to the talks to make certain that German interests would not suffer. In spite of the fact that the talks were held in Kiev, Austro-Hungarian representatives did not play any part in them; they even had difficulty following the development of the Ukrainian-Crimean dispute, inasmuch as their German colleagues were not very cooperative in keeping them informed.[123]

Obviously fighting a losing battle, the Sulkevich administration tried to postpone the opening of the talks by suggesting that one of its representatives be sent to Kiev beforehand to prepare the ground. The Hetman immediately complained to Consul General Thiel, and Corps Headquarters No. 52 in the Crimea warned Sulkevich that such tactics would not be tolerated and that the Crimean delegation must proceed to Kiev without delay.[124] Similarly, the Germans supported the Hetman in his demand that the "Great Russian" Crimean delegation, headed by the Minister of Justice, Akhmatovich, be enlarged to include Tatars and representatives of the German colonists—a request with which General Sulkevich promptly complied.[125]

When the Ukrainian-Crimean talks opened in Kiev on October 5, 1918, the Germans were extremely well represented, for in addition to Prince Reuss and other Reich officials already in Kiev, three delegates of the German colonists were in attendance.[126] The German officials remained firm in their insistence that the Crimea be attached to the Ukraine, and avowed that in the event of further difficulties the Sulkevich administration would have to be replaced by a more cooperative one.[127] According to the Ukrainian plan, the Crimea was to be united with it as an autonomous region under the common leadership of the Hetman. The Crimean representatives, on the other hand, continued to insist on full independence for the Peninsula, on which basis it could enter into a federal union with the Ukraine.[128]

It is not surprising, therefore, that the Ukrainian-Crimean talks broke down almost as soon as they started. Even before the official announcement of the failure of this conference, which the Germans anticipated, Prince Reuss worked out a specific plan for the handling of the Crimean problem following the suspension of negotiations. He advocated renewal of the Ukrainian-Crimean economic war, dismissal of the Sulkevich regime, administration of the Crimea as though it were an occupied area, the establishment of a new Crimean administration headed by V. Nalbandov or Solomon S. Krym, and then the resumption of talks with the Ukraine. All this was to be accomplished without "direct interference" by Germany! [129] By mid-October, Corps Headquarters 52 had been advised finally that the Sulkevich regime was no longer to be supported and that the establishment of a new administration, headed by someone like Krym, was not to be hindered. A new regime was also to be a provincial administration. It was not to pursue any foreign policy objectives, but rather was to be encouraged to reopen talks with Kiev, although the Germans again called for noninterference in the Crimea's internal affairs except in strictly military matters.[130]

Toward the end of October, 1918, the situation in the Crimea became extremely complicated. At a time when the formation of a new government in the Peninsula was again being contemplated, German withdrawal from the east and the rise of the Entente influence in that area were now a virtual certainty. At this point the German chargé d'affaires in Kiev, Count Berchem, came to the conclusion that Germany should no longer pursue an active policy in the Crimea; his military colleagues, however, continued to show concern over Turkish activities in that area.[131] A week or so later Berchem decided to help the Crimean representatives to establish contact with Allied spokesmen in Bulgaria; he did so, however, only following an earlier discussion of this matter with the Hetman.[132] This proved an empty gesture, since the Germans were no longer in the position to control political developments in the east. On November 12, 1918, following the terms of the armistice, they ordered the withdrawal of their forces from the Crimea and Taurida. Simultaneously, General Sulkevich was advised that he could no longer count on German support; this immediately resulted in the collapse of his regime.[133]

Thus came to an end a confusing chapter in the history of the Crimea. The selection of General Sulkevich to head the Crimean administration in the period of German military occupation was a compromise solution, from the German as well as from the Tatar point of view. The Russian circles of the Peninsula also regarded Sulkevich as acceptable for the time being and played an important role in his administration. It was not, however, until after the German withdrawal that the anti-Bolshevik Russian Whites made the Crimea into one of their strongholds in the south. The Ukrainians, on the other hand, opposed Sulkevich openly because of his refusal to cooperate with Kiev. The Tatar support of General Sulkevich, albeit with certain reservations, was based on their belief that he remained true to the idea of Crimean independence and had done all he could to strengthen the Tatar elements in that area.[134] The Germans supported General Sulkevich not so much because his plans coincided with theirs, but simply because their policy in the Crimea was even more confused and uncertain than in the Ukraine, and the general was a convenient man to help in the administration of this occupied area until a more concrete program could be developed for it.

Disengagement and Collapse: The Fall of the Hetmanate and the End of the Occupation

Austria-Hungary was eliminated by the Germans as a competitor in the Black Sea Basin quite early in the game; in fact, the Dual Monarchy eliminated itself by giving Germany a free hand in the Crimea—an area essentially within the Austrian sphere of influence in the east. True, initially some Austrians hoped to follow the Germans not only into the Ukraine but into the Caucasus and even India as well. For example, Field Marshal Langer made the following statement to his German colleagues at the Great Headquarters: "We Austrians know full well that you Germans must gain control of the route running through the Caucasus into India. Do not exclude us from this undertaking; permit us to accompany you on this road; you know that we can participate in this only on the most modest scale. . . ."[1] Even so, the early period of the occupation of the Ukraine was marred by serious Austro-German misunderstandings and rivalry. So serious were these tensions and verbal duels at times that a complete break between the two allies seemed imminent.

In spite of the fact that both the Germans and the Ukrainians continuously suspected the Austrians of long-range and sinister designs in the east, Vienna never developed a positive policy for its occupation zone in the Ukraine. These suspicions arose from a variety of sources: from Mumm's report that local Austro-Hungarian occupation authorities in the Ukraine were consolidating their zone in an attempt to free themselves of the central authorities, who were allegedly under the German influence,[2] and the assertion of a Rada leader, Arnold Margolin, that Vienna planned to organize a Tripartite Danube Empire to be composed of Austria, Hungary, and the Ukraine,[3] to the report of the Hetman's Ambassador in Vienna, V. Lypyns'kyi, that the Austrian government planned annexation of the Ukrainian territory west of the Dnieper,[4] and the repeated warnings of Ohnesseit, the German Consul in Odessa, that Vienna, and especially Field Marshal von Böltz, was determined to convert not only the Odessa district but the province of Kherson, if not the entire southern Ukraine, into an Austrian colony![5] All these rumors notwithstanding, General Krauss's report on the Ukraine of mid-June, 1918, contains a rather accurate evaluation of Austria's position in this area: "We [Austrians] do not pursue a definite political goal in the east. . . . The mere improvement of our food situation, and the desire to gain an economic foothold in the Ukraine cannot be regarded as a political goal."[6]

There were three distinct planes on which Vienna had to deal with the Ukraine: (1) the Ukraine as an occupied area; (2) the Ukraine as a somewhat obnoxious neighbor making claims to certain Austrian-controlled territories on ethnic grounds; and (3) the Ukraine as a possible partner in a larger political association (some form of federation, or even a kingdom ruled by one of the Habsburgs).

This last possibility, although rather remote, caught the imagination of certain Austrian as well as Ukrainian groups. It deserves some treatment because of the unfavorable reaction among the Germans to the plan of having a Habsburg on the Ukrainian throne. (There never was a plan to install a German prince as a ruler of the Ukraine, though the Austrians at one point suspected the Germans of such a design. The man who was allegedly slated to become king of the Ukraine was Prince Joachim of Prussia.[7] German suspicions, which had deeper roots and were taken more seriously by both Berlin and Vienna, were reinforced by the Reich's determination to maintain a dominant position in this area, not only during the war but after the general peace settlement as well.)

The controversy centered around the person of young Archduke Wilhelm von Habsburg, the son of Archduke Karl Stephan. As early as October, 1917, General Ludendorff expressed his irritation over the fact that the Archduke, who served as an officer in the Galician Ukrainian Legion, Sich Sharpshooters, and spoke fluent Ukrainian, was being groomed by Vienna for a special role in the Ukraine.[8] Although the Archduke and his Ukrainian volunteer unit were dispatched to the Ukraine in March, 1918, to join the Austrian occupation forces there, it was not until after the Hetman's coup that the Germans took note of his presence in the south and began to show concern over his activities.[9] This was prompted by the plan of a Ukrainian political group from Odessa to have the Archduke replace Skoropadsky as hetman or king of the Ukraine. The plan had strong support from the Zaporozhian Division, just back from its Crimean campaign, and the Galician Sich Sharpshooters, who were stationed at Alexandrovsk. When approached with such a proposal in early May, 1918, Archduke Wilhelm at first asked for time to think it over, but later, seeing its futility, decided to dissuade his supporters from carrying it out.[10]

Kaiser Karl, whom the Archduke informed about the incident, praised him for his tactful refusal to participate in such a dubious scheme. The Kaiser stated that the Dual Monarchy's principal aim in the Ukraine was the procurement of food and that another change of government in the country was to be avoided; however, he did not completely rule out the possibility of placing a Habsburg on the Ukrainian throne. Although he foresaw complications that could possibly result from such a choice, the Kaiser advised the Archduke to continue his friendly relations with the Ukrainians.[11]

Kaiser Karl sent a reassuring note concerning this matter to Wilhelm II several weeks later and promised that the young Archduke would soon visit him in Berlin to report more fully.[12] Moreover, the Austrian commander in the east, Field Marshal Eduard von Böhm-Ermolli, and his successor, General Alfred Krauss, as well as Ambassador Forgách and Foreign Secretary Burián were strongly critical of Archduke Wilhelm's activities in the Ukraine and openly pressed for his recall and the transfer of his Ukrainian legion to the front.[13] The Germans, for all their pretenses to the contrary, continued to show concern over the Archduke's presence in the Ukraine. Whereas the Austrians also claimed that Archduke Wilhelm was not taken seriously by the Germans, he was the object of endless correspondence between the Austrian officials in the Ukraine and their superiors in Baden and Vienna; he caused consternation in Berlin and irritation at the German Supreme Army Command and was responsible for an exchange of notes between the two Kaisers.

Even more unhappy with Archduke Wilhelm's presence in the Ukraine was General Skoropadsky. The Hetman came to regard Alexandrovsk, where the Archduke was stationed with his Galician Ukrainian legionnaires, as the center of anti-Hetman opposition in the country, and repeatedly complained to both Mumm and Forgách requesting their intervention.[14] Burián instructed Forgách to give the Hetman every assurance of Vienna's opposition to the plan of placing a Habsburg on the Ukrainian throne; however, it was not until two weeks later, on July 8 or 9, that Archduke Wilhelm was recalled from the Ukraine. The Hetman was greatly relieved and did not hide his happiness when the news was brought to him by Count Forgách.[15]

The Archduke's departure from the Ukraine was not, however, to mean the end of the controversy that centered around him. On August 8 the young man, on Kaiser Karl's request, visited Kaiser Wilhelm II to report on his Ukrainian activities and to expose "the baseless accusations and rumors to which his stay in the Ukraine had given rise." Before meeting the Kaiser, Archduke Wilhelm spoke to Kurt von Lersner of the German Foreign Office. To the query as to how the Kaiser might react if the Archduke were to raise the question of his candidacy for the Ukrainian throne, Lersner answered that "His Majesty had a strong aversion to such a plan." Consequently, the Archduke did not deal with this subject in his talks with the Kaiser confining himself rather to criticism of the Austro-Polish solution and its current promoter, Count Burián. The Archduke restated his opposition to Burián's pro-Polish policies during his meeting with the German Imperial Chancellor, asking him to regard his views as strictly confidential so as not to furnish "additional ammunition" to anti-German elements in Vienna.[16] Archduke Wilhelm's political future was thus placed in Kaiser Wilhelm's hands. The latter, apparently, was satisfied with the Archduke's explanation and did not object to the young man's returning to the Ukraine.

In the meantime, rumors about the Hetman's impending resignation and his replacement by Archduke Wilhelm continued to circulate in the Ukraine. The discussion of this possibility in Ukrainian newspapers in Austria (especially the *Nove Slovo* of Lviv) gave credence to such speculations.[17] This, no doubt, further heightened the Hetman's dislike of the Austrians and was also responsible for his greater reliance on German support at this point.

As far as the Austrian military were concerned, Archduke Wilhelm's plan to return to the Ukraine did not come to them as a surprise. In fact, they anticipated it even before his audience with Kaiser Wilhelm.[18] The Austrian Ambassador in Kiev, Count Forgách, on the other hand, was greatly surprised and annoyed when he learned that the Archduke would soon return to his Ukrainian post; he wrote a strong message to Burián urging him to prevent it and referred to the whole affair as an "incomprehensible experiment" of which he most strongly disapproved.[19] It was from Count Forgách that Mumm learned about Archduke Wilhelm's impending return to the Ukraine and of Burián's failure to persuade Kaiser Karl to prevent this. It was also Forgách who advised Mumm to urge Berlin to exert pressure on Vienna to keep the Archduke out, on the grounds that his return would seriously disturb the Hetman. The Under-Secretary of State, von dem Bussche, gave full support to such a plan of action, as did the Austro-Hungarian military command in the east.[20]

Although Mumm and Forgách continued their efforts to have the Archduke barred from the Ukraine, with General Groener giving them his full support, none succeeded.[21] Indeed, the young Archduke must have felt rather confident since, on his way back from Austria, he suggested a meeting with the Hetman in Kiev. Groener immediately decided that if the young man were to go through with his plan, the German military in Kiev would treat him like any other Austrian officer of his rank. The unpleasant task of discussing the matter with the Hetman fell to Ambassador Mumm. Luckily, the Hetman refused to have anything to do with the "pretender," and the meeting between Archduke Wilhelm and General Skoropadsky never materialized.[22] The Archduke returned to his previous post in Alexandrovsk in early September. This, in Mumm's view, meant the reestablishment of the most active anti-Hetman center in the Ukraine.[23]

One month later, however, the Galician Ukrainian Legion with its colorful and popular commander, Archduke Wilhelm, Basil the Embroidered, was recalled quietly to its East Galician base.[24] Such was the end of the Archduke's Ukrainian mission. He was destined, however, to remain an active and devoted supporter of the Ukrainian movement until his mysterious disappearance in the Soviet occupation zone of his native Austria sometime in late 1947.

German opposition to Archduke Wilhelm von Habsburg and the Kaiser-Hetman meeting in Berlin in early September, 1918, did not bring about any significant changes in German-Ukrainian relations. True, these relations may have improved somewhat, but this was attributable not so much to the Hetman's visit as to a loosening of Germany's grip on the Ukraine. As early as September 3 Count Siegfried von Roedern, the Secretary of State of the Imperial Treasury, argued that the occupation of the Ukraine was too costly to be continued and suggested that the German forces be cut to a minimum. Although his colleague, the Prussian Minister of War, General Heinrich Scheüch, opposed any drastic reduction of the German forces, shortly thereafter five German divisions were withdrawn from the Ukraine and deployed in the west.[25] Following this withdrawal, the strength of the German forces in the Ukraine was twelve infantry and three cavalry divisions, besides eight infantry divisions in other areas of the east.[26] The cut in German strength seems to have been dictated by military rather than by economic considerations. Vienna had considered the withdrawal of all its forces from the Ukraine as early as mid-August, 1918.[27] Substantial German and Austrian forces, however, remained in the country and continued to play a decisive role in the east until the collapse of the Central Powers in November, 1918.

On September 10 a new German-Ukrainian economic agreement was concluded, and for some two more months the Germans made a serious effort to retain a dominant position in the Ukraine, which they continued to regard as the key to the east. This policy was announced publicly by Vice-Chancellor Friedrich von Payer in a speech delivered at Stuttgart on September 12. While advocating the restoration of prewar frontiers in the west, the Vice-Chancellor called for a permanent separation from Russia, of Poland, Finland, and the Baltic states, and recommended endorsement of the treaties that Germany had concluded earlier in the year with the Ukraine, Russia, and Rumania.[28] Later in the month, in his conversations with General Groener, the Kaiser is reported to have manifested real concern for the Ukraine's future.[29]

German diplomats in Kiev showed great interest in the Ukraine's place in German plans for the east. Hugo Lindemann, an official at the German Embassy in Kiev, for example, though rather critical of the Reich's occupation policies in the Ukraine, advocated mantaining German preponderance in that area. Because of "future possibilities," said he, the Ukraine ought not to be abandoned as an "aimless undertaking." Like many other German leaders at the time, including those at the Supreme Army Command, Lindemann came to regard the east as the only region where the Germans would be allowed to remain active after the war, and the Ukraine was clearly the most important stepping-stone. Because of the Ukraine's importance in Germany's long-range plans Lindemann recommended better treatment of the Ukranian people and correction of past mistakes.[30]

Thus, even after their defeat in the west and the decision to sue for peace, the Germans did not abandon the hope of salvaging their wartime gains in the east. On October 5 Prince Max of Baden, the newly appointed German Chancellor, while formally accepting Wilson's Fourteen Points as the basis for future peace negotiations, declared that Poland, the Baltic states, and the Caucasian territories, as well as Finland and the Ukraine, should not be regarded as "Russian territory, strictly speaking." Discussing the withdrawal of German forces from the east, Prince Max made the following statement: "We are prepared to evacuate these territories when once guarantees have been given that they will be able to determine their future fate by means of representative bodies elected in complete freedom, to the exclusion of all terrorization by either demagogues or [the] military. . . ."[31]

At this point the Germans were prepared to recall their troops from the east on the condition that the *status quo* be maintained there. They asserted that the Ukrainians were developing greater confidence in the Reich, were friendlier than ever before toward the occupation forces, and that the prospect of a German evacuation disquieted the pro-Hetman forces.[32] The Germans in the Ukraine, however, were not satisfied with merely improving rela-

tions with the Ukrainian government. More concrete steps had to
be taken to strengthen the Hetman regime and thus insure the
Reich's continued influence in the country. This was impressed
upon the Hetman by Consul General Thiel at a meeting between
the two on October 7. Thiel urged the Hetman to work toward the
following goals: (1) immediate Ukrainization of the cabinet; (2)
speedy implementation of an agrarian reform; and (3) abandonment of the plan to organize municipal national guard units. The
Hetman accepted all these suggestions and declared that instead
of national guard units (which came to be regarded as Russian
strongholds) Ukrainian Cossack units under Ukrainian officers
would be formed.[33] In the question of an agrarian reform, Privy
Councillor Wiedfeldt, the Reich's chief economic expert in Kiev,
recommended that middle and large farms be encouraged, great
landowners be deprived of their holdings, and that these changes
should be accomplished by nonviolent methods.[34]

The result of all these German efforts, as Pavel Milyukov put it
in his memoirs, was another sharp turn toward "independence" in
the Hetman's policy, although a week earlier, when Skoropadsky
met with Count A. Bobrinskii, Milyukov, and other Kadet leaders
in Kiev, he is supposed to have stated that his aim was essentially
the same as that of these Right-oriented Russian political circles
—the restoration of Russia, one and indivisible.[35] Indeed, at this
point the Hetman's policy was especially confused and unsteady,
although, ironically, the Germans were finally developing a more
positive and consistent program for their principal satellite in the
east. On October 10 the new German Secretary of State for Foreign Affairs, Wilhelm Solf, drafted the following program for the
Ukraine:

"1) The Ukraine is to be maintained as an independent state
under our [German] hegemony.

2) The German-Ukrainian peace treaty is not to be subjected
to any revisions at the generals peace talks.

3) The Hetman is to be advised to rely on the support of the
National Union in his effort to Ukrainize his cabinet and enact an
agrarian reform; the Union is to act as a provisional national assembly. [This was the most influential organization of the former
Rada leaders.]

4) White Russian leaders and organizers as well as the Entente agents should be removed from the Ukraine.

5) The Ukraine should be induced to request, formally, the retention of our troops until complete stabilization of the political situation in the Ukraine has been achieved.

6) The peace treaty with the Ukraine is to be supplemented by additional special agreements.

7) To facilitate the implementation of all these measures, Dr. Südekum and an official of the Foreign Office will be sent to Kiev. They are to work in close cooperation with the Imperial Delegation in the Ukrainian capital.

8) Majors Hasse and Jarosch will be recalled to Berlin for consultations for the time being. Kindly advise us by wire under what pretext the two officers should be recalled to Germany. Dr. Südekum, who has contacts with the National Union, could leave for Kiev immediately." [36]

Berchem and Thiel, the two leading German diplomats in Kiev after Ambassador Mumm gave up his post, accepted this program with certain reservations. They did not think that the Russians could be removed from the Ukraine en masse, because they were too numerous and many could claim Ukrainian citizenship. Besides, these diplomats had serious doubts concerning the wisdom of taking strong measures against the Entente agents at this time. They also disapproved of the proposed mission of Dr. Südekum, fearing that the Hetman might be antagonized by such a move, although they expressed their readiness to use Südekum's contacts with Ukrainian nationalists to establish closer ties with these circles. As to the recall of Majors Hasse and Jarosch to Berlin, Berchem and Thiel advised against it. Although they acknowledged that these two aides of General Groener were greatly disliked by the Ukrainian nationalists, they advocated keeping them in Kiev, fearing that their removal would seriously disturb Groener and produce unnecessary complications among the Germans in Kiev.[37]

In the meantime, Thiel continued his efforts to Ukrainize the Hetman government and to reduce the Kadet influence in it; General Groener and his assistants worked along the same lines. To facilitate this task, Thiel urged the return to Kiev of Oleksander Sevryuk, the former Rada representative in Berlin.[38] Thiel's main efforts, however, were devoted to reorganizing the Hetman cabinet. The Hetman was, on the whole, quite cooperative in this undertaking, but he was no longer fully subservient to his German "adviser." He insisted on keeping Ihor A. Kistyakovs'kyi in his cabinet and expressed a strong preference for Dmytro I. Bahalii, a noted Ukrainian historian, to head the new cabinet. The opposition groups, however, notably the National Union through its principal leader, Volodymyr Vynnychenko, voiced their demands with a greater degree of confidence and determination than did the Hetman. They insisted on the dismissal of Kistyakovs'kyi as a *sine quo non* for their participation in the Hetman government and demanded eight seats in the cabinet.[39] Finally, in late October, a compromise agreement was reached, and a Ukrainian coalition government under the premiership of Fedir A. Lyzohub was formed. This proved to be only a temporary alliance. Soon the Russian forces around the Hetman reasserted their influence, and he clearly began to lean more and more in their direction, precipitating a complete break with the Ukrainian Union.[40] The Austrians also tried to help solve the Ukrainian cabinet crisis of October, 1918. They were at this point, however, sympathetic observers rather than advisers, and thus played but a secondary role in these efforts.[41]

At this juncture the Germans found themselves in a rather difficult position. Their plans in the Ukraine called for the maintenance of an independent Ukrainian state (which was the Ukrainian National Union's principal objective), yet they continued to regard the Hetman (who was rapidly moving away from this position) as the mainstay of their influence in the Ukraine. It was at the height of the effort to Ukrainize the Hetman government that Prime Minister Lyzohub was advised by Berchem to make a special declaration on the basic foreign policy aims of the Ukrainian state. These were the following:

"1) The Ukraine was to remain an independent state.

2) The Ukraine was to be neutral and enjoy complete freedom in dealing with other states. It had especially close relations, with Germany.

3) In the event of a coup d'état in Russia, normal friendly relations would be established between the Ukraine and the new Russian regime." [42]

Berchem further developed this line of thinking in a later memorandum in which he referred to the Hetman as "our strongest factor in the entire Ukrainian policy." [43]

While the Germans were busy trying to strengthen the Hetman's position in the country, a complete withdrawal of their forces from the Ukraine was being discussed as a real possibility. It is worth adding that such a move had not been seriously contemplated by the Germans until this point; nor had the Hetman ever raised the question of the duration of the German military contribution to the security of the state of which he was nominally the head. True, the Germans had recalled five divisions from the Ukraine in September, 1918, but the purpose of this was not so much to initiate a disengagement from this area as it was to gain forces for the more critical theater in the west. Although fully aware of the weakened morale of German troops in the east (whom he regarded as being engaged in a "stationary war"), General Groener urged keeping them in the Ukraine; and after a brief period of wavering he received full support for this policy, both from the Supreme Army Command and the German government. "The Bolshevik danger in the east" was mentioned as a factor in the German decision to postpone the military withdrawal from the Ukraine; economic considerations, however, were paramount, and the general feeling was that the Ukraine's agricultural products and raw materials were absolutely necessary for the Reich's survival after the war.[44] The German Ministry of Finance alone urged immediate withdrawal of troops,[45] but this had no effect on the Reich's policy in the Ukraine at this point.

Nevertheless, the rumors of impending German withdrawal from the east caused uneasiness in the Hetman camp, and on October 22 the Ukrainian Foreign Minister, Dmytro Doroshenko, went to Berlin to request that the German forces remain in the Ukraine. He was assured by the new Chancellor, Prince Max of Baden, that German forces would remain to protect Ukrainian frontiers.[46]

In the meantime, the over-all German position was deteriorating, and the occupation army in the east was becoming completely demoralized. Nevertheless, General Groener declared openly that the occupation of the Ukraine might continue well into the postwar period and ordered a propaganda drive in all German units to explain the situation. Groener, however, soon admitted that this "political education" failed to convince the German troops. He ruled out their possible use in the west, and he had serious doubts regarding their effectiveness and reliability even in the relatively quiet east.[47] In spite of all this, when in late

October the Austro-Hungarian forces began to withdraw from the Ukraine, the Supreme Army Command seriously contemplated the extension of German occupation to the southern Ukrainian provinces, which were being abandoned.[48]

Shortly before his take-over in the Ukraine, Hetman Skoropadsky had had to accept drastic restrictions which, in fact, amounted to a prohibition against developing an effective armed force of his own. Following the successful coup, the Germans seemingly altered this extreme stand; however, when reproached by the Austrians for this apparent breach of Austro-German policy, Ambassador Mumm explained that the military command merely allowed the organization of a token Ukrainian force for propaganda purposes, and that the Germans, just as much as the Austrians, were determined not to permit the formation of a Ukrainian army as long as the Ukraine remained under joint Austro-German occupation.[49]

Each of the two occupying powers, however, continued to suspect the other of secretly planning to develop a Ukrainian army in order to strengthen its position in the country. Feelings ran especially high when in late May Vienna announced the transfer to the Ukraine of the Ukrainian division formed in Austria from prisoners of war. Since the Germans expected this force to be Vienna-oriented, and only several weeks earlier had disbanded a similar force organized in Germany, they pressed for its dissolution.[50] As it turned out, the Austrians were even more concerned about the consequences of dispatching this division to the Ukraine and asked the Ukrainian government for various concessions and guarantees, including financial compensation and a promise to dissolve it if it should prove hostile to the Central Powers.[51] This was in keeping with Austria's earlier decision not to allow an effective Ukrainian armed force to be organized, a position that the Central Powers did not abandon until October, 1918.

Although they agreed in principle on the policy of not allowing the Ukraine to build up an armed force of its own, the Germans and the Austrians did not cooperate as closely in this important matter as one would have expected. Thus a month or so after the coup, while Vienna continued to bar the transfer of its Ukrainian prisoner-of-war division to the east, the Germans, responding to General Skoropadsky's request, gave their consent to the formation of a "small but trustworthy force." [52] Berlin, however, must have quickly developed second thoughts on the entire matter, and for a long time this was to remain merely a concession in principle. The Germans decided to keep this important project indefinitely in the planning stage, "lest the Hetman launch a drive from Kiev designed to unify the whole of Russia." [53]

Ambivalent though they were about the concession, the Germans soon began to act as if they really desired the organization of a Ukrainian army. By early June, 1918, the first draft of a German-Ukrainian military agreement was ready for signing, and in the course of the following month detailed plans for the formation of such a force were agreed upon. The Ukrainian army was to consist of eight army corps, four cavalry divisions, one independent cavalry brigade, one special guards division (the Serdyuks), heavy artillery units, and an air fleet.[54] The growth of this army, however, made very slow progress, Ambassador Mumm blaming it mainly on the lack of funds and insufficient interest on the part of the Ukrainians in joining the army.[55] Ukrainian sources, too, recognized certain domestic considerations which played a part in delaying the formation of a Ukrainian military force. Doroshenko, for example, pointed out the financial difficulties of the Ukrainian government and the political unreliability of many of the prospective recruits.[56]

Germany's reluctance to permit the organization of an independent Ukrainian force was based above all on its determination to maintain its hegemony in the country. On September 10 a German-Ukrainian military agreement had been signed, paragraph 3 of which clearly stipulated that German troops could remain in the Ukraine as long as the Supreme Army Command deemed it necessary.[57] It should also be noted that some German military leaders, notably General Ludendorff, continued to hope that Ukrainian manpower might still be made available to the Reich to save the day in the west. Naturally, the development of Ukrainian forces would rule out such a possibility once and for all. It is in the light of such plans that Ludendorff's remark, "the Ukraine has not yet succeeded in forming an army," made to Imperial Chancellor Hertling in early June, 1918, is to be fully appreciated.[58] In mid-August, 1918, the plan to recruit Ukrainians for the German army had again been revived. Mumm quickly warned that since the Hetman had difficulty filling the very limited quotas for his own force, the Germans would find it even more of a problem to recruit volunteers for their army. Even if there were any willing collaborators, Ambassador Mumm argued, their loyalty and reliability would be of doubtful value. This view was fully shared by Mumm's military colleagues in Kiev.[59]

It did not follow that the Germans were prepared to give the Hetman a free hand in building up his armed forces. In mid-September, 1918, they presented the Ukrainian government with a large bill that could seriously jeopardize Kiev's plan. The Germans demanded full compensation for training, equipping, and maintaining the two Ukrainian divisions organized in Germany prior to the occupation (disbanded shortly before Skoropadsky's coup d'état), as well as for the educational work conducted among Ukrainian prisoners of war still in German camps.[60]

The Austro-Hungarian government was similarly determined to prevent the formation of an independent Ukrainian fighting force. When General Krauss called for the organization of a large and well-equipped Ukrainian army in late September, 1918, Count Burián, the Dual Monarchy's Foreign Minister, strongly opposed this recommendation, arguing that such a force could easily become a threat to Austria-Hungary as well as to the Ukraine's other neighbors. He proposed instead the formation of a "police force," that could relieve some of the occupation troops for possible service elsewhere.[61]

These proposals and counterproposals are of interest mainly because they reflect the hopelessly confused and largely negative attitude of the German and Austrian governments toward the formation of a Ukrainian army. Obviously it was futile to go on prohibiting something that had little chance of success. (By September and October the Hetman had lost whatever popularity he might have enjoyed in the country in the beginning.) It was just as futile to "permit" the Ukrainians to develop their own defensive force at a time when it could no longer be done, though only such a force could save the Ukrainian state from collapsing after a German withdrawal. This belated decision was made jointly by Germany and Austria in early October, 1918. The two powers not only pledged their support in the form of military aid but also urged that the plan to form a Ukrainian army by calling up 85,000 men be carried out immediately.[62] All this came too late, and the Hetman's plan for the development of a dependable armed force was never realized. In November, 1918, the Hetman's forces, according to Ukrainian sources, numbered 60,000–65,000.[63] An earlier German official source which estimated the strength of the Ukrainian army at 15,000[64] apparently did not take account of the growth of this force in late October and early November, and probably failed to take into consideration the guard companies and smaller units organized throughout the country for police work and general protection. Whatever the exact strength of the Hetman's army, it was clearly insufficient to protect the Ukrainian state from internal and external enemies after the withdrawal of Austrian and German troops from the country. Moreover, it had to cope with a popular Ukrainian anti-Hetman uprising that soon won over the bulk of Skoropadsky's Ukrainian forces, leaving the Hetman government almost completely defenseless.

The disposition of the Russian Black Sea fleet was a matter closely linked to the problem of developing an effective Ukrainian army. The issue was further complicated by the fact that the Soviet regime also had claims to this fleet. Moreover, other riparian states, especially Turkey, were deeply interested in the fate of what was formerly the Black Sea's principal naval force. Finally, the fate of this fleet was linked to the broader Crimean question and the general Black Sea settlement.

During the peace talks between the Ukrainians and the representatives of the Central Powers at Brest-Litovsk the problem of the Crimea did not arise at all. The fate of Russia's Black Sea fleet—then largely in Bolshevik hands, although some units did display the Ukrainian flag—was discussed but no concrete decisions were made. Although the Ukrainization of Russia's Black Sea fleet achieved only limited success, there is no denying that many officers and sailors in this fleet were Ukrainian. This much had to be admitted even by Russian sources.[65]

On the eve of the German occupation of the Crimean Peninsula, in late April, 1918, some of the best and most modern units of the Russian Black Sea fleet escaped to Novorossiisk; a substantial part of this fleet, nevertheless, fell into German hands when they entered Sevastopol. Among the captured vessels were the following: seven battleships; two cruisers; three big modern and seven older destroyers; ten submarines; a large fleet of minelayers, minesweepers, and torpedo boats; a considerable amount (more than 100,000 tons) of merchant shipping in seaworthy condition; many general cargo vessels; and, finally, a large quantity of very valuable war matériel.[66] It was, thus, not a question of what to do with several shabby and obsolete vessels; the disposition of Russia's Black Sea fleet was an important economic, military, and political matter which no one could afford to treat lightly.

Originally, the German Foreign Office seems to have regarded the Ukraine as a natural heir to this naval force;[67] however, the Germans never really made up their minds about what to do with the Russian Black Sea units that fell into their hands. In late April the Reich's Secretary of the Navy recommended that the highly complex question of ownership of the Russian fleet be left open.[68] The Foreign Ministry's legal experts thought that Soviet Russia could be assured of eventual possession of the Black Sea fleet in return for oil and mineral concessions in the Caucasus and Turkestan's cotton. (It is not clear whether this proposal had anything to do with the Soviet protest made on April 27, 1918, following the extension of German occupation to the Crimea.)[69]

General Ludendorff, on the other hand, favored the transfer of most of Russia's Black Sea fleet to Turkey. Far from forgetting German interests, however, the general insisted that the principal Crimean port, Sevastopol, be developed into a German stronghold, that the Crimea he kept in German hands so that a colonial state could be organized in the Peninsula, and, last but not least, that the east be converted into an exclusively German economic and political sphere of influence in order to make up for the Reich's loss of its colonies overseas.[70]

General Ludendorff's views concerning the disposition of the Russian Black Sea fleet were opposed most consistently by Ambassador Mumm. In May, 1918, Mumm, who did not seem to have the Foreign Office's full support for his pro-Ukrainian Black Sea policy, tried various formulas to gain acceptance of his plan. Mumm felt at first that the Black Sea fleet could be used by the Germans without formal appropriation and that the Ukrainians could be given the task of minesweeping the Black Sea harbors; he also suggested that the use of Ukrainian naval facilities and the purchase of various marine supplies be arranged through a special agreement with Kiev.[71] Mumm returned to the question in June, urging his government to grant the Ukrainians certain minimal concessions to satisfy some of Kiev's aspirations in the Black Sea, and advised Berlin not to prohibit expressly the construction of new men-of-war in Ukrainian drydocks, so as to avoid antagonizing Kiev—especially since such a Ukrainian naval force could easily be controlled. This last proposal met with the full approval of Under-Secretary of State von dem Bussche.[72]

It was not until July 2 that Germany, at a meeting of its civilian and military leaders at Spa under the Kaiser's chairmanship, made an effort to clarify its position on various Black Sea questions. As far as the disposition of the Russian Black Sea fleet was concerned, the Foreign Office remained steadfast in its legalistic approach to the problem, maintaining that eventually the fleet would have to be handed over to Russia; General Ludendorff pressed for the acceptance of his original thesis regarding the fleet as war booty. Finally, a compromise agreement was reached whereby the ownership question was left open, but the Supreme Command was given a free hand in employing Russian Black Sea units or facilities in order to strengthen the Reich's war effort.[73]

It is interesting that already at this conference Ludendorff was ready to modify his position even further and began to speak of the transfer of some of the vessels to the Ukraine. He had more to say on this shortly after the Spa meeting. He called for an immediate transfer of small vessels to the Ukraine; large units, however, were to be retained in German hands to insure the Reich's domination of the Black Sea.[74] Ambassador Mumm continued to press for a clear and open declaration concerning Germany's view of the Ukraine's position as a Black Sea power. The Consul General in Kiev, Erich von Thiel, was even more critical of Germany's Black Sea policy and privately favored the transfer of the entire fleet to the Ukraine.[75]

The fate of the Black Sea continued to play an important part in German-Ukrainian relations during the remainder of the Hetmanate. It was one of the key items in the Hetman's talks with the Kaiser and General Ludendorff in early September, 1918. Although certain Ukrainian sources maintain that the Kaiser agreed to release a sufficient number of naval units to give the Ukraine a good start as a Black Sea power,[76] official German records present a somewhat less happy picture. Neither the Kaiser nor General Ludendorff made any specific commitments with regard to the Black Sea fleet during the Hetman's visit in Berlin. Shortly thereafter Lieutenant Captain Wülfing, the German naval attaché in Kiev, reminded the Ukrainians that once the Russian claim to the fleet had been recognized, the situation could be altered only through generous financial concessions to the Soviet government.[77]

Following the collapse of Bulgaria in early October, the Hetman was told that on the basis of a special agreement with Moscow all naval units stationed in Sevastopol would be reactivated under the German flag to bolster the Black Sea defense. The Hetman had no objections to this move at this critical moment, but was nevertheless greatly disappointed, fearing that it would further weaken Kiev's claim to the fleet.[78]

The dissatisfaction with this decision among official and naval circles of the Ukraine must have been serious enough to prompt Wülfing to recommend that some vessels be immediately transferred to the Ukrainian navy to bolster Kiev's morale.[79]

As late as November 9, however, the same Wülfing urged his superiors in Berlin to keep all naval forces in the Black Sea in German hands "for the time being." [80] Like the Ukrainian army, the Hetman's navy never advanced beyond the planning stage. Although the Germans began to transfer some naval units of the Black Sea fleet to the Ukraine shortly before the evacuation of their forces from the east, the transfer came too late to make any real difference to the already faltering Hetman state.

Although, officially, the Germans never abandoned the idea of an independent Ukrainian state, some among them, notably the military, also maintained ties with various White Russian groups which had found refuge in the Ukraine, especially after the overthrow of the Rada. These contacts were maintained by subordinate German officers with the full approval of their superiors. In early June, 1918, as General Ludendorff was to explain later, it was necessary to "get into touch with the more monarchist groups of the Right and obtain such influence over them that the monarchist movement will take the direction we want when it gets the upper hand." [81] Ambassador Mumm, too, although he continued the Reich's policy of advocating permanent detachment of the Ukraine from Russia, found it advisable to direct Consul General Thiel to maintain contacts with Prince Grigorii Laikhtenbergskii and his brother Nikolai, the two Russian monarchist leaders in the Ukraine. This was done in anticipation of a Bolshevik collapse, to insure good working relations with the most likely successors in Russia.[82] It was also with this in view that General Groener's assistant, Major Hasse, held a series of meetings with the Kadet leader Pavel Milyukov in Kiev in June and July. As it turned out, Milyukov was not in a position to speak for the Russian Volunteer Army, which remained as anti-German as ever; nor was the German representative in these talks authorized to make any new proposals to the Russian Right.[83]

Thus, even though General Ludendorff considered from time to time the possibility of drawing these Russian circles closer to the Reich, and even though this German desire (so much in keeping with the earlier foreign policy tradition) to establish closer relations with the Russian Right and the monarchists was clearly expressed at the imperial conference held at Spa on July 2–3, there was very little chance that such cordiality could develop. As long as the Germans continued their support of and domination in various new states in the east formerly under Russian control, and Milyukov and other White Russians insisted on the reestablishment of the Empire, the two parties could not get together.

Consequently, to nobody's surprise, virtually at the same time that improvement of the Reich's relations with the White Russians was being considered at Spa, the German Foreign Office came to the conclusion that all such efforts were fruitless and that the Hetman government should order Milyukov to leave the Ukraine. Mumm, who had advocated such a policy all along, was only too happy to bring these German-Russian talks in Kiev to a close.[84]

The Austrians were not directly involved in these exploratory talks with the Russian Right—which concentrated its activities in German-controlled Kiev—and were quite happy with the German decision not to continue flirting with "these hostile and unreliable elements." [85]

The Hetman's position on the attempted German-Russian *rapprochement* was not very clear. It was a rather difficult and delicate situation for him, to say the least. Some of his ministers and high governmental officials stood closer to Milyukov or Prince G. N. Trubetskoi—another Russian leader in Kiev who worked toward closer cooperation with Germany—than to him. Officially, the Hetman remained neutral and refrained from establishing contact with these Russian leaders, even though he knew many of them personally. He was thus greatly relieved to see the Germans take the initiative in this delicate matter by ending the negotiations.

Although German-Russian talks, on this level, were not to be resumed, the activities of the Russian Right in the Ukraine were by no means curtailed. From early July on, one can discern a slow return to the "old line," although in the period of the Hetmanate the idea of Ukrainian statehood, of which the Germans spoke so often, came to mean something distinctly different from the original concept. During the Rada period the concept of Ukrainian statehood was based clearly on the nationality principle, with considerable autonomy granted to the minorities, whereas under the Hetman it was based on territoriality, a principle the Germans and those around the Hetman found much more to their liking. It was based on a broader concept of nationality that included persons who did not know the Ukrainian language. The territoriality principle was also reflected in the law on Ukrainian citizenship, passed on July 3, by which any Russian subject living in the Ukraine would become a Ukrainian citizen unless he specifically refused to accept it.[86]

The fact that Kiev became a mecca for all the Russian Rightists following the overthrow of the Rada in late April, 1918, is to be credited above all to the benevolent German attitude. The Hetman's readiness to accept and accommodate these elements, however, was just as important. Although Hetman Skoropadsky does not seem to have played an active role in this movement, there is no denying that from mid-1918 until the collapse of the Hetmanate Kiev was as much a center of Russian political life as it was a Ukrainian political center. General Groener was very much aware of this, and he also knew that these circles aimed at the reestablishment of a united Russia. This did not disturb General Groener at all because he was convinced that the Hetman had, generally speaking, a similar plan for the future.[87]

A series of congresses, conventions, and conferences of various Russian monarchist, nationalist, and military organizations took place in Kiev during this period, and some of the Hetman's ministers and other high-ranking officials openly played active, and sometimes even leading, roles in these affairs. Among the organizations that made Kiev the center of their activities were the following: The Russian Kadet party, the Union for the Rebirth of

Russia, the Union of the Activists of the Ukraine, and the Kievan National Center. According to Mumm, all these organizations were in contact with German authorities in Kiev.[88]

German personnel in the Ukraine showed enough sympathy for this movement to make it necessary for Field Marshal Eichhorn to issue an order directing his officers to refrain from giving open encouragement and support to the White Russian circles active in that area.[89]

The formation of various volunteer detachments, with the Hetman's and German support, was among the most consequential activities of the Russian Right in the Ukraine. As early as mid-May (two weeks after General Skoropadsky's coup d'état), the German military command in Kiev was requested to allow the Russian officers to organize military units for service against the Bolsheviks, with the Ukraine as their base of operations. Ambassador Mumm felt that nothing of the sort could be tolerated and urged the Hetman to take the same approach in this delicate matter.[90] Soon, however, the recruitment of White Russian volunteers and the formation of special detachments on Ukrainian soil were in full swing, with similar activities taking place in the Crimea as well as in the Caucasus.[91] Both German and Russian sources agree that the recruitment seldom encountered any serious opposition from the German military.[92] According to an official Austrian source, the number of Russian officers in the Ukraine was quite impressive—well over 30,000 in the German zone of occupation and almost half that number in the Austro-Hungarian zone.[93]

Indeed, so conspicuous and widespread were these activities that Foreign Secretary Hintze, in response to Soviet complaints, urged Mumm to enlist General Groener's support to bring a halt to such activities in the occupied areas. At first, Groener's staff advised Mumm to inform the Soviet envoy in the Ukraine, K. Rakovskii, that it knew of no such recruitment taking place on the Ukrainian territory. Moreover, the Ukraine was not to be regarded as an occupied area; consequently, the German army in the Ukraine could not prohibit such activities.[94]

Groener, however, agreed with Mumm that recruitment for the Volunteer Army was to be officially forbidden, and this ban was to be extended to various Cossack military organizations (such as the Don, Kuban, and Astrakhan). The Germans were especially concerned about "open recruitment," and on August 22 the Army Group Kiev issued an order henceforth forbidding the practice.[95] This formal action was taken to meet Soviet criticism. It must be added, however, that the Germans were becoming increasingly hostile to the Volunteer Army operating in the south, especially after the capture of Ekaterinodar (now Krasnodar) in mid-August. General Groener, though he made it quite clear that the prohibition on recruitment for various Cossack formations should not be enforced too rigidly, felt that the Germans should be less cooperative as far as the Volunteer Army was concerned, lest this "hostile force become a real threat to us." [96]

Indeed, after late August open recruitment for the Volunteer Army on Ukrainian soil was largely discontinued because of the joint efforts of the occupation forces and Ukrainian authorities. At the same time the Germans and the Hetman, rather than discouraging, actually facilitated, or at least condoned, the constant movement of Russian officers southward.[97]

The continued ambivalent German policy toward the Russian Volunteer Army was caused by another important factor, namely the belief that the Soviet regime would soon collapse and that such people as Professor Pavel Milyukov or General Anton Denikin might then become the spokesmen of the new Russia. German reluctance to take stronger measures against the Russian elements in the east was also dictated by the hope, however shaky and unlikely, that the Volunteer Army might somehow be induced to move away from the Entente.[98] Soon, however, concrete steps were ordered to prevent the development of a strong anti-German military force in the south. The Germans decided to support and finance other volunteer formations in order to reduce the influx of Russian officers to the Volunteer Army in Kuban.

The most serious of these ventures was the Southern Army. Count A. Bobrinskii of Kiev had charge of recruitment, and General N. I. Ivanov was its commander. Count Fëdor Keller, another former Russian general with headquarters in Kiev, also played a part in this undertaking. The Southern Army and a similar force known as the Russian National Army (each numbering several thousand men) operated mainly in Voronezh and Saratov provinces and in August even managed to wrest from the Bolsheviks almost half of these territories.[99] These "armies" lacked popular support and had to cope with numerous peasant uprisings. As a result, they failed to attract recruits and remained badly under-staffed.[100] With the weakening of German influence in the east, in November, 1918, Ataman Pëtr Krasnov of the Don, with the Het-man's assistance (following a meeting between the two), under-took the reorganization and consolidation of these forces into a new Southern Army.[101] This venture, however, proved equally unsuccessful.

Some students of Germany's *Ostpolitik* of the World War I pe-riod have concluded that after late July, 1918, the Reich's repre-sentatives in Kiev were unable to control the situation in the Ukraine.[102] It would be difficult to deny that the Reich's military position in the Ukraine grew weaker, especially during the months of September and October; nevertheless, the Germans continued to play a decisive role in the affairs of the east until they withdrew their occupation forces. It was not until mid-October that they at long last gave permission for the organiza-tion of an effective Ukrainian armed force and not until late Oc-tober that the Hetman was given a free hand to seek closer ties with the Entente.[103]

In fact, the Germans continued to play an important role in the Ukraine until the collapse of the Hetmanate. Furthermore, they hoped, with the Entente's blessing to be sure, to carry on the role of a protecting power in the Ukraine well into the postwar period. On November 1 they decided that their military assistance to the Ukraine was to continue after the termination of hostilities in the west, in order to prevent this "allied country from falling back into chaos and lawlessness." [104]

Following closely upon the Reich's decision to keep its forces in the Ukraine after the armistice, the Hetman government formally requested the Entente to prolong the stay of German troops in the country until a Ukrainian army could be organized.[105] Another important move taken by the Hetman at this point was a meeting with the Don leader, Ataman Pëtr N. Krasnov. The two generals met on November 3 at Skorokhodovo in the Eastern Ukraine. The Ataman was accompanied by his "special adviser," Major von Co-chenhausen, and the Germans, according to the Ataman, were instrumental in arranging this meeting. The two leaders agreed upon closer cooperation, especially in the field of defense, in an-ticipation of a renewed Bolshevik attack against them. The most important result of the meeting, however, was General Krasnov's declaration hailing the Ukrainian-Don *rapprochement* as the first step in their supreme task, the restoration of a unified Russia.[106]

By early November, the Germans had also decided to give the Hetman a free hand in developing closer ties with the Kuban—an area where the Ukrainian element was much stronger than anywhere else outside the Ukraine—even though a few months earlier they had vetoed Skoropadsky's plan to send military assistance to the Ukrainians in that area.[107] As far as the Kuban was concerned, the Germans had an additional reason for encouraging the Hetman to seek greater influence there. It was the stronghold of the Volunteer Army, now led by General Denikin, and the Germans hoped to weaken it through the possible defection of the Ukrainian Kuban Cossacks, who constituted an important element of this force.[108]

This belated German decision to give the Ukrainians a free hand in the east came mainly as the result of its loss of control in this area. It was also the weakening of their position in the east that prompted the Germans to declare, on November 3, a strict neutrality in the growing Polish-Ukrainian conflict and to promise not to oppose the Galician Ukrainians in the event they should move into Kholm. The Germans formally restated their neutrality a week or so later, and urged the Hetman to refrain from giving any assistance to the Galicians to avoid complicating his already difficult position.[109] (The Hetman had quite seriously considered giving aid to the Ukrainians in Galicia in their struggle against the Poles by releasing certain Galician Ukrainian units to fight in the west. Instead, they joined the republican forces led by Petlyura in operations that ultimately resulted in the Hetman's ouster.[110])

In the meantime, the Hetman, having secured German approval for his plan to seek closer contacts with the Entente representatives, informed the German chargé d'affaires, Berchem, that because of the vague attitude of the Entente toward the Ukraine and the uncertainty of the general situation in the east, he had been in touch with Jassy and requested that someone, even an unofficial Entente representative, come to Kiev to discuss the situation with him.[111] This final phase of the Hetmanate can be understood only in the light of Skoropadsky's desperate attempts to convince the Allies, especially the French, who were expected to play a decisive role throughout the Black Sea area, that he was prepared to follow a pro-Allied course and that his regime was worthy of their recognition and support. Indeed, the Hetman's policies in the last several weeks of his rule in the Ukraine—from the appointment of S. N. Gerbel, an open anti-Ukrainian, as Prime Minister, to his November 14 declaration signifying complete abandonment of his earlier goal of a Ukrainian state—were primarily a product of this consideration.

It was at this point that the Germans decided upon a complete withdrawal of their forces from the Ukraine. "We must, of course, begin the evacuation," wrote General Hoffmann in his diary on November 12. "I am sorry for the people whose territory we are handing over to the Bolsheviks, but I cannot restrain our men— they want to get home." [112] The evacuation of the Ukraine, was not, however, such a simple matter for Prince Max of Baden, the Reich's new Chancellor. "A new eastern front would probably not arise owing to the inferiority of the Red Army, but the sacrifice of the Ukraine would presumably be regarded as a triumph for Bolshevism and would be a great source of encouragement for its propaganda." [113] General Ludendorff came to a similar conclusion. "If we do not need to live on the Ukraine, it is only a question of keeping there as many troops as can secure the frontiers against the danger of Bolshevism." [114] General Groener, who was more intimately involved in the German experiment in the east than any of the above spokesmen, voiced an even stronger opposition to the immediate evacuation of the east, arguing that "it was impossible for us [Germans] to withdraw our protecting hand from the Baltic peoples, the Finns, and the Ukrainians, whom we had liberated and whose confidence we had won." [115]

The hope that German troops would remain in the Ukraine, at least for the time being, was probably an important factor in Berlin's attempt to continue to exert its influence on the course of Ukrainian political life. On November 13, when the Hetman was planning to ban the congress of the Ukrainian National Union scheduled for November 17, Berchem warned him against this move, and in his talks with the National Union leaders this German diplomat restated the Reich's support of the Ukraine's right to separate existence.[116] The Germans, thus, even at this late stage, were determined to remain faithful to their "Ukrainian line," and their chargé d'affaires in Kiev was ready to play the role of an intermediary between the Hetman and his Ukrainian political opponents. At this point, however, German troops in the Ukraine openly proclaimed their neutrality in the growing internal conflict in the Ukraine, and this greatly complicated Berchem's already difficult mission.[117] Indeed, the proclamation of this neutrality can be regarded as ending the Reich's active role in the affairs of the Ukraine.

The Germans played no part in the Hetman's most fateful decision since his coup of late April, 1918, to abandon the idea of an independent Ukrainian state and to advocate openly a united, federated Russian state.[118] The Germans continued to show strong preference for the old course and advised the Hetman not to abandon it. Even after Skoropadsky's second coup on November 14—proclaiming union with Russia—Berchem in his talks with the Hetman expressed the hope that the new orientation of the Kiev government would not result in a complete renunciation of the Hetman's Ukrainian program.[119]

This radical shift in the Hetman's policy did little to make him more acceptable to the victorious Entente, nor did it provide him with the expected Russian support. On the other hand, it further antagonized the nationally conscious Ukrainian circles, and provided the anti-Hetman opposition, organized around the National Union, with an excellent pretext to launch a long-expected armed uprising against him. Initially, the Germans remained neutral in this struggle and did not take part in quelling anti-Hetman demonstrations in Kiev following the formation of a purely Russian cabinet headed by Gerbel, a disturbance during which some twenty students were reported to have lost their lives.[120] Nor did the Germans, following earlier instructions, in any way interfere with the Hetman's efforts to establish closer relations with the Entente. They nevertheless continued to emphasize "the Ukrainian side of this issue," protested vigorously against the Hetman's intention to arrest a number of prominent Ukrainians who opposed him politically, and made a renewed effort to Ukrainize his cabinet in the hope that the Hetman regime, while following a clearly pro-Entente course, would also remain friendly to the Germans.[121] In line with this approach, the Germans urged the Hetman to dismiss his newly appointed Commander in Chief, General Fëdor Keller, a Russian nobleman and a notorious Ukrainophobe with whom General Skoropadsky was already in a serious conflict, and promised him their "full support in case of difficulty." The Germans also urged the Hetman to declare publicly that the proposed federation with Russia did not represent a complete abandonment of his previous Ukrainian policy. Such a declaration and the dismissal of General Keller, in their view, were intended to reassure those Ukrainians who did not see eye to eye with Petlyura and thus hopefully to bring about a *rapprochement* between them and the Hetman.[122]

At first the Germans professed to be neutral during the anti-Hetman rising led by the Directory, a new Ukrainian revolutionary government in which Symon Petlyura played the key role, and even concluded a nonintervention agreement with these Ukrainian nationalist forces at Bila Tsertkva on November 17. This agreement, which neither the Germans nor the Petlyura forces honored in practice, was concluded by the representatives of the German Great Council of Soldiers, which had headquarters in Kiev.[123] A week or so later, however, they helped the Hetman forces to repel Petlyura's troops from Kiev, explaining their intervention by the necessity of preserving law and order in the city to insure a smooth evacuation of German troops from the Ukraine.[124] It was mainly because of continued German support and the failure of an anti-Hetman uprising in Kiev in late November that General Skoropadsky's regime survived until the middle of December.

On November 28, the German military command in Kiev concluded another agreement with the Petlyura forces establishing a truce line some fifteen miles southwest of Kiev, with the Germans remaining well entrenched in the city.[125] The Germans sought to maintain this precarious arrangement for several reasons. First, they continued to support the Hetman and were willing to accept his thesis that Petlyura was no more than an outlaw. Second, such allegedly was also the Entente's wish.[126] Third, the Germans wished to gain time to make another attempt to bring about a reconciliation between the Hetman and the moderate Ukrainian national circles. They tried to convince Skoropadsky that the dismissal of his purely Russian cabinet and the formation of a new Ukrainian government were the only alternatives left to him at this point.[127]

Finally, on December 5, the German chargé d'affaires in Kiev, Count Berchem, was instructed to keep his hands off the increasingly confused Ukrainian political situation and to confine his activities to the role of an impartial mediator between the various antagonistic groups and factions.[128] Several days later the Germans openly admitted that their troops in the east could no longer be regarded as a fighting force and ordered that they withdraw immediately under the protection of weak volunteer units organized for that purpose.[129] To facilitate the withdrawal from the Ukraine, a new agreement was concluded with Petlyura on December 12, promising complete neutrality of the German army.[130] These measures were essential to insure smooth evacuation of the remnants of the Reich's eastern army which was by then so completely disorganized that many of its units were no longer capable of self-defense, and the German and Austro-Hungarian troops had to move through a vast territory engulfed again by complete chaos and full of hostile guerrilla bands and other irregular forces.

On December 14, after securing the guarantee of German nonintervention, the forces of a new nationalist revolutionary government in the Ukraine—the Directory—entered Kiev, whereupon the Hetman decided to give up the struggle. Thus seven and one-half months after he assumed power and exactly one month following his declaration of reunion with Russia, Skoropadsky resigned, and the Hetmanate came to an end. His abdication statement was brief and dignified. He declared that he had been guided by the Ukraine's "best interests," and presented his abdication as irrevocable.[131] (It was not until fifteen years later, on May 16, 1933, that the Hetman, who remained a true Ukrainian patriot to the end of his days and raised his children in the same spirit, made his will appointing his son Danylo to succeed him as head of the Hetman movement in the event of his death.[132])

In the meantime, the German envoy in Kiev, Count Berchem, though he claimed that the agreement concluded with the Directory on December 12 was "a purely military arrangement," had decided to establish *de facto* relations with the new Ukrainian regime even before the Hetman's abdication. His hope was that the Directory would recognize earlier German-Ukrainian agreements and honor the economic commitments undertaken by its predecessors.[133]

Strictly speaking, however, the Germans never let Skoropadsky down. Disguised as a German soldier, the Hetman managed to escape with retreating troops and was destined to remain in Germany for the rest of his life. General Skoropadsky settled in Wann-see near Berlin, and this remained the center of his movement until the end of World War II. The Allies never forgave him his defection, and he never regretted his pro-German orientation. The end of this courageous, even though often misguided and even more often misunderstood, Ukrainian leader was as unpredictable and accidental as his reign. Ironically, if anybody's death can be termed ironic, he died in Bavaria in April of 1945—literally days before the end of World War II in Germany—in one of the final Allied air raids.

CHAPTER XII

Conclusion

A study of Germany's plans and policies in the east during World War I is largely a study of political, diplomatic, economic, and military failures. Although this may be somewhat less true of its 1918 venture in the Ukraine and the Crimea than of its occupation of other territories of the east, Germany's Ukrainian plans in the final analysis proved as defective and unrealistic as its occupation policies were crude and ineffectual.

It is not easy to sum up a venture as confused as the German occupation of the Ukraine. It generated a complex of vague and hurriedly improvised plans, a chain of unfulfilled ambitions, a series of missed opportunities. Since the venture had to be abandoned before its full development, its after-effects and results were largely inconclusive.

Frictions and rivalry between the Supreme Army Command and the German Foreign Office, which reached their peak in the year 1918, further complicated the situation in the Ukraine. The clash between Kühlmann's compromise approach and Ludendorff's total victory or total defeat position created problems during the Brest-Litovsk negotiations. Soon these differences became even more serious and Kühlmann, following his defeat at the Homburg conference on February 13, 1918, felt compelled to withdraw more and more from the Reich's decision-making process. This gradual withdrawal explains his stay of several weeks, in February and March of 1918, in Bucharest negotiating the Rumanian treaty and just plain enjoying himself in that charming Balkan capital; his silent presence at the May 11–13 Spa conference; and his absence from another such imperial consultation on July 2, even though he was still in office. In the meantime, the influence of General Ludendorff became all-pervasive, and few developments occurred in the east that did not bear his imprint. Hundreds of documents bearing the general's signature and an equally impressive collection of notes, memoranda, and the like prompted by his inquiries and proddings, leave no doubt as to where political power and responsibility were located. Of course, it would be unjust to blame Ludendorff alone for all that happened, or did not happen, in the east. In spite of his great influence, the Reich's Ukrainian undertaking was a collective gamble and should be viewed as a collective failure. Nevertheless, he must bear a major share of responsibility for it. It was, perhaps, not so much his meddling in the affairs of the Foreign Office to the point of virtual take-over of its responsibilities, as it was his narrow-mindedness and inaptness that one would hold against the general. Ironically, Kühlmann's policy of disengagement in the east could have released substantial forces for use on the western front during the spring offensive, and perhaps the destinies of the war would have taken a rather different turn. In late March, 1918, the German army in the east still numbered one million men. And no one was as much responsible for this as General Ludendorff.

Austro-German rivalry in the east was nowhere as serious as in the Ukraine. It was especially acute in the early stages of the German and Austrian advance in the east and continued throughout the period of the occupation. This factor produced more annoyance than damage, however; it is doubtful whether in its absence the exploitation of the Ukraine would have been more effective or that more German troops could have been relieved for employment in the west.

Prior to World War I the Germans, especially their eastern experts, had some familiarity with the Ukrainian problem, but German policy-makers had no special plan for this area at the outbreak of the hostilities. Initially, Austria-Hungary and, to a lesser extent, Germany tried to exploit the Ukrainian national movement for the benefit of their war effort; however, this did not mean that they aimed at the break-up and permanent dissolution of the Russian Empire. After an initial and disappointing flirtation with Ukrainian nationalist elements, and following the development of a military stalemate in the east, the Central Powers lost their enthusiasm for the Ukrainian movement but did not completely abandon it. The activities of the Union for the Liberation of the Ukraine may be viewed as a faithful index of the uncertain German and Austrian attitude toward the Ukrainian factor during this period.

That the Germans, intoxicated by early and easy victories on the eastern front, did develop some rather ambitious expansionist plans for this area in the early stages of the war can no longer be disputed. Nonetheless, Fritz Fischer's argument, developed in his well-known study of the Reich's war aims during World War I, that these extreme plans continued to dominate German official thinking throughout the war period is simply not borne out by the available documentation. Careful study of German and Austrian archives does not suggest as much continuity and consistency as Professor Fischer would have us believe. Moreover, like Soviet historians, Professor Fischer tends to ascribe too much importance to various unofficial plans and programs calling for the "rolling back of Russia," which were so common and popular in Germany during this period, forgetting that even official German plans and views were subject to constant review and revision and that many of them had never been fully developed.

The Russian Revolution did not bring about any radical changes in this cautious German view of the Ukrainian movement. The representatives of the Central Powers went to Brest-Litovsk with the intention of concluding a peace treaty with the new Soviet government, regarding it as the spokesman for all of Russia; thus, despite a series of preparatory conferences and consultations between Berlin and Vienna, they went without any special plans for the Ukraine.

After a prolonged and heated debate, the Ukrainian Rada decided, entirely on its own initiative, to send a separate delegation to Brest-Litovsk. Initially, the Germans had virtually no supporters in the Rada. The two sides were brought together mainly because of their common interest. The Bolshevik attitude played an important part in facilitating, if not necessitating, separate talks between the Central Powers and the Ukraine. Thus the Treaty of Brest-Litovsk was not the result of a carefully prepared plan for German expansion in the east, as is so widely believed. It was merely a by-product of Russia's collapse and subsequent weakness and should therefore be viewed as the real beginning of the Reich's expansionist policies in this area.

The Ukrainian treaty of Brest was negotiated on terms rather advantageous to Kiev. Certainly, the Ukrainians paid a very high price for recognition and peace, but it is to be remembered that the popular demand for peace in the Ukraine was as widespread as elsewhere in the east, perhaps more so. Moreover, some critics of the Ukrainian treaty tend to ignore the fact that for many Ukrainians the rule of Russian Bolsheviks appeared more dangerous and more distasteful than the German assistance furnished to the Rada, even at the cost of a temporary occupation of the country by the Central Powers, which would have probably taken place anyhow with or without a formal treaty. (The fact that the Germans were expected to win the war and that the Allies were nowhere in sight should also be viewed as a powerful factor in all these developmemts.) Last but not least, the Ukrainian treaty alone did not really predetermine the exact nature of Germany's Ukrainian undertaking. Indeed, events in the east might have developed along different lines had the Germans decided to follow different occupation policies, or had other people been selected to administer the undertaking.

The Germans began to develop concrete plans for the Ukraine only after the occupation of the country. Initially, even the exact form and extent of their military involvement in the Ukraine were not clear. Short-range economic considerations were paramount throughout the occupation period, although the Germans also had a genuine interest in developing a permanent basis for the exercise of economic influence in the country. There is, however, no evidence that they ever seriously contemplated keeping their forces in the Ukraine over a long period, nor did they ever consider annexation of any part of its territory, the Crimea excluded.

The overthrow of the Rada and the establishment of the Hetmanate were occasioned mainly by the Reich's inability to organize a more effective economic exploitation of the Ukraine. Ideological and national considerations played but a minor role in the

German decision to do away with the socialist Rada. General Skoropadsky's coup d'état appears to have been produced by a combination of German and Ukrainian initiative. Granting that the presence of German forces in Kiev and other points was decisive in this development, the Rada's reliance on German military support after Brest-Litovsk was just as great, even though the Rada had come into being and was reconstituted in the spring of 1918 free of any German influence or pressure and was on the whole the more independent and more popular of the two regimes.

Although the Germans decided, after a period of wavering and uncertainty, to preserve certain elements of independent statehood in the Ukraine, their policy in the country was far from consistent. The German military, especially, were constantly torn between their support of the idea of an independent Ukraine and a Russia one and indivisible—the latter being a concept most of them found easier to comprehend. The rather complex situation in the Ukraine and the equally complex political personality of the Hetman, as well as German unpreparedness for a major undertaking in the Slavic east, all contributed to this ambivalence. In spite of the fact that their plans for the Ukraine never fully crystallized, the Germans were genuinely concerned about its future even at the time of their own collapse, and they considered keeping their forces there after the armistice. Ironically, the Germans appear to have been more sincere and consistent in their Ukrainian policy from August, 1918, on, although they were no longer in a position to play a decisive role in the affairs of the east.

The Germans did not occupy the Crimea until May, 1918. Although they had no definite and clear plans for the area at that point, they soon developed a special interest in the Peninsula. In contrast to their plans for the Ukraine, which were mainly of an economic nature, the Germans—General Ludendorff in particular—seriously considered the establishment of a permanent foothold in the Crimea. The Crimea was to become a haven for German colonists of the east in the form of a *Kolonialstaat;* it was also to be transformed into a naval fortress to be used as a base for the extension of German influence into the Caucasus and the Middle East. Even though little was done to promote these bold plans, they would almost certainly have been revived and pursued

with greater vigor and determination had the Germans been allowed to remain active in this area in the postwar period.

Politically, Germany's Ukrainian undertaking proved a failure,
even though Berlin initially did have the opportunity to establish
good working relations with the first Ukrainian government, the
Rada. The Germans failed, however, as did the Hetman, to appreciate the intensity and depth of the social and political revolution
in the country and also had difficulty in understanding fully the
complexity of the Ukrainian national movement.

Militarily, the German occupation of the Ukraine was a failure
on two counts. It was relatively ineffective (General Groener himself admitted that there was a "stationary war" throughout the
occupation period); also, substantial military forces were retained in the Ukraine and other eastern areas after Brest-Litovsk
even though no major threat could be expected from this region,
which may be viewed as a major German blunder of World
War I.

Economically, Germany's Ukrainian venture was not all failure. True, the Germans and the Austrians failed completely to
exploit the Ukraine's industrial potential. (They used their own
coal to keep Ukrainian trains running; they also failed to deliver a
single tankful of oil from the Caucasus.) Ukrainian food deliveries were also short of the expected. Still, the quantities of Ukrainian foodstuffs that were shipped to Germany and Austria
through various legal and nonlegal channels (a total of 1.5 million tons) were quite significant, especially since these supplies
came at the time when they were most needed. Also, a general per
capita distribution, so often stressed by German and Austrian authors, really distorts the true picture. It is important to remember
that most of the shipments for Austria went to Vienna and other
western industrial centers of the Empire, not to Poland, Hungary,
or Croatia, and that a similar distribution principle was employed
by the Germans.

Finally, it may be useful to dwell briefly on the relationship
between the Ukrainian revolution and German plans and policies
in the east. The Ukrainian national movement matured as a result of general revolutionary upheaval in Russia. Neither the Germans and the Austrians nor the Union for the Liberation of the
Ukraine had very much to do with this development. The Rada
was a freely constituted Ukrainian administrative body—as rep-

resentative, or unrepresentative, as the Provisional Government of Russia at the time. After the German occupation of the Ukraine, the Rada lost much of its popularity and support in the country; nevertheless, it was the more popular of the two Ukrainian regimes, although perhaps somewhat less efficient than the Hetman administration.

Both Ukrainian regimes were subjected to various German controls and pressures. The Rada started as a truly independent agent and was destroyed largely because it refused to submit to more rigorous German dictates. The Hetmanate was established with direct German assistance and subjected to greater accountability and control than the Rada, but grew more independent as time went by, until the Germans finally assumed the role of mere friendly advisers and kept their hands off the incredibly complex and confused Ukrainian situation.

The best designation for the Ukraine under the German occupation in 1918 is that of "satellite." Its position was that of a state which voluntarily though reluctantly accepted a great power's protection with the inevitable imposition of certain restrictions on its sovereignty. It should be stressed, however, that this arrangement was viewed as a temporary one by both parties, that the protector was not a neighboring power, and that the satellite was too large and too distinct to be subject to any real danger of assimilation or absorption.

On balance, the Ukrainian national movement continued to make gains and the idea of Ukrainian independent statehood established stronger footing in the country despite the German-Austrian occupation. Like the Bolsheviks in the north (and one should remember that both the Russian Left and the Russian Right cooperated with the Reich at different times), the Ukrainians had won a period of respite that enabled them to consolidate their forces. The end of the Austro-German occupation of the east was followed by a renewed, and even more vigorous, effort by the Ukrainian national forces to establish themselves as masters of their land, an effort that has yet to run its full course.

APPENDICES

APPENDIX A

A Note on the Kholm Area

Kholm is not a Polish but a Ukrainian (or East Slavic) term meaning a hill or a mound. The Ukrainians considered the Kholm area one of their oldest provinces historically, and since it was the first ethnically Ukrainian area to fall into German hands in the early stages of World War I, they were anxious to develop programs there that could be applied to other Ukrainian territories should they come under German or Austrian control. The Poles, too, felt rather strongly about Kholm, fearing that their inability to secure it might harm their chances of acquiring other areas in the east, such as Galicia, the Vilno region, and parts of Byelorussia.

The province of Kholm was created in 1912 out of the formerly Uniate (that is Greek Catholic) parts of the provinces (*gubernias*) of Siedlce and Lublin. In 1915 Kholm ceased to be one of the "provinces of the Vistula." In order to appreciate the complexity of ethnic and religious relations in the Kholm area, one should keep in mind the following historical facts: Galician-Ukrainian and Orthodox background to begin with; Polish overlordship from the late fourteenth century on, accompanied by strong Polish ethnic, cultural, and religious pressures and influences; conversion to Uniate Catholicism (not always voluntary) in the late sixteenth century; inclusion of the Kholm area in the Russian Empire in 1815 resulting in the subjection of this area to Russification and forced return to the Orthodox

Church; a brief but vigorous anti-Orthodox movement following the 1905 "Toleration Edict," resulting in Polonization and conversion to Roman Catholicism of many Ukrainian-speaking former Uniates; forced evacuation of the area by retreating Russian armies in 1915, followed by the Austrian and German occupation of the province; its division into two distinct zones, and a heavy influx of settlers from western and central Poland into the Austrian zone of occupation.

The Kholm province, to which Pidlasha was added in 1915 (Podlachien in German; Pidlasha is a Ukrainian name meaning the area near Poland), was thus a typical ethnically mixed area, separating more or less homogeneous Polish and Ukrainian territories to the west and east, with some Byelorussian element in the north. The low cultural level and limited national consciousness of the local population further complicated the situation here; consequently, religion was often used to determine the national face of a given district within this area. Without going into all the arguments and theses (and disregarding both Ukrainian and Polish claims), one may conclude that on all grounds—ethnic, linguistic, historical, and religious—Ukrainian claims to Kholm were at least as well founded and justified as were those of the Poles. The best solution of this problem would have been to divide the area along ethnic lines with population exchange organized on a voluntary basis and administered by an impartial international commission composed of representatives of disinterested powers.

On the basis of recent German studies, Ukrainian claims to Kholm were better justified than it was generally believed in the west at the time. (See, for example, Beyer, *Die Mittelmächte und die Ukraine,* pp. 14–17; and Basler, *Deutschlands Annexionspolitik in Polen und im Baltikum,* p. 216.) Werner Conze, in his *Polnische Nation und deutsche Politik,* p. 21, also concluded that the eastern parts of the provinces of Siedlce and Lublin (that is, the Kholm area) were "predominantly Ukrainian." In support of this conclusion Conze cited the percentages of 1897, which, however, do not reflect various shifts and

1897	Siedlce	Lublin	1897	Siedlce	Lublin
Orthodox	15.7	21.4	Ukrainians*	16.5	21.1
Rom. Cath.	66.6	62.6	Poles	66.1	62.6
Jewish	16.0	13.5	Jews	15.6	13.4
Protestant	1.7	2.5	Germans	1.5	2.2
			Others	0.3	0.7

* Conze used the terms employed in 1897, "Great and Little Russians," but noted that they were mostly Ukrainians. For further details see his *Polnische Nation und deutsche Politik,* p. 21.

changes to which this area was subjected during the turbulent first quarter of the twentieth century. Of course, in the two provinces as a whole, the Ukrainians constituted a minority; but it should be noted that they were concentrated in a rather homogeneous and compact area in the eastern portions of these two provinces, in contrast to another important minority there—the Jews—who lived in widely scattered urban centers throughout the area.

APPENDIX B

The Fourth Universal of the Ukrainian Central Rada
January 22, 1918 *

To the People of the Ukraine:

By your strength, will, and word there has arisen in the Ukrainian land a free People's Republic. An age-old dream of your forefathers, champions of the freedom and rights of the toiling masses, has been realized. But the freedom of the Ukraine has been regained at a difficult time. Four years of destructive warfare have weakened our land and exhausted our people; plants have been closed and factories have ceased to produce; railroads have been disrupted and money has lost its value; harvests have declined and the land is threatened with famine. The countryside has been infested with bands of robbers and thieves since the collapse of the front, and these marauding soldiers have caused bloodshed, confusion, and destruction in our land. Due to these circumstances, the election to the Ukrainian Constituent Assembly as prescribed by the previous Universal could not be held; hence that Assembly, scheduled for today and expected to take over from us the supreme revolutionary authority in the Ukraine, to establish laws in the People's Republic, and to organize a new government, could not be convened. In the meantime, the Petrograd Government of People's Commissars declared war on the

* Copies of this proclamation are available in the archival collection of the Ukrainian Academy of Arts and Sciences in the United States, New York City, N. Y. Translated by the author.

Ukraine in order to place under its control the free Ukrainian Republic. It has ordered into our land its troops—the Red Guards and the Bolsheviks—who are taking away grain from our peasants and are dispatching it to Russia without payment; even the grain set aside for sowing has thus been confiscated. They are killing innocent people and spreading anarchy, lawlessness and crime everywhere.

We, the Ukrainian Central Rada, have done all in our power to prevent the outbreak of this fratricidal war between the two neighboring peoples, but the Petrograd Government refused to consider our proposals and is continuing to wage a bloody war against our people and the Republic. Moreover, the same Petrograd Government of People's Commissars is beginning to dally with peace and is calling for a new war, which it terms holy. Blood will be shed again, and once more the hapless toiling people will have to lose their lives.

We, the Ukrainian Central Rada, elected at the congresses of the peasants, workers, and soldiers of the Ukraine, cannot agree to this. We cannot support any wars, because the Ukrainian people desires peace; and democratic peace must be made as soon as possible. Therefore, in order that neither the Russian Government nor some other regime place any obstacles before the Ukraine in her efforts to establish peace, and in order to stabilize the country, to promote creative labor, to strengthen the revolution, and to uphold our freedom, we, the Ukrainian Central Rada, announce the following to all the citizens of the Ukraine:

Henceforth the Ukrainian People's Republic becomes an independent, free and sovereign state of the Ukrainian People answerable to no one. We wish to live in peace and friendship with all the neighboring states: Russia, Poland, Austria, Rumania, Turkey and others; but none of them has the right to interfere in the life of the independent Ukrainian Republic. The power in it shall belong only to the Ukrainian People, in whose name we, the Ukrainian Central Rada—the representatives of the toiling masses of the peasants, workers, and soldiers—will govern the country through our executive organ which henceforth will be called "the Council of People's Ministers."

First of all we instruct the Government of our Republic, the Council of People's Ministers, to conduct from this day on the previously initiated peace negotiations with the Central Powers, completely independently, and bring them to a conclusion regardless of any obstacles or objections from any other part of the former Russian Empire and to achieve peace so that our land can develop its economy in harmony and tranquility.

As for the so-called Bolsheviks and other invaders who are plundering and destroying our land, we instruct the Government of the Ukrainian People's Republic to launch a firm and determined struggle against them, and we appeal to all the citizens of our Republic to defend the welfare and freedom of our people, even at the cost of their lives. Our Ukrainian People's State must be cleared of the invaders sent from Petrograd, who trample upon the rights of the Ukrainian Republic.

The long and difficult war, launched by the bourgeois regime, has wearied our people, devastated our land, and destroyed its economy. We must put an end to all this. As the army is being demobilized, we recommend that some men be released now; and following the acceptance of the peace treaties, the army should be completely dissolved. Further, instead of a standing army we envisage the establishment of a people's militia; our troops should be defenders of the toiling masses and not a tool of the ruling classes.

Localities destroyed by the war and demobilization shall be rebuilt with the assistance and at the expense of the state treasury. As soon as our soldiers return home, people's councils—in villages, districts, and municipalities—shall be elected again at the prescribed time so that the soldiers will have a voice in them too. In the meantime, in order to establish an authority entitled to enjoy the general confidence, and one that is based on all the revolutionary-democratic classes of the people, the Government should invite the cooperation of the locally elected councils of workers', peasants', and soldiers' deputies.

In regard to the land question, a commission elected at our last session has already drafted a law on the transfer of land to the toiling masses without payment, basing this on the decision taken at our eighth session to abolish private property and to socialize land. This law shall be considered several days from now at a meeting of the entire Central Rada. The Council of People's Ministers shall take all the necessary measures to ensure the transfer of land to the farmers with the assistance of land committees before the spring sowing gets under way. Forests, streams, and natural resources of the land are the property of the Ukrainian toiling masses; they shall be administered by the Ukrainian People's Republic.

The war has also adversely affected the laboring forces of our country. Most of our plants, factories, and workshops were forced to produce the necessary war materiel, and the people were left without basic goods. Now the war is at an end. We are ordering the Council of People's Ministers to take immediate steps to convert all plants and factories to peaceful production to supply the toiling masses with goods of prime necessity.

The war has also produced hundreds of thousands of unemployed and disabled. In the independent People's Republic of the Ukraine there should not be a single workingman in need and distress. The Government of the Republic has been instructed to revitalize the industry of the state, to resume activities in all branches of the economy in order to provide work for the unemployed, and to take all measures necessary to protect and provide for the disabled and other victims of the war.

Under the old regime, the merchants and middlemen used to exploit the poor oppressed classes and reap huge profits therefrom. From now on the Ukrainian People's Republic shall administer the basic branches of trade and business, and all the profits from these activities shall revert to the people. Foreign trade, both imports and exports, shall also be placed under state control to forestall the possibility of the poor masses being forced to pay exorbitant prices to speculators. The Government of the Republic is accordingly instructed to draft appropriate laws on these matters, as well as to prepare legislation against monopoly in the production of iron, leather, tobacco, and other such products and goods, categories in which profits used to be unusually high—an arrangement that was especially unfair to the working classes and benefited those not engaged in productive labor.

We also order the establishment of people's state control over all banks which used to contribute to the exploitation of the working classes by advancing loans and credits to the nonworking elements. From now on, credit assistance from banks shall be provided above all to the toiling population, to promote the development of the national economy of the Ukrainian People's Republic and not for purposes of speculation or other exploitative banking practices.

Because of anarchy, general unrest, and the shortage of goods, discontent among certain segments of the population has increased. This discontent is being exploited by various dark forces among the uninformed people for the purpose of restoring the old order. These dark forces are aiming at the return of all the free peoples under the united yoke of Czarist Russia. The Council of People's Ministers should resolutely combat all the counterrevolutionary forces; anyone who advocates rebellion against the independent Ukrainian People's Republic and the restoration of the old order should be tried for high treason.

All democratic freedoms guaranteed in the Third Universal are hereby confirmed by the Ukrainian Central Rada. We further declare that in the independent Ukrainian People's Republic all nations enjoy the right to national and personal autonomy as provided in the law of January 22.

Obviously, it will not be possible for the Central Rada to realize all the programs of this Universal in a few weeks' time; these programs will be further developed and fully implemented by the Ukrainian Constituent Assembly. We order therefore all our citizens to carry out the election to this body most carefully and to make every effort to complete the tabulation of votes as soon as possible. This will make it possible for the Constituent Assembly—the supreme authority and ruler of our land—to convene within the next few weeks in order to uphold and confirm, through a constitution of the independent Ukrainian People's Republic, freedom, order, and wellbeing for all the toiling people, now and at all future times.

This supreme organ of ours shall also rule on the federative relationship with other people's republics of the former Russian state.

In the meantime, we appeal to all citizens of the independent Ukrainian People's Republic to uphold and guard without wavering the newly won liberty and the rights of our people and to use all possible means to defend their freedom against all enemies of the independent Ukrainian Republic of peasants and workers.

THE UKRAINIAN CENTRAL RADA

Kiev, January 22, 1918

APPENDIX C

The Treaty of Peace Between the Ukraine and the Central Powers*

(Signed at Brest-Litovsk, February 9, 1918)

Whereas the Ukrainian People has, in the course of the present world war, declared its independence, and has expressed the desire to establish a state of peace between the Ukrainian People's Republic and the Powers at present at war with Russia, the Governments of Germany, Austria-Hungary, Bulgaria, and Turkey have resolved to conclude a Treaty of Peace with the Government of the Ukrainian People's Republic; they wish in this way to take the first step towards a lasting world peace, honourable for all parties, which shall not only put an end to the horrors of the war but shall also conduce to the restoration of friendly relations between the peoples in the political, legal, economic, and intellectual spheres.

To this end the plenipotentiaries of the above-mentioned Governments, viz.

For the Imperial German Government: Imperial Actual Privy Councillor Richard von Kühlmann, Secretary of State of Foreign Affairs;

For the Imperial and Royal Joint Austro-Hungarian Government: His Imperial and Royal Apostolic Majesty's Privy Councillor Ottokar Count Czernin von und zu Chudenitz, Minister of the Imperial and Royal House and Minister for Foreign Affairs;

* Reprinted from *Texts of the Ukraine "Peace."* Washington, D.C.: United States Department of State, 1918.

For the Royal Bulgarian Government: Dr. Vassil Radoslavoff, President of the Council of Ministers; the Envoy M. Andrea Tosheff; the Envoy M. Ivan Stoyanovich; the Military Plenipotentiary Colonel Peter Gantcheff; and Dr. Theodor Anastassoff;

For the Imperial Ottoman Government: His Highness the Grand Vizier Talaat Pasha; Ahmet Nessimi Bey, Minister for Foreign Affairs; His Highness Ibrahim Hakki Pasha; and General of Cavalry Ahmet Izzet Pasha;

For the Government of the Ukrainian People's Republic: M. Alexander Sevruk, M. Mykola Liubinsky, and M. Mykola Levitsky, members of the Ukrainian Central Rada;—have met at Brest-Litovsk, and having presented their full powers, which were found to be in due and proper form, have agreed upon the following points:

Article I

Germany, Austria-Hungary, Bulgaria, and Turkey on the one hand, and the Ukrainian People's Republic on the other hand, declare that the state of war between them is at an end. The contracting parties are resolved henceforth to live in peace and amity with one another.

Article II

1. As between Austria-Hungary on the one hand, and the Ukrainian People's Republic on the other hand, in so far as these two Powers border upon one another, the frontiers which existed between the Austro-Hungarian Monarchy and Russia, prior to the outbreak of the present war, will be preserved.

2. Further north, the frontier of the Ukrainian People's Republic, starting at Tarnograd, will in general follow the line Bilgoray, Szozebrzeszyn, Krasnostav, Pugashov, Radzin, Miedzyzheche, Sarnaki, Melnik, Vysokie-Litovsk, Kameniec-Litovsk, Prujany, and Vydonovsk Lake. This frontier will be delimited in detail by a mixed commission, according to the ethnographical conditions and after taking the wishes of the inhabitants into consideration.

3. In the event of the Ukrainian People's Republic having boundaries coterminous with those of another of the Powers of the Quadruple Alliance, special agreements are reserved in respect thereto.

Article III

The evacuation of the occupied territories shall begin immediately after the ratification of the present Treaty of Peace.

The manner of carrying out the evacuation and the transfer of the evacuated territories shall be determined by the Plenipotentiaries of the interested parties.

Article IV

Diplomatic and consular relations between the contracting parties shall commence immediately after the ratification of the Treaty of Peace.

In respect to the admission of consuls on the widest scale possible on both sides, special agreements are reserved.

Article V

The contracting parties mutually renounce repayment of their war costs, that is to say, their State expenditure for the prosecution of the war, as well as payment for war damages, that is to say, damages sustained by them and their nationals in the war areas through military measures, including all requisitions made in enemy territory.

Article VI

Prisoners of war of both parties shall be released to their homeland in so far as they do not desire, with the approval of the State in whose territory they shall be, to remain within its territories or to proceed to another country. Questions connected with this will be dealt with in the separate treaties provided for in Article VIII.

Article VII

It has been agreed as follows with regard to economic relations between the contracting parties:

I

The contracting parties mutually undertake to enter into economic relations without delay and to organize the exchange of goods on the basis of the following stipulations:

Until July 31 of the current year a reciprocal exchange of the surplus of their more important agricultural and industrial products, for the purpose of meeting current requirements, is to be effected according to the following provisions:

(a) The quantities and classes of products to be exchanged in accordance with the preceding paragraph shall be settled on both sides by a commission composed of an equal number of representatives of both parties, which shall sit immediately after the Treaty of Peace has been signed.

(b) The prices of products to be exchanged as specified above shall be regulated on the basis of mutual agreement by a commission composed of an equal number of representatives of both parties.

(c) Calculations should be made in gold on the following basis:

1000 German imperial gold marks shall be equivalent to 462 gold roubles of the former Russian Empire (1 rouble = $\frac{1}{15}$ imperial), or 1000 Austrian and Hungarian gold kronen shall be equivalent to 393 karbovantsi 76 grosh gold of the Ukrainian People's Republic, or to 393 roubles 78 copecks in gold of the former Russian Empire (1 rouble = $\frac{1}{15}$ imperial).

(d) The exchange of goods to be determined by the commission mentioned under (a) shall take place through the existing Government central offices or through central offices controlled by the Government.

The exchange of such products as are not determined by the above-mentioned commissions shall be effected on a basis of free trading, arranged for in accordance with the conditions of the provisional commercial treaty, which is provided for in the following Section II.

II

In so far as it is not otherwise provided for under Section I hereof, economic relations between the contracting parties shall be carried on provisionally in accordance with the stipulations specified below until the conclusion of the final Commercial Treaty, but in any event until a period of at least six months shall have elapsed after the conclusion of peace between Germany, Austria-Hungary, Bulgaria, and Turkey on the one hand, and the European States at present at war with them, the United States of America and Japan on the other hand:

A

For economic relations between the German Empire and the Ukrainian People's Republic, the conditions laid down in the following provisions of the Germano-Russian Commercial and Maritime Treaty of 1894–1904,[1] that is to say:

Articles 1–6 and 7 (including Tariffs "a" and "b"), 8–10, 12, 13–19; further, among the stipulations of the final Protocol (Part I), paragraphs 1 and 3 of addendum to Article 1; paragraphs 1, 2, 4, 5, 6, 8, 9 of addenda to Articles 1 and 12 addendum to Article 3; paragraphs 1 and 2 of addendum to Article 5; addenda to Articles 5, 6, 7, 9, and 10; addenda to Articles 6, 7, and 11; to Articles 6–9; to Articles 6 and 7 paragraphs 1, 2, 3, 5, of addendum to Article 12;

---

[1] 86 British and Foreign State Papers, pp. 442, 449, 482; 97 British and Foreign State Papers, p. 1040.

further in the final Protocol (Part IV), §§3, 6, 7, 12, 12b, 13, 14, 15, 16, 17, 18 (with the reservations required by the corresponding alterations in official organizations), 19, 20, 21, and 23.

An agreement has been arrived at upon the following points:

1. The General Russian Customs Tariff of January 13–26, 1903,[2] shall continue in force.

2. Article 5 shall read as follows:

> "The contracting parties bind themselves not to hinder reciprocal trade by any kind of import, export, or transit prohibitions, and to allow free transit.
>
> "Exceptions may only be made in the case of products which are actually, or which may become, a State monopoly in the territory of one of the contracting parties; as well as in the case of certain products for which exceptional prohibitory measures might be issued, in view of health conditions, veterinary police, and public safety, or on other important political and economic grounds, especially in connection with the transition period following the war."

3. Neither party shall lay claim to the preferential treatment which the other party has granted, or shall grant to any other State, arising out of a present or future Customs Union (as, for instance, the one in force between the German Empire and the Grand Duchy of Luxembourg), or arising in connection with petty frontier intercourse extending to a boundary zone not exceeding 15 kilometres in width.

4. Article 10 shall read as follows:

> "There shall be reciprocal freedom from all transit dues for goods of all kinds conveyed through the territory of either of the parties, whether conveyed direct or unloaded, stored and reloaded during transit."

5. Article 12(a) shall be revised as follows:

> "(a) With regard to the reciprocal protection of copyright in works of literature, art, and photography, the provisions of the Treaty concluded between the German Empire and Russia on February 28, 1913,[3] shall prevail in the relations between Germany and the Ukrainian People's Republic.
>
> "(b) With regard to the reciprocal protection of trade-marks,

---

[2] New General Customs Tariffs for the European Frontiers of Russia, British Parliamentary Papers (1903), Cd. 1525.
[3] 107 British and Foreign State Papers, p. 871.

the provisions of the Declaration of July 11–23, 1873,[4] shall be authoritative in the future."

6. The provision of the final Protocol to Article 19 shall read as follows:

"The contracting parties shall grant each other the greatest possible support in the matter of railway tariffs, more especially by the establishment of through rates. To this end both contracting parties are ready to enter into negotiations with one another at the earliest possible moment."

7. §5 of Part IV of the final Protocol shall read as follows:

"It has been mutually agreed that the customs houses of both countries shall remain open on every day throughout the year, with the exception of Sundays and legal holidays."

B

For economic relations between Austria-Hungary and the Ukrainian People's Republic, the agreements shall be valid which are set forth in the following provisions of the Austro-Hungarian–Russian Commercial and Maritime Treaty of the 15 February, 1906,[5] being Articles 1, 2, and 5 (including Tariffs "a" and "b"); Articles 6, 7, 9–13; Article 14, paragraphs 2 and 3; Articles 15–24 further, in the provisions of the final Protocol, paragraphs, 1, 2, 4, 5, and 6 of addenda to Articles 1 and 12; addenda to Article 2; to Articles 2, 3, and 5; to Articles 2 and 5; to Articles 2, 4, 5, 7, and 8; to Articles 2, 5, 6, and 7; to Article 17, and likewise to paragraphs 1 and 3, Article 22.

An agreement has been arrived at upon the following points:

1. The General Russian Customs Tariff of January 13–26, 1903,[6] shall remain in force.

2. Article 4 shall read as follows:

"The contracting parties bind themselves not to hinder reciprocal trade between their territories by any kind of import, export, or transit prohibition. The only permissible exceptions shall be:

"(a) In the case of tobacco, salt, gunpowder, or any other kind of explosives, and likewise in the case of other articles

[4] 63 British and Foreign State Papers, p. 58.
[5] 99 British and Foreign State Papers, p. 599.
[6] New General Customs Tariffs for the European Frontiers of Russia, British Parliamentary Papers (1903), Cd. 1525.

which may at any time constitute a State monopoly in the territories of either of the contracting parties;

"(b) With respect to war supplies in exceptional circumstances;

"(c) For reasons of public safety, public health, and veterinary police;

"(d) In the case of certain products for which, on other important political and economic grounds, exceptional prohibitory measures might be issued, especially in connection with the transition period following the war."

3. Neither party shall lay claim to the preferential treatment which the other party has granted or shall grant to any other State arising out of a present or future Customs Union (as, for instance, the one in force between Austria-Hungary and the Principality of Liechtenstein), or arising in connection with petty frontier intercourse, extending to a boundary zone not exceeding 15 kilometres in width.

4. Article 8 shall read as follows:

"There shall be reciprocal freedom for all transit dues for goods of all kinds conveyed through the territory of either of the contracting parties, whether conveyed direct or unloaded, stored and re-loaded during transit."

5. The provision of the final Protocol to Article 21 shall read as follows:

"The contracting parties shall grant each other the greatest possible support in the matter of railway tariffs, and more especially by the establishment of through rates. To this end both contracting parties are ready to enter into negotiations with one another at the earliest possible moment."

C

In regard to the economic relations between Bulgaria and the Ukrainian People's Republic, these shall, until such time as a definitive Commercial Treaty shall have been concluded, be regulated on the basis of most-favoured-nation treatment. Neither party shall lay claim to the preferential treatment which the other party has granted or shall grant to any other State arising out of a present or future Customs Union, or arising in connection with petty frontier intercourse, extending to a boundary zone not exceeding 15 kilometres in width.

D

In regard to the economic relations between the Ottoman Empire and the Ukrainian People's Republic, these shall, until such time as a definitive Commercial Treaty shall have been concluded, be regulated on the basis of most-favoured-nation treatment. Neither party shall lay claim to the preferential treatment which the other party has granted or shall grant to any other State arising out of a present or future Customs Union, or arising in connection with petty frontier intercourse.

III

The period of validity of the provisional stipulations (set forth under Section II hereof) for economic relations between Germany, Austria-Hungary, Bulgaria, and the Ottoman Empire on the one hand, and the Ukrainian People's Republic on the other hand, may be prolonged by mutual agreement.

In the event of the periods specified in the first paragraph of Section II not occurring before June 30, 1919, each of the two contracting parties shall be entitled as from June 30, 1919, to denounce within six months the provisions contained in the above-mentioned section.

IV

(a) The Ukrainian People's Republic shall make no claim to the preferential treatment which Germany grants to Austria-Hungary or to any other country bound to her by a Customs Union and directly bordering on Germany, or bordering indirectly thereon through another country bound to her or to Austria-Hungary by a Customs Union, or to the preferential treatment which Germany grants to her own colonies, foreign possessions, and protectorates, or to countries bound to her by a Customs Union.

Germany shall make no claim to the preferential treatment which the Ukrainian People's Republic grants to any other country bound to her by a Customs Union and bordering directly on the Ukraine, or bordering indirectly thereon through any other country bound to her by a Customs Union, or to colonies, foreign possessions, and protectorates of one of the countries bound to her by a Customs Union.

(b) In economic intercourse between territory covered by the Customs Convention of both States of the Austro-Hungarian Monarchy on the one hand, and the Ukrainian People's Republic on the other hand, the Ukrainian People's Republic shall make no claim to the preferential treatment which Austria-Hungary grants to Germany or to any other country bound to her by a Customs Union and directly bordering on Austria-Hungary, or bordering indirectly thereon through another country which is bound to her or to Germany by a Customs Union. Colonies, foreign possessions, and protectorates shall in this respect be placed on the same footing as the mother country. Austria-Hungary shall make no claim to the preferential treatment which the Ukrainian People's Republic grants to any other country bound to her by a Customs Union and directly bordering on the Ukraine, or bordering indirectly thereon through another country bound to her by a Customs Union, or to colonies, foreign possessions, and protectorates of one of the countries bound to her by a Customs Union.

v

(a) In so far as goods originating in Germany or the Ukraine are stored in neutral States, with the proviso that they shall not be exported, either directly or indirectly, to the territories of the other contracting party, such restrictions regarding their disposal shall be abolished so far as the contracting parties are concerned. The two contracting parties therefore undertake immediately to notify the Governments of the neutral States of the above-mentioned abolition of this restriction.

(b) In so far as goods originating in Austria-Hungary or the Ukraine are stored in neutral States, with the proviso that they shall not be exported, either directly or indirectly, to the territories of the other contracting party, such restrictions regarding their disposal shall be abolished so far as the contracting parties are concerned. The two contracting parties therefore undertake immediately to notify the Governments of the neutral States of the above-mentioned abolition of this restriction.

Article VIII

The establishing of public and private legal relations, and the exchange of prisoners of war and interned civilians, the amnesty question, as well as the question of the treatment of merchant shipping in the enemy's hands, shall be settled by means of separate Treaties with the Ukrainian People's Republic, which shall form an essential part of the present Treaty of Peace, and, as far as practicable, come into force simultaneously therewith.

Article IX

The agreements come to in this Treaty of Peace shall form an indivisible whole.

Article X

For the interpretation of this Treaty, the German and Ukrainian text shall be authoritative for relations between Germany and the Ukraine; the German, Hungarian, and Ukrainian text for relations between Austria-Hungary and the Ukraine; the Bulgarian and Ukrainian text for relations between Bulgaria and the Ukraine; and the Turkish and Ukrainian text for relations between Turkey and the Ukraine.

Final Provision

The present Treaty of Peace shall be ratified. The ratifications shall be exchanged in Vienna at the earliest possible moment.

The Treaty of Peace shall come into force on its ratification, in so far as no stipulation to the contrary is contained therein.

In witness whereof the plenipotentiaries have signed the present Treaty and have affixed their seals to it.

Executed in quintuplicate at Brest-Litovsk this 9th day of February 1918.

[*Signatures follow*]

APPENDIX D

Secret Agreement on Galicia Committing Vienna to the Formation of a Separate Ukrainian Crownland, February 29, 1918 *

The manner in which the peace negotiations have been conducted has convinced the Austro-Hungarian delegates as well as those of the Ukrainian Republic that the two powers are animated by the wish to live henceforth in friendly and peaceful relations with one another.

Being further convinced that the desired strengthening of friendly relations between the Monarchy and the Ukraine can be promoted significantly by safeguarding an unhampered national and cultural development for their respective national minorities, plenipotentiaries of the two powers have agreed to make the following statement: The delegates of Austria-Hungary recognize the fact that the Ukrainian regime has just enacted laws guaranteeing the rights of the Poles, Germans, and Jews in the Ukraine. The representatives of the Ukraine on their part take cognizance of the Imperial and Royal Government's decision to provide the Ukrainian people in Austria with additional guarantees for further national and cultural development that would go beyond those insured by the present laws. The Imperial and Royal Government will therefore propose to the State Council [Reichsrat], not later than July 20, 1918, a draft of a bill providing that the part of East Galicia with a Ukrainian majority be

* For both German and Ukrainian copies of this document see Doroshenko, *Istoriya Ukrayiny*, II, 215–216. The above is the author's translation.

detached from this crownland and that the region together with Bukovina be organized into a special crownland. The Imperial and Royal Government will do all in its power to insure the enactment of this bill into the law.

This declaration constitutes an integral part of the general peace treaty, and it shall become null and void in the event of nonfulfillment of any of the provisions of said treaty.

This document and its contents shall remain secret.

Brest-Litovsk, February 8, 1918

Ernst Knight von Seidler,
Count Ottokar Czernin, Minister for
Foreign Affairs
Oleksander Sevryuk,
Mykola Lubyns'kyi,
Mykola Levyts'kyi

APPENDIX E

Field Marshal von Eichhorn's
Land Cultivation Order *

[*Issued in Kiev on April 6, 1918*]

All reports indicate that the spring harvest is being threatened with delay. In spite of the fact that the Minister of Agriculture appealed to the peasants and instructed the land committees to see to it that the land is cultivated, it is doubtful whether these committees have sufficient authority and it remains uncertain whether the peasants will cooperate. Local German military authorities should therefore insist most energetically that the land be cultivated in their respective districts, with the assistance of Ukrainian land committees or if necessary through the direct initiative of the local military authorities.

The broad peasant masses should be informed, in the manner best suited to reach them, about the following points, the implementation of which is viewed by the Supreme Commander of German Forces in the Ukraine as most essential:

1. The harvest belongs to those who till the land; they are to be paid for the harvested grain on the basis of fixed prices.

2. The farmer who takes possession of more land then he can cultivate fully and properly will be guilty of irreparable damage to the Ukrainian people and the Ukrainian State; he shall be severely penalized for it.

* Khrystyuk, *Zamitky i materialy do istoriyi ukrayins'koyi revolutsiyi,* *1917–1920*, II, 201–202. Translated from the Ukrainian by the author.

3. In villages where the farmers are incapable of cultivating all the land and where the landlords are still resident, the latter shall assume the task of planting the fields, without violating the right of the land committees to make a lawful division of land. In such cases the peasants shall not interfere with cultivation done by the landlords. To facilitate the sowing and harvesting, the land committees shall supply the landlords with horses, agricultural machinery, and seed. The harvest in such cases shall be equally divided between the peasants and those who cultivate the land.

4. Destruction and looting of harvest shall be severely penalized.

The lands that have been distributed by the land committees on the basis of the existing laws and with the approval of the government shall not be affected by these regulations provided such lands are actually cultivated.

Official notices dealing with the problem of land cultivation that are issued by the military authorities shall be prominently displayed in all districts, both in Ukrainian and in German versions; whenever feasible they should also be signed by the local land committees or other responsible local authorities.

The land committees should be encouraged to issue to peasants requesting them special certificates indicating the land area cultivated by them. In the event the land committees in certain localities refuse to issue such certificates, these should be furnished by the German military authorities.

All orders and regulations, their implementation and consequences, as well as the extent of land cultivation, shall be reported by the local garrisons to the Supreme Commander not later than May 15 of this year.

> *Signed:* German Supreme Commander in
> the Ukraine Field Marshal von Eichhorn

Hetman Skoropadsky's Manifesto to the Ukrainian People, April 29, 1918 *

Citizens of the Ukraine! All of you, Cossacks and citizens of the Ukraine, are well acquainted with recent events during which the blood of the Ukraine's finest sons was shed and the reborn Ukrainian State stood on the brink of collapse. It was saved thanks to the mighty support of the Central Powers, which, honoring their earlier commitment, are continuing to struggle for freedom and peace in the Ukraine. Such assistance gave all of us reason to hope that order would be restored in the country and that the economic life of the Ukraine would be normalized.

Such hopes, however, have failed to materialize. The previous Ukrainian regime proved itself incapable of further promotion of Ukrainian statehood. Disorders and anarchy continue in the Ukraine, economic decay and unemployment are on the rise and become more widespread day by day, and the once rich Ukraine is now being faced with the prospect of famine.

This situation, which threatens the Ukraine with another catastrophe, has stirred up the masses of workers in the population and they have voiced a firm demand for the organization of a governmental authority capable of guaranteeing the people peace, order, and an atmosphere conducive to constructive work. As a true son of the Ukraine, I decided to answer this call and to assume temporarily all

* Doroshenko, *Istoriya Ukrayiny*, II, 49–50. Translated by the author.

authority and power in the country. Through this manifesto I proclaim myself Hetman of all the Ukraine.

The administration of the Ukraine will be conducted through the Cabinet of Ministers, which I shall appoint, on the basis of the decree on the provisional government in the Ukraine attached to this declaration.

The Central and Little Rada as well as all the land committees are henceforth dissolved. All ministers and their deputies are dismissed. Other officials employed by various governmental institutions shall remain in their posts and shall continue their previous duties and assignments.

In the near future an electoral law will be promulgated providing for the creation of a Ukrainian Diet. Until then I shall firmly uphold law and order in the Ukrainian State, shall insist on the implementation of all the laws and regulations, and shall support the authority of the government even by the extreme means if necessary.

The private property laws, which are the basis of culture and civilization, are being restored in their entirety, and all the orders and regulations of the previous Ukrainian government as well as those of the Russian provisional government are hereby declared null and void. The right to sell and to purchase real property is also being reestablished. Laws will be passed concerning the transfer of land from large landowners to landless farmers at the prevailing market prices. The rights of the working class will also be fully safeguarded. Special attention will be devoted to improving the legal status and working conditions of railroad workers, who, in spite of difficult circumstances, never failed in the performance of their important duties. Full freedom is being reestablished in the economic, financial, and commercial fields, and private enterprise and individual initiative are again to be given a free rein.

I am fully aware of all the difficulties that lie ahead, and I pray to God to provide me with the strength to carry out in dignity this assignment which I regard as my duty toward the Ukraine at this critical moment of its history. I have no need of any personal gains or advantages and am guided solely by the interest and welfare of the people of our beloved Ukraine. With this in mind I call on you, citizens and Cossacks of the Ukraine, without regard to your nationality and religion, to assist me, my supporters, and my administration in achieving this common and vital goal.

Hetman of all the Ukraine
Pavlo Skoropadsky

Kiev, April 29, 1918

APPENDIX G

Hetman Skoropadsky's Edict Calling for the Formation of an All-Russian Federation, Kiev, November 14, 1918 *

The armistice between Germany and the Allied powers has been concluded. The bloodiest of wars has ended, and the peoples of the world are confronted with the difficult task of creating the basis for a new life.

As compared to other parts of a Russia that has suffered long, the Ukraine's fate has been considerably happier. With the friendly assistance of the Central Powers she has managed to maintain law and order until the present. Being sympathetic to all the tribulations experienced by her dear Great Russia, the Ukraine has done all in its power to aid her brothers by proffering them full hospitality and supporting them in the struggle for the restoration of a stable state authority in Russia.

We are now confronted with a new political task. The Allies were always friends of the old united Russian State. Today, following a period of turmoil and dissolution, Russia has to adopt new conditions for her future existence. The old might and power of the All-Russian State must be restored on the basis of a different principle—that of federalism. The Ukraine should assume a leading role in this federation since it was she who gave the example of law and order in the country; it was also within Ukrainian borders that the citizens of the old Russia, oppressed and humiliated by the Bolshevik despotism,

* Doroshenko, *Istoriya Ukrayiny*, II, 414–415. Translated by the author.

found freedom and security. The Ukraine took the initiative in developing friendship and cooperation with the glorious Great Don and the glorious Kuban and Terek Cossacks. These principles, which I hope are shared by Russia's allies—the Entente—and which cannot but be viewed sympathetically by all peoples, not only in Europe but throughout the world, should be the basis for the Ukraine's policy in the future. The Ukraine should thus take the lead in the formation of an all-Russian federation, the principal goal of which should be the restoration of great Russia.

The achievement of this task shall guarantee not only the well-being of all of Russia but the further economic and cultural development of the Ukrainian people as well, on the basis of national and political independence. Being deeply convinced that any other course would result in the Ukraine's collapse, I appeal to all who care about her future—so closely linked to the future and happiness of all of Russia—to unite behind me for the defense of the Ukraine and Russia. I believe that this noble and patriotic cause should be supported sincerely and strongly by the citizens and Cossacks of the Ukraine as well as by other segments of her population.

The newly formed cabinet is hereby instructed to proceed immediately with the implementation of this great historic task.

Signed: PAVLO SKOROPADSKY

GLOSSARY OF PERSONS

Antonov-Ovseenko, Vladimir A. Commander of Bolshevik troops in the Ukraine in late 1917 and early 1918; one of Soviet Russia's principal Civil War leaders.

Arz von Straussenburg, Arthur (Baron, General). Chief of the General Staff of the Austro-Hungarian Army, March, 1917–November, 1918.

Baden, Prince Max of. German Imperial Chancellor, October 3–November 9, 1918.

Bartenwerffer, Paul von (General). Chief, Political Department of the General Staff of the German Army.

Berchem, Hans von (Count). Legation Councillor in the German Foreign Office; Mumm's assistant in the Ukraine in 1918; chargé d'affaires in Kiev following the former's resignation in September.

Berckheim, Philip von (Count). Legation Secretary, Lersner's assistant at the Foreign Office's bureau at the German Supreme Army Command.

Bergen, Diego von. Legation Councillor in the German Foreign Office; the Reich's principal revolutionary expert during World War I.

Bernstorff, Johann von (Count). German Ambassador in Constantinople, 1917–1918.

Beseler, Hans Hartwick von (General). Governor-General of German-occupied Poland, 1914–1918.

Bethmann Hollweg, Theobald von. German Imperial Chancellor, 1909–1917.

Böhm-Ermolli, Eduard (Baron, Field Marshal). Commander of an Austro-Hungarian army group in the Ukraine in 1918 (with headquarters in Odessa).

Brinckmann, Friedrich (Major). Political officer attached to the German Command East; participated in negotiations of supplementary agreements with the Ukraine following the occupation.

Brockdorff-Rantzau, Ulrich von (Count). German Minister in Copenhagen, 1912–1919; played an important role in the German efforts to promote revolutions in the east.

Bülow, Bernhard von. Lieutenant of cavalry, nephew of prewar Chancellor Bülow; Baron von Rosenberg's assistant during the Brest-Litovsk negotiations.

Burián von Rajecz, Stephan (Baron). Hungarian statesman, Austro-Hungarian Foreign Minister, 1915–1916 and April–October, 1918.

Bussche–Haddenhausen, Hilmar von dem (Baron). Under-Secretary of State for Foreign Affairs; played a decisive role in the Reich's plans and policies in the east during World War I.

Cheryachukin, A. V. (General). Member of the Don delegation sent by Ataman Krasnov to Kiev in June, 1918, to negotiate with the Hetman and the Germans; later the Don envoy in Kiev.

Chicherin, Georgii V. Soviet Commissar for Foreign Affairs, 1918–1930.

Class, Heinrich. A Pan-German leader and writer during World War I; one of the foremost annexationists of the period.

Czernin von und zu Chudenitz, Ottokar (Count). Austro-Hungarian envoy in Bucharest, 1913–1916; Vienna's Foreign Minister, 1916–1918; the Dual Monarchy's principal spokesman at Brest-Litovsk.

David, Eduard. Social Democratic Reichstag deputy, generally regarded as a friend of and an expert on the Ukraine; Under-Secretary of State for Foreign Affairs following the collapse of the German Empire in November, 1918.

Deutelmoser, Erhard Eduard (Lieutenant Colonel). Chief of German Propaganda Office, 1916–1918, and Press Officer of the Imperial Chancellery, 1917–1918.

Dobry, Abraham. A Jewish Ukrainian financier who served at one time as the director of the Russian Bank for Foreign Trade; in the spring of 1918 participated as a member of the Rada delegation in economic talks with the Germans.

Dontsov, Dmytro. Ukrainian political émigré in Galicia before the war; one of the founders of the Union for the Liberation of the Ukraine; head of the Ukrainian Press and Telegraph Agency in Kiev under the Hetman.

Doroshenko, Dmytro. Ukrainian Socialist Federalist who served as Foreign Minister under the Hetman; subsequently became one of the foremost Ukrainian historians of the revolutionary period.

Eichhorn, Hermann von (General Field Marshal). Commander in Chief of German forces in the Ukraine; assassinated in Kiev by the Russian Social Revolutionaries on July 30, 1918.

Erzberger, Matthias. One of the most influential Reichstag leaders (Zentrum), with close ties to German business interests; frequent critic of Ludendorff's *Ostpolitik* in 1918.

Falkenhayn, Erich von (General). Chief of the German General Staff, 1914–1916; Commander of German forces in Lithuania, 1918–1919.

Fleischmann (Major). Austro-Hungarian military attaché in Kiev.

Forgách von Ghymes und Gacs, Johann (Count). Austro-Hungarian Ambassador in Kiev; served in the prewar period as Vienna's envoy in Belgrade.

Friedrich, Emil (General). Reich War Ministry official charged with the supervision of the Union for the Liberation of the Ukraine.

Fürstenberg, Emil (Prince). Austro-Hungarian chargé d'affaires in Kiev in late 1918.

Gerbel, Sergei N. Former Governor of Kharkov, Minister of Food Supply in the Hetman's government; appointed Prime Minister by Skoropadsky in November, 1918.

Gratz, Georg. Chief of the Economic Section in the Austro-Hungarian Foreign Office during World War I; Czernin's deputy at Brest-Litovsk.

Groener, Wilhelm (General). Chief of the Transportation Division of the German Supreme Army Command, 1914–1916; Chief of the War Production Office (Kriegsamt), 1916–1917; Chief of Staff of the Army Group Eichhorn with headquarters in Kiev; Groener was unquestionably the most influential German official in the Ukraine in 1918.

Grünau, Kurt von (Baron). Legation Councillor, special representative of the German Foreign Office at the Great Headquarters (the Imperial Train) of Wilhelm II, 1916–1918.

Gutnik, Sergei M. Jewish Ukrainian industrialist, Minister of Trade and Industry in the Hetman government.

Hasse Major. Press Officer of the Army Group Eichhorn in the Ukraine in 1918 and chief of German Military Intelligence in Kiev.

Heinze, Karl. German Consul in Lviv (officially Lemberg), the Reich official who worked closely with the Union for the Liberation of the Ukraine in the early stages of World War I.

Helfferich, Karl. Director of the Deutsche Bank; the Reich's Secretary of the Treasury, 1915–1916; Vice-Chancellor and Secretary of the Interior, 1916–1917; Ambassador to Moscow in the summer of 1918 following Mirbach's assassination.

Helphand, Alexander Israel (better known by his *nom de révolution,* Parvus). Russian Social Democrat, also active in the German Social Democratic Party. The Reich's principal agent in the east and its liaison with various Russian and non-Russian revolutionaries in Germany and abroad.

Hertling, Georg von (Count). Reichstag leader (Zentrum) and Imperial Chancellor, November, 1917–October, 1918.

Hindenburg, Paul von (General Field Marshal). German Commander on the eastern front, 1914–1916; chief of the General Staff of the Army, 1916–1919.

Hintze, Paul von (Admiral). Served in diplomatic posts in Petersburg and Peking; Secretary of State for Foreign Affairs of the Reich, July-October, 1918.

Hoetzsch, Otto. Professor of Russian history at the University of Berlin and a Reichstag deputy; the leader of the "Russian School" in wartime Germany.

Hoffmann, Max (General). Chief of Staff of the Army Command East, 1916–1918; one of the Reich's most knowledgable eastern experts and the Supreme Army Command's spokesman at Brest-Litovsk.

Hohenlohe-Schillingsfürst, Gottfried zu (Prince). Austro-Hungarian Ambassador in Berlin, 1914–1918.

Holubovych, Vsevolod. Head of the Ukrainian Peace Delegation at Brest-Litovsk; Minister of Trade and Industry in the Rada government; Ukrainian Prime Minister during the initial period of German occupation (March and April, 1918).

Hopman, Albert (Rear Admiral). Representative of the German Navy in the Ukraine in 1918; Ludendorff's unsuccessful candidate for the post of the Reich's Ambassador to Kiev.

Hoyos, Alexander von (Count). Permanent Secretary of the Austro-Hungarian Foreign Office involved in the organization of revolutionary activities among the Ukrainians in the early months of World War I.

Hrushevsky, Mykhailo. The foremost Ukrainian historian of the modern period; principal Rada leader; President of the Ukrainian Republic under the German occupation until the Rada's overthrow in April, 1918.

Hutten-Czapski, Bogdan Franz Servatius von (Count). Prussian nobleman of Polish descent with close ties to Wilhelm II and Berlin's highest governmental circles; the Reich's principal eastern expert in the initial phase of the war.

Jagow, Gottlieb von. German Secretary of State for Foreign Affairs, 1913–1916.

Jarosch (Major). Russian-speaking German political officer in the Ukraine; one of General Groener's special assistants in Kiev.

Joffe, Adolf Abramovich. Member of Petrograd's Peace Delegation at Brest-Litovsk; the first Soviet Ambassador in Berlin (1918).

Karl, Kaiser von Habsburg. The last Austro-Hungarian Emperor; succeeded Franz Josef on November 21, 1916; abdicated on November 11, 1918.

Keup, Erich. Schwerin's assistant in the Intermediary Agency of Frankfurt on the Oder through which the Union for the Liberation of the Ukraine was financed and supervised; involved with Schwerin in various annexationist schemes.

Kirchbach, Günther von (Count, General). Commander in Chief of German forces in the Ukraine following Eichhorn's assassination in July, 1918.

Kistyakovs'kyi, Ihor. The Hetman's Minister of the Interior and deputy head of the Ukrainian delegation at the peace talks with Soviet Russia in Kiev.

Krasnov, Pëtr Nikolaevich (General). Ataman of the Don Cossacks and head of the Don government, May, 1918–February, 1919.

Krauss, Alfred (General). Commander in Chief of the Austro-Hungarian Army in the Ukraine, July-November, 1918.

Kriege, Johannes. Chief of the Legal Division of the German Foreign Office during World War I.

Kühlmann, Richard von. German Secretary of State for Foreign Affairs, August 5, 1917–July 9, 1918; the Reich's chief delegate at Brest-Litovsk.

Lenin, Vladimir I. Bolshevik leader, one of the principal architects of the November Revolution, head of the Soviet Russian State, 1917–1924.

Lersner, Kurt von (Baron). Legation Councillor, special representative of the German Foreign Office at the Supreme Army Command Headquarters, 1916–1918.

Levyts'kyi, Kost'. Galician Ukrainian political leader and one of the leading Ukrainian deputies in the Austrian Diet; often served as an unofficial liaison between the Union for the Liberation of the Ukraine and Berlin.

Levyts'kyi, Mykola. Member of the Rada Peace Delegation at Brest; also served briefly as the Rada's diplomatic representative in Constantinople.

Lindemann, Hugo. Member of the Reich's economic mission in the Ukraine in 1918.

Lindequist, Friedrich von. German Colonial Secretary, 1910–1911; active during World War I in the development of various plans for the colonization of non-German areas; the principal architect of a plan for the development of a *Kolonialstaat* in the Crimea.

Lucius von Stödten, Hellmuth (Baron). German envoy in Stockholm; very active in the development of German plans for the east.

Ludendorff, Erich (General). Quartermaster General (the second highest German military leader), 1916–1918; politically, one of the most influential Germans during this period with special interest in the Reich's plans for the east.

Lübers, Walter von (Captain). General E. Friedrich's principal assistant in the War Ministry's efforts to revolutionize the east, especially the Ukraine.

Lypyns'kyi, Vyacheslav. Ukrainian ambassador in Vienna under the Hetman; later the principal ideological spokesman for the Hetman movement abroad.

Lyubyns'kyi, Mykola. Member of the Rada's Peace Delegation at Brest; Foreign Minister in the reconstituted Rada government, February-April, 1918.

Lyzohub, Fedir A. The Hetman's Prime Minister, late May to early November, 1918.

Medvedev, Ye. H. Head of the Executive Committee of the All-Ukrainian Soviet of Workers based in Kharkov in early 1918; member of the Ukrainian-Soviet Peace Delegation at Brest.

Melchior, Karl. One of the directors of the Warburg banking house in Hamburg, on loan to the Reich's Department of the Treasury (Reichsschatzamt); Germany's principal financial expert in the Ukraine in 1918.

Michaelis, Georg. Prussian official, the Reich's Food Minister, spring and summer, 1917; Imperial Chancellor, July-November, 1917.

Michelis, Theodor L. A. (Major). German political officer in the Ukraine in 1918, on loan from the War Ministry to serve as Ambassador Mumm's military adviser.

Milyukov, Pavel Nikolaevich. Russian historian and a leader of the Constitutional Democratic Party; Foreign Minister in the Provisional Government, March-May, 1917; the most influential spokesman of the Russian Right, who explored the possibility of cooperating with the Germans in 1918.

Mirbach-Harff, Wilhelm von (Count). German Ambassador in Moscow following the conclusion of the Treaty of Brest-Litovsk; assassinated there by a Russian Social Revolutionary terrorist on July 6, 1918.

Mumm von Schwarzenstein, Philip Alfons (Baron). German Ambassador in Kiev; prior to this appointment served as head of the Reich's Central Propaganda Agency in Berlin; in the prewar period was the Reich's Ambassador in Tokyo and Washington.

Nadolny, Rudolf. Privy Councillor at the Reich's Foreign Ministry and head of its Eastern Division (Referent für Ostfragen).

Naumann, Friedrich. Reichstag deputy and the author of the famous *Mitteleuropa* book, easily the most influential work of the period.

Nazaruk, Osyp. West Ukrainian (Galician) political leader; representative of the Union for the Liberation of the Ukraine in Scandinavia and the United States.

Nicholas II (Romanov). The last Russian Czar; executed by the Bolsheviks with the entire royal family on July 16, 1918.

Ostapenko, Serhii. Economic advisor to the Ukrainian Peace Delegation at Brest; also active in that capacity under the Hetman.

Paltov, Oleksander O. Under-Secretary for Foreign Affairs under the Hetman.

Payer, Friedrich von. Reichstag deputy (Progressive People's party); Vice-Chancellor, 1917–1918.

Petlyura, Symon. Secretary for Military Affairs under the Rada; principal leader in the anti-Hetman uprising in November, 1918; Petlyura subsequently became the head of the Ukrainian Directory and also continued to lead the Ukrainian nationalist movement after he was forced into exile; assassinated in Paris on May 25, 1926, by a Jewish refugee from the Ukraine.

Pyatakov, Georgii L. Bolshevik leader in the Ukraine during the Civil War period; subsequently an important Soviet official and diplomat.

Rathenau, Walter. German industrial leader and chief of the Raw Materials Department of the Reich's War Ministry during World War I.

Reuss, Heinrich (Prince). German Foreign Office's representative in the Crimea during 1918.

Riezler, Kurt. Bethmann Hollweg's secretary and adviser until the latter's resignation in July, 1917; Legation Councillor in the Reich's embassy in Moscow under Mirbach, briefly in charge of German diplomatic mission there following Mirbach's assassination on July 6, 1918.

Roedern, Siegfried von (Count). German Secretary of State of the Imperial Treasury, 1916–1918.

Rohrbach, Paul. Baltic-born German journalist and political commentator; one of Germany's best-informed eastern experts and the principal leader of the "Osteuropa School" which consistently advocated the dismemberment of the Russian Empire.

Romberg, Gisbert von (Baron). German envoy in Bern; was in charge of an extensive German information and intelligence network, in which a number of non-Russians of the east were involved.

Rosenberg, Friedrich Hans von. Ambassador in the German Foreign Office; Kühlmann's deputy at Brest-Litovsk and head of the German delegation in his absence.

Schiemann, Theodor. Baltic-born German scholar and writer; one of the Reich's leading Russian historians who exerted considerable influence on German political leaders, especially Kaiser Wilhelm II, who often sought his advice.

Schüler, Richard. Legation Councillor in the German Foreign Office, Kühlmann's assistant at Brest-Litovsk.

Schüller, Richard, Dr. Economic officer in the Austrian Foreign Office; Czernin's adviser at Brest-Litovsk.

Schwerin, Friedrich von. An influential Prussian official (Administrative President of the Frankfurt on the Oder District); head of the Intermediary Agency of Frankfurt on the Oder charged with the supervision and financing of special projects such as the Union for the Liberation of the Ukraine.

Seidahmet, Dzhafer (also Seydahmet and Seidamet, Cafer). Tatar nationalist leader in the Crimea; Foreign Affairs and War Secretary in the Tatar government organized in November, 1917, and Foreign Secretary in the Sulkevich government, May-November, 1918.

Seidler, Ernst von (Cavalier-Knight). Austro-Hungarian Prime Minister, June, 1917–July, 1918.

Sevryuk, Oleksander. First a member and then head of the Rada Peace Delegation at Brest-Litovsk; the Rada Ambassador in Berlin, February-April, 1918.

Shakhrai, Vasyl M. Ukrainian Bolshevik; Commissar for Military Affairs in the first Soviet Ukrainian government established in Kharkov in December, 1917, and its delegate at Brest.

Shelukhin, Serhii. A noted Ukrainian jurist; Minister of Justice in the Hetman government; head of the Ukrainian delegation at peace talks with Soviet Russia in Kiev, summer and autumn, 1918.

Shteingel, Fedir (Baron). The Hetman's Ambassador in Berlin.

Shul'hyn, Oleksander (also Choulguine). Secretary of State for Foreign Affairs under the Rada (resigned during the Brest negotiations because of his pro-Entente stand); Kiev's Ambassador in Bulgaria under the Hetman.

Skoropadsky, Pavlo (General). Aide-de-Camp to Czar Nicholas II; corps commander on the eastern front at the time of the Russian Revolution; the leading spirit behind the Ukrainization of the southwestern front in the summer of 1917; Hetman of the Ukraine during the German occupation, April-December, 1918.

Skoropys-Ioltukhovs'kyi, Oleksander. One of the founders of the German-sponsored Union for the Liberation of the Ukraine, head of its Berlin bureau and its most influential leader.

Solf, Wilhelm. German Colonial Secretary, 1911–1918; Secretary of State for Foreign Affairs under Prince Max of Baden, October-December, 1918.

Stein zu Nord- und Ostheim, Hans Karl von (Baron). German Secretary for Economic Affairs (Reichswirtschaftsamt), November, 1917-November, 1918.

Stein, Hermann von. Head of the Prussian War Ministry, 1916–1918.

Stolzenberg, von Colonel (Baron). German military attaché in Kiev, special representative of the Prussian War Ministry in the Ukraine.

Stumm, Wilhelm von. German Under-Secretary of State for Foreign Affairs during World War I.

Südekum, Albert. Writer and a Social Democratic Reichstag deputy; had special interest in the east and maintained close ties with Russian and Ukrainian revolutionaries abroad.

Sulkevich, Suleiman (General). Commander of a Moslem corps on the eastern front following the March, 1917, Revolution; head of the Crimean provincial government under the German occupation, May-November, 1918.

Svechin, M. A. (General). Member of the Don delegation sent to Kiev during the summer of 1918 to negotiate with the Hetman and the Germans.

Talat Pasha, Mehmed (also Talaat). Turkish Grand Vizier, the Ottoman Empire's Foreign Minister during World War I.

Tatishchev, Count. Russian conservative leader in the Crimea who held the position of Secretary of the Treasury in the Sulkevich regime.

Thiel, Erich von. German Consul General in Kiev in 1918.

Tkachenko, Mykhailo. The Rada Minister of Justice and later of the Interior.

Trautmann, Oskar Paul. Legation Councillor in the Information Division of the German Foreign Office, 1914–1918.

Trotsky, Lev. D. (Bronstein). The first Soviet Commissar for Foreign Affairs and chief delegate at Brest; Commissar for Defense and the creator of the Red Army, 1918–1925.

Urbas, Emanuel, (Consul). Austro-Hungarian official in Lviv involved in the organization and early supervision of the Union for the Liberation of the Ukraine.

Vasylenko, Mykola. The Hetman's Prime Minister in May, 1918; served later as Minister of Education in the Lyzohub cabinet.

Vasylko, Mykola (also Wassilko) (Baron). Ukrainian deputy in the Austrian Diet, often served as a go-between in negotiations between the Central Powers on the one hand and the Rada delegates on the other; a very important source of information and advice to the Ukrainians at Brest.

Vynnychenko, Volodymyr. A noted Ukrainian writer and one of the leading Social Democrats in the Ukraine; Secretary of the Rada in 1917; one of the leaders of the anti-Hetman uprising in November, 1918, and a member of the Directory—the Ukrainian government that replaced the Hetmanate.

Wedel, Botho von (Count). German Ambassador in Vienna during World War I.

Wiedfeldt, Otto. Krupp director and the Reich's principal economic expert in the Ukraine in 1918; officially the representative of the Ministry of the National Economy (Reichswirtschaftsamt).

Wilhelm II (Hohenzollern). The last German Kaiser.

Wilhelm von Habsburg, Archduke (Vasyl' Vyshyvanyi—Basil the Embroidered). Son of Archduke Karl Stephan and nephew of Kaiser Karl of Austria-Hungary; colonel in the Galician Ukrainian Volunteer Legion—Sichovi Striltsi—which was one of the Dual Monarchy's units stationed in the Ukraine in 1918; he was regarded by many at the time as Skoropadsky's chief rival for the position of hereditary ruler of the Ukraine.

Winkler I. Protestant pastor, leader of German colonists in the Ukraine; principal architect of the plan for German annexation of the Crimea.

Winterfeldt, Detlef von (Colonel). German Supreme Command's special representative at the Imperial Chancellery; worked closely with Rosenberg at Brest.

Zaliznyak, Mykola. Briefly a member of the Union for the Liberation of the Ukraine, then an independent agent working for the Austrians; served as a go-between in the talks between the Rada delegates and the Central Powers at Brest-Litovsk.

Zhuk, Andrii. One of the founders of the Union for the Liberation of the Ukraine and the head of its Vienna office.

Zimmerman, Arthur. German Under-Secretary of State for Foreign Affairs, 1911–1916; Foreign Secretary, 1916–1917.

NOTES

NOTES

Chapter I: The Ukrainian National Movement and the Outbreak of World War I

1. The best general survey of Ukrainian history in English is Dmytro Doroshenko's *History of the Ukraine*, translated by Hanna Keller. See also William E. D. Allen, *The Ukraine*, and Mykhailo Hrushevsky, *A History of Ukraine*.
2. According to the 1959 Soviet census, ethnic Russians accounted for 54.6 percent of the U.S.S.R.'s total population. Even though the results of the January, 1970, census have not been revealed as of the publication of this book, there are definite indications that the percentage of Russians is now somewhat under 50 percent. *New York Times*, April 27, 1969, and April 19, 1970.
3. This analysis pertains to the East Ukraine, that is the central Dnieper area. The history of Galicia or the West Ukraine, which followed a somewhat different course, is treated elsewhere in this chapter.
4. For a brief but reliable discussion of this problem see Ivan L. Rudnytsky, "The Intellectual Origins of Modern Ukraine," pp. 1381–1405.
5. K. Mykhal'chuk and P. Chubyns'kyi in *Trudy etnografichesko-statisticheskoi ekspeditsii v Zapadno-Russkii krai,* as cited in Rudnytsky, p. 1392.
6. One of the most comprehensive compilations of such materials is available in Volodymyr Sichynsky's *Ukraine in Foreign Comments.*

7. Cited in Walter Laqueur, *Russia and Germany*, p. 19.
8. Otto Fürst von Bismarck, *The Man and the Statesman, Being the Reflections and Reminiscences of Otto Prince von Bismarck*, I, 119–20. See also Otto Pflanze, *Bismarck and the Development of Germany*, pp. 120–21. German writings on the Ukrainian question in the nineteenth and twentieth centuries are discussed in Dmytro Doroshenko, *Die Ukraine und das Reich*, chaps. V and VI.
9. Bismarck, *Gedanken und Erinnerungen*, I, 104.
10. Kurd von Schlötzer, "Politische Berichte aus Petersburg," 17–18.
11. Eduard von Hartmann, "Russland in Europa."
12. Bismarck, *Gedanken und Erinnerungen*, I, 105–107; Gustav A. Rein, *Die Revolution in der Politik Bismarcks*, chap. V; Reinhold Wittram, "Bismarcks Russlandpolitik nach der Reichsgründung," p. 275. On the policies of Bismarck's successors see Malcolm E. Carrol, *Germany and the Great Powers, 1866–1914*, chaps. VIII–XIII; Ludwig Reiners, *In Europa gehen die Lichter aus*, chaps. I–IX; Martin Göhring, *Bismarcks Erben, 1890–1945*, chap. I.
13. Otto Hoetzsch, *Russland; Eine Einführung auf Grund seiner Geschichte von 1904 bis 1912*, p. 468.
14. According to official German estimates, there were approximately 500,000 German "colonists" in the Ukraine in the pre-war period. Document No. A. 36335, *German Foreign Office Archives*, microfilm No. 138 (hereafter cited as *GFOA*). Another, unofficial, wartime source put the number of German settlers in South Russia at 600,000 to 700,000. Alexander Faure, "Das deutsche Kolonistentum in Russland," p. 170.
15. P. V. Ol', *Inostrannye kapitaly v Rossii* [Foreign Capital in Russia], pp. 9 and 72.
16. See, for example, Ivan M. Kulinych, *Ukrayina v zaharbnyts'kykh planakh nimets'koho imperializmu, 1900–1914 rr.* [The Ukraine in the Predatory Plans of German Imperialism].
17. A. S. Yerusalimskii, *Vneshnyaya politika i diplomatiya germanskogo imperializma v kontse XIX veka* [Foreign Policy and Diplomacy of German Imperialism at the End of the Nineteenth Century], p. 204; see also Kulinych's study cited above.
18. For the background of the Ukrainian national movement see John S. Reshetar, *The Ukrainian Revolution*, chap. I. The most reliable work on the movement in the West Ukraine is Ivan L. Rudnytsky's "The Ukrainians in Galicia Under Austrian Rule," pp. 394–429.

19. Michael Yaremko, *Galicia-Halychyna*, pp. 201–202.
20. M. Stachiv, *West Ukraine and the Policy of Poland,* cited in Yaremko, p. 203.

Chapter II: German War Aims in the East and the Ukraine, 1914–1916

1. Bethmann's Reichstag speeches of August 19, 1915, and April 5, 1916, cited in Salomon Grumbach, *Das annexionistische Deutschland,* pp. 7, 8. See also Count Kuno von Westarp, *Konservative Politik,* II, 163; S. Eggert, "Die deutschen Eroberungspläne im Ersten Weltkrieg," p. 39; Henry Cord Meyer, *Mitteleuropa in German Thought and Action, 1815–1945,* p. 132; Veit Valentin, *Deutschlands Aussenpolitik,* pp. 259–60, 262–63; Arthur Rosenberg, *The Birth of the German Republic,* pp. 105, 108; Hans J. Beyer, *Die Mittelmächte und die Ukraine, 1918,* pp. 19–20.

2. For further details on the extent of German annexationist plans in the northeast see Bethmann Hollweg's secret telegram to Hindenburg, dated November 4, 1916, and Hindenburg's reply on the following day, both cited in Fritz Klein, *Die diplomatischen Beziehungen Deutschlands zur Sowjetunion, 1917–1923,* p. 18. This and a later East German study, Werner Basler, *Deutschlands Annexionspolitik in Polen und im Baltikum, 1914–1918,* should, however, be used with caution. Fritz Fischer (*Griff nach der Weltmacht,* p. 104) agrees that it was in the "second half of the war" that German plans to organize a series of buffer states in the east were extended to include the whole of *Baltikum.* The story of German plans for the Baltic region is most reliably and fully presented in the following works: Lilli Lewerenz, "Die deutsche Politik im Baltikum, 1914–1918;" Bernhard Mann, *Die baltischen Länder in der deutschen Kriegszielpublizistik, 1914–1918;* and Gerd Linde, *Die deutsche Politik in Litauen im ersten Weltkrieg.*

3. See, for example, Rosenberg, p. 96; *Das Werk des Untersuchungsausschusses der verfassunggebenden deutschen Nationalversammlung und deutschen Reichstages 1919–1928. Die Ursachen des deutschen Zusammenbruches im Jahre 1918,* fourth series, XII (1), 200 (hereafter cited as *Die Ursachen*); Hans W. Gatzke, *Germany's Drive to the West,* pp. 8, 290; Meyer, *Mitteleuropa,* p. 130; Erich Matthias, *Die deutsche Sozialdemokratie und der Osten, 1914–1918,* p. 3; Beyer, p. 8.

4. Fischer, *Griff nach der Weltmacht,* pp. 102–104.

5. Ludwig Dehio, *Germany and World Politics in the Twentieth Century,* p. 105.

6. Gerhard Ritter, *Staatskunst und Kriegshandwerk. Vol. III: Die Tragödie der Staatskunst: Bethmann Hollweg als Kriegskanzler, 1914–1917.* One of the most penetrating reviews of Fischer's work is Fritz T. Epstein's "Die deutsche Ostpolitik im Ersten Weltkrieg," pp. 381–95. Equally helpful is his "Mehr Literatur zur Ostpolitik im Ersten Weltkrieg," pp. 63–94, in which he discusses not only Fischer and Ritter, but reviews the writings of other contemporary students of this problem. In addition to Gerhard Ritter, one should mention Egmont Zechlin, Wolfgang Steglich, Karl Dietrich Erdmann, Hans Herzfeld, and Erwin Hölzle as Fischer's most persistent critics. Fritz Fischer defended his thesis in a long article, "Weltpolitik, Weltmachtstreben und deutsche Kriegsziele," 265–345. Fischer's argument and the views of several other distinguised students of the problem of German war guilt are also available in Ernst Wilhelm Lynar (ed.), *Deutsche Kriegsziele, 1914–1918: Eine Diskussion.*

7. In February, 1917, the French Propaganda Agency boasted that "wild claims" of the Pan-Germans were most useful for Allied propaganda and "had to be valued like gold." Alfred Kruck, *Geschichte des Alldeutschen Verbandes 1890–1939,* p. 95.

8. See, for example, Egmont Zechlin, "Deutschland zwischen Kabinettskrieg und Wirtschaftskrieg," pp. 408–09; and his "Probleme des Kriegskalküls," pp. 69–70, 77. See also Karl D. Erdmann, "Zur Beurteilung Bethmann Hollwegs," p. 537; and Wolfgang Steglich, *Die Friedenspolitik der Mittelmächte, 1917–1918,* Vol. I.

9. Fritz Stern, "Bethmann Hollweg and the War," pp. 269, 266.

10. Fischer, *Griff nach der Weltmacht,* pp. 114–15, 351.

11. See, for example, Gatzke, *Germany's Drive to the West,* pp. 214 ff.; and Ebba Dahlin, *French and German Public Opinion on Declared War Aims, 1914–1918,* pp. 135 ff.

12. Fischer, *Griff nach der Weltmacht,* p. 180.

13. Kruck, pp. 93–119.

14. Meyer, *Mitteleuropa,* pp. 136, 217.

15. Fischer, *Griff nach der Weltmacht,* pp. 240–42, 304, 312, 567.

16. Stern, p. 270.

17. Friedrich Naumann, "Das Jahr 1916," pp. 847–48; see also Dahlin, p. 75.

18. Beyer, p. 7 *ff*.
19. *Ibid.*, pp. 21–26; see also Meyer, *Mitteleuropa*, pp. 221, 247, 271; and Paul Rohrbach's articles in Naumann's *Hilfe*.
20. *Hilfe*, February 9, 1918.
21. Meyer, *Mitteleuropa*, p. 271.
22. *Ibid.*, pp. 271, 289–90; Fischer, *Griff nach der Weltmacht*, pp. 304, 669.
23. On Rohrbach and his school see the following: Henry Cord Meyer's *Mitteleuropa*, p. 262, his "Rohrbach and his Osteuropa," pp. 60–69, and his "Germans in the Ukraine, 1918," pp. 105–15; Beyer, pp. 21–23; Valentin, pp. 344–45; Doroshenko, *Die Ukraine und das Reich*, pp. 184–85; Fischer, *Griff nach der Weltmacht.*
24. The most useful source on Schiemann's activities is Klaus Meyer's *Schiemann als politischer Publizist.* See also Wilhelm II, *The Kaiser's Memoirs*, pp. 199–200; and Fischer, *Griff nach der Weltmacht*, pp. 233, 246, 346–47, 605, 814.
25. Paul Rohrbach, "Russland und wir."
26. Paul Rohrbach, *Russland und wir*, chap. III; and Meyer, *Mitteleuropa*, pp. 272–73. Soviet historiography has been especially critical of Rohrbach. See, for example, H. Zastavenko, *Rozhrom nimets'kykh interventiv na Ukrayini v 1918 r.* [The Rout of German Interventionists in the Ukraine in 1918], p. 5; and M. Gorkii, R. Eideman, and I. I. Mints (eds.), *Krakh germanskoi okkupatsii na Ukraine* [The Collapse of the German Occupation in the Ukraine]. This Soviet collection of German documents pertaining to the occupation of the Ukraine in 1918, made up of carefully selected but unquestionably authentic documents from German and Austro-Hungarian Foreign Office files, was until recently the most valuable source on the subject. Naturally, the opening of German and Austrian archives to researchers has greatly diminished the special value of this collection. It is also available in German under the title *Die deutsche Okkupation der Ukraine.* (The Russian edition of this source is hereafter cited as *Krakh germanskoi okkupatsii,* and its German edition as *Die deutsche Okkupation.*)
27. Rohrbach's troubles with the Pan-Germans during the war are discussed more fully in his *Die alldeutsche Gefahr* and in Martin Hobohm and Paul Rohrbach, *Die Alldeutschen.*
28. Beyer, pp. 24–25. The language of the "thesis" is Beyer's, which in turn reflects the tenor of these wartime writings.
29. Valentin, pp. 244–45.

30. Henry Cord Meyer, *Mitteleuropa*, p. 262. See also his "Germans in the Ukraine," p. 106.

31. Doroshenko, *Die Ukraine und das Reich*, p. 194; Prince Bernhard von Bülow, *Deutsche Politik*, p. 86.

32. Rohrbach in Paul Rohrbach and Axel Schmidt, *Osteuropa, historisch-politisch gesehen,* pp. 130–31. At this point Hindenburg was in charge of German forces in the east, with Ludendorff serving as his principal assistant. In August, 1916, Hindenburg became the Supreme Commander of all the German ground forces. Ludendorff accompanied him to the Great Headquarters as First Quartermaster General.

33. Paul Rohrbach, *Um des Teufels Handschrift*, pp. 219–20.

34. Rohrbach in Rohrbach and Schmidt, *Osteuropa*, p. 131. This Propaganda and Information Bureau was Germany's central coordinating agency in this field. It was headed by Baron Philipp Alfons Mumm von Schwarzenstein, who became later the Reich's ambassador to the Ukraine. Erzberger and Rohrbach were members of the Board of Directors of this agency. Klaus Epstein, *Matthias Erzberger and the Dilemma of German Democracy,* p. 104.

35. The best source on Hoetzsch's wartime activities is Fritz T. Epstein's "Otto Hoetzsch als aussenpolitischer Kommentator," pp. 9–28. See also Beyer, p. 21; and Henry Cord Meyer, *Mitteleuropa,* p. 262.

36. Beyer, p. 21.

37. Klaus Schwabe, "Zur politischen Haltung der deutschen Professoren," pp. 601, 614, 620.

38. Fischer, *Griff nach der Weltmacht*, p. 347.

39. Immanuel Birnbaum, "Deusche Ostpolitik alt und neu," p. 348.

40. Beyer, pp. 8–9; Fischer, *Griff nach der Weltmacht*, pp. 158–159, 253, 693–707; Titus Komarnicki, *Rebirth of the Polish Republic*, chaps. III and IV; Arthur Hauser, *Die Polenpolitik der Mittelmächte;* Werner Conze, *Polnische Nation und deutsche Politik.*

41. For further details see the following: Bogdan Franz Servatius von Hutten-Czapski, *Sechzig Jahre Politik und Gesellschaft,* Vol. II; Beyer, pp. 4 *ff.*; Komarnicki, chaps. III and IV; Fischer, *Griff nach der Weltmacht*, p. 123 and chap. IV.

42. Komarnicki, p. 91.

43. The Union for the Liberation of the Ukraine is sometimes referred to as the *Bund*. See, for example, Allan Moorehead, *The Russian Revolution*, p. 114, and German writings dealing with this problem. This term should be reserved for the better-

known Jewish *Bund* to avoid unnecessary confusion. For Vienna's reluctance to exploit anti-Russian forces in the pre-war period, see Helga Grebing's well-documented study "Österreich-Ungarn und die 'Ukrainische Aktion,'" p. 272.

44. A good example of this attitude is available in the article of one of the leading and most active officers of the Union, Oleksander Skoropys-Ioltukhovs'kyi, "Moyi 'zlochyny'" [My 'Crimes'], pp. 201–205.
45. Symon Petlyura, *Statti, lysty i dokumenty* [Articles, Letters and Documents], pp. 188–90.
46. Grebing, p. 277; and Skoropys, pp. 203–205. See also Volf-dieter Bihl, "Österreich-Ungarn und der 'Bund,'" pp. 505–18. This article is especially useful for the discussion of the Union's relations with Austrian Ukrainians (Galicians).
47. Fritz Fischer, "Deutsche Kriegsziele," p. 290. It appears very doubtful whether Consul Heinze was as important as Fischer claims.
48. Skoropys, pp. 201–205. See also Bihl, pp. 506–507; and Dmytro Doroshenko, *Istoriya Ukrayiny, 1917–1923,* I, 31.
49. Skoropys, pp. 202–203; and Doroshenko, *Istoriya Ukrayiny,* I, 433–34.
50. For a complete list of the Union's early publications see Document No. 2, Appendix 1, dated Vienna, December 14, 1914, containing a report on the Union's activities and bearing the signatures of O. Skoropys-Ioltukhovs'kyi and A. Zhuk, in *Österreichisches Staatsarchiv, Abteilung Haus-, Hof-, und Staatsarchiv, Politisches Archiv,* IX, 2–20. (Hereafter cited as *Politisches Archiv* (Vienna).)
51. On the contribution of the Galician Ukrainian leaders to the Union's work see the following: *Politisches Archiv* (*Vienna*), Vol. IX; Beyer, pp. 3–7; Grebing, pp. 273–74; and Bihl.
52. Doroshenko, *Istoriya Ukrayiny,* I, 32; and his *Die Ukraine und das Reich,* p. 186.
53. Skoropys, p. 205.
54. O. Skoropys-Ioltukhovs'kyi and A. Zhuk to Consul E. Urbas, "Report on the Union's finances," Vienna, December 16, 1914, *Politisches Archiv* (*Vienna*), IX, Doc. No. 1.
55. Czernin (Vienna) to Hohenlohe (Berlin), August 27, 1914, cited in Beyer, pp. 3–4. Count Czernin was at this point Vienna's envoy in Bucharest, and then from August, 1916, until April, 1918, he served as the Dual Monarchy's Foreign Minister. Prince Chlodwig von Hohenlohe served throughout the war period as the Austrian Ambassador in Berlin.

56. Hoyos to Colonel Hranilovic. Private letter dated November 14, 1914, cited in Grebing, pp. 272, 276.
57. Emanuel Urbas, Alexander von Hoyos, and the Austrian diplomatic representatives in Berlin, Sofia, Constantinople, and Bucharest were most deeply involved in the Ukrainian undertaking. See *Politisches Archiv* (*Vienna*), Vol. IX; Grebing; and Skoropys.
58. According to Beyer (p. 5), Hutten-Czapski's relations with the German Foreign Office became less close after Arthur Zimmermann's resignation in August, 1917.
59. An undated and unsigned document in *GFOA*. No. 110. See also Omelyan Terlets'kyi, *Istoriya ukrayins'koyi hromady v Rashtati* [History of the Ukrainian Community in Rastadt], p. 22; and Skoropys.
60. Both Terlets'kyi and Skoropys refer to Schwerin as the Union's most consistent supporter. For other activities of Schwerin and Keup see Fischer, *Griff nach der Weltmacht*, pp. 126, 187, 199, 346, 438.
61. Skoropys, p. 215.
62. On the League of Non-Russian Peoples see the book of one of its founders, Friedrich von der Ropp, *Zwischen gestern und morgen*, pp. 100, 109. The best work on Parvus is Z. A. B. Zeman and W. B. Scharlau, *The Merchant of Revolution*.
63. David Shub, "Lenin i Vilgelm II" [Lenin and Wilhelm II], pp. 226–27, 238.
64. See, for example, a report on Zimmermann's meeting with the head of the Central Bureau of the Union in Berlin, Skoropys-Ioltukhovs'kyi, Doc. No. A 31872–15, November 3, 1915, *GFOA*. No. 21.
65. Fischer, *Griff nach der Weltmacht*, pp. 103–104, 109–11, 123, 139–40, 149–52.
66. Friedrich von Meinecke, *Strassburg, Freiburg, Berlin*, p. 249.
67. The correspondence between the Union and the Austrian Foreign Ministry concerning their relations is available in *Politisches Archiv* (*Vienna*), Vol. IX. See also Grebing, pp. 290–91; and Doroshenko, *Istoriya Ukrayiny*, I, 33.
68. *Politisches Archiv* (*Vienna*), Vol. IX; and Skoropys, p. 212. A good source on the role of Galician Ukrainians in these talks is Bihl, pp. 511–13.
69. For German and Austrian wartime literature on the Ukraine see Doroshenko, *Die Ukraine und das Reich*, chaps. V and VI.
70. Bihl, p. 519.
71. Grebing, pp. 277–78.

72. For further details see the following: Pallavicini (Pera) to Foreign Office (Vienna), Telegram No. 1457, Secret, November 16, 1914, and Telegram No. 6659, November 19, 1914, from the Army Supreme Command (Teschen), both in *Politisches Archiv (Vienna)*, Vol. XIII; Pallavicini (Constantinople) to Hoyos (Vienna), November 27, 1914, *ibid.*, Vol. IX; Grebing, pp. 281–82.

73. Skoropys, p. 218. His name was Yevhen Heletsyns'kyi; he was a member of a Ukrainian socialist underground organization in Kiev.

74. A memorandum of the German War Ministry, Very Secret, Berlin, January 5, 1917 (signed by General Friedrich), *GFOA*. No. 109. See also Skoropys.

75. *Ibid.*, and Doroshenko, *Istoriya Ukrayiny*, I, 31.

76. Doroshenko, *Istoriya Ukrayiny*, I, 34, 39; and Beyer, pp. 14–15. Both German and Austrian documents reflect these two different attitudes. For the historical background of the Kholm area see Appendix A.

77. Zenon Stefaniv, *Ukrayins'ki zbroini syly v 1917–1921 rr.* [Ukrainian Armed Forces, 1917–1921], p. 49; German War Ministry to Foreign Office, Communication No. 697/18, Berlin, August 22, 1918, *GFOA*. No. 53.

78. Skoropys, pp. 215–17.

79. For the Union's educational work among the Ukrainian war prisoners see Terlets'kyi; he was personally involved in this program.

80. Moorehead, pp. 114–15.

81. Not only Moorehead, the author of a popular book on the Russian Revolution, but Fischer, too (*Griff nach der Weltmacht,* esp. chap. IV), tend to take the Kaiser's ideas and marginal remarks much too seriously.

82. Skoropys, pp. 230–35; Grebing's estimates (pp. 290–92), based on Austrian official documents, are virtually identical with Skoropys' figures.

83. German and Austrian documents examined in the preparation of this book fully support this thesis. See also the following: Z. A. B. Zeman (ed.), *Germany and the Revolution in Russia,* p. viii (Introduction); Ropp, p. 100; Skoropys; Axel Schmidt, *Ukraine, Land der Zukunft,* p. 191.

*Chapter III: German Plans in the East and the Russian
    Revolution*

1. Ukrainian Rada leaders to Prince Georgii Ye. Lvov, telegram
   dated March 6, 1917 (old style), cited in S. M. Dimanshtein
   (ed.), *Revolutsiya i natsional'nyi vopros* [The Revolution and
   the National Question], III, 32. For a more complete discussion of the rise of the Rada see the following: Reshetar, *The
   Ukrainian Revolution*, chap. II; Richard Pipes, *The Formation
   of the Soviet Union*, pp. 50–73; and Oleh S. Pidhainy, *The
   Formation of the Ukrainian Republic*, chaps. I–IV. This last
   item is the most ambitious and best documented work on the
   subject; unfortunately it is too polemical and not always
   reliable.
2. Doroshenko, *Istoriya Ukrayiny*, I, 11, 36; Beyer, p. 27. German
   and Austrian documents examined in the course of preparing
   this study failed to produce any evidence of direct ties between
   the Rada and the Central Powers in 1917.
3. *Die Ursachen*, fourth series, XII (1), 200.
4. Foreign Office (Berlin) to Lersner (Great Headquarters), Telegram No. 140, March 28, 1917, *GFOA*. No. 1498.
5. Erich von Ludendorff, *Ludendorff's Own Story*, II, 14; Erwin
   Direnberger, *Die Beziehungen zwischen Oberster Heeresleitung
   und Reichsleitung*, p. 48.
6. Doroshenko, *Istoriya Ukrayiny*, I, 35.
7. Walther Hubatsch, *Germany and the Central Powers in the
   World War*, p. 106; and Fischer, *Griff nach der Weltmacht*,
   p. 154.
8. Secret instructions to Councillor Storck, No. 4754, August 31,
   1917, cited in Beyer, p. 18. See also Grebing, p. 293.
9. *GFOA*. Nos. 2116–2128.
10. *GFOA*. No. 109.
11. Michaelis (Berlin) to Lersner (Great Headquarters), Telegram
    No. 1328, AS 2936, July 26, 1917, cited in Zeman, *Germany
    and the Revolution in Russia*, pp. 67–68; and Riezler (Stock-
    holm) to Hertling (Berlin), I. B. No. 11, November 16, 1917,
    GFOA. No. 110.
12. Nadolny (Brest-Litovsk) to Foreign Office (Berlin), Telegram
    No. 153, January 18, 1918; and Wedel (Vienna) to Foreign
    Office (Berlin), Telegram No. 173, January 18, 1918, *GFOA*.
    No. 110.

13. Nadolny (Berlin) to Rosenberg (Brest-Litovsk), Telegram No. 77, December 18, 1917, *ibid.*
14. Kühlmann to Lersner (to be communicated to the Emperor), Telegram No. 1925, Berlin, December 3, 1917, cited in George Katkov, "German Foreign Office Documents on Financial Support to the Bolsheviks in 1917," p. 189.
15. Skoropys, p. 233. German and Austrian documents while being incomplete, generally uphold the correctness of these figures.
16. German Embassy (Bern) to the Imperial Chancellor (Berlin), Communication No. 3706, Secret, November 30, 1917, *GFOA.* No. 110.
17. War Ministry to Foreign Office, Communication No. 697/18, Berlin, August 22, 1918, *GFOA.* No. 53.
18. Bihl, p. 515.
19. The State Secretary to his Liaison Officer at the Supreme Army Command, Telegram No. 1610, AS 3640, Berlin, September 29, 1917, cited in Zeman, *Germany and the Revolution in Russia,* p. 70; and Kühlmann's telegram cited in note No. 14 above.
20. For further details see Zeman and Scharlau, p. 231.
21. Doroshenko, *Istoriya Ukrayiny,* I, 36.
22. See, for example, the statement published in *Nova Rada* No. 118, August 22, 1917, cited in *GFOA.* No. 109.
23. *Die Ursachen,* fourth series, XII (1), 200.
24. Klaus Epstein, "The Development of German-Austrian War Aims," p. 29.
25. Robert L. Koehl, "A Prelude to Hitler's Greater Germany," pp. 43–65.
26. Rohrbach, *Um des Teufels Handschrift,* pp. 219–20.
27. *Die Ursachen,* fourth series, XII (1), 107–108.
28. Grünau (Great Headquarters) to Foreign Office (Berlin), "For the Imperial Chancellor," Telegram No. 533, April 20, 1917, *GFOA.* No. 1498.
29. Zimmermann (Berlin) to the Supreme Army Command (Great Headquarters), Telegram No. 708, April 22, 1917, *ibid.* See also *Die Ursachen,* fourth series, XII (1), 108.
30. Full text of the official report on the first Kreuznach conference (April 23, 1917), signed by Bethmann Hollweg, Zimmermann, Hindenburg, and Ludendorff, can be found in *Die Ursachen,* fourth series, XII (1), 200–202, and in Grünau (Great Headquarters) to Bethmann Hollweg (Berlin), Telegram No. 219, April 24, 1917, *GFOA.* No. 1498. An English

summary of this report is available in Klaus Epstein, "The Development of German-Austrian War Aims," pp. 31–32.

31. Ziese (Stockholm) to Erzberger (Berlin), Report No. 30, April 23, 1917, *GFOA*. No. 2091.
32. Bussche (Berlin) to Roselius (n.p.), April 13, 1917, *GFOA*. No. 109.
33. Zimmermann (Berlin) to Wedel (Vienna), April 28, 1917, *GFOA*. No. 1498. General Arz's view of the Ukrainians is discussed Wedel (Vienna) to Zimmermann (Berlin), May 5, 1917, *ibid.*
34. "Report on Ludendorff's Position," Lersner (Great Headquarters) to Foreign Office (Berlin), Telegram No. 628, April 29, 1917, *GFOA*. No. 1498.
35. *Die Ursachen,* fourth series, XII (1), 109.
36. Wedel (Vienna) to Foreign Office (Berlin), Telegram No. 224, May 5, 1917, *GFOA*. No. 1499.
37. *Die Ursachen,* fourth series, XII (1), 109.
38. For a full discussion of Bethmann Hollweg's view of the first Kreuznach conference see Klaus Epstein, "The Development of German-Austrian War Aims," pp. 31–32.
39. Fischer, *Griff nach der Weltmacht,* pp. 487, 493–95.
40. For example, German Embassy (Stockholm) to Bethmann Hollweg (Berlin), Telegram No. 466, May 3, 1917, *GFOA*. No. 2128.
41. Lersner (Great Headquarters) to Zimmerman (Berlin), April 29, 1917, *GFOA*. No. 1498.
42. Lersner (Great Headquarters) to Foreign Office (Berlin), "For the Imperial Chancellor," Telegram No. 726, Urgent, May 12, 1917, *GFOA*. Nos. 1500 and 2128.
43. Grünau (Kaiser's Great Headquarters) to Foreign Office (Berlin), "For Foreign Secretary only," Telegram No. 46, May 13, 1917, *GFOA*. No. 1499. This strange document is also discussed in Klaus Epstein, "The Development of German-Austrian War Aims," pp. 42–43. Fischer (*Griff nach der Weltmacht,* pp. 448–49) mentions a similar program prepared by the Kaiser on April 17, 1917, that is, on the eve of the first Kreuznach conference.
44. Klaus Epstein, "The Development of German-Austrian War Aims, p. 42.
45. For a complete record of this conference see *Die Ursachen,* fourth series, XII (1), 202–204.
46. Wedel (Vienna) to Foreign Office (Berlin), May 23, 1917, *Die*

Ursachen, fourth series, XII (1), 110; Czernin (Vienna) to Bethmann Hollweg (Berlin), June 18, 1917, *GFOA.* No. 1499, cited in Klaus Epstein, "The Development of German-Austrian War Aims," p. 44.

47. Report on Czernin-Michaelis talks held in Vienna on August 1, 1917, dated August 5, 1917, No. AS 3040 pr., Very Secret, *GFOA.* No. 1499.

48. Wedel (Vienna) to Michaelis (Berlin), Telegram No. 235, August 5, 1917, *GFOA.* No. 109.

49. *Die Ursachen,* fourth series, XII (1), 204–206; italics as in original.

50. Klaus Epstein, "The Development of German-Austrian War Aims," p. 46.

51. Lersner (Great Headquarters) to Foreign Office (Berlin), "A message from Ludendorff to Michaelis," Telegram No. 1207, August 13, 1917, *GFOA.* No. 1499. For the record of the Czernin-Michaelis talks see Michaelis' letter to Czernin dated August 17, 1917, in *Die Ursachen,* fourth series, XII (1), 206–209; and Georg Michaelis, *Für Staat und Volk,* pp. 333–35.

52. Ottokar von Czernin, *Im Weltkriege,* pp. 214 *ff.*; Edmund von Glaise-Horstenau, *Die Katastrophe,* p. 121; and Michaelis to Czernin, August 17, 1917, *Die Ursachen,* fourth series, XII (1), 208.

53. Michaelis, p. 336. According to Fischer (*Griff nach der Weltmacht,* pp. 528, 541), "friendly Anschluss" of the Ukraine and other eastern areas was Michaelis' definite plan during this period, an assertion which must be regarded as too sweeping.

54. Grünau (Kaiser's Great Headquarters) to the Imperial Chancellor (Berlin), Telegram No. 834, October 28, 1917, *GFOA.* No. 110.

55. The record of November 6, 1917 conference, *Die Ursachen,* fourth series, XII (1), 210–15.

56. The italics added; the date of the "thesis" was November 12, 1917. For the complete text see *GFOA.* No. 1787.

57. Wedel (Vienna) to Foreign Office (Berlin), Telegram No. 796, November 16, 1917, *GFOA.* No. 110.

58. Zeman and Scharlau, pp. 235–36. On the German role in Lenin's repatriation see Werner Hahlweg, *Lenins Rückkehr nach Russland.*

59. Lersner (Great Headquarters) to Foreign Office (Berlin), Telegram No. 1807, December 3, 1917, *GFOA.* No. 3632; also Lersner (Great Headquarters) to Ober-Ost (Army Command

East), Telegram No. 1895, December 6, 1917, *GFOA*. No. 4.
60. Minutes of the talks at the Imperial Chancellery on December 7, 1917, *GFOA*. No. 3632.
61. "On the Movements of Russia's Foreign Peoples; Situation as of December 12, 1917," submitted on December 20, 1917, *GFOA*. No. 1792.
62. Lersner (Great Headquarters) to Foreign Office (Berlin), Telegram No. 1902, December 16, 1917, *GFOA*. No. 3632.
63. The account of the December 18, 1917 talks at the Great Headquarters, dated December 22, 1917, *GFOA*. No. 1787.

Chapter IV: The Ukrainian Treaty of Brest-Litovsk

1. While relying heavily on the documents from the German Foreign Office archives and similar Austrian materials, this writer also drew upon the memoirs of German and Austrian negotiators, such as Kühlmann, Hoffmann, and Czernin, and the accounts of Ukrainian participants contained in Ivan Kedryn-Rudnyts'kyi (ed.), *Beresteiskyi myr* [The Peace of Brest]. This particular source has seldom been used and is, therefore, little known in the west. For example, John W. Wheeler-Bennett in his *The Forgotten Peace: Brest-Litovsk March, 1918,* did not take note of this source. He also failed to use an even more indispensable Soviet collection of German documents, *Krakh germanskoi okkupatsii na Ukraine* (available also in a German edition). Another study used extensively in the preparation of this chapter is Volkwart John's *Brest-Litovsk Verhandlungen und Friedensverträge*. The Soviets have published a great deal on this subject over the years, but on the whole these writings add little to the understanding of the Ukrainian treaty. See, for example, Aleksandr O. Chubar'yan, *Brestskii mir* [The Peace of Brest]. Of the recent German writings on the problem one should mention Werner Hahlweg's *Der Diktatfrieden von Brest-Litovsk, 1918;* Wolfgang Steglich's *Die Friedenspolitik der Mittelmächte, 1917–18;* and Fischer's *Griff nach der Weltmacht*.

2. Kühlmann's appearance before the Main Committee of the Reichstag on December 20, 1917, shortly before his departure for Brest. For further details see Erich Matthias and Rudolf Morsey (eds.), *Der Interfraktionelle Ausschuss*, II, 640.

3. Waldow, chief of the Wartime Food Office (Kriegsernäh-

rungsamt) to Helfferich, Secretary of the Treasury, a letter dated December 18, 1917, *Die Ursachen*, fourth series, III, 16, 18 (Von Kuhl's report).

4. Rosenberg (Brest-Litovsk) to Foreign Office (Berlin), Telegram No. 81, December 14, 1917, *GFOA*. No. 4.

5. Rosenberg (Brest-Litovsk) to Foreign Office (Berlin), Telegram No. 85, December 16, 1917, *ibid.*

6. Rosenberg (Brest-Litovsk) to Foreign Office (Berlin), Telegram No. 95, December 16, 1917, *ibid.*

7. Rosenberg (Brest-Litovsk) to Foreign Office (Berlin), Telegram No. 121, December 19, 1917, *GFOA*. No. 3632.

8. Lersner (Great Headquarters) to Foreign Office (Berlin), "A Message from General Ludendorff," Telegram No. 1910, Urgent, December 17, 1917, *GFOA*. No. 110; Bussche (Berlin) to Rosenberg (Brest-Litovsk), Telegram No. 113, December 21, 1917, *GFOA*. No. 3632.

9. Kedryn, p. 148. Since the negotiations were not in progress at the time, it was only a day or two later that the Germans learned about the presence of the Ukrainian Rada delegation at Brest and advised the Foreign Office in Berlin about it. See Telegram No. 6 from Brest-Litovsk, dated January 3, 1918, *GFOA*. No. 1787.

10. Doroshenko, *Istoriya Ukrayiny*, I, 231; Beyer, p. 31; Pavlo Khrystyuk, *Zamitky i materyaly do istoriyi Ukrayins'koyi Revolutsiyi* [Notes and Materials on the History of the Ukrainian Revolution], II, 94–95; Volodymyr Vynnychenko, *Vidrodzhennya natsiyi* [The Rebirth of the Nation], II, 199; John, pp. 31–32; Reshetar, *The Ukrainian Revolution*, pp. 103–114.

11. For the text of the Ukrainian "peace message" and the Central Powers' answer, see the above sources and *GFOA*. Nos. 3632 and 1794.

12. The text of the Soviet ultimatum is available in William H. Chamberlin, *The Russian Revolution*, I, 486–87. For further details on this stage of the Russo-Ukrainian conflict, see Reshetar, 89–97; and Pipes, 114–124.

13. George F. Kennan, *Soviet-American Relations, 1917–1920*, I, 185. See also E. Borschak, "La Paix ukrainienne de Brest-Litovsk;" Alexander Choulguine, *L'Ukraine contre Moscou*, pp. 172–77; and Général Tabuis, "Comment je devins Commissaire de la République Française en Ukraine."

14. Max Hoffmann, *Der Krieg der versäumten Gelegenheiten*, p. 207; Richard von Kühlmann, *Erinnerungen*, p. 153; Vynnychenko, II, 203; Wheeler-Bennett, p. 155.

15. Lersner (Great Headquarters) to Foreign Office (Berlin), Telegram No. 1, January 1, 1918, *GFOA*. No. 3633.

16. Kühlmann's appearance before the Main Committee of the Reichstag on January 1, 1918, Matthias and Morsey, II, 13.

17. John, p. 37; *Die Ursachen,* fourth series, XII (1), 112–13; Kühlmann, p. 526; Karl F. Novak (ed.), *Die Aufzeichnungen des Generalmajors Max Hoffmann,* II, 205–206; Ludendorff, *Meine Kriegserinnerungen,* p. 438.

18. Kühlmann (Brest-Litovsk) to the Imperial Chancellor (Berlin), Communication No. 48/4. 1.18, January 4, 1918, *GFOA*. No. 1787; also Telegram No. 1 (no date), *GFOA*. No. 1791.

19. Hoffmann, *Der Krieg der versäumten Gelegenheiten,* p. 210; Czernin, *In the World War,* p. 257.

20. Bussche (Berlin) to Kühlmann (Brest-Litovsk), Telegram No. 6, January 3, 1918, *GFOA*. No. 3633; Riezler (Brest-Litovsk) to Bergen (Berlin), January 4, 1918, *ibid.*

21. Doc. No. T. 120, January 4, 1918, and Telegram No. 31, January 5, *ibid.* Also Telegram No. 23, January 4, *GFOA*. No. 1791.

22. Kühlmann (Brest-Litovsk) to Hertling (Berlin), Telegram No. 44, January 6, 1918, *GFOA*. No. 3633. Also Czernin, *In the World War,* p. 258; and Doroshenko, *Istoriya Ukrayiny,* I, 297.

23. Hertling to Hindenburg, January 7, 1918, cited in *Die Ursachen,* fourth series, II (1), 129; Hindenburg to Emperor Wilhelm II, January 7, 1918, Ludendorff, *The General Staff and Its Problems,* II, 525–26.

24. Kühlmann (Brest-Litovsk) to the Imperial Chancellor (Berlin), probable date: January 5–8, 1918, *GFOA*. No. 1791.

25. Ludendorff (Great Headquarters) to Hoffmann (Brest-Litovsk), Doc. No. 32, January 9, 1918, *GFOA*. No. 1790.

26. Bergen (Berlin) to Kühlmann (Brest-Litovsk), January 9, 1918, *GFOA*. No. 110; and Kühlmann, p. 520.

27. Chief of the General Staff (Baden) to Foreign Office (Vienna), Telegram No. 747, Secret, January 2, 1918, *Politisches Archiv (Vienna),* VII, 27–28.

28. Wheeler-Bennett, p. 158.

29. Kedryn, p. 152.

30. John, pp. 41–42.

31. See, for example, Chubar'yan, p. 102; and Ivan S. Khmil', *Z praporom myru kriz' polumya viiny* [With the Banner of Peace Through the Conflagration of War], pp. 62–63, 74.

32. O. Sevryuk in Kedryn, pp. 152–53; John, p. 43.

33. Hertling (Berlin) to Berckheim (Great Headquarters), "For General Ludendorff," June, 1918, *GFOA*. No. 124; and G. Gratz

and R. Schüller, *The Economic Policy of Austria-Hungary During the War,* p. 88.

34. Rosenberg (Brest-Litovsk) to Foreign Office (Berlin), Telegram No. 101, January 13, 1918, *GFOA.* No. 1791; and an unsigned report sent to the Imperial Chancellor from Brest, Telegram No. 103, January 13, 1918, *GFOA.* No. 1789. See also Sevryuk in Kedryn, p. 153; and Doroshenko, *Istoriya Ukrayiny,* I, 299.

35. Max Hoffmann, *War Diaries and Other Papers,* II, 213–14; Czernin, *In the World War,* pp. 242–43, and the sources cited in the preceding footnote.

36. Rosenberg (Brest-Litovsk) to Bussche (Berlin), Telegram No. 130, January 16, 1918, *GFOA.* No. 3633; and Kühlmann (Brest-Litovsk) to Hertling (Berlin), Telegram No. 11, Personal, January 16, 1918, *GFOA.* No. 1789.

37. Kühlmann (Brest-Litovsk) to Foreign Office (Berlin), Telegram No. 209, January 17, 1918, *GFOA.* No. 1787; and Telegram No. 137, January 17, 1918, *GFOA.* No. 3633.

38. Lersner (Great Headquarters) to Foreign Office (Berlin), "A Message from Marshal Hindenburg to the Imperial Chancellor," Telegram No. 96, Urgent, January 16, 1918, *GFOA.* No. 3633.

39. For the minutes of these conferences and other details see *GFOA.* Nos. 1787 and 3634. See also John.

40. Johann Victor Bredt in *Die Ursachen,* fourth series, VIII, 223; and Zaliznyak in Kedryn, p. 80.

41. John, pp. 45–46, 125 *ff.* (Minutes of the January 19, 1918 meeting). See also Czernin (Brest-Litovsk) to Foreign Office (Vienna), Telegram No. 131, Secret, January 17, 1918, *Politisches Archiv (Vienna),* VII, 51–52; and Czernin's communication to Count Demblin (for Emperor Karl), Telegram No. 29, January 21, 1918, cited in Doroshenko, *Istoriya Ukrayiny,* I, 303.

42. John, pp. 48–49, 120–131; Sevryuk in Kedryn, p. 153.

43. Czernin, *In the World War,* p. 262; John, pp. 45–46; Wheeler-Bennett, pp. 171–72; Gratz and Schüller, p. 98.

44. Czernin, *In the World War,* p. 268 (entry for January 20, 1918).

45. The report on this meeting is available in Czernin, *Im Weltkrieg,* pp. 327–31, and in his *In the World War,* pp. 273ff. See also Edmund Glaise-Horstenau, *The Collapse of the Austro-Hungarian Empire,* p. 73.

46. Sevryuk in Kedryn, pp. 157–58; and John, pp. 49–50.

47. For the text of the *Fourth Universal* see Appendix B.

48. Rosenberg (Brest-Litovsk) to Foreign Office (Berlin), Telegram No. 205, January 22, 1918, *GFOA*. No. 110.

49. For further details on the January 23, 1918 meeting see Erich Otto Volkmann in *Die Ursachen,* fourth series, XII (1), 115. Hindenburg's letter to the Kaiser is available in Ludendorff's *The General Staff and Its Problems,* II, 525–26.

50. Radowitz to Foreign Secretary, RK 16249 K.J., Berlin, January 24, 1918, *GFOA.* No. 3270. See also *Die Ursachen,* fourth series, II (1), 135–36.

51. Imperial Chancellor Hertling to the Reichstag, January 24, 1918, cited in Kreppel (ed.), *Der Friede im Osten,* p. 145.

52. Rosenberg (Brest-Litovsk) to Foreign Office (Berlin), Telegram No. 215, January 24, 1918, *GFOA.* Nos. 5 and 1796; Bussche (Berlin) to Rosenberg (Brest-Litovsk), Telegram No. 310, January, 25, 1918, *GFOA.* No. 1787.

53. Lersner (Great Headquarters) to Foreign Office (Berlin), Telegram No. 150, January 27, 1918, *GFOA.* No. 1790; and Rosenberg (Brest-Litovsk) to Foreign Office (Berlin), Telegram No. 5, January 31, 1918, *ibid.*

54. Kühlmann (Brest-Litovsk) to Imperial Chancellor Hertling (Berlin), Telegram No. 16, Personal, January 30, 1918, *GFOA.* No. 1787.

55. See footnote No. 38 above, and Bussche (Berlin) to Rosenberg (Brest-Litovsk), Telegram No. 400, January 31, 1918, *GFOA.* No. 1787.

56. Bussche (Berlin) to Kühlmann (Brest-Litovsk), Telegram No. 403, January 31, 1918, *ibid.*

57. Kühlmann (Brest-Litovsk) to Lersner (Great Headquarters), January 31, 1918, *ibid.*

58. Rosenberg (Brest-Litovsk) to Foreign Office (Berlin), Telegram No. 189, January 21, 1918, *GFOA.* No. 110.

59. See, for example, A. V. Likholat, *Razgrom burzhuazno-natsionalisticheskoi Direktorii na Ukraine* [The Route of the Bourgeois-Nationalist Directory in the Ukraine], pp. 86–87; Chubar'yan, p. 128; Khmil', pp. 62–64, 74.

60. Rosenberg (Brest-Litovsk) to Foreign Office (Berlin), Telegram No. 197, January 22, 1918, *GFOA.* No. 3634. See also Csaky (Brest-Litovsk) to Foreign Office (Vienna), Telegram No. 183, January 22, 1918, and Hohenlohe (Berlin) to Foreign Office (Vienna), no number, January 22, 1918, *Politisches Archiv (Vienna),* VII, 59–60, 67.

61. John, p. 53; Wheeler-Bennett, pp. 209–211.

62. Hoffmann, *Der Krieg der versäumten Gelegenheiten,* p. 213;

Kühlmann (From the Field) to the Imperial Chancellor (Berlin), Telegram No. 19, Personal, February 1, 1918, *GFOA*. No. 3634.

63. Kühlmann, *loc. cit.*

64. Czernin, *In the World War*, p. 273.

65. Zaliznyak and Sevryuk in Kedryn, pp. 119–20, 160–61; also Sevryuk in John, p. 54.

66. Both Zaliznyak and Sevryuk (Kedryn, *loc. cit.*) maintain that the Ukrainians were given 24 hours to make up their minds.

67. Zaliznyak and Sevryuk in Kedryn, pp. 120–26, 161–62; John, p. 55.

68. Kühlmann (From the Field) to the Imperial Chancellor (Berlin), Telegram No. 22, February 2, 1918, *GFOA*. No. 3634.

69. Kühlmann (Brest-Litovsk) to the Imperial Chancellor (Berlin), Telegram No. 25, February 3, 1918, and Telegram No. 303, February 3, 1918, both in *GFOA*. No. 3634.

70. For a complete report on the Berlin talks and the problem of the impending treaty with the Ukraine, which he obtained from the State Archives in Vienna, see John, pp. 131–38; also *Die Ursachen*, fourth series, XII (1), 217–23. Ludendorff's and Czernin's accounts are not always accurate and reliable.

71. John, pp. 131–38.

72. Kühlmann (Brest-Litovsk) to the Imperial Chancellor (Berlin), Telegram No. 26, February 7, 1918, *GFOA*. No. 3634.

73. Gratz and Schüller, p. 104; Kühlmann, pp. 541–42; John, pp. 56–58.

74. Kühlmann (Brest-Litovsk) to the Imperial Chancellor (Berlin), Telegram No. 27, February 8, 1918, *GFOA*. No. 3634.

75. John, p. 58; Wheeler-Bennett, pp. 222–26.

76. For the text of the Ukrainian treaty and the secret agreement on Galicia see Appendices C and D. Kaiser Karl's manifesto is available in Kreppel, p. 203; for Wilhelm II talk see *Norddeutsche Allgemeine Zeitung*, February 11, 1918.

77. Kühlmann, p. 591; Hoffmann in Nowak, *Die Aufzeichnungen des Generalmajors Max Hoffmann*, II, 213.

78. Leon Trotsky, *My Life*, p. 376.

79. The literature on this problem is quite extensive. The following are the most useful sources on the subject: Erhard Walz, *Reichsleitung und Heeresleitung in der Periode des Friedens von Brest-Litowsk;* Direnberger; Schwertfeger in *Die Ursachen,* fourth series, II (1); Rosenberg; Gatzke, *Germany's Drive to the West;* and Beyer. Also more recent works: Fischer, *Griff nach der Weltmacht;* Klaus Epstein, *Matthias Erzberger;* E.

Eyck, "The Generals and the Downfall of the German Monarchy," pp. 47–67; and Militärgeschichtliches Forschungsamt (ed.), *Die Generalstäbe in Deutschland*, Vol. III.

80. John, pp. 16–23; Wheeler-Bennett, pp. 117–23.

81. Kühlmann (Brest-Litovsk) to Foreign Office (Berlin), Telegram No. 198, December 28, 1917, *GFOA*. No. 3632; Kühlmann, p. 532; Hoffmann, *Der Krieg der versäumten Gelegenheiten*, p. 197.

82. Karl Nowak, *Der Sturz der Mittelmächte*, pp. 24–25; and Kühlmann (Brest-Litovsk) to Foreign Office (Berlin), Telegram No. 180, January 20, 1918, *GFOA*. No. 3634.

83. Borschak, Part III (Conclusions).

84. John, p. 97.

85. Reshetar, p. 116.

86. Beyer, pp. 31–32.

87. John, p. 97; Ludendorff, *Ludendorff's Own Story*, II, 57.

88. Erwin Hölzle, *Der Osten im ersten Weltkrieg*, p. 46; Volkmann in *Die Ursachen*, fourth series, XII (1), 121–22.

89. Karl Helfferich, *Der Weltkrieg*, III, 320.

90. Kreppel, p. 216.

91. Wilhelm II, *The Kaiser's Memoirs*, p. 335; Hindenburg, *Out of My Life*, p. 335.

92. Interview with Prince Max of Baden in the *Norddeutsche Allgemeine Zeitung*, February 16, 1918; Kühlmann's statement in the *Berliner Tageblatt*, February 20, 1918.

93. Helfferich, III, 331; Walter Rathenau, *Politische Briefe*, p. 173; Admiral Hintze's views are discussed in Hahlweg, *Der Diktatfrieden von Brest-Litowsk*, p. 58.

Chapter V: The Occupation of the Ukraine

1. Hoffmann, *Der Krieg der versäumten Gelegenheiten*, p. 213; Kühlmann (From the Field) to the Imperial Chancellor (Berlin), Telegram No. 19, Personal, February 1, 1918, *GFOA*. No. 3634.

2. John, p. 133.

3. Czernin (Sofia) to Foreign Office (Vienna), Telegram No. 64, January 29, 1918, *Politisches Archiv (Vienna)*, VII, 78.

4. Friedrich von Payer, *Von Bethmann Hollweg bis Ebert*, p. 64; and Karl von Hertling, *Ein Jahr in der Reichskanzlei*, pp. 73–76. For Kühlmann's views see John, pp. 61–62.

5. Kühlmann, pp. 546–49; Payer, p. 64; Hertling, pp. 73–76;

Gerald Freund, *Unholy Alliance*, p. 7; Ludendorff, *The General Staff*, II, 548–51, and *Meine Kriegserinnerungen*, pp. 447–49.

6. This was Ludendorff's description of the proposed campaign. For further details see Hertling, p. 75, and Payer, p. 64.

7. Kühlmann (n.p.) to Foreign Office (Berlin), Telegram No. 54, February 14, 1918, *GFOA*. No. 5. Kühlmann's meeting with the Reichstag leaders on February 9, 1918, is discussed in Matthias and Morsey, II, 210.

8. Kühlmann (n.p.) to Bussche (Berlin), Telegram No. 55, February 14, 1918, *GFOA*. No. 5.

9. Grünau (n.p.) to Foreign Office (Berlin), Telegram No. 60, February 15, 1918, *GFOA*. No. 35; and Berckheim (Great Headquarters) to Foreign Office (Berlin), Telegram No. 304, February 16, 1918, *ibid.*

10. See, for example, Hoffmann, *Der Krieg der versäumten Gelegenheiten*, p. 217; Ludendorff, *The General Staff*, II, 549, and his *Meine Kriegserinnerungen*, p. 447; Hindenburg, *Out of My Life*, p. 336.

11. Wilhelm Groener, *Der Weltkrieg und seine Probleme*, p. 64.

12. Georg Alexander von Müller, *Regierte der Kaiser?*, p. 354.

13. Zaliznyak in Kedryn, p. 139.

14. Piedl (Brest-Litovsk) to Wiesner (Vienna), Telegram (no number), Very secret, February 17, 1918, *Politisches Archiv (Vienna)*, VII, 107–10.

15. According to the Rada Prime Minister V. Holubovych (Doroshenko, *Istoriya Ukrayiny*, I, 337), the Ukrainian "Appeal to the German People" was made on February 12. Official German records show that it was on February 15 (two days after the Homburg conference) that the Ukrainians at Brest presented the appeal to Schüler with the request that it be forwarded to Berlin. (See, for example, Telegram No. 395, *GFOA*. No. 35.) The text of the appeal is also available in the *Norddeutsche Allgemeine Zeitung* of February 17, 1918, and Doroshenko, *Istoriya Ukrayiny*, I, 334–35.

16. Grünau (n.p.) to Foreign Office (Berlin), Telegram No. 60, February 15, 1918, *GFOA*. No. 35.

17. General Hermann von Kuhl estimated the Bolshevik forces operating in the Ukraine in February 1918 at 100,000, which is undoubtedly a greatly exaggerated figure (*Die Ursachen*, fourth series, III, 20).

18. "Naïve" was Reshetar's description of the Ukrainian plans for a limited or indirect German military assistance (Reshetar, p. 117). See also Doroshenko, *Istoriya Ukrayiny*, I, 323, and his

"Getmanstvo 1918 g. na Ukraine," pp. 134–35; also Stefaniv, p. 84.

19. Schüler (Brest-Litovsk) to Foreign Office (Berlin), Telegram No. 389, February 14, 1918, *GFOA*. No. 35.

20. *Ibid.*, and Berckheim (Great Headquarters) to Foreign Office (Berlin), Telegram No. 287, February 15, 1918, *ibid.*

21. For a complete text of the order see Doroshenko, *Istoriya Ukrayiny*, I, 335.

22. Hermann von Kuhl, *Der Weltkrieg*, p. 245, and his account in *Die Ursachen*, fourth series, III, 22.

23. Colin Ross, "A Report on the Impressions in the Ukraine," March 10, 1918. (Distributed by General Hoffman). *GFOA*. No. 35; and Friedrich Freiherr Hiller von Gärtringen (ed.), *Wilhelm Groener Lebenserinnerungen*, p. 387 (henceforth cited as Groener, *Lebenserinnerungen*).

24. Kuhl, p. 247; and his testimony in *Die Ursachen*, fourth series, III, 22.

25. Kuhl in *Die Ursachen*, fourth series, III, 20.

26. Stefaniv, p. 45.

27. See the Ross report cited in note No. 23 above.

28. Schüler (Brest-Litovsk) to Foreign Office (Berlin), Telegram No. 501, February 25, 1918, *GFOA*. No. 25. See also Vynnychenko, II, 295; and A. A. Goldenweiser, "Iz kievskikh vospominaii" [Kievan Reminiscences], p. 208.

29. Isaak Mazepa, *Ukrayina v ohni i buri revolutsiyi* [The Ukraine in the Fire and Storm of the Revolution], I, 52.

30. Oleksander Udovychenko, *Ukrayina u viini za derzhavnist'* [The Ukraine in the Struggle for Its Statehood], pp. 34–36.

31. Alfred Krauss and Franz Klingenbrunner, *Die Besetzung der Ukraine*, p. 363.

32. Schüler (Brest-Litovsk) to Foreign Office (Berlin), Telegram No. 396, February 15, 1918, *GFOA*. No. 35.

33. Schüler (Brest-Litovsk) to Foreign Office (Berlin), Telegram No. 435, February 19, 1918; Telegram No. 446, February 20; and Telegram No. 452, February 21, all in *GFOA*. No. 35.

34. Hertling's memorandum on the Ukrainian treaty submitted to the Reichstag on February 19, 1918, cited in Ralph H. Lutz, *The Fall of the German Empire*, I, 814.

35. Kühlmann to the Reichstag on February 20, 1918 (the first statement), *Verhandlungen des Reichstages*, CCCXI, 4011.

36. Kühlmann to the Reichstag on February 20, 1918 (the second statement), Lutz, I, 819; see also Fischer, *Griff nach der Weltmacht*, chap. 20.

37. Khrystyuk, II, 146; Vynnychenko, II, 303.
38. Chancellor Hertling to the Rada Prime Minister Holubovych, cited in Khrystyuk, II, 146.
39. Doroshenko, *Istoriya Ukrayiny*, II, 14–15.
40. Reshetar, p. 119. [Doroshenko (*loc. cit.*) shows that this statement was made on March 7 (February 25, old style) and not February 25, as stated by Reshetar.]
41. Doroshenko, *Istoriya Ukrayiny*, I, 337.
42. Ludendorff's order is discussed in a communication from the Austrian Foreign Minister, Count Czernin, to the Dual Monarchy's Ambassador to Kiev, Count Forgách, Telegram No. 84, April 3, 1918, *ibid.*, II, 14.
43. Vynnychenko, II, 295.
44. Schüler (Brest-Litovsk) to Foreign Office (Berlin), Telegram No. 501, February 25, 1918; and Lersner (Great Headquarters) to Foreign Office (Berlin), Telegram No. 404, February 26, 1918, both in *GFOA*. No. 35.
45. Bussche (Berlin) to Rosenberg (Brest-Litovsk), Telegram No. 753, March 3, 1918, *GFOA*. No. 1790.
46. Schüler (Brest-Litovsk) to Foreign Office (Berlin), Telegram No. 437, February 19, 1918, *GFOA*. No. 1788, and Telegram No. 501, February 25, 1918, *GFOA*. No. 35.
47. Doroshenko, *Istoriya Ukrayiny*, I, 322; Zaliznyak in Kedryn, pp. 138–39; Arthur Arz, *Zur Geschichte des Grossen Krieges*, p. 234.
48. Ludendorff, *Meine Kriegserinnerungen*, p. 453; Hoffmann, *Der Krieg der versäumten Gelegenheiten*, p. 217; Gyula von Szilassy, *Der Untergang der Donau-Monarchie*, p. 290.
49. Szilassy, p. 290.
50. Glaise-Horstenau, *The Collapse of the Austro-Hungarian Empire*, p. 80; and Alfred Krauss, *Die Ursachen unserer Niederlage*, p. 262.
51. Arz, pp. 234–35; Czernin (Vienna) to Hohenlohe (Berlin), Telegram No. 81, February 18, 1918, *Politisches Archiv (Vienna)*, VII, 113 (Czernin claims to have obtained Ukrainian concessions in the Kholm area on this date). For Seidler's statement see Doroshenko, *Istoriya Ukrayiny*, I, 324.
52. Austrian Ambassador in Berlin Prince Hohenlohe to the Reich's Foreign Office, Memorandum No. 131, Berlin, February 19, 1918, *GFOA*. No. 3630; and Lersner (Great Headquarters) to Foreign Office (Berlin), "A Message from General Ludendorff," Telegram No. 335, February 19, 1918, *GFOA*. No. 35.
53. Lersner (Great Headquarters) to Foreign Office (Berlin), Tele-

gram No. 430, March 2, 1918, *GFOA*. No. 35 (this document contains a report on Ludendorff's telegram to Hoffmann, dated February 27, 1918, and Hoffmann's reply given a day or two later).

54. Karl Freiherr von Werkmann, *Deutschland als Verbündeter,* p. 184; Arz, p. 226.
55. Glaise-Horstenau, *The Collapse of the Austro-Hungarian Empire,* p. 80.
56. August von Cramon, *Unser österreich-ungarischer Bundesgenosse,* p. 146; Edmund von Glaise-Horstenau and Rudolf Kiszling (eds.), *Österreich-Ungarns letzter Krieg,* VII, 113; Krauss, 262–263; Arz, p. 226.
57. Krauss and Klingenbrunner, *Die Besetzung der Ukraine,* p. 364.
58. Arz, pp. 240, 243.
59. Storck (Baden) to Czernin (Vienna), Communication No. 27.155, February 26, 1918, *Politisches Archiv (Vienna),* VII, 123–25. See also Khrystyuk, II, 143; and Mazepa, I, 52.
60. Mazepa, I, 52.
61. See the sources cited in note No. 52 above. Also Lersner (Great Headquarters) to Foreign Office (Berlin), Telegram No. 403, February 26, 1918, *GFOA*. Nos. 35 and 3630.
62. Schüler (Brest-Litovsk) to Foreign Office (Berlin), Telegram No. 459, February 21, 1918, *GFOA*. No. 3630; and Foreign Office (Berlin) to Schüler (Brest-Litovsk), Telegram No. 681, February 21, 1918, *ibid.*
63. Ludendorff, *Ludendorff's Own Story,* II, 190.
64. See, for example, Rosenberg (Brest-Litovsk) to Foreign Office (Berlin), Telegram No. 516, February 27, 1918, *GFOA*. No. 3630.
65. Hoffmann, *War Diaries,* I, 210; Groener, *Lebenserinnerungen,* p. 389. For the Austrian side of the story see Arz, p. 240.
66. On the problem arising out of a German attempt to establish a post of the Central Powers' "Supreme Commander" in the Ukraine in March, 1918, see the following sources: Lersner (Great Headquarters) to Foreign Office (Berlin), "A Report on General Ludendorff's Views," Telegram No. 561, March 17, 1918; Mumm (Kiev) to Foreign Office (Berlin), Telegram No. 24, March 18, 1918; Lersner (Great Headquarters) to Foreign Office (Berlin), "For the Imperial Chancellor," Telegram No. 593, March 19, 1918, all in *GFOA*. No. 36.
67. Krauss and Klingenbrunner, p. 369.
68. For the text of this Austro-German agreement see the following:

an unnumbered document dated April 4, 1918, bearing signatures of Field Marshal Langer and General Groener, *GFOA*. No. 3630; and *Die deutsche Okkupation*, pp. 34–36 (Doc. No. 7). The Austrian copy of this document bears an earlier date. See Chief of the General Staff (Baden) to Foreign Office (Vienna), Telegram No. 1326, March 26, 1918, *Politisches Archiv (Vienna)*, II, 174–77.

69. Ludendorff, *Meine Kriegserinnerungen*, p. 501.

70. Hindenburg, *Aus meinem Leben*, p. 307.

71. See, for example, Schüler (Brest-Litovsk) to Nadolny (Berlin), Telegram No. 523, date: late February, 1918, *GFOA*. No. 1790; or Lersner (Great Headquarters) to Foreign Office (Berlin), "General Hoffmann's message to the Supreme Army Command," Telegram No. 403, February 26, 1918, *GFOA*. Nos. 35 and 3630.

72. See the minutes of the May 10–11, 1918 conference held at Spa in *GFOA*. No. 37; and Ludendorff, *Kriegsführung und Politik*, pp. 237–38. For an exhaustive treatment of Germany's plans and policies in the Caucasus see Winfried Baumgart, *Deutsche Ostpolitik 1918*, especially chap. III.

Chapter VI: The Aftermath: The Development of Occupation Policies

1. Gatzke, "Zu den deutsch-russischen Beziehungen im Sommer 1918," pp. 69–70.

2. Groener, *Lebenserinnerungen*, pp. 385–86.

3. Forgách (Kiev) to Foreign Office (Vienna), Telegram No. 90/594, March 29, 1918, *Politisches Archiv (Vienna)*, II, 201; and Groener, *Lebenserinnerungen*, p. 395.

4. Bülow (Berlin) to the Foreign Office representatives (Brest-Litovsk), no number, March 12, 1918, *GFOA*. No. 1790.

5. Rosenberg (Brest-Litovsk) to Foreign Office (Berlin), Telegram No. 515, February 27, 1918, *GFOA*. Nos. 35 and 1790.

6. Lersner (Great Headquarters) to Foreign Office (Berlin), Telegram No. 430, March 2, 1918, *GFOA*. No. 35.

7. Groener, *Lebenserinnerungen*, pp. 385, 389; and Dorothea Groener-Geyer, *General Groener*, p. 80.

8. Groener, *Lebenserinnerungen*, p. 385.

9. Mumm's memorandum on the Ukrainian problem, Berlin, March 1, 1918, *GFOA*. No. 35.

10. Lersner (Great Headquarters) to Foreign Office (Berlin), "A Message from General Ludendorff," Telegram No. 466, March 6, 1918, *ibid.*

11. Lersner (Great Headquarters) to Foreign Office (Berlin), "A Message from General Ludendorff," Telegram No. 476, March 7, 1918, *GFOA*. No. 1499; and Forgách (Kiev) to Foreign Office (Vienna), Telegram No. 27/163, March 22, 1918, *Politisches Archiv (Vienna)*, II, 117–18.

12. Bussche (Berlin) to Bülow (Brest-Litovsk), (discussion of a Foreign Office's earlier telegram sent to General Ludendorff) Telegram No. 770, March 8, 1918, *GFOA*. No. 1790.

13. Bülow (Brest-Litovsk) to Foreign Office (Berlin), Telegram No. 615, March 10, 1918, *GFOA*. No. 35.

14. Lersner (Great Headquarters) to Foreign Office (Berlin), Telegram No. 610, March 21, 1918, *GFOA*. No. 36.

15. Mumm (Brest-Litovsk) to Hertling (Berlin), Doc. No. A 1, March 12, 1918, *GFOA*. No. 35; and Mumm (Kiev) to Foreign Office (Berlin), Doc. No. A 3, March 16, 1918, *GFOA*. No. 36; also Groener, *Lebenserinnerungen*, pp. 394, 567.

16. Colin Ross Report (see note No. 17 below; Richard Merton, *Erinnerungswertes aus meinem Leben*, p. 44.

17. Colin Ross Report on the Ukraine, date: March 10, 1918, *GFOA*. No. 35. Ross was a German political officer attached to the Army Headquarters East. The Governor-Generalship idea was first developed by Major General Oven of the German War Ministry and discussed in a special report prepared by Erich von Thiel of the Foreign Office, dated Berlin, February 28, 1918, *GFOA*. No. 35. See also Groener, *Lebenserinnerungen*, pp. 385–386.

18. Austrian military report from Kiev, dated March 10, 1918, No. K.M. Praes. 13700/12, Very secret, *Politisches Archiv (Vienna)*, II, 95–105; and Hoffinger (Kiev) to Czernin (Vienna), Telegram No. 1/P, March 12, 1918, *ibid.*, II, 106–109.

19. For a full text of the "Directives" see Doc. No. 27.612, March 10, 1918, *Politisches Archiv (Vienna)*, II, 94–95.

20. Colin Ross Report (see note No. 17 above); and Bülow (Brest-Litovsk) to Foreign Office (Berlin), Telegram No. 605, March 9, 1918, *GFOA*. No. 35.

21. Mumm (Brest-Litovsk) to Hertling (Berlin), Doc. A 1, March 12, 1918, *GFOA*. No. 35.

22. Bülow (Brest-Litovsk) to Foreign Office (Berlin), Telegram No. 616, March 10, 1918, *ibid.*

23. See Mumm's message cited in note No. 21 above.

24. Colin Ross Report (note No. 17 above).
25. For a full text of General Ludendorff's "General Directives" see Doc. No. II/14131, dated March 18, 1918, in *GFOA*. No. 36.
26. Groener's report to Ludendorff, dated March 23, 1918. For further details see the following: Groener, *Lebenserinnerungen*, pp. 394–95; Groener-Geyer, p. 81; and Forgách (Kiev) to Foreign Office (Vienna), Telegram No. 31/168, March 22, 1918, *Die deutsche Okkupation*, pp. 28–29 (Doc. No. 4).
27. Forgách (Kiev) to Foreign Office (Vienna), Telegram No. 31/166, Secret, March 22, 1918, *Politisches Archiv (Vienna)*, III, 120–22.
28. Mumm (Kiev) to Foreign Office (Berlin), Telegram Nos. 87 and 91, March 26, 1918, *GFOA*. No. 36.
29. Kühlmann (Bucharest) to Foreign Office (Berlin), Telegram No. 222, March 25/26, 1918, *ibid*.
30. Gratz and Schüller, p. 109.
31. See Appendix C.
32. Gratz and Schüller, p. 126; Khrystyuk, II, 114.
33. Meeting of the Reichstag leaders and government officials at the Imperial Chancellery on February 12, 1918, Matthias and Morsey, II, 272–73.
34. For a more detailed discussion of the economic provisions of the treaties of Brest-Litovsk see Gratz and Schüller, pp. 117–26.
35. *Texts of the Ukraine 'Peace,'* p. 143.
36. Matthias and Morsey, II, 274–75.
37. *Texts of the Ukraine 'Peace,'* pp. 145–49.
38. Gratz and Schüller, pp. 127–28.
39. Kuhl in *Die Ursachen*, fourth series, III, 27.
40. Mumm (Kiev) to Hertling (Berlin), Communication No. 814, April 12, 1918, *Die deutsche Okkupation*, p. 100 (Doc. No. 39); Gratz and Schüller, p. 128.
41. *Ibid.*, p. 128–29. Complete texts of the Austro-German agreements on the joint economic policies in the Ukraine can be found in *Friedensverträge mit der Ukraine, Russland und Finnland*, pp. 171–215. See also Krauss and Klingenbrunner, p. 362; and Müller (n.p.) to Bergen (Berlin), Telegram No. 653, March 18, 1918, *GFOA*. No. 36.
42. Lersner (Great Headquarters) to Foreign Office (Berlin), "A Report on Ludendorff's Message to Hoffman," Telegram No. 430, March 2, 1918, *GFOA*. No. 3630.
43. Mumm (Kiev) to Foreign Office (Berlin), Telegram No. 33, March 20, 1918, *GFOA*. No. 36.
44. Krauss and Klingenbrunner, p. 371.

45. *Ibid.*, pp. 373–74; and Gratz and Schüller, p. 133.
46. Hohenlohe (Berlin) to Czernin (Vienna), Telegram No. 32/ P.S., March 25, 1918, *Politisches Archiv (Vienna)*, II, 129–34.
47. Krauss and Klingenbrunner, p. 371.
48. Bülow (Brest-Litovsk) to Foreign Office (Berlin), Telegram No. 616, March 10, 1918, *Krakh germanskoi okkupatsii*, pp. 23–25 (Doc. No. 3).
49. Mumm (Kiev) to Foreign Office (Berlin), Telegram No. 33, March 20, 1918, and Telegram No. 161, April 2, 1918, *GFOA.* No. 36.
50. Mumm (Kiev) to Foreign Office (Berlin), Telegram No. 239, April 9, 1918, *ibid.;* and Czernin (Vienna) to Forgách (Kiev), Telegram No. 84, April 3, 1918, *Politisches Archiv (Vienna)*, II, 186.
51. Groener, *Lebenserinnerungen*, p. 397.
52. Mumm (Kiev) to Foreign Office (Berlin), Telegram No. 38, March 31, 1918, *GFOA.* No. 36; and Mumm (Kiev) to Foreign Office (Berlin), Telegram No. 395, April 21, 1918, *Krakh germanskoi okkupatsii*, p. 89 (Doc. No. 41).
53. Minutes of the May 11, 1918 conference held at Spa (Ludendorff's report on the Ukraine), *GFOA.* No. 37.
54. Fischer, *Griff nach der Weltmacht*, p. 661.
55. For a complete text of this agreement see *Die deutsche Okkupation*, pp. 34–36 (Doc. No. 7).
56. *Ibid.;* and Krauss and Klingenbrunner, pp. 362, 365.
57. Krauss and Klingenbrunner, pp. 385–86.
58. *Ibid.*, p. 387.
59. Lersner (Great Headquarters) to Foreign Office (Berlin), "A Message from General Ludendorff," Telegram No. 142, January 25, 1918, *GFOA.* No. 3641.
60. Johannes (Berlin) to Stockhammern (Brest-Litovsk), Telegram No. 752, March 3, 1918, and Stockhammern's answer to Johannes given on the following day, Telegram No. 756, *GFOA.* No. 1800.
61. Ludendorff, *Meine Kriegserinnerungen*, p. 531.
62. K. Sofronenko, "Germanskie okkupanty v Polesie," p. 89.
63. Forgách (Kiev) to Czernin (Vienna), Telegram No. 80, Secret, March 28, 1918, *Politisches Archiv (Vienna)*, VIII, 133–34.
64. See Ludendorff's directive cited in note No. 25 above.
65. An unnumbered and unsigned document dated March 21, 1918, in *Die deutsche Okkupation*, pp. 30–31 (Doc. No. 5).
66. See Appendix E.
67. Bussche (Berlin) to Mumm (Kiev), Telegram No. 42, March

26, 1918, *Die deutsche Okkupation,* pp. 32–33 (Doc. No. 6); and Kühlmann (Bucharest) to Foreign Office (Berlin), Telegram No. 222, March 25/26, 1918, *GFOA.* No. 36.

68. Groener to Mumm, Communication No. 485, Kiev, March 31, 1918, *Die deutsche Okkupation,* p. 37 (Doc. No. 8).
69. Hoffmann, *War Diaries,* I, 209.
70. Mumm (Kiev) to Foreign Office (Berlin), Telegram No. 557, April 5, 1918, *Die deutsche Okkupation,* p. 42 (Doc. No. 11).
71. Arnold D. Margolin, *From a Political Diary,* p. 31.
72. Bülow (Brest-Litovsk) to Foreign Office (Berlin), Telegram No. 616, no date (a report on Colonel Stolzenberg's telegram to the Supreme Army Command), *Die deutsche Okkupation,* p. 25 (Doc. No. 3); and Groener-Geyer, pp. 82–83 (Groener's letter to his wife dated March 27, 1918).
73. Municipal order No. 2, February 28, 1918, *Die deutsche Okkupation,* p. 24 (Doc. No. 2).
74. Khrystyuk, II, 163.
75. The text of this order, issued in Kiev on April 25, 1918, can be found in *Die deutsche Okkupation,* p. 59 (Doc. No. 21); and in Doroshenko, *Istoriya Ukrayiny,* II, 32–33.
76. Schwarzkopf (Great Headquarters) to Radowitz (Berlin), an unnumbered telegram, March 6, 1918 (a report on General Ludendorff's message to Count Stirum), *GFOA.* No. 35. Chancellor Hertling's message is discussed in Khrystyuk, II, 146.
77. See, for example, Major Friedrich Brinckmann's report on the Ukraine submitted to General Ludendorff in mid-March, 1918, Lersner (Great Headquarters) to Foreign Office (Berlin), Telegram No. 599, March 20, 1918, *GFOA.* No. 36.
78. Mumm (Kiev) to Foreign Office (Berlin), Telegram No. 54, March 22, 1918, and Telegram No. 117, March 28, 1918, *ibid.*
79. Mumm (Kiev) to Foreign Office (Berlin), Telegram No. 53, March 22, 1918, *ibid.*
80. Kühlmann (Bucharest) to Foreign Office (Berlin), Telegram No. 252, March 28, 1918, *ibid.*
81. Mumm (Kiev) to Foreign Office (Berlin), Telegram No. 119, March 28, 1918, *ibid.*
82. *Ibid.*
83. Forgách (Kiev) to Foreign Office (Vienna), Telegram No. 78, March 28, 1918, *Politisches Archiv (Vienna),* II, 197–98.
84. Mumm (Kiev) to Foreign Office (Berlin), Telegram No. 300, April 13, 1918, *Die deutsche Okkupation,* pp. 48–49 (Doc. No. 15).
85. Groener, *Lebenserinnerungen,* p. 393.

86. Austro-German Agreement on the Spheres of Influence in the Ukraine, Telegram No. 1362, Secret, Baden, March 29, 1918, *Die deutsche Okkupation*, pp. 34–36 (Doc. No. 7).
87. Mumm (Kiev) to Foreign Office (Berlin), Telegram No. 293, April 12, 1918, *GFOA*. No. 36.
88. Doroshenko, *Istoriya Ukrayiny*, I, 382, 38–39.
89. *Ibid.*, II, 33; and Mumm (Kiev) to Foreign Office (Berlin), Telegram No. 296, April 13, 1918, *GFOA*. No. 36.
90. Doroshenko, *Istoriya Ukrayiny*, II, 167, and I, 38; Khrystyuk, II, 167.
91. Mumm (Kiev) to Foreign Office (Berlin), Telegram No. 3, March 17, 1918, *GFOA*. No. 1790.
92. Mumm (Kiev) to Foreign Office (Berlin), Telegram No. 325, April 15, 1918, *GFOA*. No. 36.
93. Kühlmann (Great Headquarters) to Foreign Office (Berlin), Telegram No. 856, April 16, 1918, *ibid.*; and Telegram No. 356, April 16, 1918, *GFOA*. No. 142. Also Lersner (Great Headquarters) to Foreign Office (Berlin), "A Message to General Ludendorff," Telegram No. 890, April 19, 1918, *GFOA*. No. 36.
94. Zaliznyak in Kedryn, pp. 141–42.
95. Rosenberg (Brest-Litovsk) to Foreign Office (Berlin), Telegram No. 553, March 2, 1918, *GFOA*. No. 35; Schüler (Brest-Litovsk) to Foreign Office (Berlin), Telegram No. 585, March 4, 1918, *ibid.*; Kühlmann (Bucharest) to Foreign Office (Berlin), Telegram No. 54, March 4, 1918, *ibid.*
96. Kühlmann (Bucharest) to Foreign Office (Berlin), Telegram No. 131, March 15, 1918, and Telegram No. 259, March 29, 1918, *ibid.*; Grünau (Emperor's Train) to Foreign Office (Berlin), Telegram No. 711, April 2, 1918, *ibid.*
97. *GFOA*. No. 3632; and Conze, pp. 338–39. For the background of the Kholm question see Appendix A.
98. Doroshenko, *Istoriya Ukrayiny*, I, 324; Wheeler-Bennett, p. 235; Czernin (Vienna) to Hohenlohe (Berlin) and Pallavicini (Constantinople), Telegram No. 64, February 18, 1918, *Politisches Archiv (Vienna)*, VII, 111–13.
99. Kühlmann's statement before the Budget Committee of the Reichstag made on February 19, 1918, Lutz, I, 815.
100. Complete texts of the February 18 and March 4, 1918 protocols are available in Doroshenko, *Istoriya Ukrayiny*, I, 431–32.
101. Lersner (Great Headquarters) to Foreign Office (Berlin), "General Ludendorff's messages to the Imperial Chancellor," Telegram No. 331, February 19, 1918; Telegram No. 376, February

24, 1918; and Telegram No. 430, March 2, 1918, all in *GFOA*.
No. 3630. Also Ludendorff (Great Headquarters) to Hoffmann
(Brest-Litovsk), Telegram No. 437, January 15, 1918, *GFOA*.
No. 1796.
102. Czernin (Bucharest) to Tarnowski (Vienna), March 24, 1918,
cited in Conze, 356–57; and Bussche (Berlin) to Mumm (Kiev),
Telegram No. 102, April 10, 1918, *GFOA*. No. 36.

Chapter VII: The Turning Point: General Skoropadsky's Coup d'Etat

1. Secretary Kühlmann before the Reichstag Committee, Matthias
   and Morsey, II, 255.
2. Mumm (Kiev) to Foreign Office (Berlin), Telegram No. 52,
   March 22, 1918, *GFOA*. No. 36.
3. *Ibid.*
4. Foreign Office (Vienna) to Forgách (Kiev), Telegram No. 80,
   April 3, 1918, *Politisches Archiv (Vienna)*, II, 236–37; and *Die
   deutsche Okkupation*, pp. 38–39 (Doc. No. 9); these were recommendations submitted by Field Marshal Langer.
5. Lersner (Great Headquarters) to Foreign Office (Berlin), Telegram No. 723, April 3, 1918, *GFOA*. No. 36.
6. Lersner (Great Headquarters) to Foreign Office (Berlin), Telegram No. 730, April 3, 1918, *ibid.*
7. Mumm (Kiev) to Foreign Office (Berlin), Telegram No. 200,
   April 5, 1918, *ibid.*
8. Mumm (Kiev) to Foreign Office (Berlin), Telegram No. 38,
   Secret, April 7, 1918, *ibid.*
9. Mumm (Kiev) to Hertling (Berlin), no number, April 11, 1918,
   ibid.
10. Mumm (Kiev) to Foreign Office (Berlin), Telegram No. 300,
    April 13, 1918, *ibid.*
11. Mumm (Kiev) to Foreign Office (Berlin), Telegram No. 333,
    Secret, April 16, 1918, *ibid.*
12. Lersner (Great Headquarters) to Foreign Office (Berlin), "A
    Message from General Ludendorff to Imperial Chancellor Hert-
    ling," Telegram No. 836, April 13, 1918, *ibid.*
13. A memorandum prepared by the Army Group Eichhorn bearing
    the signature of Field Marshal von Einem, Doc. No. 33, Kiev,
    April 14, 1918, *ibid.*; and Groener to his wife, April 15, 1918,
    Groener, *Lebenserinnerungen*, p. 568.

14. Mumm (Kiev) to Foreign Office (Berlin), Telegram No. 351, April 18, 1918, *GFOA*. No. 36; and *Die deutsche Okkupation,* pp. 52–53 (Doc. No. 17).
15. Forgách (Kiev) to Foreign Office (Vienna), Telegram No. 82/603, March 28, 1918, *Politisches Archiv (Vienna)*, II, 200. See also Arz (Baden) to Czernin (Vienna), Telegram No. 1329, March 30, 1918, and Czernin's reply (no number), March 31, 1918, *ibid.*, pp. 178–180.
16. Mumm (Kiev) to Foreign Office (Berlin), Telegram No. 377, April 19, 1918, and Telegram No. 382, April 20, 1918, both in *GFOA*. No. 36.
17. Groener, *Lebenserinnerungen*, p. 397.
18. Lersner (Great Headquarters) to Foreign Office (Berlin), "A Message from General Ludendorff," Telegram No. 910, April 21, 1918, *GFOA*. No. 36.
19. Groener, *Lebenserinnerungen*, pp. 397–98.
20. Forgách (Kiev) to Foreign Office (Vienna), Telegram No. 229, April 20, 1918, *Politisches Archiv (Vienna)*, III, 44–45.
21. A full report on this meeting is available in Mumm (Kiev) to Foreign Office (Berlin), Telegram No. 418, April 23, 1918, *GFOA*. No. 36.
22. Groener, *Lebenserinnerungen*, p. 398.
23. Mumm (Kiev) to Foreign Office (Berlin), Telegram No. 420, April 24, 1918, *GFOA*. No. 36, and *Die deutsche Okkupation,* pp. 56–57 (Doc. No. 19). See also Prinzig (Kiev) to Foreign Office (Vienna), Telegram No. 244, April 25, 1918, cited in Doroshenko, "Getmanstvo 1918 g. na Ukraine," pp. 153–54, and Doc. No. 1517, dated April 24, 1918, prepared by the Austro-Hungarian Supreme Army Command Opt. Abt. in *Politisches Archiv (Vienna)*, III, 164–66.
24. *Ibid.*
25. Pavlo Skoropadskyi, "Uryvok zi spomyniv'.
26. For further details on the Hetman's activities in late 1917 see Part I of his memoirs, *ibid.*, IV, 3–40. An interesting review of the period is available in the work of a former Rada minister, Mykola Kovalevs'kyi, *Pry dzherelakh borot'by* [At the Fountain of Our Struggle, especially Part II, chap. III.
27. Princess Cantacuzène Countess Speransky neé Grant, *Revolutionary Days*, pp. 297–98.
28. Skoropadsky, V, 65.
29. General Waldstätten (Baden) to Foreign Office (Vienna), Memorandum No. 1447, April 16, 1918, *Die deutsche Okkupation,* p. 133 (Doc. No. 53).

30. Burián (Vienna) to Arz (Baden), May 16, 1918, *Politisches Archiv (Vienna)*, XIV, 230–32.
31. Skoropadsky, V, 73–74.
32. Mumm to Hertling, special report dated April 29, 1918, *Die deutsche Okkupation*, p. 62 (Doc. No. 22).
33. Cantacuzène, pp. 297–98; and Mikhail A. Svechin, *Dopolnenie k vospominaniam* [Supplement to Reminiscences], II, 20.
34. Skoropadsky, Vol. V; Beyer, p. 40.
35. See, for example, Forgách (Kiev) to Burián (Vienna), June 11, 1918, *Haus-, Hof-und Staatsarchiv* (Vienna), cited in Taras Hunczak, "Die Ukraine unter Hetman Pavlo Skoropadskyj," p. 108.
36. Beyer, pp. 81–82.
37. Mumm (Kiev) to Foreign Office (Berlin), Telegram No. 461, April 29, 1918, *GFOA*. No. 37.
38. Mumm (Kiev) to Foreign Office (Berlin), Telegram No. 351, April 18, 1918, *Die deutsche Okkupation*, p. 53 (Doc. No. 17).
39. Kovalevs'kyi, p. 481.
40. For further details see Mumm (Kiev) to Hertling (Berlin), a report dated April 29, 1918, in *Die deutsche Okkupation*, pp. 60–65 (Doc. No. 22); and Prinzing (Kiev) to Foreign Office (Vienna), Telegram No. 248/2537, April 25, 1918, *Politisches Archiv (Vienna)*, III, 87–88.
41. For the text of Eichhorn's order see *Die deutsche Okkupation*, p. 59 (Doc. No. 21). Mumm's and Groener's reactions are recorded in Mumm (Kiev) to Foreign Office (Berlin), Telegram No. 437, April 25, 1918, *ibid.*, p. 58 (Doc. No. 20).
42. Stefaniv, pp. 45, 94; Doroshenko, *Istoriya Ukrayiny*, II, 33; Reshetar, p. 128.
43. Skoropadsky, V, 76; Mumm (Kiev) to Foreign Office (Berlin), Telegrams No. 459 and 460, April 28, 1918, *GFOA*. No. 37. See also Mumm's report to Hertling, dated April 29, 1918, *Die deutsche Okkupation*, pp. 62–65 (Doc. No. 22).
44. Mumm (Kiev) to Foreign Office (Berlin), Telegram No. 462, April 29, 1918, *GFOA*. No. 37.
45. For the description of Skoropadsky's "election" see Doroshenko, *Istoriya Ukrayiny*, II, chap. II. For his manifesto see Appendix F.
46. Skoropadsky, V, 90.
47. Scheidemann to Vice-Chancellor von Payer, a letter dated Berlin, April 27, 1918, *GFOA*. No. 27.
48. Grünau (His Majesty's Train) to Foreign Office (Berlin), Telegram No. 237, April 29, 1918, *GFOA*. No. 37.

49. Hoffmann, *War Diaries*, I, 214–15. A good example of the Reichstag discussion of Skoropadsky's coup is Vice-Chancellor Payer's speech of May 7 and Erzberger's statement of May 14. For further details see Lutz, I, 846 *ff.*, 852 *ff.*; and Klaus Epstein, *Matthias Erzberger*, pp. 241–42.
50. Hoffmann, *War Diaries*, I, 40.
51. Bussche (Berlin) to Mumm (Kiev), April 30, 1918, *Die deutsche Okkupation*, p. 103 (Doc. No. 42).
52. Mumm (Kiev) to Foreign Office (Berlin), Telegram No. 420, April 24, 1918, *ibid.*, p. 56 (Doc. No. 19).
53. Mumm (Kiev) to Foreign Office (Berlin), Telegram No. 474, April 30, 1918, *GFOA.* No. 37; Groener, *Lebenserinnerungen*, p. 399; Prinzing (Kiev) to Foreign Office (Vienna), Telegram No. 275, April 30, 1918, *Politisches Archiv (Vienna)*, III, 132–134.
54. Groener, *Lebenserinnerungen*, p. 569.
55. Mumm (Kiev) to Bussche (Berlin), a letter dated May 3, 1918, *GFOA.* No. 37; and May 10, *ibid.*
56. Mumm (Kiev) to Foreign Office (Berlin), Telegram No. 510, May 4, 1918, *ibid.*
57. Mumm (Kiev) to Hertling (Berlin), Communication No. 146, May 7, 1918, *ibid.*
58. See, for example, Bussche (Berlin) to Mumm (Kiev), no number, April 30, 1918, *Die deutsche Okkupation*, p. 103 (Doc. No. 42); and a memorandum from the Army Group Eichhorn to the Supreme Army Command, dated May 4, 1918, No. 30918 P, *ibid.*, p. 71 (Doc. No. 24), and *GFOA.* No. 37.
59. Mumm (Kiev) to Foreign Office (Berlin), Telegram No. 821, June 2, 1918, *GFOA.* No. 37. See also Eichhorn's memorandum cited in the preceding footnote; Khrystyuk, III, 10; and Doroshenko, *Istoriya Ukrayiny*, II, 55.
60. Mumm (Kiev) to Foreign Office (Berlin), Telegram No. 485, May 2, 1918, *Die deutsche Okkupation*, p. 68 (Doc. No. 23); Khrystyuk, III, 9–11; Doroshenko, *Istoriya Ukrayiny*, II, 53–58.
61. Mumm (Kiev) to Foreign Office (Berlin), a letter to Bussche dated May 3, 1918, *GFOA.* No. 37.
62. Kühlmann (Bucharest) to Foreign Office (Berlin), Telegram No. 411, May 4, 1918, (Kühlmann's report on his talks with Burián), *ibid.*
63. Memorandum No. 30918 P., *ibid.*; Report No. 15 of the Army Group Eichhorn, dated May 4, 1918, *Die deutsche Okkupation*, p. 70 (Doc. No. 24); and Bussche (Berlin) to Mumm (Kiev), Telegram No. 264, May 8, 1918, *Die deutsche Okkupation*, p.

72 (Doc. No. 25). See also Berckheim (Great Headquarters) to Foreign Office (Berlin), Telegram No. 1027, May 5, 1918, *GFOA*. No. 37.

64. *Die deutsche Okkupation,* documents cited above; and Bussche (Berlin) to Mumm (Kiev), Telegram No. 264, May 9, 1918, *GFOA*. No. 37.

65. Ludendorff (Great Headquarters) to Hertling (Berlin), Memorandum No. 30845 P., dated May 4, 1918 (a report prepared by Eichhorn and Groener), *GFOA*. No. 37.

66. Hoffmann, *War Diaries,* I, 217–18.

67. Mumm (Kiev) to Hertling (Berlin), Telegram No. 152, May 8, 1918, *GFOA*. No. 37. Also, Mumm (Kiev) to Foreign Office (Berlin), Telegram No. 548, May 9, 1918, *ibid.,* and in *Die deutsche Okkupation,* p. 73 (Doc. No. 26).

68. General Groener to his wife on May 8, 1918, Groener, *Lebenserinnerungen,* p. 569.

69. Mumm (Kiev) to Bussche (Berlin), May 10, 1918, *GFOA*. No. 37.

70. Khrystyuk, III, 4–5; and Doroshenko, *Istoriya Ukrayiny,* II, 49–50.

71. Khrystyuk, III, 9–10; Doroshenko, *Istoriya Ukrayiny,* II, 53–55.

72. Mumm to Skoropadsky, a note dated May 2, 1918, *GFOA*. No. 37.

73. Eichhorn's Report No. 30868 P., May 4, 1918, *ibid.*

74. Mumm (Kiev) to Foreign Office (Berlin), Telegram No. 485, Secret, May 2, 1918, *Die deutsche Okkupation,* p. 68 (Doc. No. 23); Berckheim (Great Headquarters) to Foreign Office (Berlin), "For the Imperial Chancellor," Telegram No. 998, May 2, 1918, *GFOA*. No. 37; Groener, *Lebenserinnerungen,* pp. 400, 569; Ludendorff, *Meine Kriegserinnerungen,* p. 502.

75. Army Group Eichhorn (Kiev) to Army Command East (Ober-Ost, Kovno), Communication No. Kr. 151, May 7, 1918, *GFOA*. No. 37.

76. Mumm (Kiev) to Bussche (Berlin), May 10, 1918, *ibid.*

77. Doroshenko to Mumm, a note dated May 10, 1918, *Die deutsche Okkupation,* p. 138 (Doc. No. 55); and Doroshenko, *Istoriya Ukrayiny,* II, 60.

78. For the background of political and journalistic activities of Rohrbach and Schmidt see Doroshenko, *Die Ukraine und das Reich,* chaps. VII and VIII. For Rohrbach's own account of the visit see his and Schmidt's *Osteuropa,* pp. 132–33; his "Ukrainische Eindrücke," pp. 675–680; and his *Um des Teufels Handschrift,* pp. 220–21. Axel Schmidt gives his account of the mis-

sion in his "Die Ukrainischen Parteien," pp. 781–85. See also Henry Cord Meyer, "Germans in the Ukraine," pp. 105–15.

79. Rohrbach met General Hoffmann on May 7, 1918, while on his way to Kiev (Hoffmann, *War Diaries*, I, 217), and must have arrived there on the following day. Rohrbach submitted his report to Mumm on May 13, and returned to Germany shortly thereafter. For further details see Rohrbach, *Um des Teufels Handschrift*, p. 221.

80. Rohrbach, *Um des Teufels Handschrift*, pp. 220–221.

81. There are two official copies of the "Rohrbach Report," one dated May 13, 1918, and submitted by Mumm to Chancellor Hertling (23 pages), and another sent directly to the Under-Secretary von dem Bussche on May 23 (20 pages), both to be found in *GFOA*. No. 37.

82. Mumm (Kiev) to Foreign Office (Berlin), Telegram No. 668, May 20, 1918; *ibid.*, and *Die deutsche Okkupation*, p. 139 (Doc. No. 56).

83. Mumm (Kiev) to Imperial Chancellor Hertling (Berlin), Telegram No. 215, Confidential, May 19, 1918, *GFOA*. No. 37.

84. *Ibid.*

85. A full report on this conference, dated May 25, 1918, is available in *GFOA*. No. 37.

86. See, for example, Forgách (Kiev) to Foreign Office (Vienna), Telegram No. 496, May 31, 1918, *Politisches Archiv (Vienna)*, XIV, 324–25.

87. Hoffmann, *War Diaries*, I, 218.

88. See, for example, Mumm (Kiev) to Foreign Office (Berlin), Telegram No. 668, May 20, 1918, *Die deutsche Okkupation*, p. 139 (Doc. No. 56); and Ohnesseit (Odessa) to Foreign Office (Berlin), J. No. 153, May 20, 1918, *ibid.*, pp. 107–08 (Doc. No. 45). See also Khrystyuk, III, 50–62.

89. This was Naumann's feeling recorded in his diary on May 16, 1918, Theodor Heuss, *Friedrich Naumann*, p. 551.

90. Erzberger to Kühlmann, a memorandum dated Berlin, May 21, 1918, *GFOA*. No. 37.

91. Eichhorn's order No. 386/V.B., May 22, 1918, *Die deutsche Okkupation*, pp. 74–76 (Doc. No. 27).

92. Arz (Baden) to Foreign Office (Vienna), Telegram No. 143/49, Op., May 16, 1918, *Politisches Archiv (Vienna)*, XIV, 249–50.

93. Trautmannsdorff (Baden) to Foreign Office (Vienna), Telephone message No. 29918, May 25, 1918, (a report on General Krauss's views), *ibid.*, XIV, 302–304.

94. Mumm (Kiev) to Foreign Office (Berlin), Telegram No. 818, June 1, 1918, *GFOA*. No. 37.
95. See, for example, Prinzing (Kiev) to Foreign Office (Vienna), Telegram No. 399, May 17, 1918; Foreign Office (Vienna) to Trautmannsdorff (Baden), Telephone message No. 54, May 18, 1918; and Trautmannsdorff (Baden) to Foreign Office (Vienna), Telephone message No. 29821, May 21, 1918, all in *Politisches Archiv* (*Vienna*), XIV, 263–64.
96. Mumm (Kiev) to Foreign Office (Berlin), Telegram No. 749, May 26, 1918, *GFOA*. No. 37.
97. Grünau (His Majesty's Train) to Foreign Office (Berlin), Telegram No. 271, May 29, 1918, *ibid.*
98. Berckheim (Great Headquarters) to Foreign Office (Berlin), Telegram No. 1286, May 30, 1918; and Mumm (Kiev) to Foreign Office (Berlin), Telegram No. 821, June 2, 1918, *ibid.*
99. Prinzing (Kiev) to Foreign Office (Vienna), Telegram No. 355, May 11, 1918, *Politisches Archiv* (*Vienna*), III, 209; and Forgách (Kiev) to Foreign Office (Vienna), Telegram No. 463, May 27, 1918, *ibid.*, XIV, 312.
100. Forgách (Kiev) to Foreign Office (Vienna), Telegram No. 452, May 24, 1918, *ibid.*
101. Burián (Vienna) to Forgách (Kiev), Telegram No. 388, May 30, 1918, *ibid.*, p. 318; and memoranda of the Austrian War Ministry Nos. 12029 and 3363, dated May 6 and June 15, 1918, *ibid.*, III, 173–74.

Chapter VIII: The Hetmanate: Return to "Normalcy"

1. Information Service of the Austro-Hungarian Supreme Army Command to Foreign Office (Vienna), Communication No. NA 13.078, June 6, 1918, *Politisches Archiv* (*Vienna*), XIV, 345.
2. Mumm (Kiev) to Foreign Office (Berlin), Telegram No. 836, June 3, 1918, *GFOA*. No. 37.
3. Mumm (Kiev) to Hertling (Berlin), Communication No. 280, June 5, 1918, *ibid.*
4. An extract from a stenographic report on the meeting between a delegation of Ukrainian parties and General Groener, Chief of the General Staff in Kiev, on June 10, 1918, *Die deutsche Okkupation*, pp. 142–47 (Doc. No. 58).
5. Minutes of the Imperial conference held at Spa on May 11, 1918, *GFOA*. No. 37.

6. Mumm (Kiev) to Foreign Office (Berlin), Telegram No. 966, June 13, 1918, *GFOA*. Nos. 37 and 138.

7. *Ibid.*

8. Groener, *Lebenserinnerungen*, p. 403.

9. For further details on the Russian monarchist movement in the Ukraine under the Hetman see George A. Brinkley, *The Volunteer Army and Allied Intervention*, and chap. XI of this study.

10. Document No. 11567, Secret, Great Headquarters, June 15, 1918, Chief of the General Staff of the Army, Foreign Armies Division, *GFOA*. No. 147.

11. Austro-Hungarian Embassy (Berlin) to Foreign Office (Vienna), Doc. No. 385 (Political), June 19, 1918, *GFOA*. No. 52.

12. Forgách (Kiev) to Burián (Vienna), Telegram No. 695, July 20, 1918, *Politisches Archiv (Vienna)*, VI B, 93.

13. Mumm (Kiev) to Hertling (Berlin), A 26909, June 22, 1918, (copy of Field Marshal Eichhorn's memorandum on the east, dated June 17, 1918), *GFOA*. No. 52.

14. Secret order issued by Eichhorn to German officers in the Ukraine on June 27, 1918, *ibid.*

15. Mumm to Imperial Chancellor Hertling, Berlin, June 22, 1918, *ibid.*

16. Trautmannsdorff (Baden) to Burián (Vienna), Document No. 30.455, Very secret, "Report on General Krauss's views," June 18, 1918, *Politisches Archiv (Vienna)*, XIV, 401.

17. "Minutes of the Talks on Unsettled Political Problems Held at Spa on July 2–3, 1918, Between the Representatives of the Imperial Chancellery and the Supreme Army Command, Under the Chairmanship of the Kaiser," *GFOA*. Nos. 52 and 1500.

18. *Ibid.*

19. Minutes of the Imperial conference held at Spa on May 11, 1918, *GFOA*. No. 37.

20. "Minutes of the Talks on Unsettled Political Problems," note No. 17 above.

21. *Ibid.*

22. Mumm to Groener, J. No. 3965, Kiev, July 1, 1918, (a report on Ambassador Mumm's meeting with Prime Minister Lyzohub on June 29, 1918, *Die deutsche Okkupation*, pp. 83–84 (Doc. Nos. 30 and 30 A); and Mumm (Kiev) to Hertling (Berlin), K. No. 442, July 2, 1918, *GFOA*. No. 52.

23. Colonel Beyer, Press Secretary of the Austrian Supreme Command, to His Majesty's Bureau, Foreign Office, etc., Communication No. 30.862, "Very secret, not for the Germans," June 30, 1918, *Politisches Archiv (Vienna)*, XIV, 430.

24. Mumm (Kiev) to Hertling (Berlin), K. No. 464, July 7, 1918, *GFOA*. No. 52; and Mumm (Kiev) to Hertling (Berlin), K. No. 521, July 25, 1918, *GFOA*. No. 53.
25. Mumm (Kiev) to Foreign Office (Berlin), Secret, Telegram No. 1325, July 23, 1918, *Die deutsche Okkupation*, p. 150 (Doc. No. 61); and Reshetar, p. 161.
26. For further details see the memoirs of another arrested Rada leader, Mykola Kovalevs'kyi, part II, chap. X; and K. Vishevich, Ukrainskii vopros, p. 34.
27. Thiel to Rohrbach, a letter dated July 26, 1918, Henry Cord Meyer, "Germans in the Ukraine," p. 108.
28. V. I. Gurko, "Politicheskaya situatsiya na Ukraine" [Political Situation in the Ukraine], p. 212.
29. Groener, *Lebenserinnerungen*, p. 408.
30. Mumm (Kiev) to Foreign Office (Berlin), Telegram No. 1507, August 10, 1918, (a report on General Groener's view of the Ukrainian situation), *GFOA*. No. 53; Groener to Mumm, Ia No. 3600/18, Kiev, August 8, 1918, *GFOA*. No. 143; Mumm to Groener, Kiev, August 11, 1918, (comments on Groener's memorandum of August 8), *ibid.*; Mumm (Kiev) to Hertling (Berlin), Telegram No. 610, August 10, 1918, *Die deutsche Okkupation*, p. 190 (Doc. No. 82).
31. Mumm to Groener, Kiev, August 11, 1918, *GFOA*. No. 143.
32. See, for example, *Tägliche Rundschau* or *Berliner Tageblatt* of August 19, 1918. The Hetman's "explanation," in which he restated his adherence to the idea of a free Ukraine, appeared in the German press ten days later, on the eve of his visit to Berlin (see, for example, *Kölnische Zeitung* of August 29, 1918). Prime Minister Lyzohub's clarification of his earlier interview can be found in the same German daily of August 25.
33. Mumm (Kiev) to Bussche (Berlin), Communication No. 5573, August 6, 1918, *Die deutsche Okkupation*, pp. 155–56 (Doc. No. 64).
34. For further details see the following documents in *Die deutsche Okkupation:* Nos. 49, 50, 66, 67.
35. Stumm (Foreign Office, Berlin) to Mumm (Kiev), Telegram No. 1147, August 28, 1918, *ibid.*, p. 157 (Doc. No. 65); and Mumm (Kiev) to Foreign Office (Berlin), Telegram No. 1672, Secret, August 29, 1918, *GFOA*. No. 53.
36. Hintze (Berlin) to Lersner (Great Headquarters), Telegram No. 1024, September 2, 1918, *GFOA*. No. 143; an unsigned and undated copy of this document can also be found in *GFOA*. No. 53.
37. For further details see Doroshenko, *Istoriya Ukrayiny*, II, 381–

86; "Die Reise des Hetmans der Ukraine nach Deutschland;" and Alfred Niemann, *Kaiser und Revolution*, p. 159 f.

38. Berckheim (Great Headquarters) to Foreign Office (Berlin), Telegrams Nos. 2031 and 2092, September 3 and 12, 1918, *GFOA*. No. 53.

39. Lersner (Great Headquarters) to Foreign Office (Berlin), Telegram No. 2100, September 12, 1918, *GFOA*. Nos. 53 and 143.

40. For further details see chap. XI of this study.

41. The Ukraine's foreign policy of this period is discussed by the Hetman's Foreign Minister Dmytro Doroshenko in the following of his writings: *Istoriya Ukrayiny*, II, chap. VIII; *Moyi spomyny pro nedavnye mynule*, Vol. III; and "Deshcho pro zakordonnu polityku ukrayins'koyi derzhavy v 1918 r.," pp. 49–64.

42. Lersner (Great Headquarters) to Foreign Office (Berlin), Telegram No. 1176, May 21, 1918, *GFOA*. No. 37. The line of German advance in the east, as set by General Ludendorff, was the following: Don, Donets, Ossikovka, Novo-Belaya, Grushevka, Belgorod.

43. Kühlmann (Berlin) to Mumm (Kiev), Telegram No. 368, May 23 or 24, 1918, *ibid.*

44. Foreign Office (Berlin) to Mumm (Kiev), Telegram No. 435, May 31, 1918, *ibid.*

45. Pavel N. Milyukov, "Dnevnik" [Diary], p. 14, entry for June 18, 1918.

46. Doroshenko, *Istoriya Ukrayiny*, II, 202.

47. Matthias and Morsey, II, 412.

48. Doroshenko, *Istoriya Ukrayiny*, II, 202–203, 206–207.

49. Bussche (Berlin) to Horstmann (Bucharest), Telegram No. 417, August 26, 1918, *GFOA*. No. 53.

50. Doroshenko, *Istoriya Ukrayiny*, II, 207.

51. See, for example, Mumm (Kiev) to Hertling (Berlin), Note No. 577, August 5, 1918, *GFOA*. No. 53.

52. Hohenlohe (Berlin) to Foreign Office (Vienna), (a report on Czernin's views), Telegram No. 81, Very secret, February 5, 1918, *Politisches Archiv (Vienna)*, VII, 87–89.

53. Prime Minister Seidler's statement on East Galicia made in the Austrian Diet on February 19, 1918.

54. Czernin (Szegled) to Foreign Office (Vienna), "For Wiesner," Telegram No. 1, Secret, February 22, 1918, *Politisches Archiv (Vienna)*, VII, 149; Rössler (Budapest) to Rosenberg (Berlin), Telegram No. 1, February 23, 1918, "A Message From Foreign Secretary Kühlmann," *GFOA*. No. 3630; Rosenberg (Berlin) to

Kühlmann (Bucharest), Telegram No. 81, Secret, February 23, 1918, *ibid.*

55. Mumm (Kiev) to Foreign Office (Berlin), Telegram No. 851, June 4, 1918, *GFOA.* No. 3630.
56. Kühlmann (Berlin) to Mumm (Kiev), Telegram No. 536, Very secret, June 14, 1918, *GFOA.* No. 1791; Burián (Vienna) to Forgách (Kiev), Telegram No. 502, July 1, 1918, *Politisches Archiv (Vienna)*, VI, 21.
57. Bussche (Berlin) to Wedel (Vienna), Telegram No. 714, July 12, 1918, *GFOA.* No. 3630; and Doroshenko, *Istoriya Ukrayiny*, II, 219.
58. For the complete text of the two notes see Doroshenko, *Istoriya Ukrayiny*, II, 220–21.
59. Bussche (Berlin) to Wedel (Vienna), and Mumm (Kiev), Telegrams Nos. 732 and 781, July 16, 1918, *GFOA.* No. 3630. For the "Protocol of the Burning of the 'Galician Document,'" dated Berlin, July 16, 1918, signed by Bussche and Hohenlohe, see *Die deutsche Okkupation*, p. 91 (Doc. No. 35), and Hohenlohe (Berlin) to Foreign Office (Vienna), Telegram No. 468, July 16, 1918, *Politisches Archiv (Vienna)*, VII, 170.
60. Doroshenko, *Istoriya Ukrayiny*, II, 138–39.
61. Stolberg (Vienna) to Foreign Office (Berlin), July 26, 1918, *GFOA.* No. 3630.
62. Mumm (Kiev) to Foreign Office (Berlin), August 25, 1918, *ibid.*
63. For the text of the Austrian ratification note, which had never been exchanged, see Doroshenko, *Istoriya Ukrayiny*, II, 139–40.
64. Copy of the note signed by the Hetman's Foreign Minister Dmytro Doroshenko, and sent on June 12, 1918 both to Vienna and to Austria's Ambassador in Kiev, Count Forgách, can be found in *ibid.*, pp. 225–26.
65. Mumm (Kiev) to Foreign Office (Berlin), Telegram No. 536, Very secret, and No. 1002, June 14 and 16, 1918, *GFOA.* No. 3630.
66. Burián (Vienna) to Hohenlohe (Berlin), Very secret, Copy No. 2812, June 8, 1918, *ibid.*
67. Conze, pp. 371–72.
68. Mumm (Kiev) to Foreign Office (Berlin), Telegram No. 1545, August 15, 1918, *GFOA.* No. 3630.
69. Berckheim (Great Headquarters) to Foreign Office (Berlin), Telegram No. 1933, "A report on General Ludendorff's views on Kholm," August 23, 1918, *ibid.*
70. Quoted in Ludendorff, *The General Staff and Its Problems*, II, 596 (Hintze to Great Headquarters on August 28, 1918).

71. Doroshenko, *Istoriya Ukrayiny*, II, 227–30.
72. Conze, pp. 377, 393.
73. Doroshenko, *Istoriya Ukrayiny*, II, 230.
74. *Ibid.*, chap. X.
75. Rosenberg (Brest-Litovsk) to Foreign Office (Berlin), Telegram No. 548, March 2, 1918, *GFOA*. No. 35.
76. Doroshenko, *Istoriya Ukrayiny*, II, 162, 164.
77. *GFOA*. No. 118.
78. Berckheim (Great Headquarters) to Foreign Office (Berlin), Telegram No. 1255, "A report on General Ludendorff's views," May 28, 1918, *ibid.*
79. Berckheim (Great Headquarters) to Foreign Office (Berlin), Telegram No. 1081, May 11, 1918; and Mumm (Kiev) to Foreign Office (Berlin), Telegram No. 748, May 26, 1918, both in *GFOA*. No. 118. See also Doroshenko, *Istoriya Ukrayiny*, II, 181.
80. Doroshenko, *loc. cit.*
81. Mumm (Kiev) to Foreign Office (Berlin), Telegram No. 793, May 30, 1918, *GFOA*. No. 118.
82. Foreign Office (Berlin) to Mumm (Kiev), Telegram No. 435, May 31, 1918, *GFOA*. No. 37.
83. For further details see "Draft of a German Memorandum to the Ukraine," Kiev, June 1, 1918. (It was prepared by Privy Councillor Wiedfeldt and addressed to Prime Minister Lyzohub.) *Die deutsche Okkupation*, pp. 109–10 (Doc. No. 46).
84. Berckheim (Great Headquarters) to Foreign Office (Berlin), Telegram No. 1333, July 4, 1918, "A message from General Ludendorff," *GFOA*. No. 118; and Kühlmann (Berlin) to Mumm (Kiev), Telegram No. 481, June 6, 1918, *GFOA*. No. 37; and Mumm (Kiev) to Foreign Office (Berlin), Telegram No. 924, June 10, 1918, *ibid.*
85. Gatzke, "Zu den deutsch-russischen Beziehungen," p. 76.
86. Groener, *Lebenserinnerungen,* p. 570; Groener to Mumm, Ia No. 3600/18, Kiev, August 8, 1918, *GFOA*. No. 143; and Ludendorff (Great Headquarters) to Hintze (Berlin), August 5, 1918, *GFOA*. No. 85, cited in Freund, p. 24.
87. Fischer, *Griff nach der Weltmacht,* chap. XXI.
88. Lersner (Great Headquarters) to Foreign Office (Berlin), Telegram No. 2567, October 25, 1918, *GFOA*. No. 118.
89. Doroshenko, *Istoriya Ukrayiny*, II, 207–08.
90. *Ibid.*, p. 208.
91. Mumm (Kiev) to Foreign Office (Berlin), Telegram No. 3, March 17, 1918, *GFOA*. No. 1790.

92. Berchem (Kiev) to Foreign Office (Berlin), Telegram No. 1071, June 24, 1918, *GFOA*. No. 52.
93. Foreign Office (Berlin) to German Embassy (Kiev), no number, June 29, 1918, *ibid.*
94. Forgách (Kiev) to Burián (Vienna), No. 69/Pol., July 16, 1918, *Politisches Archiv (Vienna)*, VI B, 66–68.
95. For further details see Doroshenko, *Istoriya Ukrayiny*, II, chaps. VIII, X, XI.

Chapter IX: Economic Exploitation of the Ukraine: A Balance Sheet

1. Gratz and Schüller, p. 136.
2. Mumm (Kiev) to Foreign Office (Berlin), Telegram No. 474, April 30, 1918, *GFOA*. No. 37.
3. Wiedfeldt (Kiev) to Department of National Economy (*Reichswirtschaftsamt*, Berlin), and Mumm (Kiev) to Foreign Office (Berlin), Note No. 498, May 3, 1918, *Die deutsche Okkupation,* p. 101 (Doc. No. 40).
4. Winterfeldt (Supreme Army Command's representative at the Imperial Chancellery) to Imperial Chancellor, "A message from General Ludendorff," Berlin, May 23, 1918, *GFOA*. No. 37; and General Kress (Tiflis) to Foreign Office (Berlin), Telegram No. 53, August 8, 1918, *GFOA*. No. 144.
5. Kühlmann to Winterfeldt, Berlin, May 25, 1918, *GFOA*. No. 37.
6. For the complete text of the draft of a special warning to Ukrainian railroad workers, dated May 3, 1918, and bearing signatures of Velsen and Hasse, see *Die deutsche Okkupation,* pp. 77–78 (Doc. No. 28).
7. *GFOA*. No. 37.
8. Zastavenko, pp. 52–53; and *Texts of the Ukraine "Peace,"* pp. 153–154.
9. Kuhl in *Die Ursachen*, fourth series, III, 32–33.
10. For Eichhorn's order, dated May 17, 1918, see Zastavenko, pp. 53–54. The agreement of mid-August is discussed in Krauss and Klingenbrunner, p. 387.
11. Ludendorff to Groener, letter dated May 19, 1918, Groener, *Lebenserinnerungen,* pp. 400–401.
12. Stefaniv, pp. 98–99.
13. Thiel (Kiev) to Foreign Office (Berlin), Telegram No. 1878, September 19, 1918, *GFOA*. No. 53.
14. Khrystyuk, III, 48–49.
15. Berckheim (Great Headquarters) to Foreign Office (Berlin),

"A message from General Ludendorff," Telegram No. 990, May 1, 1918, *GFOA*. No. 143.

16. For further details see the following: "The Appointment of General Krauss as the Supreme Commander of Austria-Hungary in the Ukraine," Telegram No. 143149, Secret, May 18, 1918, signed by General Arz, *Die deutsche Okkupation*, pp 182–83 (Doc. No. 78); Krauss, pp. 253–58; Arz, p. 218; Beyer, p. 49.

17. An unsigned report prepared for the Legation Councillor Trautmann, dated June 18, 1918, *GFOA*. No. 52.

18. Gratz and Schüller, p. 134.

19. Krauss and Klingenbrunner, pp. 376–77.

20. For further details see Gatzke, "Zu den deutsch-russischen Beziehungen im Sommer 1918," pp. 77–78, and Stresemann's note of July 7, 1918, reproduced in this article (pp. 79–83).

21. Deutelmoser's memorandum concerning the problem of propaganda, Berlin, August 19, 1918, *Die Ursachen*, fourth series, II (2), 356–58.

22. Krauss and Klingenbrunner, pp. 375–76.

23. Merton, p. 43.

24. Gratz and Schüller, p. 136.

25. Czernin, *Im Weltkriege*, pp. 345–46.

26. Krauss and Klingenbrunner, pp. 384–85.

27. Krauss, p. 256. See also Telegram No. 143149, Secret, May 18, 1918, an order signed by General Arz, *Die deutsche Okkupation*, pp. 182–83 (Doc. No. 78).

28. Arz (Baden) to Burián (Vienna), June 13, 1918, "General Krauss's Report on the Ukrainian Situation," *Die deutsche Okkupation*, pp. 79–82 (Doc. No. 29).

29. Bussche (Berlin) to Mumm (Kiev), April 30, 1918, *ibid.*, p. 103 (Doc. No. 42).

30. Mumm (Kiev) to Stein (Berlin), Telegram No. 638, May 1918, *ibid.*, p. 104 (Doc. No. 43).

31. Ludendorff (Great Headquarters) to Groener (Kiev), letter dated May 19, 1918, Groener, *Lebenserinnerungen*, pp. 400–401.

32. Kühlmann to Winterfeldt, Berlin, May 25, 1918, *GFOA*. No. 37; and Wiedfeldt to Prime Minister Lyzohub, a memorandum dated Kiev, June 1, 1918, *Die deutsche Okkupation*, pp. 109–10 (Doc. No. 46).

33. A more comprehensive discussion of Germany's long-range economic plans for the east is available in Fischer's *Griff nach der Weltmacht*, especially chaps. XX and XXI.

34. *Ibid.*, p. 720.

35. For further details and sources on the May 16, 1918 Stahlhoff meeting see V. G. Bryunin, "Sovetsko-germanskiye otnosheniya nakanune noyabrskoi revolutsii," in Kul'bakin, p. 204.
36. *Ibid.*, p. 205.
37. See, for example, Chamber of Commerce of the City of Hamburg to German Ambassador in Kiev, Baron Mumm, Hamburg, August 29, 1918, *Die deutsche Okkupation*, pp. 122–23 (Doc. No. 51).
38. Baumann (Ministry of the Interior) to Foreign Office, Communication No. 8292, Berlin, June 14, 1918, *ibid.*, pp. 111–13 (Doc. No. 47).
39. Ludendorff, *Kriegsführung und Politik*, p. 240.
40. Gratz and Schüller, pp. 129–30. For the complete text of the agreement see *Friedensverträge mit der Ukraine*, Supplement No. 1. (1 pood is equivalent to 36.11 pounds.)
41. *Ibid.*
42. Mumm (Kiev) to Foreign Office (Berlin), also Wiedfeldt and Melchior (Kiev) to the Ministry of National Economy (Berlin), Telegram No. 1755, September 5, 1918, *Die deutsche Okkupation*, pp. 124–25 (Doc. No. 52).

Chapter X: German Plans and Policies in the Crimea and the Black Sea Basin

1. For example, Werner Daya, *Der Aufmarsch im Osten.*
2. Rohrbach in *Deutsche Politik*, III, 869–71.
3. Bussche (Berlin) to Kühlmann (Brest-Litovsk), Telegram No. 86, December 23, 1917, *GFOA*. No. 1787.
4. General Ludendorff to General von Seeckt on March 15, 1918, and to General von Lossow on May 11, 1918, cited in C. Mühlmann, *Das deutsch-türkische Waffenbündniss im Weltkrieg*, pp. 196–97.
5. Mumm to Hertling, Berlin, June 22, 1918 (this message contains Field Marshal von Eichhorn's memorandum on Russia and the Ukraine prepared on June 17, 1918), *GFOA*. No. 52. General Groener's views are discussed in a special report on the Ukrainian situation prepared by the Commander in Chief of the Austro-Hungarian Eastern Army, General Alfred Krauss. General Arz (Baden) to Burián (Vienna), June 13, 1918, *Die deutsche Okkupation*, pp. 79–82 (Doc. No. 29). General Groener's memoirs, incidentally, do not reveal such thinking on his part at the time.

6. Cited in Edige Kirimal, *Der nationale Kampf der Krimtürken*, p. 2.
7. Headquarters of the Army Command East (Ober-Ost), Doc. No. A 27111, June 12, 1918, *GFOA*. No. 107.
8. For the discussion of Ukrainian-Crimean relations in the Rada period see Doroshenko, *Istoriya Ukrayiny*, II, 209; and Kirimal, pp. 121–26.
9. Kirimal, p. 127.
10. Lutz, I, 821.
11. Ludendorff to Seeckt on March 15, 1918, cited in Mühlmann, p. 193.
12. Bussche (Berlin) to Mumm (Kiev), Telegram No. 43, March 25, 1918, *GFOA*. No. 36.
13. Kühlmann (Bucharest) to Foreign Office (Berlin), Telegram No. 229, March 26, 1918, *GFOA*. Nos. 36 and 142.
14. Mumm (Kiev) to Foreign Office (Berlin), Telegram No. 86, Secret, March 26, 1918, *ibid.*
15. Lersner (Great Headquarters) to Foreign Office (Berlin), Telegram No. 706, April 1, 1918, *ibid.*; and Mumm (Kiev) to Foreign Office (Berlin), Telegram No. 156, April 1, 1918, *GFOA*. No. 36, (a report on the Supreme Army Command's communication to the Army Command East).
16. Bernstorff (Constantinople) to Foreign Office (Berlin), Telegram No. 447, March 30, 1918, *GFOA*. No. 142.
17. Bernstorff (Constantinople) to Foreign Office (Berlin), Telegram No. 459, April 1, 1918, *GFOA*. No. 36.
18. Bussche (Berlin) to Mumm (Kiev), Telegram copy No. A 14227, April 2, 1918, *ibid.*
19. Lersner (Great Headquarters) to Foreign Office (Berlin), "A message from General Ludendorff," Telegram No. 744, April 5, 1918, *GFOA*. Nos. 36 and 142.
20. Lersner (Great Headquarters) to Foreign Office (Berlin), "A message from General Ludendorff," Telegram No. 766, April 7, 1918, *ibid.*
21. Foreign Office's memorandum on the Crimea, dated April 9, 1918, Copy No. 15175, *GFOA*. No. 36, and an unnumbered document in *GFOA*. No. 142; Lersner (Great Headquarters) to Foreign Office (Berlin), Telegram No. 807, April 11, 1918, "A message from Radowitz," *GFOA*. Nos. 36 and 142; Bussche (Berlin) to Lersner (Great Headquarters), Telegram No. 622, April 13, 1918, *GFOA*. No. 142.
22. Lersner (Great Headquarters) to Foreign Office (Berlin), Telegram No. 874, April 15, 1918, *GFOA*. No. 36.

23. Kirimal, p. 214.
24. *Ibid.*, pp. 193–94.
25. Lersner (Great Headquarters) to Foreign Office (Berlin), Telegram No. 898, April 20, 1918, "A message from General Ludendorff," *GFOA.* No. 36.
26. Udovychenko, pp. 36–37.
27. The order was signed by General Hoffmann on April 22, 1918, Copy No. A 27111, *GFOA.* No. 143.
28. Mumm (Kiev) to Foreign Office (Berlin), Telegram No. 453, April 27, 1918, *GFOA.* No. 37.
29. Memoranda on the Crimean question prepared by Trautmann and Nadolny (both of the German Foreign Office), Copy No. A 18575, May 1, 1918, *GFOA.* Nos. 143 and 147.
30. Chicherin began to protest the movement of German and Ukrainian units in the direction of the Crimea even before they entered it. See, for example, radiogram sent by Chicherin to the German Foreign Office on April 21, 1918, Doc. No. 202 in S. Dörnberg *et al.* (eds.), *Sovetsko-germanskie otnosheniya* [Soviet-German Relations], I, 511. See also his note of April 26, 1918, *ibid.*, pp. 512–14 (Doc. No. 205).
31. Berckheim (Great Headquarters) to Foreign Office (Berlin), Telegram No. 979, April 30, 1918, "A message from General Ludendorff," *GFOA.* No. 143; and Kühlmann (Bucharest) to Foreign Office (Berlin), Telegram No. 396, May 2, 1918, *ibid.*
32. Bernstorff (Constantinople) to Foreign Office (Berlin), Telegram No. 717, May 4, 1918, *GFOA.* Nos. 143 and 147.
33. Kühlmann (Bucharest) to Foreign Office (Berlin), Telegram No. 408, May 4, 1918, *ibid.*; and Bernstorff (Constantinople) to Foreign Office (Berlin), Telegram No. 653, May 6, 1918, *GFOA.* No. 143.
34. Mumm (Kiev) to Foreign Office (Berlin), Telegram Nos. 530 and 530 A, May 7, 1918, *GFOA.* Nos. 37 and 143, resp.
35. Kirimal, p. 182.
36. Bernstorff (Constantinople) to Foreign Office (Berlin), Telegram No. 672, May 9, 1918, *GFOA.* No. 143.
37. Kirimal, pp. 183–85.
38. Minutes of the May 11, 1918 Spa conference, *GFOA.* Nos. 37 and 143.
39. *Ibid.*; and Lersner (Great Headquarters) to Foreign Office (Berlin), Telegram No. 1118, May 16, 1918, "A message from General Ludendorff," *GFOA.* No. 143.
40. Mumm (Kiev) to Foreign Office (Berlin), Telegram No. 702, Very secret, May 23, 1918, *GFOA.* No. 143.

41. Berckheim (Great Headquarters) to Foreign Office (Berlin), Telegram No. 1208, May 23, 1918, "A message from General Ludendorff," *ibid.*
42. Foreign Office (Berlin) to Berckheim (Great Headquarters), Telegram No. 1110, May 29, 1918; and Bussche to the Department of the Navy, Doc. No. A 23783, Berlin, June 12, 1918, *ibid.*
43. These figures were supplied by the Berlin Bureau of the Union of German Colonists, Doc. No. A 36335, entitled "German Colonists in Russia," *GFOA*. No. 138.
44. The Headquarters of the German Army Command East (Ober-Ost), Doc. No. A 27111, June 12, 1918, *GFOA*. No. 107.
45. J. Schleuning, *In Kampf und Todesnot*, p. 57.
46. Lersner (Great Headquarters) to Foreign Office (Berlin), "A message from General Ludendorff," Telegram No. 744, April 5, 1918, *GFOA*. Nos. 36 and 142.
47. Berckheim (Great Headquarters) to Foreign Office (Berlin), Telegram No. 848, April 15, 1918, *GFOA*. No. 138.
48. Lersner (Great Headquarters) to Foreign Office (Berlin), "A message from Lindequist to General Ludendorff," Telegram No. 786, April 9, 1918, *GFOA*. No. 36.
49. Mumm (Kiev) to Foreign Office (Berlin), Telegram No. 306, April 13, 1918, *ibid.*
50. From a report of Christian E. Weiser (identified as an American-German) to the German Foreign Office on the activities of Reverend Winkler, Berlin, April 13, 1918, *ibid.*
51. Ludendorff, *Meine Kriegserinnerungen*, p. 532.
52. Groener, *Lebenserinnerungen*, p. 401.
53. Mumm (Kiev) to Foreign Office (Berlin), Telegram No. 756, May 28, 1918, *GFOA*. Nos. 37 and 138.
54. Bussche (Berlin) to Mumm (Kiev), April 30, 1918, *Die deutsche Okkupation*, p. 103 (Doc. No. 42); and Mumm (Kiev) to Foreign Office (Berlin), Telegram No. 756, May 28, 1918, *GFOA*. Nos. 37 and 138.
55. Bussche (Berlin) to Mumm (Kiev), Telegram No. 471, June 4, 1918, *ibid.*
56. Trautmann's report on the meeting between the former Colonial Secretary Lindequist and Imperial Chancellor Hertling held on June 8, 1918, in Berlin. Note No. A 24332 in *GFOA*. No. 37. Trautmann sent a copy of this note to Mumm in Kiev on June 10, 1918; it is available in *GFOA*. No. 138.
57. Ludendorff (Great Headquarters) to the Imperial Chancellery (Berlin), Note No. 24499, June 9, 1918, *GFOA*. No. 37.

58. Mumm (Kiev) to Foreign Office (Berlin), Telegram No. 945, Secret, June 12, 1918, *GFOA*. Nos. 138 and 143.

59. Mumm (Kiev) to Foreign Office (Berlin), Telegram No. 913, Very secret, June 9, 1918, *ibid.*

60. Mumm (Kiev) to Foreign Office (Berlin), Telegram No. 966, June 13, 1918, *GFOA*. Nos. 37 and 138.

61. Arz (Baden) to Burián (Vienna), "General Alfred Krauss's report on the Ukraine," June 13, 1918, *Die deutsche Okkupation*, pp. 79–82 (Doc. No. 29).

62. Foreign Office (Berlin) to Mumm (Kiev), an unnumbered document prepared some time in mid-June, 1918; Mumm (Kiev) to Foreign Office (Berlin), Telegram No. 1008, June 17, 1918; Mumm (Kiev) to Foreign Office (Berlin), "A report on General Groener's views," Telegram No. 957, Very secret, June 18, 1918; and Bussche (Berlin) to Berckheim (Great Headquarters), June 16, 1918, all in *GFOA*. No. 138.

63. Groener, *Lebenserinnerungen*, p. 401.

64. Bussche (Berlin) to Horstmann (Bucharest), Doc. No. A 26434, June 23, 1918, *GFOA*. No. 52.

65. Groener, *Lebenserinnerungen*, p. 570.

66. Lersner (Great Headquarters) to Foreign Office (Berlin), "A message from General Ludendorff," Telegram No. 1596, July 2, 1918, *GFOA*. No. 138.

67. Minutes and reports on this conference can be found in the following documents of the German Foreign Office archives: *GFOA*. No. 52; Doc. No. A 3086, July 9, 1918, and Doc. No. AS 3114, July 11, 1918, both in *GFOA*. No. 138; and *GFOA*. No. 1500.

68. Minutes of the Spa July 2, 1918 conference, *GFOA*. No. 52.

69. "Results of Talks Held at Spa on July 2 and 3, 1918," para. No. 6, *GFOA*. No. 1500.

70. Minutes of the July 2–3 Spa conference, *GFOA*. No. 138. Also Rosenberg (Great Headquarters) to Foreign Office (Berlin), Telegram No. 1595, July 2, 1918, *ibid.*

71. Minutes of the Crown Council held at Spa on July 2–3, 1918, under the Kaiser's chairmanship, *ibid.*

72. German Consul (Odessa) to the Imperial Chancellor (Berlin), J. No. 1865, K. No. 41, July 4, 1918, *GFOA*. No. 52; and Mumm (Kiev) to Foreign Office (Berlin), Telegram No. 1161, July 4, 1918, *ibid.*

73. Foreign Office to the Imperial Chancellor, Doc. No. A 30295, Berlin, July 5, 1918, *ibid.*

74. The memorandum, dated August 22, 1918, and addressed to

Foreign Secretary von Hintze, was signed by Winkler and ten other leaders of "eastern Germandom" representing the colonists in the Ukraine, Bessarabia, Caucasus, Volga, and Siberia. For further details see the complete text of the memorandum, *GFOA.* No. 52.

75. Foreign Office to the Chairman of the Society for German Settlement and Migration, Berlin, September 14, 1918, *ibid.*
76. "Krymskoe kraevoye pravitel'stvo v 1918/19 g. (Zapiski Nalbandova)" [The Crimean Regional Administration in 1918/19 (Nalbandov's Notes)], p. 100.
77. Bogdanov in James Bunyan (ed.), *Intervention, Civil War, and Communism in Russia,* p. 57.
78. Kirimal, p. 193.
79. See, for example, *ibid.*, p. 210.
80. Doroshenko, *Istoriya Ukrayiny,* II, 210–13.
81. *Ibid.*, p. 213.
82. For the composition of the Sulkevich government, organized on June 25, 1918, see Kirimal, p. 195.
83. Berchem (Kiev) to Foreign Office (Berlin), Telegrams Nos. 1030, 1031, and 1034, June 18, 19, and 20, resp., *GFOA.* No. 143.
84. Berckheim (Great Headquarters) to Foreign Office (Berlin), Telegram No. 1513, June 23, 1918, "A message from General Ludendorff," *ibid.*; and Berchem (Kiev) to Foreign Office (Berlin), Telegram No. 1069, June 24, 1918, *GFOA.* Nos. 52 and 143.
85. General Kosch to General Sulkevich, Doc. No. K 485, June 25, 1918, *GFOA.* No. 143; and Berchem (Kiev) to Foreign Office (Berlin), Telegram No. 1075, June 25, 1918, *ibid.*
86. Mumm (Kiev) to Foreign Office (Berlin), Telegram No. 1122, June 29, 1918; and Lersner (Great Headquarters) to Foreign Office (Berlin), Telegram No. 1579, June 30, 1918, *ibid.*
87. "Krymskoe kraevoe pravitel'stvo," p. 104.
88. D. S. Pasmanik, *Revolutsionnye gody v Krymu* [Revolutionary Years in the Crimea], pp. 104–105.
89. Berchem (Kiev) to Foreign Office (Berlin), Telegram No. 1241, July 12, 1918, *GFOA.* No. 143.
90. Lersner (Great Headquarters) to Foreign Office (Berlin), Telegram No. 1704, July 17, 1918, "A message from General Ludendorff," *ibid.*
91. Mumm (Kiev) to Foreign Office (Berlin), Telegram No. 1303, July 19, 1918, *ibid.*
92. "Krymskoe kraevoe pravitel'stvo," p. 111.

93. Lersner (Great Headquarters) to Foreign Office (Berlin), Telegram No. 1109, July 26, 1918, "A message from Hindenburg to Hertling," *GFOA*. No. 143.

94. Mumm (Kiev) to Foreign Office (Berlin), Telegram No. 1371, July 29, 1918, *ibid.*

95. Hausschild (Consul General, Moscow) to Foreign Office (Berlin), Telegram No. 166, August 26, 1918, *GFOA*. No. 143.

96. Lersner (Great Headquarters) to Foreign Office (Berlin), Telegrams Nos. 1692 and 1795, July 15 and 31, 1918, "A message from General Ludendorff," *ibid.*

97. Rosenberg to Berckheim, Note No. A 35474, Berlin, August 28, 1918, *ibid.*

98. For further details see Doroshenko, *Istoriya Ukrayiny*, II, 213–214; and Kirimal, pp. 229–30.

99. Kirimal (p. 231) maintains that the blockade hurt the Crimea seriously, while Pasmanik (pp. 104–105) argues that its effectiveness was limited because the Ukrainian custom officials were rather lax in fulfilling their duties.

100. Groener to Mumm, Division Ia 2518/18, Headquarters of the Army Group Eichhorn, July 20, 1918, *GFOA*. No. 143.

101. Kirimal, p. 231, and the sources cited therein.

102. Mumm's report on his meeting with Doroshenko, J. No. 4842, Kiev, July 26, 1918, *GFOA*. No. 143.

103. Mumm (Kiev) to Foreign Office (Berlin), Telegram No. 1370, July 29, 1918, *ibid.*

104. Groener to Mumm, Ia No. 3600/18, Kiev, August 8, 1918; and Mumm to Groener, Kiev, August 11, 1918, *ibid.*

105. Ludendorff (Great Headquarters) to Hintze (Berlin), M.J. No. 35133 P.I., August 15, 1918, *ibid.*

106. Foreign Office (Berlin) to Mumm (Kiev), Telegram No. 1109, August 24, 1918; Foreign Office memorandum No. A 35722, August 24, 1918; and Hintze (Berlin) to Berckheim (Great Headquarters), Telegram No. 2065, August 28, 1918, "A message from General Ludendorff," *ibid.*

107. Mumm (Kiev) to Stumm (Berlin), August 29, 1918, *GFOA*. No. 53.

108. Kirimal, pp. 238–39.

109. For the discussion of Talat Pasha's stay in Berlin see *ibid.*, pp. 239–41.

110. *Ibid.*, p. 240.

111. Hintze (Berlin) to Berckheim (Kiev) and Lersner (Pera), No. A 37670, September 9, 1918, (A report on his talks with Talat Pasha concerning the Crimea), *GFOA*. No. 143.

112. Mumm (Kiev) to Foreign Office (Berlin), Telegram No. 1835, September 13, 1918, (A report on the Supreme Army Command's message presumably to German military representatives in Kiev), *ibid.*

113. Hintze (Berlin) to Lersner (Great Headquarters), Telegram No. 1024, September 2, 1918, (Directives for the forthcoming Kaiser-Hetman talks), *GFOA.* Nos. 53 and 143.

114. Lersner (Great Headquarters) to Foreign Office (Berlin), Telegram No. 2100, September 12, 1918, (A report on the talks between General Ludendorff and the Hetman), *ibid.*

115. Sulkevich (Crimea) to Tatishchev (Berlin), A 38351, September 6, 1918, *GFOA.* No. 143; and Kirimal, p. 243. See also Mumm (Kiev) to Foreign Office (Berlin), Telegram No. 1811, September 11, 1918, (A report on his talks with Lyzohub); Mumm (Kiev) to Foreign Office (Berlin), Telegram No. 1826, September 12, 1918; and Mumm (Kiev) to Hertling (Berlin), Telegram No. 1825, September 12, 1918, all in *GFOA.* No. 143.

116. Mumm (Kiev) to Foreign Office (Berlin), Telegram No. 1827, September 13, 1918, *ibid.*

117. Groener, *Lebenserinnerungen,* p. 396.

118. Kirimal, pp. 207–208.

119. This was exactly the order in which these national groups were listed, the Ukrainians again being excluded. Consul General Thiel (Kiev) to Foreign Office (Berlin), Telegram No. 1854, September 14, 1918, *GFOA.* No. 143.

120. *Ibid.*

121. Thiel (Kiev) to Foreign Office (Berlin), Telegram No. 1900, September 21, 1918, *ibid.*

122. Thiel (Kiev) to Foreign Office (Berlin), Telegram No. 1863, September 16, 1918; and Telegrams Nos. 1882 and 1908, September 19 and 22, 1918, resp., *ibid.*

123. Thiel (Kiev) to Foreign Office (Berlin), Telegram No. 1920, September 23, 1918, *ibid.*

124. Thiel (Kiev) to Foreign Office (Berlin), Telegram No. 1914, September 23, 1918, *ibid.*

125. Thiel (Kiev) to Foreign Office (Berlin), Telegram No. 1958, September 27, 1918; and Sulkevich to Akhmatovich, Head of the Crimean delegation in Kiev, October 1, 1918, *ibid.*

126. They were Friedmann, minister of communication in the Sulkevich administration, former minister of agriculture, Thomas Rapp, and one Nefer, Kirimal, pp. 244–45.

127. Corps Headquarters No. 52 (Crimea) to Army Group Kiev, Ia No. 540, early October, 1918, *GFOA.* No. 143.

128. Kirimal, pp. 248–49.
129. Thiel (Kiev) to Foreign Office (Berlin), Telegram No. 2041, October 10, 1918, *GFOA*. No. 143.
130. Thiel (Kiev) to Foreign Office (Berlin), Telegram No. 2084, October 16, 1918, *ibid.*
131. Berchem (Kiev) to Foreign Office (Berlin), Telegram No. 2188, October 29, 1918, *GFOA*. Nos. 143 and 188; and Telegram No. 2208, October 31, 1918, *GFOA*. Nos. 142 and 144.
132. Berchem (Kiev) to Foreign Office (Berlin), Telegram No. 2272, November 7, 1918, *GFOA*. No. 143.
133. Berchem (Kiev) to Foreign Office (Berlin), Telegram No. 2319, November 12, 1918; and German Consulate (Nikolaev) to the Imperial Chancellor (Berlin), J. No. 1017/18, K. No. 62, November 12, 1918, *ibid.* Kirimal (p. 276) maintains that General Kosch's declaration and the fall of the Sulkevich regime took place on November 16, 1918.
134. This included the encouragement of repatriation of the Crimean Tatars from other areas into the Peninsula (Kirimal, p. 109).

Chapter XI: Disengagement and Collapse: The Fall of the Hetmanate and the End of the Occupation

1. Lersner (Great Headquarters) to Foreign Office (Berlin), Telegram No. 693, March 31, 1918, *GFOA*. No. 36.
2. Mumm (Kiev) to Foreign Office (Berlin), Telegram No. 811, Secret, June 1, 1918, *Die deutsche Okkupation*, pp. 184–85 (Doc. No. 79).
3. Arnold Margolin, p. 32.
4. Berchem (Kiev) to Foreign Office (Berlin), Telegram No. 1264, July 15, 1918, *GFOA*. No. 3630.
5. Ohnesseit (Odessa) to Hertling (Berlin), K. No. 30, June 21, 1918, *GFOA*. No. 52; and Ohnesseit (Odessa) to Hertling (Berlin), K. No. 170, Secret, November 10, 1918, *GFOA*. No. 99 and *Die deutsche Okkupation*, pp. 223–24 (Doc. No. 101).
6. Arz (Baden) to Burián (Vienna), June 13, 1918, "General Alfred Krauss's Report on the Ukraine," *Die deutsche Okkupation*, pp. 79–82 (Doc. No. 29).
7. Burián (Vienna) to Forgách (Kiev), Telegram No. 464, Secret, June 21, 1918, and Forgách (Kiev) to Burián (Vienna), Telegram No. 602, Secret, June 23, 1918, *Politisches Archiv (Vienna)*, XIV, 412.
8. Foreign Office representative at the Kaiser's headquarters to

Michaelis (Berlin), Telegram No. 770, October 12, 1917, "A message from General Ludendorff," *GFOA*. No. 109.

9. Mumm (Kiev) to Hertling (Berlin), Telegram (no number), Confidential, May 13, 1918, and Mumm (Kiev) to Hertling (Berlin), K. No. 188, May 14, 1918, both in *GFOA*. No. 37.

10. Nykyfor Hirnyak, *Polkovnyk Vasyl' Vyshyvanyi* [Colonel Basil the Embroidered], pp. 10, 19–20.

11. Kaiser Karl (Vienna) to Archduke Wilhelm (Alexandrovsk, Ukraine), a personal handwritten letter dated May 25, 1918, (this was the Kaiser's answer to Wilhelm's notes of May 9 and 11), in Marsovszky to Burián, Telegram No. 156, Secret, May 26, 1918, *Politisches Archiv* (*Vienna*), VIII, 146. An abridged version of this note is also available in *Die deutsche Okkupation*, p. 181 (Doc. No. 77).

12. Kaiser Karl to Kaiser Wilhelm II, July 1918, no number, *Politisches Archiv* (*Vienna*), VIII, 146.

13. See, for example, General Cramon (Kiev) to Supreme Army Command (Spa), Division Ia. No. 1687/18, Secret, May 26, 1918, *GFOA*. No. 52; Forgách (Kiev) to Burián (Vienna), Telegram No. 499, Very secret, June 1, 1918, *Politisches Archiv* (*Vienna*), VIII, 146–47, and an unnumbered "very secret" telegram dated June 16, 1918, *ibid.*, pp. 148–49. Also, Burián (Vienna) to Forgách (Kiev), Telegram No. 491, Very secret, June 26, 1918, *ibid.*, p. 153.

14. See, for example, Forgách (Kiev) to Burián (Vienna), Very secret, Telegrams Nos.: no number, 604, and 658, June 16, 24, and July 9, 1918, resp., *Politisches Archiv* (*Vienna*), VIII, 148–149, 152–54.

15. Burián (Vienna) to Forgách (Kiev), Telegram No. 491, Very secret, June 26, 1918; and Forgách (Kiev) to Burián (Vienna), Telegram No. 658, Very secret, July 9, 1918, *ibid.*, pp. 153–54. See also Wedel (Vienna) to Foreign Office (Berlin), Telegram No. 451, July 8, 1918, *GFOA*. No. 52.

16. Lersner (Great Headquarters) to Foreign Office (Berlin), Telegram No. 409, August 8, 1918, *GFOA*. No. 53.

17. Trautmannsdorff (Baden) to Burián (Vienna), Telegram No. 31640, August 3, 1918, *Politisches Archiv* (*Vienna*), VIII, 154–155.

18. *Ibid.*

19. Forgách (Kiev) to Burián (Vienna), Telegram No. 791, Secret, August 11, 1918, *ibid.*, pp. 156–58.

20. Mumm (Kiev) to Foreign Office (Berlin), Telegram No. 1520, Secret, August 11, 1918, *GFOA*. No. 53; and Bussche (Berlin)

to Berckheim (Great Headquarters), Telegram No. 1948, August 14, 1918, *ibid.*

21. Forgách (Kiev) to Burián (Vienna), Telegram No. 851, Very secret, August 23, 1918; and Trautmannsdorff (Baden) to Burián (Vienna), Telephone message No. 32211, Very secret, August 23, 1918, *Politisches Archiv (Vienna)*, VIII, 161–62, 164.

22. Forgách (Kiev) to Burián (Vienna), Telegram No. 912, Secret, September 3, 1918, *ibid.*, p. 170; and Mumm (Kiev) to Foreign Office (Berlin), Telegram No. 1730, September 4, 1918, *GFOA.* No. 1520.

23. Mumm (Kiev) to Foreign Office (Berlin), Telegram No. 1776, September 8, 1918, *GFOA.* No. 1520.

24. Zitkovszky (Odessa) to Foreign Office (Vienna), Telegram No. 31, October 9, 1918, *Politisches Archiv (Vienna)*, VIII, 172.

25. Report on the meeting of the Royal Prussian State Ministry held on September 3, 1918, in Berlin, signed by Heinrichs, Doc. No. AS 4743, September 26, 1918, *GFOA.* No. 99. On the size of German occupation forces in the east at this point see Kuhl in *Die Ursachen,* fourth series, III (4), 23.

26. Kuhl in *ibid.*

27. Burián (Vienna), to Forgách (Kiev), Telegram No. 541, Urgent, Secret, August 18, 1918, *Politisches Archiv (Vienna)*, VI B, 173.

28. *Berliner Tageblatt*, September 13, 1918.

29. Groener, *Lebenserinnerungen,* p. 413 (report on his meeting with the Kaiser on September 24, 1918).

30. Lindemann (Kiev) to Bussche (Berlin), no number, September 27, 1918, *GFOA.* No. 99.

31. Maximilian, Prince of Baden, *The Memoirs*, II, 34–35.

32. Report of the Foreign Armies Division of the General Staff of the Army, Secret, no number, October 6, 1918, *GFOA.* No. 99.

33. Thiel (Kiev) to Foreign Office (Berlin), Telegram No. 2008, October 7, 1918, *ibid.*

34. German Ukraine-Delegation (Kiev) to Hertling (Berlin), Telegram (number illegible), October 2, 1918, *ibid.*

35. Milyukov, p. 198 (entry for October 10, 1918), and pp. 188–90 (entry for October 2).

36. Solf (Berlin) to either Berchem or Thiel (Kiev), Telegram No. 1449, October 10, 1918, *Die deutsche Okkupation,* p. 160 (Doc. No. 68).

37. Thiel (Kiev) to Foreign Office (Berlin), Telegram No. 2049, October 11, 1918, *ibid.*, pp. 161–62 (Doc. No. 69) and *GFOA.* No. 99.

38. Thiel (Kiev) to Foreign Office (Berlin), Telegram No. (illegible), October 11, 1918, and Telegram No. 2046, October 11, 1918, *GFOA.* No. 99.
39. Thiel (Kiev) to Foreign Office (Berlin), Telegram No. 2078, October 15, 1918, *Die deutsche Okkupation,* pp. 166–67 (Doc. No. 71).
40. For a detailed discussion of these developments see Doroshenko, *Istoriya Ukrayiny,* II, 395–403. See also Thiel (Kiev) to Foreign Office (Berlin), Telegram No. 2091, October 17, 1918, *GFOA.* No. 99; and two lists of candidates for the Hetman cabinet, dated October 8, 1918, and bearing von Thiel's signature, in *Die deutsche Okkupation,* pp. 214–15 (Docs. No. 95 and 96).
41. See, for example, Fürstenberg (Kiev) to Burián (Berlin), No. 114/Pol., Confidential, October 15, 1918; and Telegram No. 1114, October 16, 1918, *Politisches Archiv (Vienna),* VI B, 328–329 and 335, resp.
42. Berchem (Kiev) to Foreign Office (Berlin), Telegram No. 2126, October 22, 1918, *GFOA.* No. 99.
43. Berchem (Kiev) to Foreign Office (Berlin), Telegram No. 2209, October 31, 1918, *Die deutsche Okkupation,* pp. 217–18 (Doc. No. 98).
44. For Groener's views on the retention of German forces in the east, see: Groener, *Lebenserinnerungen,* p. 411; and Thiel (Kiev) to Foreign Office (Berlin), Telegram No. 2052, October 12, 1918, *GFOA.* No. 99. The views of the Reich's principal governing bodies are expressed in the following: Bismarck (Great Headquarters) to Imperial Chancellor (Berlin), "A message from the Chief of General Staff," Telegram No. A 42628, October 11, 1918; Hintze (Great Headquarters) to Foreign Office (Berlin), Telegram No. 2464, October 16, 1918; The War Food Department (Kriegsernährungsamt) to Foreign Office, Berlin, October 16, 1918; Department of National Economy (Reichswirtschaftsamt) to Foreign Office, Berlin, October 17, 1918, all in *GFOA.* No. 99.
45. Count Roedern to the Chief of General Staff, Doc. No. IV A 6347, October 23, 1918, *ibid.*
46. Doroshenko, *Istoriya Ukrayiny,* II, 405.
47. Groener, *Lebenserinnerungen,* p. 411.
48. Berchem (Kiev) to Foreign Office (Berlin), Telegram No. 2197, October 31, 1918, *GFOA.* No. 99; Fürstenberg (Kiev) to Foreign Office (Vienna), Telegram No. 1165, Secret, October 30, 1918, and German Embassy (Vienna) to Foreign Office of the Austro-

Hungarian Empire, Note No. B.A. 2551, October 30, 1918, *Politisches Archiv (Vienna)*, VIII, 74 and 75, resp.

49. Mumm (Kiev) to Foreign Office (Berlin), Telegram No. 506, May 4, 1918, and Telegram No. 530, May 6, 1918, both in *GFOA*. No. 37.

50. Lersner (Great Headquarters) to Foreign Office (Berlin), Telegram No. 1168, May 20, 1918, *ibid.*

51. Austrian Supreme Army Command (Baden) to Ukrainian General Staff (Kiev), Communication No. 146.603, August 6, 1918, *Politisches Archiv (Vienna)*, VIII, 16–19.

52. Foreign Office (Berlin) to Berckheim (Great Headquarters), no number, late May, 1918, *GFOA*. No. 37; Berckheim (Great Headquarters) to Foreign Office (Berlin), "A message from General Ludendorff," Telegram No. 1284, May 30, 1918; and Mumm (Kiev) to Foreign Office (Berlin), Telegram No. 849, June 4, 1918, *ibid.* See also Doroshenko, *Istoriya Ukrayiny*, II, 234–235.

53. Foreign Office (Berlin) to Berckheim (Great Headquarters), (For General Ludendorff), no number, May, 1918, *GFOA*. No. 37.

54. For the full text of this agreement, dated June 1, 1918, see *GFOA*. No. 37; and Mumm (Kiev) to Hertling (Berlin), Telegram No. 497, July 16, 1918, *GFOA*. No. 53.

55. Mumm (Kiev) to Hertling (Berlin), Telegram No. 555, August 1, 1918, *GFOA*. No. 53.

56. Doroshenko, *Istoriya Ukrayiny*, II, 235, 250–51.

57. For the complete text of this document, dated September 10, 1918, see *GFOA*. No. 53.

58. Ludendorff to Hertling on June 9, 1918, Ludendorff, *The General Staff*, II, 572.

59. Mumm (Kiev) to Foreign Office (Berlin), Telegram No. 685, August 20, 1918, *GFOA*. No. 53.

60. Thiel (Kiev) to Hertling (Berlin), Telegram No. 850, September 19, 1918, *GFOA*. No. 99.

61. Burián (Vienna) to Trautmannsdorff (Baden), Telegram No. 317, September 20, 1918, *Politisches Archiv (Vienna)*, VIII, 127–29. See also Beyer, pp. 55–56.

62. Ludendorff's interest in the organization of a Ukrainian army at this point is recorded in General Cramon to General Arz, Telegram No. 148.252, October 4, 1918, *Politisches Archiv (Vienna)*, VIII, 54. For General Groener's recommendations, see Waldbott (Kiev) to Austrian Supreme Army Command (Baden), Note No.

3889, October 9, 1918, *ibid.*, pp. 53–54; and Hintze (Great Headquarters) to Foreign Office (Berlin), "A message from General Ludendorff," Telegram No. 2454, October 15, 1918, *GFOA.* No. 99.

63. Doroshenko, *Istoriya Ukrayiny*, II, 248; Stefaniv, pp. 105–106; and Udovychenko, p. 42.

64. Chief of the General Staff of the Army, Secret, Doc. No. 19210, Great Headquarters, November 1, 1918, *GFOA.* No. 99.

65. See, for example, N. Krishevskii, "V Krymu" [In the Crimea], p. 99; and V. K. Zhukov, *Chernomorskii flot* [The Black Sea Fleet], chap. VII.

66. Kirimal, p. 201.

67. See chapters VIII and X of this study for a general discussion of the Ukraine's foreign policy goals during the period of German hegemony in the east.

68. Secretary of the Navy to Secretary for Foreign Affairs, Doc. No. 6568, Berlin, April 26, 1918, *GFOA.* No. 37.

69. For further details see *US Foreign Relations, 1918; Russia*, II, 512–13. The Foreign Office's proposal that the Black Sea fleet be returned to Soviet Russia in return for certain economic concessions is contained "Memorandum" No. A 18575, May 1, 1918, *GFOA.* Nos. 143 and 147. (The author of this plan was Trautmann.)

70. For Ludendorff's earlier views on the Black Sea, especially on the disposition of the Russian fleet, see the following: Lersner (Great Headquarters) to Foreign Office (Berlin), Telegram No. 1118, May 16, 1918, *GFOA.* No. 143, and Telegram No. 1167, May 20, 1918, *ibid.*, No. 37; Chief of the General Staff of the Army, Political Division (Great Headquarters) to Colonel Winterfeldt (no place), Doc. No. N.J. R 419 P., June 10, 1918, *GFOA.* No. 138; Berckheim (Great Headquarters) to Foreign Office (Berlin), Telegram No. 1416, June 13, 1918, *GFOA.* No. 37; and Mühlmann, pp. 193–94.

71. Mumm (Kiev) to Foreign Office (Berlin), Telegram No. 598, May 14, 1918, *GFOA.* No. 37.

72. Mumm (Kiev) to Foreign Office (Berlin), Telegram No. 847, June 3, 1918, *GFOA.* No. 418, and Telegram No. 1102, June 27, 1918, *ibid.*, No. 52; and Mumm's memorandum dated Berlin, June 22, 1918, *ibid.*

73. Minutes of the imperial council held at Spa on July 2–3, 1918, Doc. No. Rk. 197 prepared at the Great Headquarters, *GFOA.* No. 1500.

74. Mumm (Kiev) to Foreign Office (Berlin), Telegram No. 1172,

July 6, 1918 (a report on the Supreme Command's views), *GFOA*. No. 52.

75. *Ibid.*; and Thiel to Rohrbach, August 1, 1918, cited in Henry Cord Meyer, "Germans in the Ukraine," p. 110.

76. See, for example, Udovychenko, p. 43.

77. The Chief of Naval Staff to Secretary for Foreign Affairs, Doc. No. 28089 B II, Berlin, September 25, 1918, *GFOA*. No. 99.

78. Thiel (Kiev) to Foreign Office (Berlin), Telegram No. 1994, October 5, 1918, *ibid.*

79. Department of the Navy to Foreign Office, Doc. No. A IV 17173, Berlin, October 15, 1918, *ibid.*

80. Berchem (Kiev) to Foreign Office (Berlin), Telegram No. 2305, November 9, 1918, *GFOA*. No. 143.

81. Ludendorff, *The General Staff*, II, 572.

82. Mumm (Kiev) to Hertling (Berlin), Telegram No. 361, June 15, 1918, *GFOA*. No. 147.

83. For further details see Milyukov, pp. 16–27, 84 *ff.*; Mumm (Kiev) to Foreign Office (Berlin), Telegram No. 1055, June 22, 1918, *GFOA*. No. 147; and Berchem (Kiev) to Foreign Office (Berlin), Telegram No. 1253, July 13, 1918, *ibid.* A reliable discussion of Milyukov's activities in Kiev at this point, and the development of the Russian movement in the Ukraine in general, is available in Brinkley, pp. 43–45, and chap. II.

84. Milyukov, pp. 78–116, 118; Mumm (Kiev) to Foreign Office (Berlin), Telegram No. 1156, July 3, 1918, *GFOA*. No. 147; and Imperial and Royal Ambassador (Berlin) to Foreign Office (Vienna), Telegram No. 417, Confidential, July 5, 1918, *GFOA*. No. 52.

85. See, for example, the Royal and Imperial Command of the Eastern Army to Forgách (Kiev), Memorandum No. Op. 6530, July 8, 1918; and Forgách (Kiev) to Burián (Vienna), Doc. No. 71/Pol., July 17, 1918, *Politisches Archiv (Vienna)*, VI B, 77, 76.

86. Doroshenko, *Istoriya Ukrayiny*, II, 158 *ff.*

87. Groener, *Lebenserinnerungen*, p. 402.

88. Mumm (Kiev) to Foreign Office (Berlin), Telegram No. 1354, July 26, 1918, *GFOA*. No. 144; and S. Dolenga, *Skoropadshchyna* [The Skoropadsky Period], pp. 78–86. For a more complete account of the White Russian movement in the entire southwest, including the Don, Kuban, and Caucasus, see Brinkley.

89. A secret order issued by Field Marshal von Eichhorn to officers

of the German army in the Ukraine, dated June 27, 1918, *GFOA*. No. 52.

90. Mumm (Kiev) to Foreign Office (Berlin), Telegram No. 631, May 16, 1918, *GFOA*. No. 37.

91. Chief of Naval Staff to Foreign Office, Secret, No. 19342 B II, Berlin, July 6, 1918, *GFOA*. No. 147; and General Kress (Tiflis) to Foreign Office (Berlin), Telegram No. 21, July 25, 1918, *ibid*. See also Brinkley, chap. II.

92. See, for example, Milyukov, p. 31 (the entry for June 23, 1918); and Mumm (Kiev) to Foreign Office (Berlin), Telegram No. 1559, Rush! August 17, 1918, *GFOA*. No. 144.

93. Forgách (Kiev) to Burián (Vienna), Communication No. 71/Pol., July 17, 1918, *Politisches Archiv (Vienna)*, VI B, 76–7.

94. Hintze (Berlin) to Mumm (Kiev), Telegram No. 1069, August 20, 1918, *GFOA*. No. 147; and Mumm (Kiev) to Foreign Office (Berlin), Telegram No. 1589, August 21, 1918, *ibid*. No. 144.

95. Mumm (Kiev) to Foreign Office (Berlin), Telegram No. 1595, August 21, 1918; and Telegram Nos. 1599 and 1604, August 22, 1918, *GFOA*. Nos. 53 and 144.

96. Mumm (Kiev) to Foreign Office (Berlin), Telegram No. 1580, August 20, 1918, *GFOA*. No. 144; and P. N. Krasnov, "Vsevelikoe Voisko Donskoe," p. 209. General Groener's views are discussed in Mumm (Kiev) to Foreign Office (Berlin), Telegram No. 1595, August 21, 1918, *GFOA*. No. 144.

97. Mumm (Kiev) to Foreign Office (Berlin), Telegram No. 1604, August 22, 1918, *ibid.*; Ivan Vyslots'kyi (ed.), *Het'man Pavlo Skoropads'kyi v osvitlenni ochevydtsiv* [Hetman Pavlo Skororopadsky as Seen by His Contemporaries], pp. 23–24; and Pasminik, pp. 106, 109.

98. Bassewitz (Pleskau) to Foreign Office (Berlin), Telegram No. 716, September 9, 1918; and Waldburg (Constantinople) to Foreign Office (Berlin), Telegram No. 1470, September 9, 1918, *GFOA*. No. 144.

99. P. N. Krasnov, p. 209; V. I. Gurko, "Iz Petrograda cherez Moskvu," [From Petrograd Through Moscow], p. 30. Another similar formation, the Astrakhan Army, according to Count Bobrinskii, numbered a mere 800 men. Cited in Milyukov, pp. 185–86.

100. On the Southern Army see G. Pokrovskii, *Denikinshchina* [The Denikin Period], p. 36; G. N. Laikhtenbergskii, "Kak nachalas' 'Yuzhnaya Armiya'" [The Origin of the "Southern Army"], pp. 180–81; and Brinkley, chap. II.

101. Laikhtenbergskii, p. 181. According to Brinkley (p. 57), this new force incorporated all three "armies" of the southwest and was known as the "South Russian Army."
102. For example, Beyer, p. 53.
103. Fürstenberg (Kiev) to Foreign Office (Vienna), Telegram No. 1115, October 16, 1918, *Die deutsche Okkupation*, p. 213 (Doc. No. 94) and *Politisches Archiv (Vienna)*, VIII, 50; and Berchem (Kiev) to Foreign Office (Berlin), Telegram No. 2209, October 31, 1918, *Die deutsche Okkupation*, p. 218 (Doc. No. 98) and *GFOA*. No. 99.
104. Hintze (Great Headquarters) to Foreign Office (Berlin), Telegram No. 2669, November 1, 1918, (report on the Supreme Army Command's communication to its representative in the Don, Major von Cochenhausen), *GFOA*. Nos. 99 and 144.
105. Berchem (Kiev) to Foreign Office (Berlin), Telegram No. 2215, November 1, 1918, *GFOA*. No. 99.
106. Krasnov, p. 237 *ff.*; Doroshenko, *Istoriya Ukrayiny*, II, 411–12.
107. Even General Denikin admitted in his memoirs that political circles of the Kuban showed "strong Ukrainian tendencies." A. I. Denikin, *Ocherki russkoi smuty* [Notes on the Russian Time of Troubles], III, 69. For a more comprehensive treatment of the Volunteer Army's activities in the Kuban, see Brinkley, chaps. II and III. A useful source on the Ukrainian movement in the Kuban is the work of one of its leaders, Vasyl' Ivanys, entitled *Stezhkamy zhyttya: spohady* [The Paths of My Life: Reminiscences], 5 vols.
108. Berchem (Kiev) to Foreign Office (Berlin), Telegram No. 2243, November 4, 1918, *GFOA*. No. 99.
109. Foreign Office (Berlin) to Berckheim (Great Headquarters), Telegram No. 2942, November 3, 1918; and Berchem (Kiev) to Foreign Office (Berlin), Telegram No. 2299, November 8, 1918, *GFOA*. No. 99.
110. Osyp Nazaruk, *Rik na Velykii Ukrayini* [One Year in the Central Ukraine], p. 6 *ff.*
111. Berchem (Kiev) to Foreign Office (Berlin), Telegram No. 2209, October 31, 1918, and Telegram No. 2811, November 10, 1918, *GFOA*. No. 99.
112. Hoffmann, *War Diaries*, I, 246.
113. Maximilian, Prince of Baden, II, 135.
114. *Ibid.*, p. 120.
115. *Ibid.*, p. 274.
116. Berchem (Kiev) to Foreign Office (Berlin), Telegram No. 2320, November 13, 1918, *GFOA*. No. 99.

117. Berchem (Kiev) to Foreign Office (Berlin), Telegram No. 2348, November 14, 1918, *ibid.*
118. For the full text of the Hetman's edict of November 14, 1918, see Appendix G.
119. Berchem (Kiev) to Foreign Office (Berlin), Telegram No. 2356, November 15, 1918, *GFOA.* No. 99; and Telegram No. 2366, November 17, 1918, *ibid.*
120. Thiel (Kiev) to Foreign Office (Berlin), No. A 48973, November 17, 1918, *GFOA.* No. 99.
121. *Ibid.*; and Thiel's letter to Paul Rohrbach, dated Kiev, November 20, 1918, cited in Henry Cord Meyer, "Germans in the Ukraine," pp. 111–13.
122. Berchem (Kiev) to Foreign Office (Berlin), Telegram No. 2424, November 25, 1918, *GFOA.* No. 99.
123. Doroshenko, *Istoriya Ukrayiny*, II, 421–22.
124. Berchem (Kiev) to Foreign Office (Berlin), Telegram No. 2428, November 26, 1918, and an unsigned memorandum addressed to the Under-Secretary of State Eduard David, Doc. No. A 50607, Berlin, November 27, 1918, both in *GFOA.* No. 99.
125. Berchem (Kiev) to Foreign Office (Berlin), Telegram No. 2439, November 28, 1918, *ibid.*
126. Berchem (Kiev) to Foreign Office (Berlin), Telegram No. 2444, November 30, 1918, *Die deutsche Okkupation,* pp. 226–27 (Doc. No. 103); and Consul Emile Henno's telegram sent to Major Jarosch and the Council of German Soldiers in Kiev, *ibid.* See also Brinkley, pp. 78–87.
127. Berchem (Kiev) to Foreign Office (Berlin), Telegram No. 2462, December 4, 1918, *GFOA.* No. 99.
128. Berchem (Kiev) to Foreign Office (Berlin), no number, December 5, 1918, *ibid.*
129. Lersner (Spa) to Foreign Office (Berlin), Telegram No. 213, December 11, 1918, *ibid.*
130. Berchem (Kiev) to Foreign Office (Berlin), Telegram No. 2499, December 12, 1918, *ibid.*
131. Doroshenko, *Istoriya Ukrayiny*, II, 424.
132. Ivan Isayiv (ed.), *Za Ukrayinu, podorozh V. P. Het'manycha Danyla Skoropads'koho do Zluchenykh Derzhav Ameryky i Kanady* [For the Ukraine; The Trip of Hetmanych Danylo Skoropadsky to USA and Canada], p. 23.
133. Berchem (Kiev) to Foreign Office (Berlin), Telegram No. 2504, December 14, 1918, *GFOA.* No. 99.

BIBLIOGRAPHY

I. Unpublished Documents

German Foreign Office Archives—cited in the notes as *GFOA*. The documents contained in this collection constituted the principal source in the preparation of this book. Formerly these secret files of the Reich's Foreign Office were known as "Captured German Documents" and were deposited in the Archives of the United States of America, Washington, D.C., and several locations in Great Britain. Before their return to the West German Federal Archives in Bonn in the late 1950's, the documents were microfilmed and are now available in that form in Washington. Specifically, the following microfilm reels were used in this study: Nos. 4, 5, 21, 27, 35, 36, 37, 43, 52, 53, 55, 85, 99, 107, 109, 110, 118, 124, 138, 142, 143, 144, 147, 188, 418, 1498, 1499, 1500, 1787, 1788, 1789, 1790, 1791, 1792, 1794, 1796, 1800, 2091, 2116, 2128, 3270, 3630, 3632, 3633, 3634, 3641.

Politisches Archiv (*Vienna*), documents from the Austrian Foreign Office archives available in their original form in Vienna. The official title of this collection is *Österreichisches Staatsarchiv, Abteilung Haus-, Hof-, und Staatsarchiv, Politisches Archiv*. The documents from this collection dealing with the Ukraine have been reproduced by the W. K. Lypynsky East European Research Institute in Philadelphia; it is this particular collection that I used in the preparation of this book. Volume numbers shown in the notes refer to the folders as arranged by the Philadelphia Institute prior to the appearance of this collection in print. These documents have been published under the title *Ereignisse in der Ukraine, 1914–1922*. 3 vols. Horn, Austria: F. Berger, 1966–1968.

II. Published Documents

Bunyan, James (ed.). *Intervention, Civil War, and Communism in Russia*. Baltimore: The Johns Hopkins University Press, 1936.

Bunyan, James, and Fischer, Harold H. (eds.). *The Bolshevik Revolution*, Stanford: Stanford University Press, 1934.

Die deutsche Okkupation der Ukraine. See Gorkii, M., *et al.* below.

Dörnberg, S., *et al.* (eds.). *Sovetsko-germanskie otnosheniya ot peregovorov v Brest-Litovske do podpisaniya Rapal'skogo Dogovora: sbornik dokumentov* [Soviet-German Relations from the Brest-Litovsk Negotiations to the Conclusion of the Treaty of Rapallo: Collection of Documents]. Vol. I, the years 1917–1918. Moscow: Izdatel'stvo Politicheskoi Literatury, 1968.

Friedensverträge mit der Ukraine, Russland und Finnland samt den dazugehörigen wirtschaftlichen Vereinbarungen. Vienna: Generalkommissariat für Kriegs- und Übergangswirtschaft im K. K. Handelsministerium, 1918.

Gorkii, M., Eideman, R., and Mints, I. I. (eds.). *Krakh germanskoi okkupatsii na Ukraine* [The Collapse of the German Occupation in the Ukraine]. Moscow: Ogiz, 1936. This source is also available in German under the title *Die deutsche Okkupation der Ukraine: Geheimdokumente*. Strasbourg: Prométhée, 1937.

Krakh germanskoi okkupasii. See above.

Kreppel, Josef (ed.). *Der Friede im Osten*. Vienna: Der Tag, 1918.

Lutz, Ralph H. (ed.). *The Fall of the German Empire, 1914–1918*. 2 vols. Stanford: Stanford University Press, and London: Oxford University Press, 1932.

Matthias, Erich, and Morsey, Rudolf (eds.). *Der Interfraktionelle Ausschuss, 1917–1918*. Düsseldorf: Droste, 1959.

Mints, I. I., and Gorodetskii, E. W. (eds.). *Dokumenty o razgrome germanskikh okkupantov na Ukraine v 1918 godu* [Documents on the Rout of the German Occupiers in the Ukraine in 1918]. Moscow: Gosudarstvennoye izdatel'stvo politicheskoi literatury, 1942.

Petlyura, Symon. *Statti, lysty i dokumenty* [Articles, Letters and

Documents]. New York: Ukrainian Free Academy of Arts and Sciences in the United States of America, 1956.

Scherer, André, and Grunewald, Jacques (eds.). *L'Allemagne et les problèmes de la paix pendant la Première Guerre Mondiale.* Vol. I. Paris: Presses Universitaires de France, 1962.

Texts of the Ukraine "Peace." Washington, D.C.: United States Department of State, 1918.

United States Senate Documents, 66th Session (1918). *United States Foreign Relations, 1918. Russia II.* Washington, D.C., 1937.

Verhandlungen des Reichstages. Berlin, 1918.

Das Werk des Untersuchungsausschusses der verfassungsgebenden deutschen Nationalversammlung und deutschen Reichstages, 1919–1928: Die Ursachen des deutschen Zusammenbruches im Jahre 1918. Berlin: Deutsche Verlagsgesellschaft für Politik und Geschichte, 1929. (This source is referred to in this study as *Die Ursachen.*)

Zeman, Z. A. B. (ed.). *Germany and the Revolution in Russia, 1915–1918.* (Documents from the Archives of the German Foreign Ministry.) New York: Oxford University Press, 1958.

III. *Memoirs, Diaries, and Biographies*

Arz, Arthur von. *Zur Geschichte des Grossen Krieges.* Vienna, Leipzig, and Munich: Rihola, 1924.

Bismarck, Otto Fürst von. *Gedanken und Erinnerungen.* Stuttgart: Cotta, 1898.

————. *The Man and Statesman: Reflections and Reminiscences of Otto Prince von Bismarck.* 2 vols. Edited and translated by A. J. Butler. London: Smith, Elder, 1898.

Bülow, Bernhard Heinrich Martin, Prince von. *Deutsche Politik.* Berlin: Reimar Hobbing, 1916.

Cantacuzène, Countess Speransky, née [Julia Dent] Grant. *Revolutionary Days: Recollections of Romanoffs and Bolsheviks, 1914–1917.* Boston: Small, Maynard, 1919.

Czernin, Ottokar von. *Im Weltkriege.* Berlin and Vienna: Ullstein, 1919.

————. *In the World War.* London and New York: Harper, 1920.

Denikin, A. I. *Ocherki russkoi smuty* [Notes on the Russian Time of Troubles]. 5 vols. Berlin: "Slovo," 1924–1925.

Doroshenko, Dmytro. *Moyi spomyny pro nedavnye mynule* [My Reminiscences of the Recent Past]. 4 vols. Lviv: Chervona Kalyna, 1923–1924.

Epstein, Fritz T. "Otto Hoetzsch als aussenpolitischer Kommentator während des Ersten Weltkrieges," *Russlandstudien, Gedankenschrift für Otto Hoetzsch.* Stuttgart: Deutsche Verlags-Anstalt, 1957.

Epstein, Klaus. *Matthias Erzberger and the Dilemma of German Democracy.* Princeton: Princeton University Press, 1959.

Erzberger, Matthias. *Erlebnisse im Weltkriege.* Stuttgart and Berlin: Deutsche Verlags-Anstalt, 1920.

Groener, Wilhelm. *Lebenserinnerungen.* Edited by F. F. H. von Gärtringen. Göttingen: Vanderhoeck & Ruprecht, 1957.

Groener-Geyer, Dorothea. *General Groener: Soldat und Staatsmann.* Frankfurt am Main: Societäts-Verlag, 1954.

Helfferich, Karl. *Der Weltkrieg.* 3 vols. Berlin: Ullstein, 1919.

Hertling, Karl von. *Ein Jahr in der Reichskanzlei.* Freiburg: Herdersche Verlagshandlung, 1919.

Heuss, Theodor. *Friedrich Naumann.* Stuttgart and Berlin: Deutsche Verlags-Anstalt, 1937.

Hindenburg, Paul von. *Aus meinem Leben.* Leipzig: Hirzel, 1920.

————. *Out of My Life.* London: Cassel, 1920.

Hirnyak, Nykyfor. *Polkovnyk Vasyl' Vyshyvanyi* [Colonel Basil the Embroidered]. Winnipeg: Mykytyuk, 1956.

Hoffmann, Max. *Der Krieg der versäumten Gelegenheiten.* Munich: Verlag für Kulturpolitik, 1923.

————. *War Diaries and Other Papers.* 2 vols. London: Martin Secker, 1929.

Hutten-Czapski, Bogdan Franz Servatius von. *Sechzig Jahre Politik und Gesellschaft.* 2 vols. Berlin: E. S. Mittler, 1936.

Ivanys, Vasyl'. *Stezhkamy zhyttya: spohady* [The Paths of My Life: Reminiscences]. 5 vols. Neu-Ulm, Germany: Ukrayins'ki Visti, 1959.

Kedryn-Rudnyts'kyi, Ivan (ed.). *Beresteiskyi myr* [The Peace of Brest]. Lviv-Kiev: Chervona Kalyna, 1928.

Kovalevs'kyi, Mykola. *Pry dzherelakh borot'by* [At the Fountain of Our Struggle]. Innsbruck: M. Kovalevsky, 1960.

Krauss, Alfred. *Die Ursachen unserer Niederlage.* Munich: J. F. Lehmann, 1921.

Kühlmann, Richard von. *Erinnerungen.* Heidelberg: Lambert Schneider, 1948.

Ludendorff, Erich von. *Ludendorff's Own Story.* 2 vols. New York: Harper, 1919.

————. *Meine Kriegserinnerungen.* Berlin: E. S. Mittler, 1926.

Margolin, Arnold D. *From a Political Diary: Russia, Ukraine and*

America, 1905–1945. New York: Columbia University Press, 1946.

Maximilian, Prince of Baden. *The Memoirs of Prince Max of Baden.* 2 vols. London: Constable, 1928.

Mazepa, Isaak. *Ukrayina v ohni i buri revolutsiyi, 1917–1921* [The Ukraine in the Fire and Storm of the Revolution]. 2 vols. [n. p.] Prometei, 1950.

Meinecke, Friedrich von. *Strassburg, Freiburg, Berlin, 1901–1919: Erinnerungen.* Stuttgart: K. F. Köhler, 1949.

Merton, Richard. *Erinnerungswertes aus meinem Leben, das über das Persönliche hinausgeht.* Frankfurt am Main: Fritz Knapp, 1955.

Meyer, Klaus. *Schiemann als politischer Publizist.* Frankfurt am Main: Welt- und Geschichtsbild, 1956.

Michaelis, Georg. *Für Staat und Volk, eine Lebensgeschichte.* Berlin: Furche, 1922.

Müller, Georg Alexander von. *Regierte der Kaiser? Kriegstagebücher, Aufzeichnungen und Briefe des Chefs des Marine-Kabinetts Admiral G. A. v. Müller.* Edited by W. Görlitz Göttingen: Musterschmidt, 1959.

Nazaruk, Osyp. *Rik na Velykii Ukrayini* [One Year in the Central Ukraine]. Vienna: Vydannya "Ukrayins'koho praporu," 1920.

Niemann, Alfred. *Kaiser und Revolution: Die Entscheidungen: Ereignisse im Grossen Hauptquartier.* Berlin: Scherl, 1922.

Nowak, Karl F. (ed.). *Die Aufzeichnungen des Generalmajors Max Hoffmann.* 2 vols. Berlin: Verlag für Kulturpolitik, 1929.

Pasmanik, D. S. *Revolutsionnye gody v Krymu* [Revolutionary Years in the Crimea]. Paris: Imprimerie de Navarre, 1926.

Payer, Friedrich von. *Von Bethmann Hollweg bis Ebert.* Frankfurt am Main: Frankfurter Societäts Druckerei, 1923.

Rathenau, Walter. *Politische Briefe.* Dresden: Karl Reissner, 1929.

Rohrbach, Paul. *Um des Teufels Handschrift: Zwei Menshenalter erlebter Weltgeschichte.* Hamburg: Hans Dulk, 1953.

Ropp, Friedrich von der. *Zwischen gestern und morgen.* Stuttgart: Steinkopf, 1961.

Skoropadsky, Pavlo. "Uryvok zi spomyniv" [A Fragment from Reminiscences]. *Khliborobs'ka Ukrayina* [Agrarian Ukraine], IV and V (1923–25), 3–40 and 31–92.

Skoropys-Ioltukhovs'kyi, Oleksander. "Moyi 'zlochyny' " [My 'Crimes']. *Ibid.*, II (1920–1921), 201–205.

Trotsky, Leon. *My Life.* New York: Scribner's, 1930.

Vynnychenko, Volodymyr. *Vidrodzhennya natsiyi* [The Rebirth of the Nation]. 3 vols. Vienna: Dzvin, 1920.

Westarp, Count Kuno von. *Konservative Politik.* Berlin: Deutsche Verlagsgesellschaft, 1935.

Wilhelm II, German Emperor. *The Kaiser's Memoirs.* Translated by Thomas R. Ybarra. New York: Harper, 1922.

Zeman, Z. A. B., and Scharlau, W. B. *The Merchant of Revolution: The Life of Alexander Israel Helphand (Parvus), 1867–1924.* London: Oxford University Press, 1965.

IV. *General Works and Monographs*

Allen, William E. D. *The Ukraine: A History.* Cambridge (England): The University Press, 1940.

Basler, Werner. *Deutschlands Annexionspolitik in Polen und im Baltikum, 1914–1918.* Berlin: Rütten und Löning, 1962.

Baumgart, Winfried. *Deutsche Ostpolitik, 1918; Von Brest-Litowsk bis zum Ende des Ersten Weltkrieges.* Vienna and Munich: R. Oldenbourg, 1966.

Beyer, Hans J. *Die Mittelmächte und die Ukraine, 1918.* Munich: Isar, 1956.

Blücher, Wipert. *Deutschlands Weg nach Rapallo.* Wiesbaden: Limes, 1951.

Brinkley, George A. *The Volunteer Army and Allied Intervention in South Russia, 1917–1921.* Notre Dame, Indiana: University of Notre Dame Press, 1966.

Carroll, Malcolm E. *Germany and the Great Powers, 1866–1914.* New York: Prentice-Hall, 1938.

Chamberlin, William H. *The Russian Revolution, 1917–1921.* 2 vols. New York: Macmillan, 1935.

Choulguine, Alexander. *L'Ukraine contre Moscou.* Paris: F. Alcan, 1935.

Chubar'yan, Aleksandr O. *Bretskii mir* [The Peace of Brest]. Moscow: "Nauka," 1964.

Conze, Werner. *Polnische Nation und deutsche Politik im Ersten Weltkrieg.* Köln and Gratz: Böhlau, 1958.

Cramon, August von. *Unser österreich-ungarischer Bundesgenosse im Weltkriege.* Berlin: E. S. Mittler, 1920.

Dahlin, Ebba. *French and German Public Opinion on Declared War Aims, 1914–1918.* Stanford: Stanford University Press, 1933.

Daya, Werner. *Der Aufmarsch im Osten, russisch Asien als deutsches Kriegs- und Wirtschaftsziel.* Dachau bei München: Einhorn, 1918.

Dehio, Ludwig. *Germany and World Politics in the Twentieth Century.* New York: Knopf, 1959.

Dimanshtein, S. M. *Revolutsiya i natsional'nyi vopros* [The Revolution and the National Question]. 3 vols. Moscow: Ogiz, 1930.

Direnberger, Erwin. *Die Beziehungen zwischen Oberster Heeresleitung und Reichsleitung von 1914–1918.* Berlin: Junker & Dünhaupt, 1936.

Dolenga. S. *Skoropadshchyna* [The Skoropadsky Period]. Warsaw: M. Kunyts'kyi, 1934.

Doroshenko, Dmytro. *Die Ukraine und das Reich.* Leipzig: Hirzel, 1942.

————. *History of the Ukraine.* Translated by Hanna Keller. Edmonton, Alberta: The Institute Press, 1939.

————. *Istoriya Ukrayiny, 1917–1923* [History of the Ukraine, 1917–1923]. 2 vols. Uzhhorod: Svoboda, 1930.

Faure, Alexander. "Das deutsche Kolonistentum in Russland," *Westrussland in seiner Bedeutung für die Entwicklung Mitteleuropas.* Leipzig and Berlin: Teubner, 1917.

Freund, Gerald. *Unholy Alliance: Russian-German Relations from the Treaty of Brest-Litovsk to the Treaty of Berlin.* New York: Harcourt and Brace, 1957.

Fischer, Fritz. *Griff nach der Weltmacht; Die Kriegszielpolitik des kaiserlichen Deutschland, 1914–1918.* Düsseldorf: Droste, 1961.

Gatzke, Hans W. *Germany's Drive to the West.* Baltimore: The Johns Hopkins University Press, 1950.

Glaise-Horstenau, Edmund von. *The Collapse of the Austro-Hungarian Empire.* London: J. M. Dent; New York: E. P. Dutton, 1930.

————. *Die Katastrophe.* Zurich: Amalthea, 1929.

Glaise-Horstenau, Edmund von, and and Kiszling, Rudolf (eds.). *Österreich-Ungarns letzter Krieg.* Vienna: Verlag der militärwissenschaftlichen Mitteilungen, 1938.

Göhring, Martin. *Bismarcks Erbern, 1890–1945.* Wiesbaden: Franz Steiner, 1959.

Gratz, Gustav, and Schüller, Richard. *The Economic Policy of Austria-Hungary During the War in Its External Relations.* New Haven: Yale University Press, 1928.

Groener, Wilhelm. *Der Weltkrieg und seine Probleme.* Berlin: Georg Stilke, 1920.

Grumbach, Salomon. *Das annexionistische Deutschland.* Lausanne: Payot, 1917.

Hahlweg, Werner. *Der Diktatfrieden von Brest-Litowsk 1918 und die*

Bolschewistische Weltrevolution. Münster: Aschendorff, 1960.
————. *Lenins Rückkehr nach Russland.* Leiden: Studien zur Geschichte Osteuropas, 1957.
Hausner, Arthur W. *Die Polenpolitik der Mittelmächte und die österreichisch-ungarische Militärverwaltung in Polen während des Weltkrieges.* Vienna: Brüder Hollinek, 1935.
Hobohm, Martin, and Rohrbach, Paul. *Die Alldeutschen.* Berlin: Engelmann, 1919.
Hoetzsch, Otto. *Russland. Eine Einführung auf Grund seiner Geschichte von 1904 bis 1912.* Berlin: Georg Reimer, 1913.
Hölzle, Erwin. *Der Osten im Ersten Weltkrieg.* Leipzig: Köhler und Amelang, 1944.
Hrushevsky, Mykhailo. *A History of Ukraine.* New Haven: Yale University Press, 1941.
————. *Yakoyi my khochemo avtonomiyi i federatsiyi* [What Kind of Autonomy and Federation We Desire]. Kiev: n. p., 1917.
Hubatsch, Walther. *Der Weltkrieg 1914/1918 in Handbuch der deutschen Geschichte.* Vol. IV. Konstanz: Athenaion, 1955.
————. *Germany and the Central Powers in the World War, 1914–1918.* Lawrence: University of Kansas Press, 1963.
Isayiv, Ivan (ed.) *Za Ukrayinu, podorozh V. P. Het'manycha Danyla Skoropads'koho do Zluchenykh Derzhav Ameryky i Kanady.* [For the Ukraine: The Trip of Hetmanych Danylo Skoropadsky to America and Canada]. Edmonton: n. p., 1938.
John, Volkwart. *Brest-Litowsk Verhandlungen und Friedensverträge im Osten, 1917 bis 1918.* Würzburg: Richard Mayr, 1937.
Kann, Robert A. *The Multinational Empire: Nationalism and Reform in the Habsburg Monarchy, 1848–1918.* 2 vols. New York: Columbia University Press, 1950.
Kennan, George F. *Soviet-American Relations, 1917–1920.* 2 vols. Vol. I: *Russia Leaves the War.* Princeton: Princeton University Press, 1956.
Khmil', Ivan S. *Z praporom myru kriz' polumya viiny* [With the Banner of Peace Through the Conflagration of War]. Kiev: Academy of Sciences of the Ukrainian SSR, 1962.
Khrystyuk, Pavlo. *Zamitky i materyaly do istoriyi Ukrayins'koyi Revolutsiyi, 1917–1920* [Notes and Materials on the History of the Ukrainian Revolution]. 4 vols. Vienna: Seriyi Ukrayins'koho Sotsiolohichnoho Instytutu, 1920–1921.
Kirimal, Edige. *Der nationale Kampf der Krimtürken mit besonderer Berücksichtigung der Jahre 1917–1918.* Emsdetten, Germany: Lechte, 1952.
Klein, Fritz. *Die diplomatischen Beziehungen Deutschlands zur*

Sowjetunion, 1917–1932. Berlin: Rütten und Löning, 1952.

Komarnicki, Titus. *Rebirth of the Polish Republic*. London: Heinemann, 1957.

Krauss, Alfred, and Klingenbrunner, Franz. *Die Besetzung der Ukraine: Die Militärverwaltung in den von den österreichischungarischen Truppen besetzten Gebieten*. In *Wirtschafts- und Sozialgeschichte des Weltkrieges*, österreichische und ungarische Serie. Vol. XI. Shotwell, J. T. (gen. ed.). Vienna and New Haven: Carnegie Endowment for International Peace, 1928.

Kruck, Alfred. *Geschichte des Alldeutschen Verbandes, 1890–1939*. Wiesbaden: Franz Steiner, 1954.

Kuhl, Hermann von. *Der Weltkrieg, 1914–1918*. Berlin: Wilhelm Kolk, 1929.

Kul'bakin, V. D. *et al.* (eds.). *Noyabrskaya Revolutsiya v Germanii* [The November Revolution in Germany]. Moscow: Izdatel'stvo Akademii Nauk SSSR, 1960.

Kulinych, Ivan M. *Ukrayina v zaharbnyts'kykh planakh nimets'koho imperializmu, 1900–1914 rr.* [The Ukraine in the Predatory Plans of German Imperialism, 1900–1914]. Kiev: Vydavnytstvo Akademiyi Nauk Ukrayins'koyi RSR, 1963.

Laqueur, Walter. *Russia and Germany: A Century of Conflict*. London: Weidenfeld & Nicolson, 1965.

Likholat, A. V. *Razgrom natsionalisticheskoi kontrrevolutsii na Ukraine, 1917–1922 gg.* [The Rout of the Nationalist Counterrevolution in the Ukraine, 1917–1922]. Moscow: Gosudarstvennoe izdatel'stvo politicheskoi literatury, 1954.

Linde, Gerd. *Die deutsche Politik in Litauen im Ersten Weltkrieg*. Wiesbaden: Harrassowitz, 1965.

Ludendorff, Erich von. *The General Staff and Its Problems*. 2 vols. London: Hutchinson, 1920.

———. *Kriegsführung und Politik*. Berlin: E. S. Mittler, 1923.

Lynar, Ernst Wilhelm (ed.). *Deutsche Kriegsziele, 1914–1918: Eine Diskussion*. Frankfurt am Main: Ullstein, 1964.

Mann, Bernhard. *Die baltischen Länder in der deutschen Kriegszielpublizistik, 1914–1918*. Tübingen: Mohr, 1965.

Matthias, Erich. *Die deutsche Sozialdemokratie und der Osten, 1914–1918*. Tübingen: Arbeitsgemeinschaft für Osteuropaforschung, 1954.

May, Arthur J. *The Passing of the Hapsburg Monarchy, 1914–1918*. 2 vols. Philadelphia: University of Pennsylvania Press, 1966.

Meyer, Henry Cord. *Mitteleuropa in German Thought and Action, 1815–1945*. The Hague: Nijhoff, 1955.

Militärgeschichtliches Forschungsamt (ed.). *Die Generalstäbe in*

Deutschland, 1871–1945: Beiträge zur Militär- und Kriegsgeschichte. Stuttgart: Deutsche Verlags-Anstalt, 1962.
Moorehead, Alan. *The Russian Revolution.* New York: Harper, 1958.
Mühlmann, C. *Das deutsch-türkische Waffenbündniss im Weltkrieg.* Leipzig: Köhler und Amelang, 1940.
Naumann, Friedrich. *Mitteleuropa.* Berlin: G. Reimer, 1915.
Nowak, Karl. *Der Sturz der Mittelmächte.* Munich: Verlag für Kulturpolitik, 1921.
Ol', P. V. *Inostrannye kapitaly v Rossii* [Foreign Capital in Russia]. Petrograd: Gosudarstvennaya tipografia, 1922.
Pflanze, Otto. *Bismarck and the Development of Germany.* Princeton: Princeton University Press, 1963.
Pidhainy, Oleh S. *The Formation of the Ukrainian Republic.* Toronto and New York: New Review Books, 1966.
Pipes, Richard. *The Formation of the Soviet Union: Communism and Nationalism, 1917–1923.* Cambridge: Harvard University Press, 1964.
Pokrovskii, Georgii. *Denikinshchina* [The Denikin Period]. Berlin: Grzhebin, 1923.
Rein, Gustav A. *Die Revolution in der Politik Bismarcks.* Göttingen: Musterschmidt, 1957.
Reiners, Ludwig. *In Europa gehen die Lichter aus.* Munich: Beck, 1954.
Reshetar, John S. *The Ukrainian Revolution, 1917–1920.* Princeton: Princeton University Press, 1952.
Ritter, Gerhard. *Staatskunst und Kriegshandwerk.* Vol. III. *Die Tragödie der Staatskunst: Bethmann Hollweg als Kriegskanzler, 1914–1917.* Munich: Oldenburg, 1964.
Rohrbach, Paul. *Die alldeutsche Gefahr.* Berlin: Engelmann, 1918.
————. *Russland und wir.* Stuttgart: J. Engelhorns Nachf., 1915.
Rohrbach, Paul, and Schmidt, Axel. *Osteuropa, historisch-politisch gesehen.* Potsdam: Rütten und Löning, 1942.
Rosenberg, Arthur. *The Birth of the German Republic, 1871–1918.* New York: Oxford University Press, 1931.
Schleuning, J. *In Kampf und Todesnot: Die Tragödie des Russlanddeutschtums.* Berlin-Charlottenburg: Bernard und Gräfe, 1930.
Schmidt, Axel. *Ukraine, Land der Zukunft.* Berlin: Reimar Hobing, 1939.
Sejdamet, Dzafar. *Krym* [The Crimea]. Warsaw: Wydawnictwo Instytutu Wschodniego, 1930.
Sichnysky, Volodymyr. *Ukraine in Foreign Comments and Descriptions.* New York: Ukrainian Congress Committee of America, 1953.

Stefaniv, Zenon. *Ukrayins'ki zbroini syly v 1917–1921 rr.* [Ukrainian Armed Forces, 1917–1921]. [n. p.] Biblioteka "Ukrayins'koho Kombatanta," 1947. (This is an enlarged edition of the work first published in 1935.)

Steglich, Wolfgang. *Die Friedenspolitik der Mittelmächte, 1917–1918.* Vol. I. Wiesbaden: F. Steiner, 1964.

Stern, Fritz. "Bethmann Hollweg and the War: The Limits of Responsibility," in Krieger, Leonard, and Stern, Fritz (eds.). *The Responsibility and Power (Historical Essays in Honor of Hajo Holborn).* Garden City, N.Y.: Doubleday, 1967.

Szilassy, Gyula von. *Der Untergang der Donau-Monarchie.* Bern: Neues Vaterland, 1921.

Terlets'kyi, Omelyan. *Istoriya ukrayins'koyi hromady v Rashtati* [History of the Ukrainian Community in Rastadt]. Kiev-Leipzig: Ukrayins' ka Nakladnya, 1919.

Udovychenko, Oleksander. *Ukrayina u viini za derzhavnist'* [The Ukraine in the Struggle for Its Statehood]. Winnipeg: Mykytyuk, 1954.

Valentin, Veit. *Deutschlands Aussenpolitik von Bismarcks Abgang bis zum Ende des Weltkrieges.* Berlin: Deutsche Verlagsgesellschaft für Politik und Geschichte, 1921.

Vishevich, K. *Ukrainskii vopros, Rossiya i Antanta* [The Ukrainian Question, Russia and the Entente]. Helsinki: Central Publishing Co., 1918.

Volkmann, Erich Otto. *Die Annexionsfragen des Weltkrieges.* In *Das Werk des Untersuchungsausschusses der verfassungsgebenden deutschen Nationalversammlung und deutschen Reichstages, 1919–1928. Die Ursachen des deutschen Zusammenbruches im Jahre 1918.* Fourth series, Vol. XII (1). Berlin: Deutsche Verlagsgesellschaft für Politik und Geschichte, 1929.

Vyslots'kyi, Ivan (ed.). *Het'man Pavlo Skoropads'kyi v osvitlenni ochevydtsiv* [Hetman Pavlo Skoropadsky as Seen by His Contemporaries], Toronto: Vydavnytsvo "Ukrayins'koho Robitnyka," 1940.

Walz, Erhard. *Reichsleitung und Heeresleitung in der Periode des Friedens von Brest-Litowsk.* Düsseldorf: G. H. Nolte, 1936.

Werkmann, Karl Freiherr von. *Deutschland als Verbündeter.* Berlin: Verlag für Kulturpolitik, 1931.

Wheeler-Bennett, John W. *The Forgotten Peace: Brest-Litovsk, March 1918.* New York: William Morrow, 1939.

Yaremko, Michael. *Galicia–Halychyna (A Part of Ukraine): From Separation to Unity.* Toronto, New York, Paris: Shevchenko Scientific Society, 1967.

Yerusalimskii, A. S. *Vneshnyaya politika i diplomatiya germanskogo imperializma v kontse XIX veka* [Foreign Policy and Diplomacy of German Imperialism at the End of the Nineteenth Century]. Moscow: Izdatel'stvo Akademii Nauk SSSR, 1951.

Zastavenko, H. *Rozhrom nimets'kykh interventiv na Ukrayini v 1918 r.* [The Rout of German Interventionists in the Ukraine in 1918]. Kiev: Ukrayins'ke vydavnytstvo politychnoyi literatury, 1959.

Zeman, Z. A. B. *The Break-up of the Habsburg Empire, 1914–1918.* London: Oxford University Press, 1961.

Zhukov, V. K. *Chernomorskii flot v revolutsii 1917–1918 gg.* [The Black Sea Fleet in the Revolution of 1917–1918]. Moscow: Molodaya Gvardiya, 1931.

V. *Articles and Essays*

Bihl, Volfdieter. "Österreich-Ungarn und der 'Bund' zur Befreiung der Ukraina." In *Österreich und Europa: Festgabe für Hugo Hantsch zum 70 Geburtstag*, pp. 505–526. Graz, Vienna, and Köln: Styria, 1965.

Birnbaum, Immanuel. "Deutsche Ostpolitik alt und neu." *Forum* (Vienna), no. 22 (October, 1955), 348–351.

Bondarchuk, S. "Ukraina v planakh germanskogo imperializma" [The Ukraine in the Plans of German Imperialism]. *Bor'ba klassov* [The Class Struggle], XII (1933), 13–23.

Borschak, Elie. "La Paix ukrainienne de Brest-Litovsk." *Le Monde Slave*, II, no. 4 (April, 1929), 33–62; III, no. 7 (July, 1929), 63–84; III, no. 8 (August, 1929), 199–225.

Doroshenko, Dmytro. "Deshcho pro zakordonnu polityku ukrayins'koyi derzhavy v 1918 r." [Notes on the Foreign Policies of the Ukrainian State in 1918]. *Khliborobs'ka Ukrayina* [Agrarian Ukraine], II (1920–1921), 49–64.

———. "Getmanstvo 1918 g. na Ukraine" [The Hetmanate in the Ukraine, 1918]. *Golos minuvshego na chuzhoi storone* [The Voice of the Past in Exile], VIII, no. 5 (1927), 133–164.

Eggert, S. "Die deutschen Eroberungspläne im Ersten Weltkrieg." *Neue Welt*, II, no. 4 (20) (February, 1947), 33–58.

Epstein, Fritz T. "Die deutsche Ostpolitik im Ersten Weltkrieg." *Jahrbücher für Geschichte Osteuropas*, X (1962), 381–395.

———. "Mehr Literatur zur Ostpolitik im Ersten Weltkrieg." *Ibid.*, XIV (March, 1966), 63–94.

Epstein, Klaus. "The Development of German-Austrian War Aims in the Spring of 1917." *Journal of Central European Affairs*, XVII, no. 1 (April, 1957), 24–47.

Erdmann, Karl Dietrich. "Zur Beurteilung Bethmann Hollwegs." *Geschichte in Wissenschaft und Unterricht*, XV (September, 1964), 525–540.

Eyck, E. "The Generals and the Downfall of the German Monarchy, 1917–1918." *Transactions of the Royal Historical Society* (London), 5th series, II (1952), 47–67.

Fischer, Fritz. "Deutsche Kriegsziele." *Historische Zeitschrift*, CLXXXVIII, no. 2 (October, 1959), 249–310.

————. "Weltpolitik, Weltmachtstreben und deutsche Kriegsziele," *Historische Zeitschrift*, CXCIX, no. 2 (October, 1964), 265–346.

Gatzke, Hans W. "Zu den deutsch-russischen Beziehungen im Sommer 1918." *Viertelsjahrhäfte für Zeitgeschichte*, III, no. 1 (January, 1955), 67–98.

Goldenweiser, A. A. "Iz kievskikh vospominanii' [Kievan Reminiscences]. *Arkhiv Russkoi Revolutsii* [Archives of the Russian Revolution] (22 vols. Berlin: "Slovo," 1921–1937), VI (1922), 161–303. This source is referred to throughout this study as the *ARR*.

Grebing, Helga. "Österreich-Ungarn und die 'Ukrainische Aktion.'" *Jahrbücher für Geschichte Osteuropas*, VII, no. 3 (1959), 272–291.

Gurko, V. I. "Iz Petrograda cherez Moskvu, Parizh i London v Odessu, 1917–1918 gg." [From Petrograd Through Moscow, Paris, and London to Odessa, 1917–1918]. *Arkhiv Russkoi Revolutsii* [Archives of the Russian Revolution], XV (1924), 5–84.

————. "Politicheskaya situatsiya na Ukraine pod get'manom" [Political Situation in the Ukraine Under the Hetman]. In Alekseev, A. S. (ed.), *Revolutsiya na Ukraine po memuaram belykh* [Revolution in the Ukraine as Reflected in the Memoirs of the Whites]. Moscow: Gosizdat, 1930, pp. 212–221.

Hartmann, Eduard von. "Russland in Europa." *Gegenwart*, XXXIII, nos. 1–3 (January, 1888), 1–4, 24–25, 36–39.

Herzfeld, Hans. "1871–1918—Literaturbericht." *Geschichte in Wissenschaft und Unterricht*, XIV, no. 7 (July, 1963), 450–466.

Hölzle, Erwin. "Das Experiment des Friedens im Ersten Weltkrieg." *Geschichte in Wissenschaft und Unterricht*, XIII, no. 8 (August, 1962), 465–522.

Katkov, George. "German Foreign Office Documents on Financial Support to the Bolsheviks in 1917." *International Affairs* (London), XXXII, no. 2 (April, 1956), 181–189.

Koehl, Robert L. "A Prelude to Hitler's Greater Germany." *American Historical Review*, LIX (October, 1953), 43–65.

Krasnov, P. N. "Vsevelikoe Voisko Donskoe" [The Great Don Army]. *Arkhiv Russkoi Revolutsii* [Archives of the Russian Revolution], V (1922), 190–321.

Krishevskii, N. "V Krymu" [In the Crimea], *ibid.*, XIII (1924), 71–124.

"Krymskoe kraevoe pravitel'stvo v 1918–1919 gg. (Zapiski Nalbandova)" [The Crimean Regional Government in 1918–1919 (Nalbandov's Notes)]. *Krasnyi Arkhiv* [Red Archives] (Moscow), XXII (1927), 92–152.

Lehmann, Hartmut. "Czernin's Friedenspolitik, 1916–1918." *Die Welt als Geschichte*, XXIII, no. 1 (1963), 47–59.

Laikhtenbergskii, G. N. "Kak nachalas' 'Yuzhnaya Armiya' " [The Origin of the "Southern Army." *Arkhiv Russkoi Revolutsii* [Archives of the Russian Revolution], VIII (1923), 166–182.

Meyer, Henry Cord. "German Relations with Southeastern Europe." *American Historical Review*, LVII (October, 1951), 77–90.

————. "Germans in the Ukraine, 1918." *American Slavic and East European Review*, IX (April, 1950), 105–115.

————. "Rohrbach and His Osteuropa," *Russian Review*, II, no. 1 (August, 1942), 60–69.

Petzold, Joachim. "Ludendorff oder Kühlmann; Die Meinungsverschiedenheiten zwischen Oberster Heeresleitung und Reichsregierung zur Zeit der Friedensverhandlungen in Brest-Litowsk." *Zeitschrift für Geschichtswissenschaft*, XII, no. 5 (1964), 817–832.

Raumer, Kurt von. "Zwischen Brest-Litowsk und Compiègne: die deutsche Ostpolitik vom Sommer 1918." *Baltische Lande* (Leipzig), IV (1939), 1–14.

"Die Reise des Hetmans der Ukraine nach Deutschland, September 1918." *Mitteilungen des Ukrainischen Ministeriums des Äussern* (Kiev), nos. 1–2 (1918).

Rohrbach, Paul. "Russland und wir." *Das grössere Deutschland*, December 25, 1914.

————. "Ukrainische Eindrücke." *Deutsche Politik*, III (1918), 675–680.

Rudnytsky, Ivan L. "The Intellectual Origins of Modern Ukraine." *The Annals of the Ukrainian Academy of Arts and Sciences in the United States*, VI, nos. 3–4 (1958), 1381–1405.

————. "The Ukrainians in Galicia Under Austrian Rule." *Austrian History Yearbook*, III, part 2, 394–429. Houston, Texas: Rice University Press, 1967.

Schlötzer, Kurd von. "Politische Berichte aus Petersburg." *Preussische Jahrbücher*, CCXIX (January-March, 1930), 1–27.

Schmidt, Axel. "Die Ukrainischen Parteien." *Deutsche Politik*, III (1918), 781–785.
Schwabe, Klaus. "Zur politischen Haltung der deutschen Professoren im Ersten Weltkrieg." *Historische Zeitschrift*, CXCIII, no. 3 (December, 1961), 601–620.
Shub, David. "Lenin i Vilgelm II: novoe o germansko-bol'shevitskom zagovore 1917 g. [Lenin and Wilhelm II; New Light on the German-Bolshevik Conspiracy of 1917]. *Novyi Zhurnal* [The New Journal], LVII (June, 1959), 226–267.
Sofronenko, K. "Germanskie okkupanty v Polesie" [German Occupiers in Polesie]. *Krasnyi Arkhiv* [Red Archives], XCI (1938), 89–105.
Sweet, Paul R. "Germany, Austria-Hungary and Mitteleuropa: August, 1915–April, 1916." In Hantsch, H., and Novotny, A. (eds.), *Festschrift für Heinrich Benedikt*, pp. 180–212. Vienna: Notring, 1957.
Tabuis, Général. "Comment je devins Commissaire de la République Française en Ukraine." In *Spohady* [Reminiscences]. Warsaw: *Proceedings of the Ukrainian Learned Society*, VIII (1932), 142–164.
Wittram, Reinhold. "Bismarcks Russlandpolitik nach der Reichsgründung." *Historische Zeitschrift*, CLXXXVI (1958), 261–275.
Zechlin, Egmont. "Deutschland zwischen Kabinettskrieg und Wirtschaftskrieg." *Historische Zeitschrift*, CXCIX, no. 2 (1964), 347–458.
————. "Probleme des Kriegskalküls und der Kriegsbeendigung im Ersten Weltkrieg." *Geschichte in Wissenschaft und Unterrricht*, XVI, no. 2 (February, 1965), 69–83.

VI. *Unpublished Materials*

Hunczak, Taras. "Die Ukraine unter Hetman Pavlo Skoropadskyj." (Unpublished Ph.D. dissertation.) Vienna: University of Vienna, 1960.
Lewerenz, Lilli. "Die deutsche Politik im Baltikum, 1914–1918." (Unpublished Ph.D. dissertation). Hamburg: University of Hamburg, 1958.
Milyukov, Pavel N. "Dnevnik [Diary]. New York: Columbia University, The Russian Archives. (Typewritten.)
Svechin, Mikhail A. "Dopolnenie k vospominaniam" [A Supplement to Reminiscences]. 2 vols. New York: Columbia University, The Russian Archives. (Typewritten.)

VII. *Newspapers and Magazines*

Berliner Tageblatt
Deutsche Politik
Hilfe
Kölnische Zeitung
New York Times
Norddeutsche Allgemeine Zeitung
Nova Rada
Tägliche Rundschau
Ukrainische Ministerium des Äussern, Mitteilungen (Kiev)

Index

The text of this book was set in Primer Linotype and printed by Letterpress on Warren's # 1854 Regular Text manufactured by S. D. Warren Company, Boston, Mass. Composed, printed and bound by H. Wolff Book Manufacturing Company, Incorporated, New York, N. Y.